The **Retail**
Value Chain

The **Retail Value** Chain

How to gain competitive advantage through Efficient Consumer Response (ECR) strategies

SAMI FINNE & HANNA SIVONEN

KOGAN
PAGE

London and Philadelphia

Publisher's note
Every possible effort has been made to ensure that the information contained in this book is accurate at the time of going to press, and the publishers and authors cannot accept responsibility for any errors or omissions, however caused. No responsibility for loss or damage occasioned to any person acting, or refraining from action, as a result of the material in this publication can be accepted by the editor, the publisher or any of the authors.

First published in Great Britain and the United States in 2009 by Kogan Page Limited

120 Pentonville Road
London N1 9JN
United Kingdom
www.koganpage.com

525 South 4th Street, #241
Philadelphia PA 19147
USA

© Sami Finne and Hanna Sivonen, 2009

ISBN 978 0 7494 5456 2

British Library Cataloguing-in-Publication Data

A CIP record for this book is available from the British Library.

Library of Congress Cataloging-in-Publication Data

Finne, Sami.
   The retail value chain : how to gain competitive advantage through efficient consumer response (ECR) strategies / Sami Finne and Hanna Sivonen.
       p. cm.
   Includes index.
   ISBN 978-0-7494-5456-2
   1. Retail trade--Management. 2. Consumers. 3. Competition. 4. Consolidation and merger of corporations. I. Sivonen, Hanna. II. Title.
   HF5429.F4973 2008
   338.8'9--dc22
                                                  2008028275

Typeset by Saxon Graphics Ltd, Derby
Printed and bound in India by Replika Press Pvt Ltd

Contents

Foreword

If ECR is to progress beyond the considerable strides already made, then it has to focus hard on extending the search for knowledge on an industry-wide basis. How do we best understand consumers' needs? How do we operate supply chain processes to create most value and least waste? Sustainability is a key challenge for the supply chain and ECR can help attain it. At Tesco, we build our business back from the customer – but we need our supplier partners to help us to do this. Knowledge is key, but sharing the knowledge makes it useful and this is why ECR continues to be important.

Sir Terry Leahy
Chief Executive
Tesco plc

Acknowledgements

The Retail Value Chain was an extensive project involving several people we would like to thank sincerely.

The Retail Value Chain is largely based on an original Finnish book by Sami Finne and Tuomas Kokkonen. Special thanks to Tuomas who has been closely involved in this project, reviewing and commenting on all chapters. Your uncompromising and constructive style contributed much to the quality of the book and, as always, it has been a pleasure to work with you.

The inspiration for this project came from the efficient consumer response (ECR) community. Thanks especially to Professor Saara Hyvönen from the University of Helsinki and Professor Arto Lindblom from the Helsinki School of Economics, Kristina Metso from ECR Finland and Antti Sippola, Co-chairman of ECR Finland, as well as Bernard Karli and Stephanie Pfenning from ECR Europe – your supporting comments encouraged us to undertake this project.

We would also like to thank the following retail industry leaders and experts who were willing to share their experiences and views for this book: Saliha Barlatey, Chairman of ECR Operations Committee (Nestle); Kenneth Bengtsson, Chief Executive Officer and President of ICA AB; Stefan Fröberg, Supply Chain Business Unit Director for Aldata; Dr Brian Harris, Chairman of the Partnering Group; Peter Kabuth and Ralf Kern from SAP; Bernard Karli from ECR Europe; Matti Karlsson, CEO of Sello; Rob Turtle, Director of Pricing and Promotions at dunnhumby; Jenni Virnes, Product Marketing Manager of Corporate Venturing at UPM-Kymmene Corporation, and all 22 other interviews carried out for the original Finnish version of the book. We also thank the 16 retailers from 11 countries participating in our shopper-information sharing study, and several Capgemini colleagues who helped with the interviews on this fascinating topic and provided interesting results never seen before.

As non-native speakers of English, we are grateful to many people for helping us with the language. Thanks to Maarit Tillman for the first version of the translation for most chapters. Without your help this project would not have been possible in the tight time span. Special thanks to publishing manager Priscilla Donegan from Capgemini, who has contributed greatly to the quality and readability of this book. You are absolutely great! Thanks to our commissioning editor Annie Knight and all others at Kogan Page, who stretched with our tight schedules and always had a very positive attitude. The awesome cartoons starting each chapter were drawn by Huib Jans. We have always been fans of your cartoons, so it was a great honour to have your work in this book. Special thanks for finding the time and squeezing work for our book into a very tight schedule.

The biggest thanks belong to our friends and colleagues who have commented on the book, contributing considerably to the quality of the text and the richness of the content. Thanks to Olli Ek, Miia Finne, Anton Helander, Harri Hovi, Kees Jacobs, Tuomas Kokkonen, Antti Syväniemi, Päivi Vuorensyrjä and Edward Westenberg for your comments, questions and suggestions that have undoubtedly made this book significantly better. Anton also provided the case study example in Chapter 4.

A great number of Capgemini colleagues around the world have contributed to this book, directly or indirectly. We want to specially thank Brian Girouard, the global leader of the Retail & Consumer Products Sector in Capgemini for support and guidance, and Vice President Jyrki Veranen and Sales Director Elja Kirjavainen for their encouragement and support for this project. Alongside these, we also thank all our colleagues in Capgemini, our customers and partners with whom we have had the honour to work. The way we see the retail industry has been significantly shaped by the experiences and lessons learned from you. The journey continues, thank you.

Finally, and most importantly, we want to thank our families and friends for all the support. Warm thanks to Miia, Camilla, Melinda and Olli who have been our support and joy, and understood us during the long process.

Introduction

The retail industry is changing all over the world at a fast pace. Internationalization, consolidation and intensive price competition, especially driven by different value retailing formats, have defined new benchmarks for competition. On the other hand, premium retailing and local initiatives are also gaining share. New, increasingly heterogenous consumer and product trends constantly set new requirements for retailers, sustainability being a major theme for both retailers and manufacturers. As convergence continues new entrants enter retailing, and many retailers also expand to new business areas such as banking, insurance, healthcare, mobile telecommunications and travel. Online retailing gains share in many categories, and personalization enabled by customer loyalty programmes transform the customer dialogue. Small micro-segments can be targeted ever-more precisely, and special assortments for them grow constantly. Retailing polarizes as some formats become more and more complex, hedonistic experience centres, and at the other end some players, such as hard discounters, count on very simplified formats and operational models. There will be several formats for success, and totally new players will also emerge.

This book discusses the above topics and several other key trends occurring in the retail industry. The book is largely based on the original Finnish version *Asiakaslähtöinen kaupan arvoketju – kilpailukykyä ECR-yhteistyöllä* by Sami Finne and Tuomas Kokkonen, published by WSOY in 2005. Tuomas has also been heavily involved in this project, and has reviewed and commented on all chapters.

The Retail Value Chain consists of the following eight chapters.

Chapter 1: Change drivers in the retail value chain. The retail value chain is changing at an ever-increasing pace, as for example industry consolidation, internationalization, value chain integration and convergence drive the rise and fall of different players in the industry. This chapter introduces key change drivers in the retail value chain including these trends, as well as consumer behaviour and product trends and key areas of sustainability in the retail value chain. Also, the key effects of the e-business are analysed – which players will gain most using the 'long tail'?

Chapter 2: Retail formats. The best retail formats are memorable for customers and have a clear value proposition delivered consistently throughout all customer contacts – the moments of truth. There are several ways to differentiate a store in the market: service and staff, price, in-store experience and continual assortment renewal are among some of the key areas where retailers may differentiate to meet the needs of the target customer segments. This chapter focuses on key success factors of retail formats and options available for differentiation. Also, key retail format types are described, and selected retail growth areas including value retailing formats, premium grocery retailing, convenience stores and malls are discussed in more detail.

Chapter 3: Collaboration in the retail value chain. This chapter introduces the key discussions in the retail value chain collaboration, such as quick response (QR) and efficient consumer response (ECR). The core areas of ECR are also presented, including the ECR scorecards. One size still doesn't fit all – there are several types of successful retailer–manufacturer relationships. The end of the chapter covers the key retail partnership levels in retailer–manufacturer collaboration.

Chapter 4: Demand management. This activity is essential for all retailers, and covers areas like how to drive value to the target shopper segments, and how to differentiate from competitors. Which categories and services should be included in the product range, and how can a retailer drive growth in different categories? These questions and several other areas of retail demand management, such as assortment management, space management, product development, new product introductions and activity management are discussed. A holistic framework for shopper-oriented demand management in retail is also presented and it guides the structure of the chapter.

Chapter 5: Store operations. Efficient implementation of new concepts and operational models is vital for all retailers. Most retail variable costs are personnel costs, and competence building in a low-pay industry with high employee attrition is a real challenge. However, constant concept renewal with efficient, low-cost implementation is a key sustainable competitive advantage for retailers. This chapter discusses the key store operations practices, such as product replenishment, store management, customer service, as well as campaign and assortment change implementations. In addition, the latter part of the chapter includes areas like store refurbishment, chain-level execution and the manufacturer's role in store operations.

Chapter 6: Information technology trends in the retail value chain. Retail is detail, and efficient information systems enable totally new efficiency levels in several retail processes. Customer loyalty programmes make possible the collection and analysis of data specific to the target group, increasing the possibilities for fact-based management. This chapter describes the main IT trends affecting the industry, including for example offshoring, international IT operations and the development of identification standards. Key trends in retail enterprise resource planning (ERP) and other selected solution development areas are also discussed. The chapter introduces a framework for fact-based management with shopper information, and describes its key components, which is essential for all retailers running loyalty programmes.

Chapter 7: Loyalty programmes and shopper information sharing. Loyalty programmes are key differentiators for some retailers enabling, for example, personalized dialogue with customers. The programmes also enable collection and use of shopper information. The key retail customer-facing processes can be redefined to truly serve the target shopper segments when shopper data is available and actively used. This chapter examines key loyalty programme types and their core areas, and discusses the use of shopper data in retail customer portfolio management and in other key retail processes. Interesting results of the shopper information sharing study of 16 retailers from 11 countries are published and address the question: Do the retailers 'walk the talk' in ECR? The end of the chapter discusses future trends in customer loyalty programme development.

Chapter 8: The future. The last chapter summarizes the key retail development trends and discusses the authors' views of the future development of retailing in areas such as globalization and consolidation, operational efficiency, innovation and exclusivity and adapting to local environment. Seven possible future success formats are also described to illustrate the key development trends in practice.

We wish to give a holistic and understandable big picture about the retail value chain, and the key operational models and success factors of its main players. As there are quite a few discussed topics – actually most of them would deserve their own book – only some of the areas are covered in detail. Our objective in the book is to provide a holistic description of the modern retail value chain, its players and steering models, and provide insights into successful retail formats and operational models. We are passionate about retailing, and we hope that this book will inspire others to join this interesting industry, and also provide some new insights for experienced retail practitioners.

1 Change drivers in the retail value chain

The retail value chain is changing all over the world. Internationalization and consolidation of retailers and manufacturers are changing the balance of power in collaboration. The key change drivers are both intra-industry and even intra-company factors, but there are also drivers outside the industry with an impact on retailing. Retailers are expanding to new areas such as banking, insurance and foodservice, and new players are also entering the retail arena. Retail infrastructure is affected by many external factors such as technology and product trends, forcing the players to rethink their conventional models.

Customers are ever-more demanding and retailers are competing to please them, and the consumer demand in the market becomes increasingly heterogeneous. The internet has changed the availability of information in the retail value chain; consumers have more knowledge about products and services than ever, and can sometimes even participate in retail processes such as development of products and the choice of products offered (referred to as the assortments).

The key challenge for retailers and manufacturers is to identify the most important trends affecting their operations, assess the effects and take actions to respond to them. Figure 1.1 summarizes some key trends affecting the retail value chain and its players. Some selected trends will be discussed in more detail in this chapter, and several trends relating to retail competition and format development in Chapter 2. The key retail technology trends are discussed in Chapter 6.

Industry consolidation

Like many other industries, retailing is facing a strong consolidation trend, affecting both retailers and suppliers. An increasingly large part of food retailing is concentrating in the hands of global giants. Retailing is a business mostly based on large volumes, and as consolidation increases volumes, retailers have a better position in negotiations with suppliers. This translates into better purchasing terms, leading to competitive advantage in the market. As for suppliers, a large size enables economies of scale in production and economies of scope, for example, in marketing.

US-based Wal-Mart is a statue of the economies of scale that facilitates consolidation. With net sales of US~$345 billion in 2007, it has grown to become the largest company in the world, bigger than global giants such as General Electric or Exxon. The tremendous size of Wal-Mart can be illustrated with the help of a few comparisons. The net sales of Wal-Mart are about the size of the GDP of Austria or Saudi Arabia, and it has more employees globally than many small countries such as Iceland have inhabitants. For many product brands Wal-Mart accounts for over 20 per cent of the brands' sales volume. Consequently, Wal-Mart plays a remarkable role as a distribution channel to suppliers. This in turn gives Wal-Mart a good negotiation position and enables even lower purchase prices.

Other key retail giants include Carrefour, Metro Group, Tesco, Seven & i and Ahold. In recent years, these companies have grown aggressively, in part through mergers. Table 1.1 outlines retail consolidation rates in different European countries by showing the combined market shares of the three biggest players in a certain market.

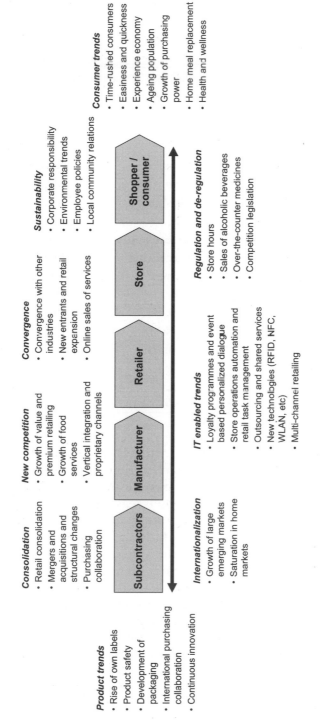

Product trends
- Rise of own labels
- Product safety
- Development of packaging
- International purchasing collaboration
- Continuous innovation

Consolidation
- Retail consolidation
- Mergers and acquisitions and structural changes
- Purchasing collaboration

New competition
- Growth of value and premium retailing
- Growth of food services
- Vertical integration and proprietary channels

Convergence
- Convergence with other industries
- New entrants and retail expansion
- Online sales of services

Sustainability
- Corporate responsibility
- Environmental trends
- Employee policies
- Local community relations

Consumer trends
- Time-rushed consumers
- Easiness and quickness
- Experience economy
- Ageing population
- Growth of purchasing power
- Home meal replacement
- Health and wellness

Subcontractors → Manufacturer → Retailer → Store → Shopper / consumer

Internationalization
- Growth of large emerging markets
- Saturation in home markets

IT enabled trends
- Loyalty programmes and event based personalized dialogue
- Store operations automation and retail task management
- Outsourcing and shared services
- New technologies (RFID, NFC, WLAN, etc)
- Multi-channel retailing

Regulation and de-regulation
- Store hours
- Sales of alcoholic beverages
- Over-the-counter medicines
- Competition legislation

Figure 1.1 Key change drivers in the retail value chain

Table 1.1 Share of the three largest players in the retail market (Source: ACNielsen, 2007)

	Number 1	Number 2	Number 3	%
Denmark	Coop	Dansk Supermarket	Supergros	86
Finland	SOK	Kesko	Tradeka	86
Sweden	ICA	Kf-coop	Axfood	84
Norway	Norgesgruppen	Coop	Ica	81
Switzerland	Migros	Coop	Denner	79
Austria	BML-REWE	Spar	Hofer-Aldi	77
Belgium	Carrefour	Delhaize	Colruyt	69
Germany	Edeka	Rewe	Aldi	61
UK	Tesco	Sainsbury's	Asda	58
Netherlands	Albert Heijn	TSN	Laurus	55
France	Carrefour	Leclerc-systeme U	Intermarche	55
Spain	Carrefour	Mercadona	Eroski Group	51
Ireland	Tesco	Dunnes	Supervalue	48
Portugal	Sonae	JMR	Intermarche	47
Slovakia	Coop	Tesco	Billa	46
Greece	Carrefour	Alfa Beta	Lidl	38
Czech R	Ahold	Kaufland	Tesco	35
Hungary	Tesco	CBA	Coop	35
Italy	Coop	Conad	Carrefour	28
Poland	Tesco	Biedronka	Real	16

As the table shows, retailing is particularly concentrated in the Nordic countries. The combined market share of the top three players is 80 per cent or more in each country. One reason for this is the relatively small size of the national markets, and some other reasons are the geography, with long distances and the Baltic Sea separating the countries from continental Europe. According to the Herfindahl-Hirschman Index (HHI), a key measure for market concentration, the value of Finnish food retailing at the current company market shares goes up to more than 2,981 points. To put that result in perspective, a market with an HHI exceeding 1,800 points is considered to be very concentrated. The index is calculated by squaring the market share of each firm competing in the market and then adding the resulting numbers (for example, $41^2 + 34^2 + 12^2 = 2,981$). The results are used, for instance, in anti-trust assessments in merger and acquisition activities.

The consolidation trend goes on and small players are continually bought out of the market. Increased concentration is a universal trend.

Rarely do completely new retailers come in to markets, especially in food retailing. If new chains are established, they are usually new banners of existing large retailers, launched to new segments to ensure market share and economies of scale. It is difficult for new small players to reach critical mass quickly enough, whereas large retailers can afford the required investments. Consequently, the number of retailers in the market is decreasing as large players buy competitors out of the market.

There is a host of recent examples of big mergers and acquisitions. CVS bought Caremark, resulting in an extremely strong player in the drugstore sector in the United States. Similarly, Kmart and Sears merged. Earlier, Ahold bought into the ICA group in Sweden as well as the Norwegian food retailer Hakon. Italian retailing has also significantly consolidated during the past few years, even though the market has been one of the most heterogeneous in Europe. There are also persistent rumours of corporate reorganizations in many markets. Sainsbury's, for example, has often been speculated to be a potential target of corporate takeovers. Also, an interesting merger took place in the United States with Whole Foods buying Wild Oats in 2007. The merger was not certain from the beginning because of concerns by the Federal Trade Commission that Whole Foods would become too dominant in the organic food market, even though the size of both companies was small compared with the biggest retailers. They are both considered pioneers in the strategic, fast-growing, organic food market, and possess valuable own label lines in these areas.

A similar consolidation trend is taking place among suppliers and manufacturers. Large companies are buying smaller ones both at local and global levels. The phenomenon is already rather old in the consumer products sector. International conglomerates such as Procter & Gamble (P&G), Nestlé and Unilever went through mergers as early as the mid-1990s to reach their current size. Merger and acquisition activity continues in the consumer products space, due to three key reasons, which are to:

- gain size and achieve economies of scale;
- divest – focus on key areas and sell everything else;
- buy innovations and leverage the global 'marketing and sales machine'.

Gaining size and achieving economies of scale has been the key reason for merger and acquisition activity in the past, and is likely to remain important in balancing the power in the retail value chain.

Especially in food manufacturing, many companies are still very regional and consolidation provides synergy benefits in areas such as manufacturing and sourcing. In durables, production is increasingly outsourced to the Far East, and acquiring traditional big players with production plants in Western countries is not as attractive as in the past. Merger and acquisition activity in this space focuses more on buying brands and innovations and achieving economies in scale in marketing and sales. One of the biggest recent company reorganizations was the acquisition of Gillette by P&G. The acquisition of Body Shop in 2006 gave L'Oreal a new strong brand in the portfolio, but also provided a significant retail channel and competences, even though cross-sales opportunities between internal brands are scarce because of brand dissimilarities.

Now let's consider the aim to divest – focus on key areas and sell everything else. At the same time that consumer products companies are gaining size and economies of scale in their core areas, many of them are divesting non-core product lines and business. Only megabrands will survive in the future, and company resources are heavily prioritized for building them. Non-core business is often still the core business for some other company. An example of a recent large divestiture was Pfizer divesting its consumer products arm to Johnson & Johnson in 2006. A similar move can be seen in retailing where many retailers are moving away from new markets where they cannot achieve the number 1 or 2 position, as they divest their units and focus on core markets. Examples of this are mentioned in the following section on the internationalization of retailing.

The desire to buy innovations and leverage the global 'marketing and sales machine' is relatively new, but is expected to be a long-lasting trend. P&G's chairman of the board, A G Lafley, has demonstrated the trend well by saying: 'We will acquire 50 per cent of our innovations from outside P&G... we can be better at anything than anybody, but we can't be better at everything than everybody.'

Small companies with new innovations do not often have the power to negotiate good contracts with retailers and build strong consumer brands. On their own the innovations are likely to be marketed in a small regional area, with limited economies of scale, and they also risk being copied soon after coming to market by bigger players. A natural choice is to sell the innovations to large global companies such as P&G, Unilever, L'Oreal and Johnson & Johnson, which can leverage their well-established global sales relationships with retailers to sell new products, and use their marketing power in building new megabrands from new innovations. The big players in the market are actively searching for new innovations, and a growing amount of innovation spend will be on small company acquisitions.

There are also examples of failed consolidations in the retail industry. Ahold, which has rapidly internationalized mainly through acquisitions, has not always succeeded in reaping sufficient synergy benefits for its chains, and has been compelled to give up some of its investments. Similarly, Coop Norden in Scandinavia, a consortium of many Nordic cooperative retailers, has not reaped the benefits promised by the consortium.

It is, however, to be assumed that the consolidation trend will go on both among retailers and consumer product manufacturers. Food retailing is still relatively regional, and there are as yet few truly global-level (or even

European-level) players. The consolidation trend is influenced by high barriers of entry for new players. Setting up stores is a capital-intensive effort, and it may take years for a new store to break even. Owners are seldom patient enough to wait for five or more years before the new chain becomes profitable. Additionally, large retailers may easily copy the new ideas of smaller chains and execute them efficiently at a large number of stores. As mentioned earlier, there should be no rush of new players, but growth will mainly take place in the form of existing players expanding their operations. New entrants are mainly seen in non-food retailing, food-service or other areas close to retailing.

Internationalization

The trends of consolidation and retailer growth have been accompanied by a closely connected trend – internationalization. While growing in size, retailers and manufacturers have actively looked for new sales potential beyond their national boundaries. In particular, companies operating in mature markets seek additional growth in emerging, fast-growing markets. Internationalization can take place both organically by opening new units abroad and inorganically through acquisitions.

The internationalization strategies in retailing are often divided into three main categories. Investors (like Ahold) expand their business by acquiring retailers in new target markets and developing them as independent units. Replicators (such as IKEA, Costco and Lidl) develop a business concept and model, and leverage it in a potential market. This strategy enables a relatively simple way of expanding abroad and achieving economies of scale. However, it is also a slow method because of the challenges of organic growth in new markets. Many retailers have also used franchising to speed up internationalization. Adaptors (like Carrefour and Tesco) master many business concepts and adapt them as needed in local markets. Often, the challenge in reinvention is in understanding new markets, adapting concepts to markets and linking them to standardized processes. In Europe, internationalization has mainly happened through acquisitions and investments where the player is among the first in the market to launch a new attractive format.

Figure 1.2 shows the share of international sales of the total sales for some selected grocery and speciality retailers that have international operations. Overall, grocery retailing in particular is still distinctly local business, and if we would add companies on the list, the tail would be long with minimal percentages, as the ones shown represent a major part of the most global players. On the contrary, in speciality retailing we could find a number of other truly global retailers as well. Some retailers have acquired

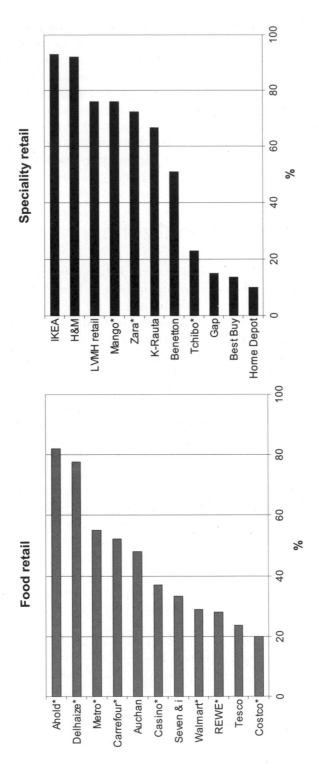

Figure 1.2 Selected examples of share of international sales percentages (other than domestic market in 2007 (*2006))

over 90 per cent of the sales abroad, for instance IKEA and H&M that have been very successful in international operations. In speciality retail, many of the companies are truly international, and operate with a multi-channel strategy. For example, LVMH is a luxury brand house with over 50 top brands, including Louis Vuitton, Christian Dior, TAG Heuer and Hennessy, sold often in department stores, but LVMH also has its own retail channel with selected brands such as Sephora and Thomas Pink. All of its operations are truly international.

Notably, the share of international operations of US retailers is lower than their European counterparts. One reason for this is the large size of the US domestic market, which lowers the overall internationalization percentages. Also, because of the large domestic market the retailers haven't had similar need to search for growth from abroad. For example, Footlocker operates athletics shoe stores with mall formats and has about 80 per cent of the stores in the United States, even though mall formats are one of the most suitable formats for internationalization. Most US retailers start their internationalization from markets nearby, such as Canada and Mexico. Expansion attempts to Europe and Asia have not always been successful. For example, Wal-Mart has had its share of challenges in internationalization. It expanded to Germany by acquiring Wertkauf and Interspar but did not succeed in increasing its market share as expected. In 2006, it sold the unprofitable business to Metro, for which the store locations were well-suited for the expansion of the Real chain.

The conquest of the UK through the acquisition of Asda has succeeded slightly better, but even there the growth rate has been lower than expected, and market share is far behind Tesco's. Wal-Mart has also faced challenges in Japan where it owns the majority of the Seiyu chain. After the initial difficulties, the situation seems better, though, for Seiyu has started to show positive signs. In spite of the challenges, Wal-Mart can be expected to continue its internationalization. With its enormous resources, the company is a potential threat to competitors all over the world. New focus areas for internationalization have been South America, India and China.

Carrefour is one of the pioneers in the internationalization of food retailing. Brazil, Argentina, and Spain were some of the company's first targets outside France. When entering new markets as a greenfield operation, Carrefour has typically operated several pilot stores before a large-scale launch. The company policy has been not to expand in any country unless several pilots have proved to be successful. Closing unprofitable stores in the United States, for example, reflects this policy. Carrefour's internationalization has been done with multiple formats. Hypermarkets and hard discounters have been and are the most important formats for greenfield operations. Focus for hypermarkets has been in emerging markets and hard discounters have succeeded in more mature markets, but the group has also completed several acquisitions and established strong presence in supermarket retailing outside its home market, especially in Greece, Italy and Argentina. Carrefour adapts the formats and product assortments to the local environment and consumer demand, complemented with global sourcing in own labels to gain economies of scale.

Carrefour has set a target to be among the three leading players in each of the markets where it has a presence. In line with the strategy, Carrefour has withdrawn recently from several markets: it pulled out of Japan and Mexico in 2005; South Korea, Slovakia and the Czech Republic in 2006; and Switzerland and Portugal in 2007. While doing so, the group strengthened its position with acquisitions in Brazil, Poland and Spain. According to Carrefour investor information, new store openings will focus on key markets where the group aims to become a leading player, in China, Brazil, Indonesia, Turkey and Poland in particular.

Emerging markets attract many players because of the potential for rapid growth and an easier competitive situation. In food retailing, growth in emerging markets has focused on hypermarkets and large supermarkets. They can be used to stake out markets and achieve large volumes right from the start. Expanding these concepts in conventional markets can be slow because of restrictive legislation, difficulties in getting construction permits and high costs.

Key emerging markets today are India and China, which now enjoy huge growth, driven by a large middle class with increasing purchase power. China, for instance, has about 100 million people who may be considered rich and about 300 million people considered to belong to the middle class. The number keeps growing, and it is estimated that as much as 40 per cent of the population will belong to the middle class by 2020. The market potential is immense and as yet largely unexploited.

However, expansion into these emerging markets is not without challenges. Many countries in emerging markets have passed legislation to restrict the direct entry of foreign competitors into the market. Thus, Western companies wishing to enter the market must establish joint ventures with local companies, as Wal-Mart has done with Bharti Group in India.

Differences in culture, language and business practices can pose additional challenges to expansion. Though competition is so far not very tough in India, local companies operating in other industries are building new retail businesses at an unprecedented rate. Some examples of these companies include Reliance Retail and Birla Group, which have briskly proceeded to get their retail chains up and running before the entry of international competitors. For example, Reliance announced in 2006 that it will invest US~$5 billion in retailing operations. Since then, it has systematically built one of the leading retail groups in the country.

Russia is another expansion area that has aroused interest, especially among European chains. Russia is a huge market, and price competition is not nearly as tough as in many other European markets. Russian retailing is as yet very fragmented, and a strong consolidation wave and expansion of international chains are to be expected during the next few years. Expansion into Russia also involves many kinds of challenges: the country is geographically large and challenging in terms of logistics, and many retailers have found that store site acquisition takes time and involves red tape. However, IKEA and Stockmann, for example, have worked systematically for a long time in Russia, building stores in several areas, and have established a good business in rapidly growing markets. Stockmann has used its competences in Russian retailing also by operating Zara as a franchising concept there for several years successfully, until Zara bought back operations.

Tesco and Carrefour have also been very active in the developing markets of Asia and Eastern Europe as soon as the markets opened. Their rapid growth is largely based on the hypermarket format, which has been missing from certain markets. After Tesco sold its stores in Taiwan to Carrefour in return for stores in the Czech Republic and Slovakia, it has become evident that retailers concentrate on different areas in their geographical expansion. Many markets are already going through the second wave of internationalization, in which phase the chains are expected to succeed. Typically, if a retailer is not the biggest or the second biggest player in a regional market, it buys market share by acquiring competitors, or sells its stores to another player.

Expanding into more developed Western markets needs a different approach from expanding into emerging markets. The legislation often prevents the building of large stores, or at least makes the process long and cumbersome. One alternative is to acquire local retailers to get store sites, but finding the correct store profiles may be difficult. Moreover, price competition is tough in many markets. These factors have contributed to the emergence of hard discounters and convenience stores that are key formats in internationalization in Western markets. As an example, the internationalization of Lidl (Schwartz Group) has been very systematic in Europe. The company now operates in as many as 24 countries and is one of the most global food retailers in the world. The hard discounter format does not require more than 1,000 square metres of store space, and the properties do not have to be situated in prime locations. Suitable lots are usually fairly easily available, especially when the traditional small supermarket is disappearing from those areas as customers move into larger supermarkets or hypermarkets. Whereas hard discounters in Europe most often operate as separate units, in the United States they are often located in retail parks or shopping centres.

Convenience stores are also spreading quickly in developed markets. Requiring little store space, they are easy to set up. As for operations, convenience stores closely resemble fast-food restaurants, most of which are international like McDonald's, Subway and KFC. Many convenience store formats rely heavily on pharmacy operations, but differences in drug sales legislation efficiently hinder the internationalization of these chains in some markets. To cite an example, 7-Eleven has already expanded to 18 countries, especially in Asia. The company shifted into Japanese ownership in 2005.

Tesco has entered the United States with its new convenience store concept Fresh & Easy. This will be a real test for Tesco's abilities in the very competitive US market, and the company will face competition ranging from value retailers and premium retailers to many convenience stores. Tesco has launched extensive management bonus schemes to support the move into the United States, ensuring the focus and attention of senior management. However, even with several hundred shops, Fresh & Easy would remain relatively small in terms of volume compared with the competition. The concept will not be significant for Tesco's overall growth in terms of net sales until the chain has approximately 1,000 stores.

What makes the concept particularly interesting, though, is the possibility of introducing the Tesco.com online store to the US market. This can be used to expand sales into new product categories and services, with Fresh & Easy used as a local service and pick-up point. This enables Tesco to utilize online experience gained in the domestic market. This form of grocery retail-driven online retailing may have a significant demand and potential in the US market as there are few similar local concepts with significant sales. However, competitors are not letting Tesco off easily. For example, Wal-Mart has opened several Marketside stores close to Tesco's stores. Sales volumes of either player are minimal compared with the big picture, but the success of the first few hundred stores will more or less determine success of Tesco's US investment in the eyes of investors.

Many rapidly internationalized retailers operate in mall environments with well-differentiated retail formats, which are easy to replicate in new markets. Typically, own labels account for a high share, sometimes up to 100 per cent, of their total sales. Assortment in this case strongly differentiates the retailer from its competitors and is one of the primary marketing tools. Good examples of these companies include Body Shop, Benetton and the Sunglass Hut. Strictly managed international replicators control most of the retail value chain with their private label (own label) products. The business model is especially typical of channels selling fashion and seasonal products. Quick integrated operations reduce response time to demand. This is a key requisite of success if product stockouts are common or obsolescence costs are high.

Many retailers have flexible formats, which can be tailored not only to shopping malls but also to downtown locations. The latter requires much more work in store site acquisition and renovation but the business model as such can be similar to that of mall formats. The model is typical for European chains like H&M and Zara, which are used to operating in

European city centres. When a retailer has the capability of customizing stores in challenging old downtown properties, the mall format is easy to implement.

On the other hand, a retailer can also proceed with own-store properties and a systematic approach. IKEA is perhaps the best example of this. It has operations in as many as 36 countries and the concept is similar all over the world, but the structure of local demand is naturally taken into account. IKEA is one of the best differentiated chains in the world, and it has not so far faced any direct challengers at the global level. The company continues to grow at a strong rate all over the world. Another example, Costco, has grown tremendously during the last few years and has started internationalization with a large-scale value retailing format. Its focus has been mainly on Mexico, Canada, the UK and the Far East. One challenge it will face in Europe might be finding sufficiently large warehouses to operate its stores. On the other hand, customers may be willing to drive a long way for low prices, as has been shown by the success of smaller hard discounter chains.

In non-food retailing, many European formats have already become global, whereas most concepts originated in the United States seem to remain focused on domestic or nearby markets for quite some time. Because of large domestic markets, US retailers often focus on reaching a strong local position, and only after that does the focus shift to international operations. Internationalization is often started in markets nearby in Canada or Latin America. Fashion concepts are likely to start internationalization in the UK and a few European metropolises or Japan. From there, the retailer slowly starts spreading to other markets, as the flagship stores are in place. European retailers typically have a business model that supports multinational operations; to them the US market is just one market among others.

One interesting concept and case of internationalization is German Tchibo. The business focuses on mail-order retailing and coffee shops that have started to sell various kinds of ancillary products to customers. Products carrying the TCM brand are manufactured by contractors and are not sold anywhere else. A key part of the Tchibo concept is a highly varied product mix and a hefty element of surprise, where themes vary according to season and include, for example, gardening, office supplies or jewellery. There are 15–20 theme products at a time, and they can represent almost any category from clothes to electronics. Assortments change weekly, so customers have a good reason to visit the store frequently.

Tchibo operates in a true multi-channel environment, with products also sold by mail order and through the online store. One indication of success was the company's nomination as 'The distant retailer of the year 2004' in Germany. Tchibo also supplies its products to other retailers and has become a significant non-food supplier. Tchibo shop-in-shop modules are found in many supermarket chains, bakeries, pharmacies and magazine outlets, and they sell not only coffee but also non-food items. International operations started in some markets through mail-order retailing and in some as free rider alongside German food retail chains. Products are sourced centrally and the assortment is mainly the same in different countries and sales channels.

In the near future the internationalization of retailing can be expected to continue, and consolidation will shift from regional to international arrangements. In food retailing, many local chains will become international, as several non-food retailers have already done. Over the long term, China, India and Russia will form extremely important mass markets, and it is hard to imagine a value retailer that could afford to ignore this number of consumers in its quest for economies of scale. Premium retail both in food and non-food will also become international, but the development will be supported by new product development and premium private label products. An increasingly large share of customers will be willing to pay for the exclusivity. More suppliers will sell at least some portion of their products through their own formats, thereby gaining access to the customer interface in various markets. Malls provide a venue and easy access for this. Value chain integration is discussed in more detail in the next section.

Value chain integration

In addition to geographical growth, companies are increasingly active in extending their role in the value chain. Vertical integration refers to expanding company ownership upstream or downstream in the value chain. A supplier can set up a retail chain of its own, or a retailer may start manufacturing the products it sells. New business models make it possible to eliminate unnecessary non-value-adding agents, representatives or other intermediaries and the manufacturer can start importing the products on its own.

Typical business models are franchising and direct retailing by suppliers. For instance, Nike and Adidas have set up large own stores where all the products are own brands. This is in many ways a logical extension in the operations of these companies: they have practically no production of their own, and all manufacturing is bought from subcontractors wherever production is cheap, such as the Far East. The core competences of these companies consist of brand management and the identification of customer needs. By establishing stores of their own they get access to the customer interface and ensure that the brand is displayed to the final customer in exactly the desired form. A store is, in other words, a display window for a carefully protected brand. Own stores can also be a significant source of sales and may operate either wholly owned or on the franchising principle. Concept stores, however, are rarely the only distribution channel; products are also sold via other channels. As an example, Hallmark cards are sold at many supermarkets and other formats, but the company also has its own stores in malls and other shopping centres.

Concept stores are key opportunities to promote manufacturer brands, and are usually situated in prime locations. Their display is particularly well groomed and the products are the manufacturer's top brands, not seconds or the previous season's stock. In concept stores the manufacturer gets a chance to display all its offered products in the way it wants, and also observe the shopping behaviour of consumers and get direct feedback on new products, services and activities. Classic examples of manufacturer flagship stores include Niketown in London and the Apple Store in New York. Both stores are well-designed with big money and focus on promoting the brand and the products. High ceilings and the use of glass make them open and enjoyable to shop in. Both stores are favoured by locals and tourists alike, and they are often crowded with customers.

Speaking of concept stores, a clear distinction has to be made between flagship stores and a concept store chain that may consist of hundreds or thousands of stores. A major supplier can set up 5–10 flagship stores in the biggest metropolises in the world for marketing purposes, but if it establishes a chain of several hundred stores, they should be profitable as such. The purpose of a flagship store is to act as an advertisement and a display window to the world for the brand. For example, at Samsung's Experience Store, you cannot buy anything, only test products and collect experiences. Still, the concept has been estimated to yield a significant amount of additional sales through other sales channels.

Large concept store chains aim at increasing not only brand visibility but also direct sales and profitability of the manufacturer. Many fashion retail brands have strengthened their retail channel considerably. For example, Hugo Boss directly owned store sales has rapidly grown to 15 per cent of total sales, and is expected to continue to grow. Concept stores may also be used for targeting and securing certain customer segments. For example, Sherwin-Williams, the largest paint manufacturer in the United States, operates over 3,000 own stores that focus on serving architectural and industrial painting contractors, residential and commercial builders, property owners and managers and DIY homeowners. Own retail channel is a key enabler of growth, as some of the segments could not be reached effectively through traditional channels and in the pressure of retailers' private labels.

Concept stores should not be confused with manufacturer-driven factory outlets either. These also aim to communicate about the supplier's brand, but the primary aim is to sell out surplus stock from the previous season at a price consumers find reasonable. Consumers know the factory outlet concepts, and when products are sold there at a discount instead of cutting their prices in traditional channels, a better overall price image can be maintained for the brand. Factory outlet concepts are often located as large clusters including dozens or even hundreds of stores where consumers can come bargain shopping. Clusters of this kind are usually located outside cities by major highways, but sometimes also downtown. To cite an example, Atlantic City, New Jersey, houses a large factory outlet area right in the middle of the casino area. With the factory outlet concept, brands can reach new target groups who cannot be reached through conventional channels and the normal price level. The factory outlet concepts are particularly typical for fashion products with continually changing assortments. Many apparel manufacturers have concepts of their own. Examples include Timberland Outlet, Nike Factory outlet, Guess Factory Store, and Tommy Hilfiger Company Store. Similar concepts are seen in shoes (for example, Reebok and Ecco) and bookshops (such as Borders' outlet stores).

A kind of miniature form of the concept store is the ever-increasing use of shop-in-shop concepts, where products are presented in a way that permits visibility for the manufacturer's brand. The shop-in-shop model has been extensively used in cosmetics, but it has also become more common in electronics, brand apparel and decor items. Shop-in-shop concepts often include tools facilitating the buying process, such as product data, mirrors and testers in cosmetics, or different customer communication tools, such as shelf information lists and touch screens. In shop-in-shops manufacturers can ensure the customer service experience for their products. At large department stores, manufacturer-branded departments may have dedicated sales assistants whose pay may be partly or totally paid by the supplier. Shop-in-shop concepts are discussed in more detail in Chapter 4.

During the past few years, vertical integration has been actively practised, especially by technology companies. One of the best success stories has been Apple, which operates over 200 concept stores in malls and is expanding rapidly. High sales volumes and space profitability give freedom to choose the most suitable store locations in malls. The chain operates not only in the United States but also in Canada, Japan and several European countries. At the moment, Apple is one of the fastest growing large retailers. The success of Apple in this sector has mobilized competitors as well. Dell has responded by opening service outlets in shopping malls. These service outlets can also be used to buy products through the conventional Dell online store. These outlets are usually well located in shopping malls, in the middle of hallways or plazas and close to high shopper flows. Similar service outlet concepts have been established by many mobile operators. Dell has also piloted a mall concept store, and it seems as though it may well take the road paved by Apple.

Vertical integration also happens in grocery retailing, but there retailers are often in the driver's seat. Extreme examples of vertical integration are

RETURNS

TOTAL

PLEASE ADD APPLICABLE POSTAGE

For your own protection we suggest you return items UPS or insured parcel post. Should the items be lost or damaged in transit, carriers require that you file the tracer or claim. Postage is non-refundable.

N/07/07

FOR YOUR ORDER

If you are not satisfied with your order, you may return it within 14 days of the delivery date. For your convenience, items may be returned to the address on the packing slip or returned to your local Barnes & Noble store (check the local store refund policy for details).

0510011273080090101

04/14/2009 11:00PM (CL)

From:

BEV HORGAN
BEV HORGAN
13405 33RD AVE NE
SUITE 1A
BELLEVUE, WA 98005
UNITED STATES

To:

BARNES & NOBLE #2607
B&N.COM Customer Returns
1 Barnes & Noble Way
Monroe Township, NJ 08831

0510011273080090101

4/13/2009   9:06:53PM

return instructions

REASON FOR RETURN (PLEASE CHECK ONE)

◯ Damaged in Transit   ◯ Defective   ◯ Wrong Quantity

◯ Wrong Merchandise Received   ◯ Other (explain below)

COMMENTS:

---

easy returns

We are committed to bringing you not only the best values, but also the best service.

If for any reason you are not satisfied with your order and would like to return an item, please use the form below.

Please call 1-800•THE•BOOK for routing instructions.

FOR RETURNS: PLEASE CUT OUT LABEL ON DOTTED LINE AND ADHERE TO CARTON BEING RETURNED

QTY	DESCRIPTION	ITEM #	UNIT PRICE	AMOUNT

hard discounter business models. Hard discounters keep 600 to 1,000 low-price items in their assortments, consisting mainly of private labels, bought from contract manufacturers with clear retailer-driven specifications. In this way hard discounters exert a centralized and extremely efficient control over their value chain. Chapter 2 looks in closer detail at the factors affecting the competitiveness of hard discounters and the opportunities for other players to compete against them.

Food retailers have also entered manufacturing in some cases. Premium retailers such as Publix and Waitrose have their own manufacturing facilities, and these products are mainly positioned in premium segments. However, it is worth mentioning that vertical integration is by no means an automatic or 'one-way' trend. A good example of vertical disintegration is cooperative retailers giving up manufacturing. As late as the 1980s, several of these retailers had factories and bakeries. Nowadays, it is very rare to see retailers with these operations.

To summarize, the current trend seems to be vertical integration towards the consumer interface in order to gain access to final customers, get information on their behaviour and secure the customer experience. Some companies integrate vertically for differentiation purposes, and some also to secure resources in the retail value chain. The trend partly reflects the goal to eliminate unnecessary intermediaries from the value chain.

Convergence

In addition to vertical integration, the structure of retailing has been altered by the change in conventional distribution channel solutions. The familiar distinction between food and non-food stores is no longer valid. Non-food items in particular are sold at unusual locations and also often at lower than usual prices. For example, hypermarkets have had household appliances in their assortments for quite some time, but computer supplies and home decor products have also found their way into the permanent assortments of superstores, bringing their own worlds into the stores. Superstores offer possibilities for paint tinting – a service that has traditionally been the expertise of DIY stores. Similarly, a confectionery stand is now found at almost every sales location, including post offices and gardening shops. Consequently, the distinction between food and non-food is becoming increasingly blurred, and new store concepts consciously battle against conventional retail models.

Besides internal convergence within retailing, industries also intermingle. Retailers' share of the consumer's wallet has decreased considerably during the past few decades. In the 1980s, around 20 per cent of income was spent on food and non-alcoholic beverages. Nowadays it has dropped to about 15 per cent in many mature markets. At the same time, communication, home, travel and entertainment have become more important. In emerging markets the relative share of retailers is as yet significantly higher. To be able to compete with other industries for share of the consumer's wallet, new products and services are needed in retail. On the other hand, other players are also entering the retail sector, and they actively acquire retail expertise. For example, mobile operators are present at almost all shopping malls, petrol stations have become grocery stores, and many foodservice players have started to sell products like retailers.

The categories of retailers, restaurants and cafés are moving toward each other. For example, Starbucks coffee can also be bought at a retail store beside its own stores. Home meal replacement (HMR) is one of the biggest threats to retailing, but it is also one of its biggest opportunities. The buying habits of customers have shifted more clearly to ready meals. Also, consumption is moving away from the home to outlets where meals are not self-cooked. Restaurants are also entering this sector with their take-away offerings, aimed at selling not only sit-down meals at lunchtime but also meals to be taken home. If retail wants to compete for these consumer pounds, dollars or euros, it must respond to daily eating needs at different times of day and in different contexts. The challenge for retailers is to find out what makes customers spend time at a café, for example, and to see if the same effect could be created at a retail store. If this trend grows, it may have a big impact, especially on the sales of conventional top-up shopping outlets.

Whole Foods and Wegmans Food Markets are examples of retailers that have a dining area at the store after the checkouts. Customers can make their own salad or buy a warm meal at a counter and enjoy it at the store. Varied café services are also offered. Many small gourmet shops have started as a café, and have then grown into a whole store. Adding a wine bar in a retail store is an idea seen in Italy and the UK. Customers may pause at a wine department to have a glass of wine and then continue shopping. At the same time, they have the opportunity to test new wines and buy them to bring home. A wine bar may increase the time spent at a store and the enjoyment of shopping. Selfridges in London has positioned the wine bar next to the ladies' fashion department.

Foodservice may be a significant source of additional revenue in non-food retailing as well, as the example of IKEA shows. In 2004, the worldwide food sales of IKEA amounted to 515 million euros and it has risen at the annual rate of more than 25 per cent. According to Jan Kjellman, Vice President of IKEA Food Services, customers who visit the restaurant spend 20–30 minutes more time at the store itself, so the restaurant business seems to support the traditional concept. Café services are also offered in non-food retailing. Many bookshops and clothing stores have a coffee shop where customers may sit down for a while during shopping. These services can be owned by the non-food retailer, as in the case of IKEA, or offered by a partner.

Many retailers have expanded their operations into service stations either with a partner or on their own. Partners have been used to attend to fuel retailing, whereas retailers have focused on the running of convenience stores and cafés. In collaboration with Repsol, Spanish department store chain El Corte Inglés has established a chain of service stations. Repsol takes care of the service station operations and El Corte Inglés runs the food retailing operations. The service stations of El Corte Inglés follow the same principles as the department stores: they offer high-quality products and first-rate customer service. The fresh produce assortment is wide and the price level is higher than average, but still reasonable. In France, the market share of service stations owned by food retail chains amounted to 35 per cent. The biggest player was Carrefour with more than 1,200 service stations. Most of them are situated beside the retailer's hypermarkets, supermarkets and convenience stores, and only a few are freestanding outlets.

At least in some cases, a retailer may rely on its brand and its loyalty programme to expand its service offering. This is an attractive option, particularly when the cost of customer acquisition is high or when the product brand has little impact on the customer's quality image. A club member may then be exposed to the marketing of new products or services in conjunction with other communication for customers. On the other hand, billing can rely on the systems and customer data that are used at the company for other purposes as well. Tesco, for example, uses loyalty data in cross-selling financial services.

Table 1.2 lists examples of the most common new services. Industry boundaries have largely overlapped during the last few years as retailers have started to operate as mobile operators, banks or health clinics.

Banking services maintained by retailers have grown significantly during the past few years, and many of them have proved successful. Tesco, for example, had 1.7 million credit card customers and carried 1.4 million car

Table 1.2 Examples of retail expansion into new service areas

New service area	Examples
Banking	Tesco Financial Services, Migrosbank
Credit card	Target Visa, M-Budget Mastercard (Migros)
Insurance	Seguros El Corte Inglés, Carma (Carrefour)
Travel agency	Costco Travel, Voyages U (Système U)
Web store	Tesco.com, leshop.ch (Migros)
Mobile operator	Carrefour Mobile, Migros Mobile
Clinics	Target Clinic, Wal-Mart, Publix

insurance policies by 2004. It has over 20 different banking or insurance products covering everyday financial services. Marks & Spencer significantly increased its banking operations, but as the number of its customers went up to 2.4 million, it sold half of its banking operations to HSBC. The two companies continue to develop services in close cooperation. The Visa Card of German Metro is one of the most popular in Germany, and the bank established by Migros in Switzerland is the sixth largest in the market. In Finland, the grocery retail market leader S-Group opened its own bank at the end of 2007. The trend is also affecting US markets where, for instance, Wal-Mart and Kroger each offer a wide range of financial services.

Typically, retailers' financial services offerings cover consumption credits and mortgages as well as pension fund services. Many retailers rely on partners in banking operations: services are produced by a partner, or products designed and branded by partners are sold to customers. In many countries, working with a partner significantly facilitates the launch of operations as financial services are subject to strict administrative requirements. Traditional retail banking players already master these routines and have the necessary standard products; retailers then offer a new sales and service channel for the products.

The credit card business is often a significant area of expansion for retailers. The business is often profitable as such but it also increases revenues indirectly. The aim of launching a credit card may be to increase shopping visits and shopping basket size or to improve brand image. Some customers may not like the idea of using a combined credit and loyalty card at a competitor's store, which helps to strengthen customer loyalty. A retail credit card is usually sold on a 'one-card principle', helping to decrease the number of cards in the wallet.

Credit cards are often linked with loyalty programmes and used to enhance customer loyalty. Club members with a credit card may receive additional benefits, such as larger discounts and surprise benefits at the store. Many retailers give a bonus whenever customers use the card, regardless of where the card is used. However, the biggest rewards are given when the customer buys at the retailer's own stores. The terms and conditions of the cards are usually better than for standard credit cards: there is generally no annual or subscription fee and customers may also be given time for payment without interest. A credit card may also be targeted at a particular consumer segment. For instance, Printemps offers not only the basic card but also the Printemps à 2 card for couples getting married. The couple may open an account where wedding guests may donate money. The card also offers many additional benefits.

Credit cards are usually offered in cooperation with a major credit card company or bank. For example, Real-chain (part of Metro-Group) offers Visa options with its PAYBACK Premium card. Credit card partners may take care of billing and application processing, while the retailer takes care of distribution and marketing. Retail credit cards combined with basic financial services will pose a genuine risk to traditional banking players.

In addition to banking services, some retailers also offer a wide range of insurance products. Common insurance products include car, home, sickness, life, travel and pet insurance, but El Corte Inglés also offers insurance related to hobbies, such as downhill skiing and hunting. The competitive tools of many retailers are lower than average prices and in some cases also more wide-ranging benefits. For example, Tesco life insurance provides a price guarantee: if a customer finds a lower priced insurance policy somewhere else, the customer will receive 1,000 Clubcard points. Tesco has also made it easy for club members to buy travel insurance: insurance policies are available at the stores, and the customer may pay for insurance at the checkout, after which the insurance immediately takes effect. At El Corte Inglés, travel and home insurance may also be linked to the credit card.

Retailers can be very successful in the insurance business because they can choose their target groups and customers to be contacted among loyalty club members. Based on the knowledge of a customer's behaviour, a retailer has different information from the traditional insurance companies, which usually get their information from external data sources. The hit rate of campaigns carried out by traditional insurance companies is usually low, and retailers have good opportunities to be more effective. Typically, the role of retailers in insurance services is limited to selling and marketing insurance, and insurance claims handling is outsourced to a partner as the retailer seldom has experience in this area.

Loyalty programmes usually create a good foundation for online business, offering retailers a way of expanding their offering to customers. Nowadays few major online shops rely on food sales alone but also sell items such as electronic products and books. Tesco.com, considered by many to be the most successful grocery online retailer, offers a wide selection of non-food products and services. In 2007, Tesco.com exceeded the milestone of £2 billion in sales, and strong growth continues. Online retailing will be looked at in greater detail at the end of this chapter.

Many retailers have expanded operations into online services in addition to product sales. Common online services include ticket service, music downloads and digital photo service. These services can rely on the online channel or a combination of online and brick and mortar store channels. An online photo service may be used to order photos to be delivered to the customer's home or to the nearest store. Alternatively, or in addition, there may be a terminal device at the store where customers may order photos for home delivery or pick up at the store.

One of the newest expansion areas are mobile phone subscriptions. Many retailers aim to offer a basic subscription model responding to the needs of the masses. Affordable pricing and simple services are the competitive tools behind many subscriptions. The subscription offered by

Migros is one of the cheapest in the market; as is the one offered by Delhaize. Carrefour advertises its subscriptions as simple, clear and affordable. Simple products aimed at the mass market enable low prices and respond to the need of consumers to get a simple and reliable basic subscription. Tesco goes further by investing in excellent customer service. This has also been something consumers have desired; the response times of operators have been too long and customers have become frustrated with queuing. Many subscriptions are pre-paid, which enables a simple offering and the selling of additional usage time at the stores. Recently, retailers have also started selling post-paid subscriptions.

Mobile phone subscriptions are usually offered with mobile operators that provide the network and often also take care of billing and customer service, while the retailers focus on marketing and distribution. Over the long term, a retailer may have other reasons for being interested in acting as an operator for it may use the mobile phone in its own communication, especially if it adopts an ad-financed subscription model. The mobile phone and mobile portals may become a communication channel used for delivering information to customers on products, services and events. Suppliers can possibly buy advertising time on these channels.

Some retailers also offer travel services online or at separate outlets, located either at stores or as independent units. Many retailers use partners for these services – Tesco offers travel services together with lastminute.com, and Système U with a travel agency called Fram Voyages. Retailers may also have very different business models in travel services. Carrefour chooses travel services from the offerings provided by major travel agents and offers them to customers. Printemps focuses on luxury travel and honeymooners, whereas El Corte Inglés tailors travel services as needed by the customer. Tesco travel products are sold only online. The service offering can be very wide: package tours, just flights, hotels, car hire and other travel-related services are available at many chains. Expansion into travel has often been successful, for example Viajes El Corte Inglés is the leading travel agency in Spain and forms a considerable part of the business of El Corte Inglés, and Printemps is one of the biggest honeymoon sellers in France.

Fitness and healthiness are dominant trends in many markets, and retailers have expanded into them as well. Migros, something of a pioneer in this area, established the first fitness centres as early as 1977. Now it operates a host of centres with an abundant offering of services all over Switzerland. Various kinds of indulgence services are also popular, especially at upscale department store chains, where they naturally fit with the product and service offering and help maintain the store's overall image. Whole Foods has introduced a spa to one of its stores recently.

In the United States, supermarket and drug store chains have also started to diversify into health care. For instance, Target, Wal-Mart and

Publix have healthcare clinics at some of their stores. Drug stores, such as CVS and Walgreen Co, are also opening in-store clinics. Shoppers with minor ailments, such as strep throat or bladder infections, can easily visit the clinics during their shopping trip. Target clinics can be visited without an appointment and prices are lower than average.

One important motive for retailers to offer this service is attracting new customers to the store. In the United States, many retailers also run pharmacy operations at a convenience store, supermarket or hypermarket. In the long term, these services may have a big influence on the dynamics of welfare services and the development of the industry structure. For example, Wal-Mart has announced its intentions to roll out 2,000 in-store clinics in the next five to seven years. Healthcare-related services at stores are, however, tightly regulated in many countries. In-store clinics have also raised questions about possible drawbacks. However, it seems in most markets that the consumer demand for these services exists, but retailer participation is mainly governed by legislation.

Another example of innovative diversification is providing car hire services at retail stores. Système U in France has set up a car rental service called Location U. Cars are booked and rented at a store, and cars are also picked up and returned to the store. The service is available at about half of the retailer's stores, and the range offered includes both passenger cars and pick-up trucks. Low prices, a large store network and the lack of competitors in some areas have ensured the success of Location U. Short-term car rental is also offered at many DIY, furniture and home appliance stores, where a pick-up or trailer is needed for transporting the products, and it is a natural part of the service offering of the store.

Stores may also offer many other value-adding services like installation services or tickets for events. Some services become profitable quickly, such as music downloads, ticket services, online photo service and DVD rental. Some of the services, such as different types of consultation services, are offered for free and are aimed at adding value to the customer. Even if services are free, they may help to enhance customer loyalty and give a professional image for the retailer. Value-adding services will be discussed in more detail in Chapter 2.

The new services require retailers to develop new competences in service business and customer contact centres. Naturally enough, this development is generally pioneered by companies with a loyalty programme and strong expertise in multi-channel customer services that expand the relationship with customers to new services, by capturing a larger 'share of life'. A loyalty programme and shopper data form the foundation of the operations for targeting the communication and the offering at the right customers. The same billing system and support services may be used for new services, leading to cost advantages compared with one-industry companies. A smoothly running online shop with established customer flows also supports the expansion of operations. A trusted and expandable brand is also another key requirement for a successful service business. This may present a challenge to some companies in the market, both in terms of brand image and brand quality.

To sum up, retailing has expanded and will expand systematically into many new industries. During the past 10 years, retailers' share of the consumer's wallet has become significantly smaller, especially in mature markets in relation to other industries. New services may offer an opportunity to gain additional revenues and recapture some of the lost positions. Each new service area should still constitute a clear business case. Many extensions so far have been successes and some have even climbed to top positions in the market. In saturated markets, reaping additional revenues from existing stores with new offerings and services is a real challenge, but also a key focus area of retail strategy.

Consumer and product trends

Consumer trends and product changes are additional forces driving the retail industry. Changes in the needs and wants of customers may be slow and hard to detect, but they should be taken into account in the operations and product offerings both of retailers and manufacturers. As mentioned earlier, retailers are losing their share of the consumer's wallet and consumption is shifting elsewhere. This is partly due to the increase in income level; there is money to spend on non-obligatory purchases. On the other hand, however, the prices of necessities like electricity have risen and take an increasingly larger share of consumers' spending. Time pressure and consumers' convenience orientation have meant an increase in eating out and the buying of ready-made meals. Also, more and more money is spent on services like cleaning and beauty care. Retailers and manufacturers must become better at responding to the needs of the changing consumer to be able to defend their share of the consumer's purchases.

The list below highlights some key consumer facts and trends facing retailers:

- eating out – home-meal replacement;
- time-rushed consumers;
- cultural awareness and adoption of ethnic foods;
- health and healthiness;
- 'welfare diseases', such as obesity, diabetes and allergies;
- an ageing population with free time and capability to consume;
- growing singles and 'dinks' (dual income, no kids) segment with ability to consume;

- experience economy and hedonistic consumption;
- online shopping;
- product and price information availability;
- the new and growing iPod generation;
- social networks;
- sustainability and 'green' values;
- ethical consumption.

However, many of these trends may differ country by country. Consumer markets are still very local, and so are many consumer trends. However, key mega trends, such as sustainability, are affecting all markets to some extent.

Products develop at a fast pace, and there have been significant changes in product offerings during the past 10 years or so. Thanks to new product development and international sourcing, consumers are offered products they could not even dream of in the past. Products are becoming ever-more sophisticated and new materials among other things are continually taken into use. Examples include 'intelligent' clothes with embedded microchips, or Adidas running shoes where a small computer controls the degree of attenuation based on how hard the ground or running surface is. At the same time, a typical product lifecycle has become considerably shorter and new innovations are launched at an accelerating rate. These changes bring opportunities to manufacturers and retailers but they also require them quickly to adopt innovations and know how to develop products without delay.

Internationally known brands, mega brands, have spread all over the world and have replaced old local brands in many categories. Brand management is no longer so much about product development as marketing and creating an image among the desired target groups. Fashion and trends are now more international, with the same trends occurring all over the world. Even multinational giants have cut back some of their brands and increasingly focus on developing a few strong brands. As an example, Unilever has announced that it will dramatically decrease the number of brands. Instead, it will emphasize the group's own brand. On the flip side, there is a myriad of product copies and fakes, the number of which has risen at least at the same rate as global brands have strengthened.

Private labels act as a sort of counterforce to mega brands, and their share in retail assortments is continually rising. Traditionally, most private labels have been basic products, which have eaten market share from weaker-selling 'B brands' and have also improved margins. Over the long term, this reflects a significant change in the retail value chain, as the product development process shifts from manufacturers to retailers, at least partially. This is natural as retailers with customer interface and insight can make new product development an integral part of category management. With private labels, retailers have started to differentiate and selectively target certain consumer groups. Good examples include Tesco's Finest and Value product lines, which target different shopper segments. Private labels will be covered in more detail in Chapter 4.

What makes responding to consumer needs particularly challenging is the heterogeneity of the consumer base. Demographic factors are no longer sufficient to explain the consumer's behaviour. Instead, all age groups include many micro segments. As an example, young people can be further divided into representatives of many subcultures such as brand-conscious consumers, fitness fanatics and organic products consumers. These groups can also include people of various ages. The core family is no longer the standard, the daily rhythms differ and individual needs vary. Life in a family with two adults and three children is very different from that of five students in a city commune. Similarly, the shopping habits of individual consumers may vary to a significant degree, and they may be very different on weekdays from habits at the weekend. Moreover, the same consumers may emphasize quality in some purchases and just price on others, even during the same shopping trip. Many people want to eat healthy but they also want to enjoy the food experience. In some cases, retailers have even managed to identify yo-yo dieters based on their purchasing behaviour: sometimes they buy nothing but diet foods, while at other times they indulge in loads of delicious high-calorie goodies.

One of the most dramatic demographic changes is the ageing of the population. The average age of the population is rising in the industrialized countries, with an increasing share of people retiring. A significant difference from earlier generations is that 'old people' now retiring are usually in good physical condition and interested in using their time actively. Some use the expression 'free 2', the second free period in life, or the third age, starting for a person, for example, when the children have left home and the career is already past. Moreover, the generation soon to retire has a considerable amount of money, making it an attractive shopper segment to retailers. In fact, those belonging to this age group are used to spending money and demand that they get their money's worth. An increasing share of the money spent by the ageing population goes to services that make life easier, such as cleaning, and to hobbies and travelling. Retailers are in a position to capitalize on this, if they take the needs of older consumers into consideration.

From an overall economic perspective, the situation is not quite as sunny. This is because a smaller number of those working have to support an increasingly large amount of retirees. The situation also poses major challenges to local administrations. However, retailers may play new roles in developing the necessary local services, such as home delivery of groceries. One trend related to the growing number of retirees is the fact that more and more people have second homes and live there part of the year. The trend poses new challenges and opportunities to retailers operating in locations that are popular for second homes. Consumers who are used to city store offerings may spend considerably more at a local store if the retailer has the ability to listen to their needs. Some retirees also move to another area either permanently or for part of the year. For example, Florida in the United States and the Malaga area in Spain are popular destinations for retirees.

In addition to retirees, the number of singles has also been growing, making them an attractive market segment with a high purchasing power. Smaller packs and individually packed foods are favoured by singles for the simple reason that mega packs meant for families with children easily perish in a single-person household. The assortment in convenience stores located in a town centre looks very different from that at supermarkets located in a residential area full of families with children. In addition to singles, the number of 'dinks' (dual income, no kids) is also increasing. Dinks focus on indulgence and gathering experiences, and they often have the money to do so. Dinks may also have more time for shopping and cooking as a hobby than do busy families with children.

Furthermore, retailers have to be prepared to serve the consumers of the future, including the iPod generation. This consumer group will behave in quite different ways from today's consumers, and they already influence their parents' shopping behaviour. This generation is thirsty for information, and with the web having always been present in their lives, they expect to get information easily. Instead of indulging in a passive activity such as watching television, they have become used to interactive services and having a say, a trend further strengthened by the development of Web 2.0. Peer group opinions and recommendations are also important, and the new consumer generation wants to make decisions based on available information and not just be on the receiving end of conventional push marketing communication. They know how to pick the information, which poses challenges to retail operations. The consumer of the future can be approached with a well-targeted event-based communication, for example through virtual communities.

The new generation is also accustomed to a wide assortment as, thanks to the internet, the whole world is open to them. New technology is nothing to be feared; they are open to try anything new, and are generally more informed and thus also more demanding customers. In many countries, the new generation has a healthy attitude towards working and desires to have free time, too. Leisure time is optimized, so products and services making everyday life easier are in high demand. Thus, the new generation is willing to buy many kinds of services. Unlike the baby boom generation, they find the buying of cleaning services, for example, natural.

Many ethnic groups today are more visible in society than before. In many areas, Chinese communities are a classic example of a distinct ethnic group, but today there are a large number of other groups as well. Spanish is the number one language in many areas in the United States. Similarly, there are now more than 2.5 million Turks in Germany; and the Swedish capital of Stockholm has areas where more than 80 per cent of inhabitants are immigrants. International crises continually increase the number of refugees, and the flow of immigrants from Africa to Europe, for instance, is ongoing. In addition, new generations are more willing to relocate when studying or working.

The trends related to ethnicity force retailers to reconsider their product offering and labelling. The number of languages in product labelling reflects not only the needs of ethnic groups, but also the internationalization of sourcing. The aim is to design a product package that can be used in as many countries as possible. Ethnic food has been included in almost every retailer's assortment, but it seems that its share is still on the rise. Ethnic food trends vary and TV shows featuring celebrity cooks also play a role in building new trends. The needs of ethnic groups will drive 'genuine' ethnic foods in the assortment and not only adapted versions targeted at the mainstream population. On the other hand, the demand for ethnic food has grown among the mainstream population as well. Real food lovers often buy original ingredients at small speciality shops, which help to maintain the wide range of retailing. But also big retailers can play this game. For example, Wal-Mart operates Arab-America's store, where several hundred additional stock keeping units (SKUs), including falafel, Halal meats and Islamic greeting cards, are presented in addition to the traditional supercentre assortment. Wal-Mart has also hired several Arabic speaking people for customer service.

Consumer income level has risen steadily all over the world. In addition, emerging markets, like China and India, have a large number of middle-class consumers who can afford luxuries. The number of wealthy consumers is increasing in the West as well, and the demand for luxury and designer products is on the rise. Consumption rates vary in different countries and customer groups; while expensive bags and designer clothes are important status symbols for some, others may prefer a state-of-the-art phone or MP3 player. Luxury brands have also become important to many consumers, even to those who actually cannot afford them. Consumer credit has become increasingly common, although there are big differences depending on how developed a market is. As some formerly exclusive brands are now owned by almost everyone who has an interest in them, the rich and famous are trying to find new exclusive products to show their status. Some brands have suffered from their popularity as they have become too common.

With the increase in consumer income levels, time pressures have increased and most people have little time left, for example, for cooking. Over the years, the number of weekly shopping trips has declined in many markets. At the same time, the value of each grocery purchase trip has increased considerably. The trend is closely connected to the growing presence of large hypermarkets and shopping centres; it is now possible and desirable to spend a larger amount of money on each shopping trip.

Time pressures have also affected product offerings; the number of convenience food items has gone up, for example. Convenience food that is quick to heat up makes everyday routines considerably easier. There is a wide selection of convenience foods, ranging all the way from hot dogs to complete gourmet meals. Recent development has put a particular emphasis on high-quality ready meals. These products have increasingly often been developed by retailers as part of their private label offerings.

Time pressures have also boosted the demand for snack products. With no time for a decent meal, consumers have many small snacks during the day. They are often bought on the go: at a grocery store, service station, fast-food outlet, school or work. The snack offering is very wide, ranging from conventional chocolate bars and crisps to sandwiches and biscuits. New products are mushrooming as consumption grows and is more varied. Though snacking is usually thought to be unhealthy, there are also healthy snack options: diced fruit and vegetables are available in many places.

Healthfulness is a key trend having a strong impact on marketing and product development, both in retail and food service operations. Among the most popular health products are light products containing less fat and sugar than their standard version. Their popularity has grown steadily, and nearly all products now have a light version. There are light versions of basic foods such as cheese and meat, but also of food normally considered unhealthy, such as sweets. At one extreme, you can even buy 'fatless fat'. With the current technology, almost any kind of product can be created. However, not all light products are healthy and low calorie. For instance, light bologna sausage is very fatty compared with no-fat turkey slices. Likewise, the healthfulness of synthetic non-fats and sugar substitutes has been questioned.

There is a growing need for light products, since more than 60 per cent of US adults and about half of Europeans are overweight. Among major markets, the United States and UK consumers are most likely to be overweight, but the increase is fastest in France and Germany. The number of overweight consumers in the United States will also continue to grow rapidly. In addition, childhood obesity is a growing concern. The increase in obesity rates in many Western countries (and increasingly also in developing countries) has boosted the popularity of diets and light foods. The consumer products industry has also been criticized for the increased obesity rate. During the past few decades, packages have grown in size, and many unhealthy foods such as confectionery and crisps are sold in mega packs. Advertising also often emphasizes manufacturer brands with indulgence, but as retailers often handle marketing of perishables themselves with little manufacturer monetary support, fruit and vegetables have not gained much visibility in marketing.

Organically produced products with no preservatives are also considered healthy. Many consumers have started to fear potential dangers caused by heavily processed food. For example, sweets may contain dozens of different colouring agents and additives. Many sweeteners have been suspected of causing concentration difficulties, especially when used in large amounts. Consumers have also been biased against GMO (genetically modified organisms) products though there is so far no strong evidence of health hazards. In Europe, consumer resistance is currently so strong that many retailers would not take GMO products in assortments even if the EU legislation did not impose any restrictions on them. It is, however, still likely that GMO products will be accepted at some point, and the product offerings will continue to be developed. Non-additive products may bring competitive advantage in certain customer groups, and many children's foods, indeed, contain no additives or preservatives. The popularity of organic foods has been rising for some time, and constitutes a significant trend. Organic products will be dealt with in more detail in the next section.

The increasing number of so-called welfare diseases, as well as allergies and the ageing of the population, cause retailers to address new needs, which can also be seen as a new business opportunity. Obesity causes many kinds of welfare diseases such as diabetes and cardiovascular diseases.

Consumers are often willing to pay a higher than average price for products that are considered healthy. Manufacturers have tried to respond to the prevention of welfare diseases by launching functional foods, or foods that promote health benefits. These refer to preparations that have an intrinsic health-promoting effect or that together with added ingredients have a healthy effect. Examples that have aroused a lot of attention include cholesterol-lowering Benecol margarine and Danone's Actimel products. Health-promoting ingredients such as vitamins and digestives are often added to juices, milk products and margarines. For instance, Kroger carries cholesterol-reducing milk in its assortment. Besides functional foods, various performance-increasing products have grown in popularity. Sports drinks have been on the market for a long time, but performance drinks and foods are being consumed by other consumers, too. Various kinds of waters and juices are advertised to improve concentration, raise the energy level or help people slow down and relax.

The growth of allergies and other conditions requiring special diets leads to increased requirements for products and labelling. Packages contain more – and more detailed – information on the products and the ingredients used, partly due to legislative requirements. The challenge is to present information in a simple form in spite of increased information requirements. The label space available does not increase, and small fonts make labelling hard to read. Manufacturers might also use vague terms, like 'spice', and technical terms, such as 'casein' instead of milk, or 'albumin' instead of eggs, which make it difficult to know what the product actually contains. There is a continuing stream of new products related to special diets as the customer base grows and requirements rise. For instance, more than 5 per cent of US adults have food allergies; the most common food allergens are milk and other dairy foods, fish, eggs, crustaceans such as lobster and shrimp, tree nuts such as walnuts, peanuts, soy and wheat. The number of multi-allergic people is also increasing.

Health and a healthy diet are accompanied by different fashion diets emphasizing a certain type of foods, such as the Atkins diet, which encourages avoiding carbohydrates. Many retailers have answered to this call with low-carb products in assortments. Protein has been added to some surprising products, such as pasta. Though some diets have a very short life, retailers may enhance customer satisfaction and sales by offering products compatible with them. The low-carb fervour has calmed down but new diets are introduced continually. Some consumers are interested in the GI (glycaemic index) values of foods, whereas others wish to follow the South Beach Diet, or 'Stone Age' diet.

On the other hand, consistently following a healthy diet is also catching on. Fairly commonplace products can be branded to suit a particular diet. For example, WeightWatchers has had products made with its own brand. Moreover, retailers have built services around various diets. For example, Tesco's web service helps customers follow their preferred diet by providing recipes and product lists to make shopping easier. The K-Supermarket chain in Finland offers its customers a service called Food Code, which uses receipt data to analyse the nutritional values of the shopping basket compared with recommended levels. The service is subject to a fee, and customers may analyse their shopping trolley over the internet either for a single shopping visit or over a longer period. The service enables those watching their weight to pay attention to 'challenging points' in their own shopping, such as products containing a lot of sugar and fats.

Besides healthfulness, self-care and indulgence are a rising trend. Different health and luxury products have grown in popularity, as consumers seek to add those aspects to their lives. Indulgence products may be healthy but they do not entail abstinence. Food needs to be more than something to fill your stomach. Indulgence embraces many gourmet products, such as high-quality cheese and wines. High-quality chocolate is also in fashion, and some even savour chocolate in the same way as wines are tasted. Indulgence may also involve a good convenience meal, sparing the customer from having to cook. On the other hand, time pressures and fast food are offset by the trend for slow food. In some cases, the focus is shifting towards cooking and slow enjoyment of food. Many consumers are obliged to resort to fast food on weekdays, but offset it by focusing on slow food on weekends. Various home-spa products are also related to the healthiness trends. Time-rushed consumers do not necessarily have time to go to a spa, but they can create a similar experience at home with the help of retailers.

Consumers also seek adventure and experiences in products. Shopping is not supposed to be boring, but surprising and inspiring, and retailers can use this trend in many ways. The whole concept may be based on adventure. An excellent example is Stew Leonard's, also called the Disneyland of grocery stores. Service at the store is excellent, and walking through the store's departments offers inspiration and certainly leaves nobody cold. Individual products can also be used to create experiences. Many stores use storytelling to add a sense of adventure to products, and local products in particular often have a story behind them. Regularly renewed assortments and novelties also enhance customer experience. Retail concept development and category management are discussed in greater detail in Chapter 4.

In an internationalizing world, product safety is an issue that has received increasing attention. BSE (mad cow disease), avian influenza and other plagues as well as terrorist attacks have received considerable media coverage and made consumers cautious. Likewise, products manufactured in countries with low-cost production, especially in China, have recently hit the headlines because of product safety issues. The challenges have been caused by, for instance, the use of prohibited ingredients in manufacturing, dangerous electric devices and poisonous animal feed. Dangers are usually linked to a particular product category, such as poultry or beef, which may cause significant changes in the structure of demand.

In response to growing doubts, retailers and manufacturers have to work together to ensure that the products have a risk-free and safe flow in the retail value chain. A safe product offering may be used as a competitive advantage. Carrefour, for example, has advertised the retailer's safety policies in China, where negligence has led to increased attention paid to product safety. With new packing methods, the shelf life of fresh products in particular has been greatly improved. Dates by which these products need to be consumed have become longer, and a considerable number of meat and fish products are now sold in manufacturer packages and not in the traditional way, at a service counter. 'Intelligent packages' are also emerging, especially for fresh products. These are packages that monitor the state of products and may issue an alarm if the cold chain is disrupted or if the amount of bacteria in the product is too high.

Product safety involves the tracking of product flow right from the beginning. This may, however, be difficult, particularly in the case of processed food. The fact that products are local may be a value as such and increase the trust level among customers. The same product may arouse suspicion if it has been produced abroad even though there are no differences in quality. Locality is sometimes a value in itself. An example is the Pro Mustard movement in Finland, which arose to protest against Unilever's decision to move the manufacturing of the most well-known mustard in Finland first to Sweden and then to Poland. Former employees re-opened the factory with a new local brand. Another example is Superquinn in Ireland, that portrays the local meat producers and other farmers in pictures on the wall. This is a way of selling a story instead of just a product. At the same time, product safety has been translated into a differentiating factor and even a competitive advantage.

Green values and social responsibility are examples of other rising trends, which have a considerable impact on the product offering. Corporate responsibility and its consequences will be looked at in greater detail in the following chapter. To sum up, there is a host of consumer trends affecting retailers' product and service offerings. Consumer groups become more heterogeneous, and the trend is strengthened by retailers with their differentiated offerings. Offerings are targeted at increasingly small segments with a wide spectrum of lifestyles. On the other hand, an individual customer may be interested in many things: the same consumer may have an interest in green values, state-of-the-art technology and fast food. With new technologies and loyalty programmes, retailers can reach the niche groups they identify through effectively focused communication. This will be covered in more detail in Chapter 7.

Sustainability

International investment markets require companies to report on corporate responsibility. Consumers are also increasingly aware of the social and ecological consequences of business operations, and various non-governmental organizations (NGOs) efficiently spread related information in the media. Global warming and its effects have stirred much discussion. This is why corporate responsibility has aroused attention among retail companies as well. Corporate responsibility involves 'triple bottom-line thinking': companies take into account economic, environmental and social responsibility. Economic responsibility involves meeting the financial expectations of the owners and shareholders and contributing to the economic well-being of society. In other words, a company should be profitable, efficient and competitive. Management of the company's impact on the environment and the use of natural resources in a sustainable way are considered in environmental responsibility. Social responsibility can be executed by implementing good business practices in the relations with all stakeholder groups, from employees to local communities and consumers. Corporate responsibility may be visible both in a company's operations and its products and services. Voluntary programmes and charity are other elements involved in putting corporate responsibility into practice. The current critical issues in retail include transportation impact, eco-efficiency (energy and water usage) and recycling. Social issues are also important in retail because of its labour-intensive nature.

For some pioneer companies, corporate responsibility provides the opportunity to stand out from the competition. The image benefit may have far-reaching implications not only among consumers but also in the form of increasing attractiveness in the recruiting market. On the other hand, weakly managed corporate responsibility is a key risk factor for a company if it is exposed through the media and highly visible investigative journalism. Therefore, ongoing monitoring of corporate responsibility belongs on the agenda of every competent board in the retail industry. Finnish retailer Kesko has been in the vanguard of corporate responsibility reporting. Many years ago, it started to prepare environmental reports for its customers and interest groups. The company has won many awards with its reports and has raised environmental consciousness as a visible theme in its operations. More recently, Kesko has emphasized the conditions of workers in the sourcing countries, and other local retailers have followed suit.

During the last few years, the most visible area of corporate responsibility has been 'green retailing'. Global warming and carbon dioxide emissions have affected the thinking among retail management as well. Many of our interviewees believe that sustainability will be one of the key themes in the development of ECR (efficient consumer response) collaboration during the next few years. One environmental development theme that was considered common for the whole industry was efficient transportation. This key cost driver can also be promoted on the basis of green values and carbon dioxide emissions, as has been done in the airline industry in Europe. At the same time, retailers should be prepared for one key risk factor, which is the dramatic rise in fuel costs and the accompanying increase in logistics costs.

In addition to intra-company projects, discussions have been underway among different retail groups on possibilities to combine transportation to increase volumes and utilization rates. This would be particularly efficient in sparsely populated areas where distances are long and demand is relatively small. On the other hand, there is no point in driving with half-empty loads in big-city traffic jams. Good loading degrees have an impact on both pollution and traffic jams. Pollution can also be affected by using alternative means of transportation and fuels. For instance, Sainsbury's has announced that by September 2008, 20 per cent of its online deliveries will be made using electric vans, saving 45 tons of CO_2 emissions in the first year. Another way of influencing pollution and traffic jams is good store site planning, ensuring that customers can come to the store on foot or using public transport.

Some retailers provide customers the opportunity to make green choices in terms of carbon dioxide emissions. As an example, customers are often offered the option of buying local fruit instead of items transported from far away. Marks & Spencer informs customers of this by adding air-freight labels to products that have been transported by air. This supports the consumer to make pro-environmental choices.

Corporate responsibility is reflected in the retail product offering in many ways. The aim is to take responsibility into account throughout the lifecycle of a product, from raw materials to recycling of old products. Efforts have been made to reduce the use of harmful materials, and alternative materials have been developed. This is especially important in many durable commodities, such as refrigerators and washing machines. Another goal is to reduce the amount of packaging waste. Finally, disposing or recycling of used products and their packages should be made easy and as environmentally friendly as possible. In transport, pallets have long been recyclable, but increasingly other transport packages are standardized and recyclable at least on the national level. In Finnish retailing, the bottle deposit system used for soft drinks has been used for dozens of years, and Finns are keen to return their bottles: as many as 98 per cent of deposit bottles are returned to be washed and refilled. Glass bottles are recycled an average of 33 times and plastic bottles an average of 18 times.

Another good example of product lifecycle management is the milk bag. Waitrose plans to sell milk in bags to reduce the amount of plastic bottles used. The bags will be sold alongside a jug into which the milk can be decanted and kept in the fridge. The bags contain 75 per cent less plastic than the milk bottles, and thus less energy is used in making them. They also take up far less space when disposed of, helping to reduce waste. Milk bags are popular, for example, in Canada and some South American countries. The goal is to cut down the use of plastic in many other areas. For example, Tesco rewards its club members for using their own bags instead of buying new ones. In the United States, many seashore cities like San Francisco and Annapolis (MD) have set up a plastic bag ban to protect their sensitive maritime wildlife. Recently China banned using thin plastic bags in retail stores. The paper bag production process does not consume any oil, and recycled paper can often be used. Sainsbury's has also replaced some plastic containers with bio packaging made from maize, sugar cane or starch, which can naturally break down in a compost heap at home.

An especially strong trend at the moment is organic products. Organic foods are produced according to certain production standards that are usually legally regulated. Currently, for instance, the United States, the European Union and Japan require producers to obtain organic certification in order to market food as organic. In some countries, the government has also set targets to increase organic production. There are organic products ranging from vegetables, fruit and processed food to home decor. Selling organic products is nothing new; Carrefour marketed organic Carrefour Bio products as early as 1997. However, the popularity of organic products keeps rising. Almost every retailer has included some organic products in its assortments, and stores like Whole Foods sell nothing but organic products. For example, organic food sales in the United States have enjoyed a growth rate of up to 20 per cent for the past few years while sales of conventional food have grown only a few per cent a year. The strong growth is expected to continue as new players enter the market. Consumers are generally willing to pay more for organically produced products, but these products' high prices have also been criticized.

With added emphasis on green values, store solutions have also been reconsidered. Buildings create a lot of indirect carbon dioxide emissions both during construction and when in operation. Sainsbury's has been one of the pioneers in environmental friendliness of buildings with its energy-saving green house pilot as early as the end of the 1990s. Recently, many other retailers have piloted eco properties. Tesco's energy-efficient property uses 20 per cent less electricity than normal stores. Electricity is produced by wind turbines located on the store roof. The store also saves energy by reusing the air from refrigeration equipment in ventilation, by maximizing the use of natural light and by using energy-saving ovens in the bakery department. Wal-Mart also aims at maximizing the use of renewable resources in its pilot and reuses air heated by refrigeration equipment. Refrigeration equipment contains motion-sensing LED lights, which automatically go off when there are no customers in front of a shelf and turn on when customers appear. Furthermore, the use of lights can be regulated automatically depending on the amount of natural light. Another innovative solution is the recycling of oil that has been used to fry chickens, using it in heating the property.

These solutions are said to have brought in significant energy savings, but they are not yet widely used. Building pilot sites is easy, and they have been exploited visibly in marketing. But implementing the ideas in the hundreds or thousands of stores is a totally different exercise in terms of costs. On the other hand, even small improvements may lead to significant benefits in the energy efficiency of properties, when implemented on the chain level. Pilots are needed for discovering these areas and validating the benefits.

Social responsibility is also important in the labour-intensive retail sector. Because of long opening hours, working hours pose challenges for many people in their personal lives. Industrial safety, humane working conditions and self-development opportunities are the key focus areas of social responsibility. Retailing is largely a low-paid industry where employees are clearly less organized than in other industries. Consequently, typical challenges in low-wage industries can be covered in the media using retailing as an example. In particular, value retailing companies with their tight cost discipline and rigid rules have been attacked by the media because a large majority of employees work at almost minimum pay. Many retailers have been suspected of preventing the unionization of the workforce, and in many countries trades unions are very weak in retailing. Retailers are studied more often in courts or in the media than labour unions or trades unions. For example, Wal-Mart recently appeared in court because of charges relating to alleged sex discrimination and the alleged use of illegal immigrants. The tough workforce rules of hard discounters have also been covered in the media in many countries all over Europe. On the other hand, satisfied and respected employees can be a competitive advantage for retailers. Employees as a competitive factor will be covered in greater detail in Chapter 2.

Unfortunately, the efficiency and low prices of large-scale retail stores also have negative consequences, of which one has to do with local communities. Typically as soon as a new large-scale store opens, many conventional small stores lose customers and often shut down, with Darwinian principles. This also leads to unemployment and migration, and the total salary level in the area goes down because large-scale stores employ fewer employees than do conventional, service-based small stores. Large-scale retail stores also often pay lower salaries than conventional players and the lower total payroll amount has consequences in the community and decreases purchasing power in the area. Town centres may become empty as one store after another closes and services move elsewhere. Besides empty small-town centres, the same trend has brought a new side effect: dead malls, with malls being deserted first by shoppers and little by little also by stores.

During the past few years, this trend has been noted particularly in small towns. In the United States the number one scapegoat has been Wal-Mart, though similar developments can be seen all over the world. Many towns across the United States have seen the birth of opposition movements aiming at preventing Wal-Mart from entering the town. Their goal is to maintain the local small-town community, and in some cases the movements have achieved their goal. In other cases, a large-scale store has been built next to the town boundary. The consequences at the local level are almost the same, but the tax money goes to the neighbouring town. Though Wal-Mart is the most maligned in this respect, the same trend is also true for other countries and other retailers with large-scale stores. An increasing number of retail players have started programmes to support the local community to ensure its future vitality. Perhaps the most important individual form of these programmes is local sourcing, which will be covered in more detail later.

Sustainability also affects manufacturers. Key issues in the consumer goods industry are somewhat different from those in retailing because of the different nature of the business. The consumer goods industry is facing the challenges of manufacturing while retailers' issues are related more to the services industry. The most significant areas for manufacturers include, for instance, product lifecycle management, sustainable agriculture and biodiversity, animal welfare, genetic engineering and transport impacts. Social responsibility is also important, with human rights, employment issues, employee education and workplace safety among the most important areas.

On the other hand, the social responsibility of retailers also involves supplier relationships. While an increasing amount of production has moved to countries offering cheap labour, notably the Far East, the working conditions have started to arouse more attention. Whenever a cheaper alternative is found, production is moved. This has also raised criticism both because of the loss of jobs and the working conditions in countries where production is cheap. Thanks to efficient international sourcing, large value retailers are actually the major reasons for shifting production to countries where it is cheap. Struggling with price pressures, conventional Western suppliers also have to move production there; if not, sourcing is done directly from local suppliers. The use of a child workforce and destruction of the local environment are other themes that have been given visibility in the media, forcing companies to pay attention to them.

In some markets, social responsibility is linked with charity. Many retailers donate money or employee time for charity purposes. Employees may use working hours for participating in voluntary activities. For instance, Starbucks has a volunteer programme called 'Make Your Mark' where baristas and customers come together to work on projects that directly affect the community. Baristas organize projects like park clean-ups and AIDS walks with local non-profit organizations.

Big retailers like Wal-Mart, Tesco and Carrefour annually donate large sums to charity. For example, Wal-Mart provides financial and volunteer support to more than 100,000 charitable and community-focused organizations. Many also have foundations to support the charitable activities, such as Tesco Charity Trust and Carrefour International Foundation. Each year, Tesco selects a national charity with a strong community network to become their Charity of the Year. This becomes the main focus for staff fundraising. The Carrefour International Foundation has an annual budget of 4.57 million euros, and it is focused on two main missions: emergency reconstruction aid and the fight against social exclusion. It is active in countries where the Carrefour Group operates and supports local teams, based on the involvement of employees, stores and local charity organizations.

So far, most companies have responded to consumers or interest groups mainly when they have been compelled to do so, but there are companies whose business is based on ethical principles. A case in point is The Body Shop, with its business idea of offering naturally manufactured and non-animal tested cosmetic products to consumers. Indeed, The Body Shop has been a huge success and the concept has spread all over the world. Another example is Whole Foods, which sells natural fresh produce and organic products. It has enjoyed a staggering rate of growth in the United States. The Fair Trade trademark is another expression of the rising social responsibility among Western consumers and of the need for retailers to respond to this sentiment.

Full-scale execution of corporate responsibility throughout the organization is a challenging task. It requires good quality standards and efficient follow-up routines. A company, if it wishes to preserve its competitiveness, often needs to balance the cost advantages with corporate responsibility actions. Currently there is a lack of clear metrics, and corporate responsibility communication is an exceptionally challenging task because some consumers have a sceptical attitude towards it. Spreading faulty information may harm a company's reputation even more than abstaining from communication. Consumer activists are not ready to believe in the sincerity of companies unless they see evidence of responsible actions. Implementation also poses practical challenges at stores. For example, a significant increase in recycling creates issues in reverse logistics and store space usage, which may be a challenge particularly for small stores.

Corporate responsibility is a theme that receives increasing attention. It is a major risk factor to large retailers, as individual visible mistakes in this respect may have a considerable impact on reputation. There is and will be a lot of activists who bring the problems to the surface. Visible activists like Naomi Klein, the author of several bestsellers such as *No Logo* and *The Shock Doctrine: The rise of disaster capitalism*, arouse a lot of social discussion. It is much easier for retailers to respond proactively by operating in a high-quality fashion in the first place, and not have to make up for damage already done. The internet speeds up the activities of NGOs, and the information on products or companies to be boycotted spreads at a fast rate. Activists focus on different themes, such as animal rights, anti-globalization or human rights. Besides big international organizations, small organizations also arise, and some of them have radical approaches.

It is clear that retailers will try to better anticipate the social reactions of their measures. Some may aim at profiling themselves as supporters of a certain social idea, or even as pioneers. Environmental consciousness and attention to local conditions may soon be important criteria for people choosing where to shop. Over the long term, environmental friendliness will grow in importance and consumers will be more and more enlightened. Products may be assigned new metrics, such as 'consumption values' or 'ecological footprint', corresponding to CO_2 emission values for cars.

Global standardization is still missing, but getting it will only be a matter of time. Standardization will entail costs and tests, so manufacturers are hardly eager to promote it. Various research institutions have studied the degree of products' ecological friendliness, and, for instance, in Sweden the amount of ecological load has been calculated for different products. Environmental effects can be determined by using a lifecycle assessment, investigating key areas of the production chain from the manufacturing of production inputs like fertilizers to farming, refining, packing and retail distribution. The environmental load caused by the use of the product may be evaluated in a similar fashion, for example the impact on climate warming, acidification and eutrophication. Still, legislation or directives are needed before large-scale use of product analyses. Retailers are business players responding quickly to new legislative consequences, but they will not actively promote new rules and regulations unless these produce direct business benefits.

Few retailers have publicly written down their full corporate responsibility mission and the related guidelines and principles for different areas. The future attitude towards animal rights, for instance, may vary to a large degree among companies. Some will leave the choice to customers and offer the alternatives available on the market, whereas others may reject ethically precarious products or products that do not meet the sustainability criteria set by them. These are major value choices, which can be used to steer demand. One interesting recent case is from the United States, where premium supermarket retailer Wegmans Food Markets banned the sale of cigarettes and other tobacco products in its stores. 'As a company, we respect a person's right to smoke, but we also understand the destructive role smoking plays in health', said Danny Wegman, CEO. This will affect the company's bottom line as cigarettes are a small but profitable category for most grocers. But it also will distinguish Wegmans as a socially responsible company that cares about the health of its customers, which could increase customer loyalty among non-smokers – (however, the solution might also have its consequences among smokers).

It has been interesting to see that consumers have a tremendous power over the solutions of retailers, but this power is now rarely used. Using it collectively is a challenging task, and many markets lack suitable forums and opinion builders. Activists in this area are often too extreme for the mass market to follow. With the current efficient category management and store replenishment methods, a simple decision by consumers not to buy a certain product, or shifting consumption to some other product has a very quick impact, but few consumers understand or believe it. Public debate, newspapers and the media in general will have a weighty role in these choices. With an increased focus on sustainability, consumers may use more discretion in filling shopping trolleys and choosing which stores to visit. Some ideological segments are already very conscious, but it remains to be seen when the mainstream with big money start to choose their shopping place based on ethical values.

E-business

Around the turn of the 2000s, with the IT craze in full swing, it was expected that the internet would revolutionize the whole infrastructure of retailing. When the IT bubble burst and most expectations were left unmet, many traditional retailers were willing to bury the whole idea of e-retailing. Consumer trade over the internet has, however, quietly continued to grow. Its annual growth is clearly faster than the overall retail average. E-retailing brings many benefits, which have contributed to its growth. The internet knows no borders, and customers may often buy the same products at a clearly cheaper price abroad than in their home country. Comparing competing products is easy and price comparison programs help in finding the best offer. The web stores often have huge assortments, impossible for conventional retailers to match. Moreover, you can often find special products and rarities that are not sold anywhere else, and several online retailers have made a business of 'the long tail', selling small volumes of hard-to-find items to many customers, instead of only selling large volumes of a reduced number of popular items as typical brick and mortar retailers.

E-commerce also gives benefits to retailers and suppliers. Some e-stores only operate over the net, but many retailers have a multi-channel strategy. Using a well-known brand in online commerce is one key success factor as customers are more willing to order products from a well-known, trustworthy source. For a successful retailer, starting an online store may be a natural way of extending the brand. An online store is often profitable as such, but it may also bring other benefits. The value of a shopping basket may be considerably higher in the online environment than at brick and mortar stores. Also, the internet is a cheap and easy channel to use for communication and product testing. It can be used for marketing and brand-building activities as well, offering information to customers and communicating with them. The web can also serve as a channel for selling products on commission, which helps to offer customers a wider-than-normal assortment. Some companies test products over the net before including them in store assortments. This is a low-cost way of testing the success of a new product before full-scale distribution, and customer views may be exploited using active customer segments. Testing global brands over the net is cost efficient and simpler than testing them locally, separately in each country. Customers may also be committed to a brand through different clubs such as the Harley-Davidson club, which has an online community of more than a million customers.

The identification of customers at an online store enables personalization of customer communication. Retailers can generate product and service recommendations based on a customer's earlier purchases and interests. Unidentified customers may also be given recommendations according to their browsing behaviour on the basis of the behaviour of other customers who have visited similar pages. Optimized offers and other messages may also be personalized by the visited pages. The time of day and the quickness of mouse movements may also have an impact on the content and timing of communication.

A classic example of personalization is Amazon, which continually uses personalized recommendations. Customers may also influence the offers by notifying the site of their interests. Personalization is used also in e-mail messages as an automatic and cost-efficient way of activating customers to visit the site and make additional purchases. Amazon also lets customers prevent personalization if they so wish. Additionally, information collected over the web can be used in marketing and for improving the site. On the other hand, excessive marketing needs to be avoided as frequent pop-ups only annoy customers and cause them quickly to move elsewhere.

E-commerce is very close to conventional mail-order selling, and the net just complements or replaces older technologies, such as catalogues in product demonstration and the telephone or coupons in making an order. The main principles and logistical background processes are largely the same, and so are the challenges. An often-cited hindrance to the success of online retailing is the last-mile problem, as the delivery to the doorstep of the customer is distinctly more expensive than in self-service retailing where the customer goes to the 'warehouse' (that is, the store), collects and pays for the products and takes them home. It is a challenge in online retail to figure out how to gather the products ordered by consumers and deliver them at an acceptable price. The sales of digital media such as music and movies are simple over the web, as customers may download the products directly, and there is no last-mile problem.

Delivery time and security are also potential challenges in distance retailing, especially when products are ordered from abroad. Delivery times have perhaps been given vaguely, and ordering from unknown companies may be risky. Here is a distinct niche for international courier companies, which can, thanks to large volumes, deliver products quickly and at a relatively low cost all over the world.

Another challenge in online retailing is a low conversion rate. The site may have a lot of visitors, but only a fraction of them ends up buying something. It is easy to look at products on the internet and perhaps proceed all the way to the checkout without ultimately buying anything. Some customers use the web to search for information and then buy the products somewhere else. This may be caused partly by web pages that are poorly designed and difficult to use or by technical challenges. Then again, there is no social pressure to buy on the internet; it is easy to reject products just before payment if you change your mind. This is rare at a store checkout.

Another challenge for an online retailer is that consumers are cautious about privacy and security issues. Many retailers selling products over the net are unknown to consumers. The selling party may be a small company or private person whose reliability is a question mark. Credit data thefts have eroded trust in e-commerce. Differences in legislation and customs clearance may also cause problems in international orders. When expensive goods are bought, exchange risk is also something to take into account. In addition, consumers may not be willing to buy products if they are not convinced of the quality or if they can't examine the items as they would at a store. An example that is often mentioned is clothes, which customers wish to try on. However, clothes and shoes are still among the most popular categories purchased at online stores together with books and music. They are in some markets even more popular than services like travel and accommodation bookings, which are relatively easy to buy online. This suggests that many customers who have used traditional mail-order selling have shifted to using the net as an ordering channel; clothes have, after all, been a popular product category in mail-order selling.

On the other hand, an online store may provide such a wide selection that it is easy for consumers to find the products they need. Moreover, online shopping is also possible in areas that lack certain speciality stores or have a limited assortment. Many active online shoppers buy products that would otherwise not be available to them. A wide selection is one of the key success factors of an online store, compared with a conventional store. For example, beside a large book assortment, Amazon has expanded its offering to many new product areas, such as consumer electronics, apparel and jewellery. In addition, Amazon has collected a large group of partners under its brand, adding further to the site's appeal. Local bookshops only have a fraction of Amazon's selection. Thanks to volume, Amazon and other major internet retailers can also serve the long-tail, niche groups with very small local demand but who may be very appealing at the national or global level.

Another successful internet retailer is the computer manufacturer Apple. It made a break-through with its iTunes service, showing that a large-scale music service over the web can be a profitable business. In many markets, the distribution of music, movies and other services has already shifted largely to the internet. Popular services include music downloading, ticket office, online photo service and DVD rental. Other successful internet services include the Delhaize wine site, with an average of 3,000 customers each day, and Carrefour ticket office, the largest in France.

The internet auction site eBay has also had tremendous success in many countries. Through eBay, consumers and companies can sell and purchase almost anything; eBay takes care of the payment traffic and when needed, also handles transport on behalf of its trading partners. eBay has focused on popular and high-margin products, such as novelties and collectible rarities, but also on products at the end of the lifecycle that sellers want to get rid of at almost any price. Internet auction stores can be a useful channel for conventional retailers in disposing of left-over products.

In many cases, online retailing is just basic transactional business, but more advanced online stores may offer sophisticated value-added services to customers. To cite an example, many kinds of services have been created to help customers in fashion shopping. The My Virtual Model service enables customers to create their own 3-D model for trying on clothes. The model can be used for trying on clothes made by H&M and Adidas, for example. Preferred combinations can be created from the assortments of different apparel stores, and it is also possible to set up a virtual dressing room for trying on clothes. An interesting application is the creation of a motivational self-image during weight watching, where customers can make their own picture lose weight by 10 kilograms and see how well clothes fit. Other services that facilitate shopping include price comparison sites, product tests and recommendations given by other customers. These value-added services may be provided by the retailer or third parties.

The internet is also a channel for C2C (consumer to consumer) commerce. Consumers can easily sell goods they do not need in the second-hand market. Various auction shops and second-hand stores sell everything imaginable from old wedding suits to used tractors. The internet is a treasure trove particularly for collectors and those seeking rarities. Rarities can be found in a few seconds by 'googling' instead of travelling all over the world looking for them. However, C2C commerce over the web has also faced challenges as the security of shopping is difficult to guarantee. The internet has also enabled a huge black market for products such as concert tickets.

Inter-company (B2B) commerce is also growing, but it has not become the kind of retail success that was expected. Some of the most well-known examples have been WWRE (WorldWide Retail Exchange) and 1SYNC (formed by the combination of UCCnet and Transora), where suppliers and retailers can exchange bids for products to be included in assortments. They have strengthened their position especially as sourcing channels for private labels. The process works as follows: a retailer announces an invitation for bids on a product meeting certain criteria. After the application period has expired, the supplier with the best bid is allowed to manufacture the product during the contract period. A similar model may also be used in sourcing industrial raw materials.

Contrary to the expectations at the beginning of the millennium, online grocery shopping has taken off slowly. A key challenge in online grocery retailing is the product requirements: fresh produce and frozen goods require cold transportation and a cold-storage location at the customer's home. Retailers specializing in online retailing, such as Webvan and Peapod, have had severe trouble, and Webvan even had to close down. A notable exception to the rule is Tesco, which has succeeded in the UK in developing an efficient and highly popular store-based online system. Another successful grocery online store is Leshop, the online supermarket of Swiss Migros. Many grocery retailers have added non-food products to their online stores or set up separate non-food online stores; the goal is to increase sales and use the existing distribution network. The trend is also accompanied by the growth of non-food at grocery stores. Tesco, for instance, has increased the sales of non-food products, and it is expected that its non-food online store Tesco Direct will gain a significant position in the market. Other recently established non-food online stores include Boostore, the electronics store of Carrefour.

In summary, it is important for retailers to consider how they can use the internet in their own multi-channel operations, and how they should respond to the competition brought about by the internet. This is one of the areas on which retailers cannot postpone decisions for long. The web offers tremendous assortments and huge amounts of product information. The consumers of the new generation are used to the benefits of the net, and will also demand them at brick and mortar stores; if they do not get them, they will shop somewhere else.

In-store technology solutions will facilitate purchasing, and the internet via the mobile phone platform will make it even easier, enabling customers to check data while shopping at a store, whether the retailer is in the loop or not. The ease of getting information poses challenges for training retail salespeople as customers have access to ample product information. The net also facilitates to radical change in the sales of some categories, especially in digital services such as music. For sophisticated retail players with well-functioning customer relationships, online selling may also open up opportunities to expand business into new service areas.

2 Retail formats

In retailing, as in all business, operations management and development are based on the strategy chosen. Though a successful trader 'buys for 1 euro and sells for 2', as the saying goes, business planning is not easy and the accompanying decisions are not self-evident. In a tough competitive situation, each retailer needs to consider its strategy and sources of competitive advantage carefully. As many differentiators are fairly easy to copy, a successful retailer must be able continually to update and adapt its business model.

Strategic planning starts with the definition of the business idea, consisting of three basic questions: to whom, what and how. 'To whom' refers to the target customer group, whose needs are used as the basis for planning the operations. 'What' refers to the format, assortments and services offered to the target customer group. 'How' covers the business models and processes applied to implement the answers to the two previous questions. The basic philosophy of hard discounter Lidl is a good example of a clear business idea: 'Our business is simplicity itself: We buy and sell with the sole aim of offering our customers the highest quality everyday products at the lowest prices. Customer satisfaction drives our action. Quality is big and prices are small at Lidl.' (Source: www.lidl.co.uk)

This chapter examines various competitive weapons used by retailers as well as business models related to them. The focus is on retail formats, which largely set the guidelines for operations, assortment management and customer relationship management. In addition, selected retail formats and their core features are evaluated. They include value retailing, premium retailing, convenience stores and malls, which are all key growth areas in retail.

Chain operations

A retail chain consists of stores operating according to a consistently defined retail format under management of the central chain unit. The Food Marketing Institute (FMI) in the United States defines the minimum size of a chain as 10 stores, but in practice the number of stores in a chain may vary from a few to several thousand. As a result of the success of chain operations, the market share of small independent retailers in many markets is just a few per cent.

The chain model offers clear advantages over the conventional whole-sale-retail model where management and decision making have been decentralized to many different levels and units. Chain operations seek the benefits of centralization and economies of scale shifting a large part of planning and administrative tasks to the central unit, which will save time and resources in stores. This development has increased the retailers' negotiating power in sourcing, with one party planning assortments and agreeing upon purchase terms with suppliers. Similarly, the chain model brings considerable savings in customer communication through central-ized marketing. The advantages of chain operations are also undeniable in logistics, where demand forecasting and store deliveries gain significant efficiency. Shared information systems enable information to be trans-ferred extensively from chain operations to stores and the other way around. Efficient communication and information processing are the main prerequisites for well-functioning retail chain operations.

A retailer's key operating principles are usually drawn together in a chain concept, describing the business idea and its components in the form of a clear operational model – a manual of the retail format. This is done to ensure that customers will be offered a consistent set of products and services at all chain outlets. The chain concept, in other words, details the value promise to the consumers and how it will be applied in daily retail operations. The consumer should see the retail format as a uniform brand, with the chain's stores and their general appearance in line with the retailer's value proposition.

Often a retailer has an umbrella brand and may have several retail formats operating under it. Examples include Wal-Mart, Carrefour and Tesco, which operate many chains, each with different principles and product ranges. Some chains have names that reveal the parent (such as Carrefour hypermarkets). Others have names that bear no resemblance to the chain operator, like Victoria's Secret – part of Limited Brands, and One Stop stores – part of Tesco.

Both approaches have their advantages. With separate brands customers rarely know about the ownership of chains. This enables retailers to expand operations with new formats into new markets and new customer segments that might otherwise not be aligned with the company's positioning and value promise. For example, few consumers associate The Body Shop with L'Oréal. Having all chains under the same umbrella brand brings significant economies of scale in marketing, private labels (own labels) and communication, but it also adds to vulnerability. For example, many large players in retailing are under criticism from various activist groups. Even if the image of the umbrella brand may suffer, individual chains may avoid the harm, if separate brand names are used.

Chain management models and levels of decision making may vary greatly by company and markets. At one extreme are the truly international chains such as IKEA and Mango, which are managed by the same principles all over the world. An even more extreme concept is McDonald's, which carries essentially the same product assortment all over the world. Another approach is illustrated by Spar, which is primarily a joint marketing name and operates in European countries with widely different store concepts and different ownership structures. The brand and some sourcing are international, but decision making is largely local. Likewise, Intersport is a consortium concentrating on joint sourcing and marketing, but Intersport retailers in different countries are essentially free to make their own decisions.

A slightly different approach is used by localized chains such as DIY companies K-Rauta and Bauhaus. Both have stores in many countries and the business models have been adapted for each country or market. However, many elements of the retail format are the same and sourcing synergies are gained for a large part of the product range. In grocery retailing, the biggest European retailer Carrefour has internationalized by adapting formats to suit demand in local markets. Furthermore, there is a large group of purely local chains, like KF in Sweden and Bashas in the United States, which operate only regionally and have adapted their operations to local conditions. Efficient chain operations require balancing between local adaptation and synergy benefits achieved through centralized operations.

The chain models vary highly in terms of how tightly and centrally coordinated they are. In an extreme case, all decisions down to the pricing and display of individual products are made centrally, whereas at the other end of the spectrum a chain only offers a shared brand and stores may operate relatively autonomously. The degree of chain control is not automatically linked to ownership. For example, franchising concepts are often controlled and instructed more tightly than stores under same chain ownership.

The degree of retailers' chain discipline is the key collaboration factor with suppliers, as it largely dictates how well the agreed plans, such as new product introductions, product displays and marketing campaigns, can be implemented in the stores. A well-managed chain can assure a supplier a certain store penetration and visibility of its products. In a traditional retailing model, suppliers have used product demonstrators and field sales to ensure product availability at individual stores. Most retail chains do not allow supplier store-specific operations anymore, and the dialogue with suppliers takes place through chain management or sourcing.

A local focus is often seen as the opposite of chain operations. However, a chain operating centrally may adapt its operations at least partly based on local needs and characteristics. In practice this might mean the use of the store's local name in connection with the chain logo or including local products in store assortments. The chain can also 'mass customize' its concept and offer centrally designed alternative elements for stores. Ranges in different categories may consist of smaller components, and stores can adjust them to satisfy local demand. The level of chain control may vary greatly by product area, for example the centre-floor products can be relatively fixed, but a considerable amount of local touch is allowed in some perishable categories. The principles of the chain model and operations need to be clear to enable efficient mass customization. Best retailers with centrally operated mass customization practices have often started operations with totally centralized product ranges, where there is no room for local flavour, and added freedom to stores in small steps.

Shopper segmentation and target group selection

An integral part of the chain operations planning and retail format development lies in shopper segmentation and the target segment selection. All chain activities should be based on a clear understanding of what customer groups the retailer primarily targets and with what kind of offering and customer value promise. For example, for a modern convenience store it might be of vital importance to be able to provide a wide range of services to the customers living in the neighbourhood, but still with limited depth of product assortment. Customer traffic is important for these stores as their catchment area is fairly limited. By contrast, hypermarkets usually arouse and collect consumption demand in larger area so the customer base becomes correspondingly wider.

Food retailers typically need to reach a significant share of the customers in the catchment area and do not desire to intentionally exclude any segments from the potential customer base, so strong differentiation becomes difficult. Therefore, shopper segmentation is in practice done inside the store, offering suitable products and services to the different target groups. Shopper segmentation also has a significant role in the targeted customer communication, which is discussed in Chapter 7.

Customers can be segmented by various criteria. Traditionally, segmentation has taken place largely on the basis of demographic factors, such as age, sex, domicile and income level. These facts are unambiguous and often fairly easy to get from external data sources. However, they do not necessarily tell much about the customers' buying behaviour, desires or the decision-making criteria on the point of purchase. Hence, an increasingly common segmentation approach is shopping missions, indicating the consumer shopping baskets. The same customer may shop in different roles at different times. For example, average weekend purchase is often large, whereas top-up shopping purchases during the week are considerably smaller. Different shopping missions are associated with different needs, and consumers choose stores depending on the need at a given time. Especially small stores need to focus on certain shopping missions, as their space is very limited.

An old but good example of shopping missions is given by the study conducted in 2000 by Roland Berger & Partnering Group for ECR Europe, where convenience stores were found to have the following six customer segments: main shopper, top-up shopper, impulse shopper, distress shopper, grab-and-go shopper and habitual shopper. The needs of segments differ a lot. A top-up shopper may value only certain products, such as fresh bread and convenience food, whereas a main shopper values a sufficiently wide offering in the most important categories to be able to do one-stop shopping. For an impulse shopper, some attraction is needed, for example in the display window or street advertising to prompt him or her to enter the store. A grab-and-go shopper wants to do his or her shopping in a minimum amount of time, whereas a distress shopper goes for certain individual products that he or she clearly needs. Habitual shoppers enter the store to buy, for example, a daily pack of cigarettes or evening paper, but it is important for the retailer concerned also to sell impulse products to increase this shopper's average purchase.

Large stores often serve multiple segments so it is beneficial to create separate solution areas for the customer segments inside the store. As an example, shoppers buying lunch may be offered a short shopping path in a store, with ready-made lunches, drink and daily paper close to the entrance and the checkout. Another way to offer a similar service is to set up a separate take-away stand beside the store, where the purchase may be done quickly and the customer is left with enough time for eating. In this case, the strongest competitor is rarely another retailer but rather an outlet offering ready-made food, such as a staff canteen, coffee shop or fast-food supplier.

Retail shopper segmentation can also be based on customer relationship, where the retailer actively seeks to build and extend the relationship with customers. Tesco is one of the most well-known retailers to pursue this strategy, and it offers several new products and services linked to the everyday life of customers, such as bank and insurance services, electricity sale and a wide range of non-food items. Modern loyalty programmes enable the collection of extensive behavioural data that can be used effectively for segmentation and targeting. One of the key benefits of behaviour-based segmentation is that almost all customers in the database may be 'scored' in one or more segments. The customer behaviour and trends in all segments can then be measured accurately, even on a daily basis if needed, and the information used in key retail planning processes. It is possible and also recommended to complement segment data with more traditional methods, based on the use of external data sources, such as in-depth interviews, focus groups and other customer studies. Behaviour-based segmentation is discussed in more detail in Chapter 7.

Key success factors in retailing

Identifying the core target segments and their needs are key factors of any retailer. The retailer needs to assess consumers' expectations and define the differentiators that can make the retailer stand out from the competition. As an example, Figure 2.1 shows the main factors consumers consider when choosing where to shop for groceries. This consumer data is collected from the Finnish market, but similar results have been seen in other markets as well.

As Figure 2.1 shows, convenient location is clearly the most important selection criterion in food retailing, but assortment (range of products offered), loyalty benefits and price–quality ratio are also essential factors in the decision making. However, many of these factors will be totally different, for example, in DIY, sports, apparel and home electronics retailing. Factors affecting the competitiveness and success of a retail format are dealt with in

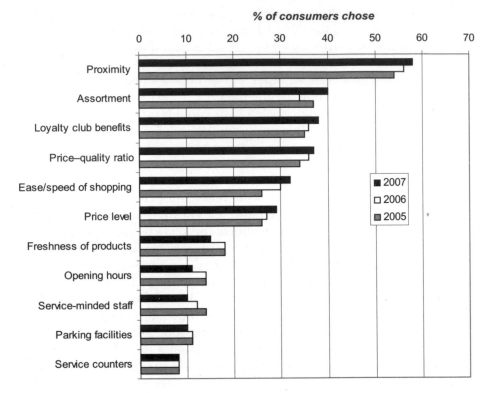

Figure 2.1 Main grocery store selection criteria (Source: PTY/ACNielsen, 2007)

more detail in the following sections. The retailer has the power to make an impact on some of these factors, while others are still largely dictated by external circumstances. The key differentiation factors in a retail format strategy are summarized in to a few main categories as shown in Figure 2.2. These are examined in more detail on the following pages.

Location

As said already for decades, the three primary retail success factors are location, location and location. There is still a lot of truth in this, as a suitable location is in practice a prerequisite for the survival of a store. In many retail formats, the number of potential customers is largely based on the location of a store. 'Catchment area' is the term used to describe the area from which the store is expected to draw its permanent customer base.

Catchment areas differ considerably depending on store format and location. A superstore can attract customers from a distance of dozens of

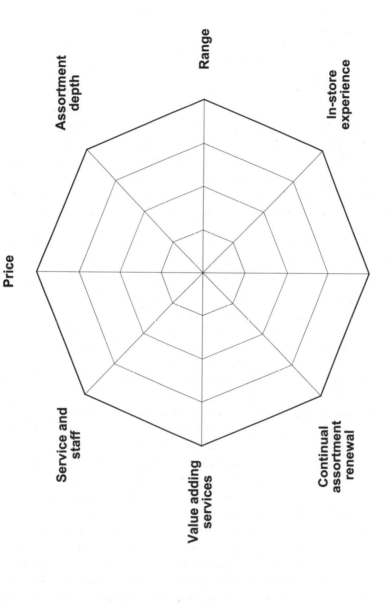

Figure 2.2 Key retail differentiation factors

miles, whereas the customer base of a convenience store is based on a considerably smaller area, often less than a mile. A modern convenience store at a railway station, for instance, may draw its customers from a distance of less than 100 metres. An interesting example of a large catchment area is the village store Keskinen in Finland, situated in Tuuri, which has only 500 inhabitants. By sales it is the second largest store in Finland, and offers over 250,000 products. It became the most famous tourist attraction in Finland with over 5.8 million visitors in 2005. The catchment area of the store is huge, as an average customer drives 150 kilometres to get there.

In many cases, most grocery customers go shopping by car, which is natural as purchases are heavy. For those who drive to work, it is practical to make shopping trips on the way home. Also, in terms of purchasing power, these households are usually better than households without a car. In social terms, the present retail structure in many markets favours higher-income consumers who can go shopping at superstores and hypermarkets. In some places, those who lack transport, have low incomes or suffer from physical disabilities may have to use services close to their neighbourhood. The prices there may be distinctly higher and assortments more limited than in hypermarkets.

Especially in speciality retailing, the catchment area of a store may be very wide. A good example is IKEA, which does not need dozens or hundreds of outlets in all countries where it operates, as customers are willing to come to its stores from far and wide. Mega malls also have wide catchment areas. For example, the success of Mall of America in Minnesota was very much in question before its launch, as it was built in the middle of fields in a small state. The mall is nowadays visited annually by more than 40 million customers, about eight times the population of Minnesota. The mall employs more than 12,000 people, and is a destination for shopping with a very wide catchment area.

Speciality stores with well-targeted shopping segments, for example enthusiasts of golf, cycling or sailing, can also survive in a distant location where rents per square metre are low. In these locations retailers can use the space for large displays and product testing, for example demonstrating golf simulators, that enhance the customer experience. In addition to selling and informing about products, a speciality store can be transformed into an experience provider and may include service elements to the concept.

An important metric in terms of store location is space profitability, which is normally measured by sales margin achieved per square metre or square foot. This measure is the main reason why hypermarkets normally are situated out of town where the price or rent is relatively low. In contrast, speciality stores usually get higher sales margins and can therefore afford high street locations with a lot of customer traffic.

It is rare to find very large grocery stores in city centres because business premises are expensive relative to sales and profitability in the space. There is also often a shortage of parking space, and the average purchases of customers without a car are smaller. The concentration of grocery retailing in stores out of town drives customer traffic away from city centres, since grocery retailing has the greatest purchase frequency. Because of this, many shopping malls have grocery stores, notably hypermarkets, as the anchors of the mall. However, in the United States, malls are more likely to have large department stores as anchor stores. Department stores and downtown malls are the only large retail units that are often situated in city centres.

Large retail properties are available quite rarely and it may take some hard work to find suitable ones. Smaller units are easier to build, but good sites for these are in scarce supply. Legislation in many countries affects the number of available store sites, especially new store openings. Store site acquisition is, therefore, one of the focal expertise areas and competitive factors in retailing. Considering that town planning decisions are often made locally, store site acquisition is also closely related to having a say in regional and municipal politics. In a mature industry, a significant part of market share growth is often due to new store sites.

Conducting store site analyses requires special expertise where a large set of variables needs to be taken into account including customer flows and traffic connections as well as the local competitive situation. A store site analysis relies on syndicated store directories and various geo-demographical analyses, but the knowledge and field experience of the person doing the analysis is also important. To understand customer and traffic flows, the analyst needs to be familiar with town planning and road projects. In the case of city centres, public traffic plans such as railway projects can offer valuable information. For optimization of the store network, cannibalization effects within the chain also need to be analysed.

One alternative is to outsource store properties to investment companies, to lighten the balance sheet and thereby improve stock performance and key performance indicators (KPIs). Capital thus relieved can be used to accelerate the growth of core business operations, especially the capital-intensive new store acquisition. Additionally, rent agreements are often long term, spanning more than 10 years, and they do not necessarily create a problem for the decision makers. However, as location has a significant impact on retail success, it is relevant to ask who will reap the biggest rewards in the future.

If properties are always rented at market prices, the company with the best space profitability can get on to more property possibilities and thereby increase sales and sales margin, thus achieving economies of scale, enabling even lower prices. In other words, space profitability is a key measure of retail competitiveness. It is also relevant to consider whether outsourcing property ownership will be profitable for retailers in the long term. Nowadays, retailers spend a lot of time and resources on store site acquisition and permit processes, and the property investment company reaps the fruit after the valuable work done by the retailer. Should investors also learn to look at new metrics when studying the retail industry?

In-store experience

In-store experience is becoming more and more important, as shopping becomes a hedonistic activity. Retailers need to think about how to delight consumers day after day as consumers come back to the store. Best differentiators in terms of in-store experience can be mainly found from non-food chains. For instance, IKEA, Abercrombie & Fitch, and Best Buy have distinct characteristics that help differentiation, and consumers will recognize the store easily. In-store experience should also reflect customer expectations. In value retailing the property should not be fancy, or customers may feel that the retailer is expensive. Similarly, in a premium department store customers do not expect to see transport boxes and pallets on the floors.

The best retail facilities are more like amusement parks than retail stores. In these, customers do not only buy a product, they buy an experience. One of the great examples is Build a Bear Workshop, which offers an unique approach to customer entertainment in retail industry. Children can make their own teddy bears in an eight-phase process, involving customers actively participating in each phase. The teddy bear theme is carried throughout the whole store with teddy bear fixtures, murals and artwork. Cross-selling is done cleverly in each phase of the bear-making process: the bear itself is reasonably priced but product extensions, for example clothes and voice, are available in most phases. As the children are enjoying themselves and want the complementary parts for their own teddy bear, only few adults will deny the fun, so they pay a bit extra. Customer emotions, both children's and adults', are strongly linked to the bear-building experience.

In addition to speciality retailers, grocery stores have also managed to add some flavour to their concepts. One good example is Stew Leonard's; a grocery store where, some say, a dairy store meets Disneyland. Indeed, it is a place where children love to shop. It has costumed characters greeting customers in the store. Children can dance in the aisles to the songs performed by audio animatronics characters. It has the only in-store milk-processing plant in the world and customers can watch milk caps fly through the tubes before they land on the milk cartons. In addition, there is a petting zoo with sheep, calves and goats next to the store. There are also several seasonal happenings, for example during Hallowe'en, Christmas and Easter.

Another good example is the Pike Place Fish Market in Seattle. It is world famous for its excellent and fun service. In addition to just selling fish, the employees have fun with the customers by throwing fish and joking with each other. When a customer orders a fish, a fishmonger at the ice-covered fish table picks up the fish and hurls it over the counter, where another employee catches it and prepares it for sale. The philosophy of Pike Place is to make the customer's day every time he or she comes there. Customers do not even have to buy anything to enjoy the show. The 'flying fish' have also become a famous tourist attraction. Pike Place has its own website where you can watch the fishmongers in their work through a webcam.

Not all stores need to be as exciting as amusement parks to attract customers. Time-rushed consumers need easy and quick solutions. Store layout also affects the efficiency of in-store operations. In an ideal situation, each store is identical in terms of layout. This makes planning easy and leads to economies of scale both during building and later on during operations. Similarly, displays and even product replenishment can be optimized in accordance with store structure. Castor pallets and other transportation tools can be packed at the warehouse or cross-docking terminal in the shelf order, which enables rapid replenishment at the store. This is one reason large, tight chain concepts such as Lidl seek to build their stores to the same pattern. Similar layouts also help customers to navigate in the stores since the departments are always placed similarly in every store.

The reality is, however, that in many markets most properties have already been built, and it is rare to be able to affect the layout solution or other crucial aspects of the property. It is difficult and expensive to move external doors and parking lots, so it is necessary to be able to adapt the store format to widely different properties. There are many different factors that require concept adaptation on a case by case basis: the number and location of entrances vary greatly depending, among other things, on whether the store is located on a lot owned by the store or whether it is part of a larger mall or quarter. Also, the direction of customer shopping path and the locations and number of gondolas and other shelf fixtures vary greatly from store to store. Therefore, it may be necessary to plan the locations of whole departments on a store by store basis. The leading beauty chain in Europe, Sephora, is a good example of a retailer that has been able to adapt into many different kinds of locations. The retail format is easily recognizable, but at the same time, the facilities and its surroundings are taken into account in the store design.

Furthermore, refrigeration equipment and service counters have usually been firmly located during the set-up of the store. In particular, moving technical HVAC (heating, ventilating and air conditioning) solutions may require a major renovation and make changes expensive to implement. In an existing property, renovation often requires the store to be shut down for a certain time. This results in lost sales and high shrinkage costs, especially with perishables. Thus, the retail format needs to be adapted to suit local circumstances to avoid large renovation costs. Concept adaptation to local conditions is discussed in more detail in Chapter 4.

The number of parking places is an important factor affecting customer satisfaction and potential customer base. This again is directly linked to the location and availability of the store: if the store is situated out of the town centre and mostly reached by car, it is simply obligatory to have a sufficient number of parking spaces, which in practice dictate the upper limit of customers during peak hours. Covered parking facilities may sometimes emerge as a competitive factor because customers value the possibility of going to the store and back to the car on a rainy day without getting wet. Also, families with children can enter the store with lighter clothing as there is no need to take weather into account. The parking facilities are, however, expensive, especially in covered car parks built in big cities and towns. For a superstore situated out of town, the situation is often considerably easier.

When retail chains are highly similar, the freshness of the store and property is often the differentiating factor among competitors on a local level. The newness of a store might be a better profile-building factor than the actual retail format, which sometimes is quite similar to a competitor's format. Sometimes properties may, however, have solutions that are distinctly different from those adopted by the competition. One example is premium retailer Whole Foods that in some stores has only one customer queue for checkouts, where customers are directed to the next available cashier. This solution has been noticed to be more efficient than traditional solutions, but also requires a totally different store layout close to cashiers. Another example is IKEA. Most IKEA stores are built in a way that the shopping path goes through the whole store, and there are a lot of impulse purchases on the way. Many other players in furniture retail rely on open store layouts where the customer makes the choices of the route in store.

Instructions and best practices in setting up a new store are an important part of the chain concept. The chains of hard discounters often aim at very standardized solutions, enabling the store to be built fast and at low cost. In supermarkets costs are raised by different kinds of service counters and other factors meant to improve customer experience. In speciality stores interior design is an especially expensive cost element where the aim is to make customers enjoy their stay and where the products offered are emphasized with displays and aesthetic means. Renovating and furnishing are also among the core competences of a retailer, though they are often not thought of as such. Key fixture solutions like gondola types form the basis for display solutions and the implementation of the chain concept. The management of store space is examined in greater detail in Chapter 4.

The team implementing the fixture solutions is one of the key retail expert groups creating the retail format. In addition to actual fixture installation, the team can also act as experts for certain product areas, such as bakery products, fruit and vegetables, meat or industrial foodstuffs. Furthermore, the team can instruct store employees on the building of merchandise displays, thereby increasing product knowledge and display competences in the store. At the same time, it is possible to get feedback from the retailer as to how well different solutions work, which helps the team to develop its operations.

The advantages of having in-house installation and renovation teams include secured and competent resources, but often also cost efficiency and flexibility in implementing solutions. Retailing concepts are renewed all the time, and greenfielding and retail site renovation ensure an ongoing workload for a skilled team. When in-store solutions are implemented by a small and chosen group of experts, implementation will be of equal quality and cost efficient. With a small team, however, travel costs may rise significantly because of long distances. Even so, the benefits achieved through quality and efficiency often outweigh these costs.

Some store departments can also be outsourced, in which case it is wise to engage the partners early – at the building stage. Examples include bakery and seafood departments in hypermarkets or superstores. Another option is to define a franchising concept and to offer it to an independent entrepreneur. In speciality retailing, various shop-in-shop concepts have become common. This means branded products of a manufacturer are displayed in a special fixture provided by the manufacturer. The brand may stand out from the competition this way, raise the brand profile and attract brand-loyal customers. Many retailers use these solutions, as the brand image of the premium products can also help to lift the retailer's own brand image.

Product and service offering

The product and service offering is one of the central competitive weapons of a retailer. The retail offering has two key dimensions: product range breadth, also called variety (the number of product lines included) and assortment depth (how many product items are included in each category). These have been illustrated at a general level in Figure 2.3, which shows the usual differences between some common retail format types. The figure includes mall, even though this is not really a retail format but a one-stop shopping experience, a collection of different retail formats.

Range management means allocating resources among product categories, and an essential part of it is to define the product categories to be sold. The starting point for this is customer needs. To meet customers' expectations, the range has to be in line with the profile of the store, and the desired product categories must be included in the product mix. On the

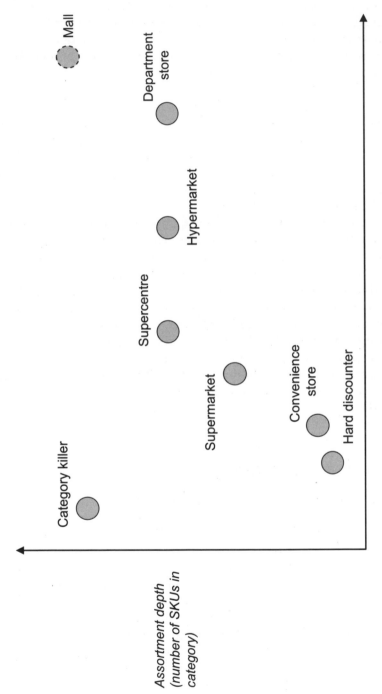

Figure 2.3 Breadth of product range and assortment depth in different retail formats

other hand, as the inventory turn rate has improved significantly during the last few years, space is freed up to be used for new products. Introducing a new category may then be a more profitable solution than expanding existing categories with new variants. The latter might increase cannibalization within the category and have no impact on total profitability.

Assortment management refers to defining items in a category – in other words, choosing products within the given category. Assortment management is not easy nor cheap though it must be said that there is often no competence or willingness to take its costs into account. Supplier cooperation alone drives some costs, especially if there are many suppliers and a lot of time is spent on supplier meetings. In a hard discounter chain, there may be few suppliers and the variety bought from them is limited. In this case, the costs of assortment management and sourcing remain low.

On the other hand, the use of sourcing companies serving a variety of chains might blur acquisition costs and may also conceal overly expensive sourcing. A question worth asking is how to allocate sourcing costs fairly to different chains. If the use of a buyer's or assortment manager's time varies significantly among categories, this should somehow be taken into account in pricing or at least in profitability calculations. Activity-based costing can be used for estimating and allocating these costs.

The target in many chains should be to automate a certain standardized part of assortment planning or to implement it in countries offering cheap labour. Calculating space profitability and optimizing planograms, for example in India or Eastern Europe, may be significantly cheaper in the long term than using the local workforce. For international, centrally managed retailers this is a feasible business model, and shared service activities also make it easier to keep the concept uniform.

Another fundamental question is the collaboration level at which sourcing and assortment decisions will be made in the future. International cooperation in sourcing has rapidly become common, but many different levels of sourcing exist, such as:

- international sourcing cooperations (eg Associated Marketing Services – AMS);
- international retailers (eg Ahold and Carrefour);
- country-specific retailers or sourcing companies (eg Sainsbury's or Système U);
- retail chains (eg Albert Heijn – part of Ahold);
- regional sourcing (eg regional cooperatives);
- store-level sourcing.

In practice, the degree of sourcing cooperation may vary even by category, and it is customary to use a combination of many options. Hard discounters and centrally operating chains are often the most cost efficient in sourcing, but all chains make some regional decisions, at least at country level. Even Lidl, known for its strict chain discipline, operates in this way.

Store-level sourcing is far too expensive on a large scale and even entrepreneur-based chains have made efforts to shift the entrepreneur's role from full-time sourcing and supplier bargaining into customer service and running the 'retail machine' offered by the chain. For suppliers, it is extremely important to decide on which retail sourcing channels to focus their limited sales and marketing efforts. This is naturally dependent on how the sourcing decisions for each category are made, and who really buys the products.

Various sourcing levels need different kinds of support from suppliers in collaboration. There is a notable difference in whether products are sold to an individual store or a chain, not to mention a centralized sourcing organization of an international chain. In some retail groups, assortment planning is concentrated at the retail group level, whereas others use the chain level. Category management is clearly the primary task of retailers, so a big manufacturer aiming at collaboration in this area can hardly bypass the retail chain level.

The number of retailers' private labels has risen considerably during the last decade, and retailers have adopted a more active role in product development. Private labels can be a true differentiator and make it more difficult to make comparisons between competitors. Even though many private labels are bulk products and replace 'B brands' (products with weaker sales) in shelves, some private labels are true innovations that can help a retailer to differentiate from competitors. Target, for example, has done a good job of positioning its private labels in a different way from competitors Wal-Mart and Kmart. In small markets, the retailer volumes are often not large enough to justify own product development to any significant degree. Therefore, international horizontal sourcing collaboration is a good option. This also promotes consolidation within retailing. On the other hand, as the share of private labels rises, 'B brands' can be expected to suffer because they will find it difficult to justify being included in the choice of products (or assortment). The position of private labels is especially strong in hard discounters. In the case of Aldi, more than 90 per cent of the products in the assortment are private labels. Supermarkets may also have a large share of private labels. This is particularly true in UK supermarket chains. The forerunners in this area have been Marks & Spencer and Sainsbury's, and in some of their formats private labels account for more than 70 per cent of the product mix.

Different sourcing levels also offer opportunities for small manufacturers. A company can specialize in a wide regional assortment and build a strong local brand in its target groups. Sales will take place at the local level, either to individual stores or, more likely, to regional units. For a small regional player, finding a local niche is vital. To succeed, you have to be the best at something and a strong local brand makes a supplier well equipped for collaboration with retailers. The sustainability trend in retailing increases the opportunities available to local suppliers. Retailers would often be interested in even wider local collaboration if only suppliers had delivery capacity to satisfy higher demand.

Another option is to focus on the contract manufacturing of private labels. In this case, a company has practically no need for a marketing organization and sales resources can also be very thin. What matters is cost efficiency. The game with the big retailers is ruthless; manufacturing contracts can be rapidly shifted to a new player that is found to be more efficient. Many local subcontractors have suffered during the past few years both in Europe and the United States as retailers have moved an increasing share of sourcing to China and other countries where production is cheap. The consumer products industry has also been compelled actively to shift production to cheaper countries to maintain competitiveness. The continuing efforts, by value retailers in particular, to achieve better cost efficiency and low-price products will continue to drive production to cheap import countries. Other retailers cannot but follow the same path at least partly; if they do not, the cost efficiency and price competitiveness will differ too much from that of the value retailers.

Value-adding services

In addition to the product assortment, retailers can offer a host of different value-adding services, which may have a crucial role in customer service. Value-adding services can also be used to increase customer flows. Typical examples include postal services, lottery ticket sales and small coffee corners. A small store may sell products on commission, ordering products from catalogue assortments to enable one-stop shopping.

The goal of providing value-adding services is to facilitate the lives of customers by offering them services related to the products included in the store assortments. Home delivery is a good example of a value-adding service that a customer may get at a store besides actual products. Home delivery is relevant, for example, in the sale of household appliances, furniture and DIY stores where products are too large for the customer to transport. Many retailers offer not only home delivery but also pick-up or trailer rental services. An interesting example of transport services in grocery retailing is the campaign of French Monoprix and Coca-Cola: customers who bought Coca-Cola Light had their purchases delivered to their home at no cost. The stores are located in areas where it is difficult to get a parking space and customers usually walk to the store. Since soft drinks are heavy to carry, the service truly adds value for to the customer.

Besides home delivery, installation services such as furniture assembly or household appliance installation services may be offered. Installation services have been normal in furniture solutions, but they are now also making their way to home decoration. They are usually sold as part of an integral package. These services have usually been outsourced to a subcontractor. It is important that a subcontractor is capable of delivering the service in a high-quality fashion in line with the retailer's image.

In product installation services, retailers still have a lot to gain. Capgemini's Future Consumer study (2007) found that there will be an increasing appreciation in the coming decade for services around the product, particularly on-site guidance, installation and assembly. Approximately 60 per cent of respondents said those services will be valuable or extremely valuable over the next 10 years in influencing their buying decisions. For instance, in DIY retailing most suppliers offer installation services but retailers have traditionally rarely taken responsibility for the final installation. There are exceptions, most notably in sales of kitchens and bathrooms. A growing number of customers today are willing to buy installation on a turnkey basis if they are offered this as an option. Similarly, in sales of musical instruments such as pianos the customer can get a voucher for the tuning of the instrument. Good service increasingly involves usage or installation training and, for example, in DIY retailing special theme nights have been organized for different hobbyist groups.

In fashion retailing, apparel consultants are a good example of value-adding services. They are common in department stores where they can increase sales significantly. In grocery retailing, store employees can help customers choose suitable meals or wines. For example, Delhaize stores in the Netherlands have wine consultants who help customers choose wine for a certain occasion or a certain dish. This adds wider expertise to traditional selling, and may translate into a significant increase in customer satisfaction. Similar solutions have been used in decoration design. El Corte Inglés offers many services related to decoration and renovation, such as planning and implementation of a home improvement project. Consultative customer service appointments are one form of value-adding service that busy people hold in high esteem.

An interesting type of consultation service is provided by Hy-Vee dietitians who advise on healthy eating and help customers choose the correct products at a store. Some stores have kitchen facilities where cooking courses can be arranged. Courses are arranged for consumers interested in healthy diets, children and those interested in a certain cuisine. At 'make and take' events, customers prepare meals and bring them home.

In-store rental services are also expected to mushroom. Rental services are in active use in sports shops located close to ski slopes, for example, but there is a host of other suitable areas within speciality retailing. Equipment rental is a natural way of expanding the service assortment of a DIY store, and it can increase customer shopping frequency significantly during a renovation project. An interesting example is also the Sherpa chain of

Carrefour, which rents fondue and raclette pans primarily to tourists. Sherpa stores are usually situated in mountain villages, visited by large numbers of skiing tourists.

In food retailing, the significance of value-adding services has been so far relatively small. ATMs and bottle recycling are everyday services and facilitate customers' routine actions. Some stores have their own kitchens, enabling a significantly wider range of value-adding services, for instance selling convenience food, but also offering catering services to order. Today it is rare to see top cooks employed by retailers, but this could be an option for enhancing the profile of retailers, at least in premium grocery retailing. It is also possible to offer shopping aid services for special groups like seniors and disabled people. The shopping visits of families can be made easier by arranging child care or interesting activities for children.

Value-adding services can be tailored to the specific needs of each customer. Examples include tailor-made clothes or various kinds of decoration services based on the specifications and measurements provided by the customer. However, individualized service can impact store profitability and may be selectively offered only to the retailer's best customers. Nevertheless, at some speciality stores individual customer service may be a good way of standing out from the competition and serving the target customer group.

Value-adding services can also be offered by a partner. A store may house a florist, bank, post office, shoemaker, pharmacy, bakery or travel agency. These services enable the customer to run multiple errands during the same shopping trip. These services can also be offered by the store itself. Many retailers have an own pharmacy chain, for example Wal-Mart and Target, or a gas station, for example Carrefour and Système U. Stores can also be enhanced with new services such as Target's health clinics, Whole Foods' day spa or Système U's car rental services. Also, car windshield repair or car wash can be done at a mall's garage while the car owner is shopping. There are several ways to delight customers with different services, and often these services might be the key reason to visit the store.

The biggest challenges for retailers are to build the competences and operational model for offering value-adding services and to provide them in a cost-efficient way. There is a high demand for installation services related to home improvement, but DIY stores have in many markets not yet been able to meet the demand by hiring or training installation employees who are able to do consistent quality work in line with customer expectations and still have a competitive price. In many cases, store services are not necessarily a significant source of income, but they can be used to delight the customer and have an impact on customer loyalty. In this case they can be considered as marketing spend to ensure customer loyalty and should be compared with other marketing activities as such.

Marketing and customer communication

Marketing is a substantial investment in retailing, used to attract customers and stand out from the competition. Grocery retailers often rely on newspaper and television ads, focusing on product offers. However, retailers' share of total advertising has fallen considerably during the past decade in most markets. Other industries such as telecommunication, consumer electronics and retail banking in turn have gained share. In retailing, loyalty programmes have become an essential customer communication channel. Rebates on purchases have been the tradition in retail cooperatives, but today different kinds of programmes are to be found in almost all areas of retailing. Their basic principles, however, may vary widely.

The price of loyalty programmes has aroused criticism, both among retailers and consumers. The costs of developing and maintaining customer databases and the operative loyalty programme solutions are high, and club members are paid considerable bonuses or rebates, even over 5 per cent of the value of purchases in some markets. Even bigger rebates or bonus percentages have been seen in department store retailing. From a consumer perspective, bonuses and rebates can often be looked at as an 'acquired advantage' which cannot easily be taken away. Loyalty programmes are a true marketing cost, which should be visible when prices are compared among retailing groups. However, very few consumer price studies take loyalty programmes into account at all.

Loyalty programmes and the related rewards granted to customers have swelled retail marketing budgets considerably. Some of these costs are shared with loyalty programme collaboration partners or suppliers. In many chains, marketing communication costs may add up to several per cent of turnover. This may bring a clear competitive advantage for players not involved in loyalty programmes. Big-box retailers without loyalty programmes, such as Wal-Mart, often spent less than 0.4 per cent, and some retailers even below 0.3 per cent of the net sales on marketing.

Speciality retailing also features loyalty programmes, but many other forms of customer communication are at least as significant. Word of mouth is especially important, and various kinds of hobbyist circles or communities and special magazines can be used in customer communication. Sporting goods manufacturers have taken image marketing the furthest, with products sponsoring celebrity athletes, for example.

The store itself is also an efficient medium. Colours, display and general appearance express a clear message about the retailer and its way of operating. Spartan decor may convey efficiency and a focus on the basics with no frills, whereas various details make the environment pleasant and may turn a shopping visit into an interesting experience. The clothes and appearance of employees may also contribute to the environment in the store. In-store audio advertisements or televisions are efficient media, almost impossible for customers to overlook.

The focus of advertising seems to be shifting more towards in-store marketing. According to several studies over the years, as high a share as 75 per cent of purchase decisions are made at the store. Consequently, in-store marketing efforts would seem appropriate. Besides actual products, stores usually display a tremendous amount of marketing materials, seeking to arouse customers' attention and influence their purchasing behaviour. Some of the materials come from suppliers and are often product centred. Others are general advertisements related to a specific season or event. However, most chains are not keen to have supplier promotional material in stores, or at least its use has to be agreed upon with chain management. Stores as media will be dealt with in more detail in Chapter 4, and customer loyalty programmes and personalized communication in Chapter 7.

Service and staff

An area that is often more or less ignored in connection with the competitive factors in retailing is store employees. As a whole, the retail sector is a significant employer, with typically high attrition rates. The large share of part-time employees is one reason for the high turnover of employees, and another is their readiness to change jobs as soon as the opportunity arises. To many, work at a store is just an interim stage during studies, for example. Long opening hours can make it challenging to get suitable, competent resources. In addition, it is a low-paid industry, which deters some potential employees. Overall, employee turnover varies greatly by geographical location, even within a city.

Employee satisfaction will be even more important for retailers in the future as the industry in many countries or regions suffers from a chronic shortage of competent employees. Where employee retention can be increased from one year to three, for example, customer satisfaction often improves as employees know both the store and the products. At the same time, the store can save the initial employment and recruitment costs. Recruitment is an important part of the HR strategy because the most competent and permanent people choose the best employers. Research shows that job satisfaction also has an impact on customer loyalty. As discovered in a study conducted by Coca-Cola Research Group (2006), retailers with satisfied employees also often have loyal customers.

An important issue for retailers is how to get a high-performance team in all stores. In supermarkets with a high-quality service level, a notably larger share of employees are typically full-time employees than the industry average. This naturally increases the expenditure of the store, but also provides a workforce with expertise and commitment. Particularly in speciality retailing, expertise can be a genuine differentiator as the role of product knowledge and service ability grows. Therefore, high employee retention is usually desired and it may be a real competitive advantage.

Employees can be supported and their commitment enhanced in many different ways. Both monetary and non-monetary means can be used for motivation. Entrepreneur-based chains have traditionally been one way of empowering and committing the retail level, and they have been in some respects very efficient. The challenge in this model is that empowerment only applies to the entrepreneur, and the impact on all other employees often remains limited. There are often good leaders among entrepreneurs, but opposite examples are also seen. Differences within a chain may be significant, making it difficult to identify a consistent business culture.

Mercadona, a Spanish retailer operating mainly small supermarkets, has emphasized employee satisfaction in many ways. The company has taken action to earn employees' trust. The whole staff is employed with permanent contracts. Mercadona keeps supermarkets closed on Sundays to ensure quality of life for employees, and also operates a standard staff plan: shifts are either mornings or evenings, and staff are aware of their shifts one month in advance. The company also invests heavily in training and internal promotions. Good employee satisfaction is one of the key enablers for Mercadona's fast growth (over 15 per cent compound annual growth rate in 2005–07), even though operating in the small supermarket segment that has been in severe trouble in many other markets.

Stores owned by entrepreneurs abound, but the motivating impact of this form of ownership for all employees may often be questioned. Employee ownership is not uncommon in retailing either. To cite some examples, many of the employees in Starbucks and Whole Foods own company stock options. John Lewis Partnership is an example of a staff-owned retailer that has earned a good reputation in the market with the Waitrose grocery chain and the John Lewis department store chain. This arrangement certainly affects the corporate culture and the way of working together. When employee retention is good, it enables learning and personal relationships with customers. Waitrose is growing fast and was nominated as the UK Supermarket of the Year in 2007.

Many companies use merit pay to improve employee commitment, and this approach is used extensively in retailing. As an example, Tesco distributed a total of £57 million as merit pay in 2003. What is interesting in Tesco's model is that merit pay is given to employees as shares in proportion to pay. It is given to employees who have worked for the company for at least a year. Besides merit pay, employee commitment can be strengthened with different kinds of support and benefits. To give an example, Wegmans has put in place extensive retirement support programmes.

Pay and other monetary rewards are one way of improving employee commitment, but 'soft' rewards are often more important in making employees satisfied and willing to stay in the company. Non-monetary rewards (recognition, Employee of the Month prizes, etc) may even be more important than pay. Motivation is also enhanced by a feeling that a person's work is important and contributes to the success of the company. Moreover, a genuine possibility to have an impact adds to satisfaction and motivation. These things can be addressed through leadership culture. It is important to convey the message that everybody's work is an important contribution to the big picture. Creating a positive empowerment culture is one way of retaining good employees.

For job motivation, the working standards in key operations need to be raised high enough. Employees can be proud of their company if it meets high quality standards. On the other hand, people need to get a chance to develop and apply their own knowledge. Employee empowerment is very important for staff motivation. This is a threatening factor for tightly controlled value retailing concepts that need employees who work often with predefined instructions and standard operating procedures. Experienced staff who value variety or individual responsibility seek work at other companies where they have better possibilities to fulfil themselves.

Values and core operating principles can play a key role in retail management. The significance of values rises when management truly lives them in all operations. For example, Tesco's main themes of 'Every little helps' and 'Nobody tries harder for customers' have worked in an excellent way since 1995, judging by Tesco's track record for growth and customer loyalty since then. When company top management strongly supports these principles and applies them in the daily management of business, employees also start to believe in them.

The leverage of personnel practices and culture varies greatly among retail chains and especially among cultures. The success of many chains in the United States is based on the empowerment of employees: they are granted fairly wide authority to make decisions. Wal-Mart implements principles launched by Sam Walton: respect the individual, give service to customers and strive for excellence. These principles can be implemented relatively freely within the range of the chain concept, even though management is very results-oriented. Wal-Mart has had some culture clashes, when the conventional approach was more hierarchical and predefined. In the German chains the company bought, most employees were regarded more as shelf stackers than as respected individuals providing service to customers. Wal-Mart's culture involves actively testing new things and taking risks if needed, decisions that in German management culture are often done more hierarchically from the chain management, not from the store level.

An apt example of employees taking initiative and of an exceptional sort of social responsibility is the Home Depot chain in the United States. According to Roush (1999), when a bomb attack was made in 1995 against a federal building, local Home Depot store managers immediately went to the accident site to help and they arranged necessary clearance and other supplies from the chain's stores. This kind of willingness and ability to help cannot be acted on or commanded from above. It springs from the corporate culture and from each employee committing to it. All Home Depot stores regularly participate in socially useful activities in the local community. It also heightens esprit de corps among employees and, as a by-product, positive attention from potential customers.

Value retailers also have many cultural principles that are worth noting. Their operations strive for extreme simplification and clear targets. Cost efficiency is visible in all operations, and it is forbidden, for example, for employees to have lunch with suppliers. A good example of frugality is served by IKEA founder Ingvar Kamprad, who tries to save company costs in all operations and, for example, always flies economy class. Wal-Mart founder Sam Walton is also known to have been extremely cost conscious. On occasion, he even cancelled or postponed supplier negotiations if they had been arranged at hotels considered to be too expensive. It is easy for top management to require a disciplined cost-efficiency approach from the staff if management itself sets an example.

Employer brand has a big impact on recruiting, and the best retail companies are very desirable employers. HR strategy can indeed be one of the sources of competitive advantage; employee satisfaction and customer satisfaction are often strongly correlated. In addition, there are many examples of good retail employers held in high esteem. Tesco, for example, has been one of the most admired companies in the UK for many years.

The '100 Best Companies to Work For' published yearly by *Fortune* includes many retailing companies. Wegmans has appeared on the list every year since it was first published in 1998 and has ranked among the top 10 for six consecutive years. The company is a premium food retailer operating along the US East Coast. Though the retailer operates only in five states, its net sales sum up to US~$4.1 billion. The family-run company has relatively large units as the net sales have been achieved through only 71 stores.

It is almost unbelievable that a company operating in a low-pay industry like retail can place so high on the *Fortune* list and rank well from year to year. Wegmans rewards its employees in many ways, and the service culture and respect for others have been purposefully built since the 1950s. The former chairman of the board, Robert Wegman, has said that 'All investments in personnel always pay back'. Generally, the United States can be looked at for inspiration in the field of good customer service. Nordstrom is an almost legendary example of good customer service. In grocery retailing, good customer service examples include Whole Foods and Hy-Vee, both veterans in the *Fortune* list, just like Nordstrom and Wegmans. Though many valued employers are premium grocery retailers, the list also includes other well-differentiated companies such as IKEA and Starbucks.

In large retail organizations, the reality of store operations may be easily forgotten unless management visits stores often enough to see how key initiatives have been implemented and how they operate in practice. The owner of the Superquinn chain in Ireland and a unique personality, Feargal Quinn, talks with customers and has had Superquinn's top management meetings while walking around the stores. Happy customers have also elected him a senator – a role that few grocers are up to.

It is also important that management has hands-on experience in store operations. Most of the current management trainee programmes in modern retailing companies include a long in-store period. Every future manager and expert spends time in a store, learning daily in-store operations. There has been speculation as to whether those with a long in-store career will bypass those graduated from universities when management positions are filled in the future. Not all of the senior executives have a university degree, but instead a long background in store operations and management. Knowledge of business at shop-floor level may be a key to the success of retail executives in the coming years, if growth is achieved with successful organic growth instead of through mergers and acquisitions.

Pricing

Pricing strategy is one of the fundamental competitive tools in retailing, and a key to retail profitability. It is based on the chosen target customer segments and their price awareness. Pricing is also largely a question of retail image and competitive situation. The truth is that the average customer only remembers a very limited number of prices. Loyalty programmes and the related special offers as well as private labels, not found at the competitors' stores, also have an impact on the consumer's ability to create a price image.

Price awareness varies greatly by category and naturally also by consumer. As a rule of thumb, the more important a product is to a customer, the more its price affects the customer's decision making. In grocery products, this often refers to products that are bought frequently or the price of which is distinctly higher than that of other products. Good examples are milk, bread, beer and coffee, which are purchased regularly and which retailers often use in their campaigns. These products, however, vary a lot by market, as does consumer purchase behaviour.

Retailers may have an impact on customers' perception of price by using 9 as the last digit (eg €5.99) which makes the customer imagine that the price is lower than it is. An interesting example of price image comes from China, where the last digit of a price can be affected by superstition. Figures often end with lucky numbers and certain numbers are avoided because they bring bad luck. Affecting the price images of a customer in this way is called psychological pricing.

The retail pricing focus areas can be divided into three sub-areas: shelf pricing, activity and promotional pricing, and markdowns. The shelf pricing refers to everyday prices without discounts. Activity-based and promotional pricing are temporary price discounts or other ways to add value, for example 'buy one, get one free' (BOGOF), with the aim of enhancing demand. Markdowns are discounts granted to sell out products that are becoming outdated.

Price optimization is a challenge for retailers as the number of products can add up to tens of thousands, and factors to be taken into account for each product include campaigns, markdowns and any local pricing differences. A retailer must, therefore, make continual decisions on up to hundreds of thousands of prices. Prices should support the retail strategy and allow for demand forecasting. Unnecessary markdowns and stockouts can be avoided when both demand forecasting and pricing work well. Retail pricing is also important for suppliers as category captains in particular are expected to support retailers in pricing decisions. Successful pricing can improve margins, decrease markdowns and enhance customer satisfaction when prices are consistent and customers feel they are getting value for money.

Different pricing models are in use in retailing. The traditional retail pricing model has been to use special offers to attract customers into the store, also called high-low pricing. In this model, product prices are normally at general market level or even higher, but select product prices are cut down significantly at times, emphasizing them especially in marketing. This usually leads to a momentary increase in demand, which levels off when the special offer is over. The aim is to build and maintain a price image of the retailer, but only a small number of items are used to create it. In very competitive markets, these items may be sold below cost (if allowed by law).

Another important form of pricing is the everyday low pricing (EDLP). Campaigns or markdowns are not used at all, and the price level is steadily low for all products. The customer can trust not paying too much for products and there is no need to shop around in other stores to find the best offer. However, consistently low pricing does not mean that the same margin base would be applied in all categories. The basis for the price setting is often determined individually for each category or subcategory.

The use of EDLP has grown considerably, and value retailers in particular use it extensively. One of the biggest challenges is that it tends to cause few impulse purchases as there are no price surprises. Because of this, many retailers have begun to use a hybrid EDLP model, where EDLP pricing is complemented with high-low pricing. Hard discounters often offer constantly changing hard-line products at campaign prices. Hypermarkets often have price aisles with a lot of campaign-priced products. The hybrid EDLP model, however, loses many of the advantages of the pure EDLP model in terms of demand forecasting and delivery flow management.

Besides everyday shelf pricing, markdowns and continual price changes are also important to certain categories and store types. Fruit and vegetable prices, for example, vary by season and availability. Markdowns are common for products with a short lifecycle. Certain foodstuffs perish quickly and they are sold at a markdown when the best before date approaches. Fashion clothes are also quickly sold at markdown prices as soon as the season is over. The prices of electronics products often go down fast as new, more advanced models are launched. The markdowns are also used in high-low pricing. Some products and brands are often sold at reduced prices, whereas for other brands it may be important to maintain the premium price image. Therefore, these products might not be offered with significant markdowns. On the other hand, even top designers' clothes are sold at reduced prices in factory outlets without their image suffering.

Part of pricing may also be linked with bulk purchases. It is typical to get several products at an exact sum of money, motivating the customer to buy a larger number of products at a time. Another option is BOGOF. In the UK, particularly Asda has strongly used bundled offers in its pricing and marketing communications. In fashion retailing, H&M and Lindex commonly use a similar approach, for example with campaigns offering 'buy two and get the third free'.

Whatever the general pricing model, it should be able to adapt to the local price level and competitive situation. Though the principles of chain operations also include price-level unification, it may not be possible all the time and throughout the chain. Or simply, local pricing for certain products might be more profitable. Even large retailers like Wal-Mart use local pricing to some extent. Local pricing has its problems, though. Changing prices at different stores may arouse opposition among customers and make it difficult to convey a consistent image. An extreme case of local pricing is predatory pricing, which is used, for example, in establishing a store in a new area and killing consumer demand for competitors. In predatory pricing most of the known value items are priced below the competitors' prices. After competitors have moved away or are out of business, pricing may be changed to a more profitable model. Many traditional retailers have noticed that they cannot compete on price against big-box discounters, as they will always go lower with their prices.

It is important to note that retail pricing always involves several layers and, to work efficiently, retailers need to use several of them simultaneously. Table 2.1 summarizes some key components of retail pricing. Retailer pricing strategy should involve clear business rules for each layer, and identify all products and categories belonging to them. This is important, as often there are quite a few decision makers for pricing decisions, and pricing in many layers might be decided separately.

Dynamic pricing is one of the latest trends in scientific retailing and, if well executed, can yield considerable profits. In dynamic pricing product

Table 2.1 Key components of retail pricing

Retail pricing component	Key objectives
Destination products for megacampaigns	Attract customer flows to store and enhance customer price image. Always priced below competitor prices.
Impulse campaigns	Increase value of customer shopping basket with additional items. Visibility of campaign often more important than price reduction. Bundled pricing used often.
Seasonal products	Manage pricing dynamically during season to ensure category profitability. Optimize markdowns to sell out obsolete stock soon enough.
Private labels (own labels)	Secure always good price for customer (especially price fighter own labels) that is consistent with the own label brand across categories. Often priced with EDLP using some key A-brands in the category as benchmark.
Shelf pricing/core assortment	Ensure retailer profitability. Price level depends on retailer overall pricing strategy, but also on consumer price awareness of the product. Often done as EDLP pricing that will not create additional demand fluctuations.
Locally priced assortment	Adapt to local competitive situation. Mainly implemented for some key *known value items* and locally sourced products. Sometimes aggressive predatory pricing used to drive competitors out of business.
Differentiated pricing	Reward club members for customer loyalty and introduce new products and services to selected shopper segments. Personalized coupons for club members is one key option to implement differentiated pricing.
Pricing of services	Use yield management pricing principles to ensure good use of service capacity and especially generate new demand for quiet hours.

prices can vary by store and date based on actual demand. The competitive situation of the store can vary a lot depending on location, and also by customer portfolio. The same store format in a small city and next to a hypermarket can have a totally different customer base and needs. Traditionally, these store-level price settings have been done by store employees based on personal expertise. In modern retailing advanced mathematical models are used for optimizing the right prices for each product in the category based on real demand and competitive pressure. The prices can be managed centrally, even though price tags still have to be set up by store employees, as most stores do not use electronic price tags. Dynamic pricing can be seen mostly in perishables, where products' supply and purchase prices change constantly, but other categories are also gaining share. Non-food retailers with a lot of new product introductions and markdowns can also significantly benefit from dynamic pricing.

Price discrimination among different customer groups is also part of a pricing model. The goal is also to attract those who would perhaps not buy the product at the 'normal' price. Usual targets include students and retired people, whose income level is often lower than in other segments. Markdowns might be offered only to selected club members of the loyalty programme. A traditional method, used especially in the United States, is the use of discount vouchers and money-off coupons to give price reductions. Voucher-based marketing was almost finished in many European countries but loyalty programmes and individualized marketing have given them a chance for a new boom.

Price differentiation in terms of time is also possible in certain situations. This can involve giving discounts to customers who shop outside rush hours and thereby help the store in allocating store resources evenly throughout the day. Most checkouts are underused for most of the day, because the checkout capacity has been planned according to peak hours. However, it might be hard to educate consumers to visit the store another time, and changing prices might also cause irritation among other customers, especially if prices are higher during peak hours. Lower prices during certain times may be accepted more easily. Department stores are often good at creating new seasons and shopping situations for otherwise low sales days. For example, Stockmann's in Finland uses special shopping nights for Exclusive Club members, when club card holders receive special benefits. These nights can be arranged on low sales days to create new customer traffic to the store.

It is also to be expected that retailers will begin to emphasize the principles of yield management, commonly used in other service industries such as hotels and airlines. The idea is to price services cheaper at times when capacity is used the least to attract more customers. One example is a car wash that is sold at a discount during night time, as the service would otherwise be on low demand. One key enabler for dynamic pricing and yield management in retailing is electronic shelf edge labels. They allow all prices to be changed easily without burdening any store resources. A similar solution is giving Christmas sale vouchers, which shift the moment of shopping to an earlier time and also encourage customers to concentrate their purchases at one store.

Price discrimination can be taken a step further with personalized pricing; prices are set individually for each customer. This solution is, however, very hard to implement in a retail environment, as most price markings are not dynamic, and the customer is not identified during shopping. In online shopping the situation is different, and this approach is technically easy to implement. However, personalized pricing is also ethically precarious as the basis for setting prices can basically be chosen freely, and is very hard to control if there are several decision makers. Effects on customer trust needs to be carefully considered if implementing this approach. The ethical challenges may also be avoided by involving the customer in the pricing process. An interesting example of customer-specific pricing is Carrefour's loyalty programme in France, where a customer may freely choose 25 products, which he or she will get at a permanent discount.

Pricing also needs to take into account loyalty rebates that are paid afterwards. They represent considerable sums and resemble traditional distribution of cooperative capital. One can ask whether they are profitable in business terms or merely a way to entice customers and make them committed to the chain. Also, it has to be remembered that loyalty rebates are usually not taken into account in price comparison studies, though they can play a significant role in reality. Club member rebates limit the retailer's freedom in other marketing activities, because they consume an often relatively large amount of the total marketing spend. Without a very clear strategy there is a danger to distribute the marketing efforts in too many places, and be 'stuck in the middle' compared with the competition.

Within retailing, syndicated data pools are often used as a base data for pricing, even though competitive authorities have recently set limitations to their usage, for example as in Norway and Finland. An example is AC Nielsen's ScanTrack reporting, which in many countries covers tracking a large part of retail sales, and can be easily used to monitor product price changes. Still, many chains, especially value retailers, are not included in syndicated data sources. Also, since it is used by most players in the market, one can ask whether it is an optimal tool to gain competitive advantage.

Retailers also use own shopper data in the planning and monitoring of prices. The lack of competitor price data is naturally a challenge, but shopper data is still well suited for monitoring and evaluating the retailer's pricing within a category. Shopper data is also useful for suppliers, who can use it to monitor the planned and actual retail prices of individual products. Average product price is not always at the assumed level, and the retailer sales data can be analysed to gain insight as to whether this is due to an incorrect ordering rhythm, in which case products get outdated and have to be sold at a discount. Retailers have no resources to monitor the prices of individual products manually, but suppliers can help them to define optimal prices and follow up on how they affect demand. However, pricing optimization tools will change the game and enable retailers to plan price changes efficiently.

Pricing is one tool of differentiation, and can be used to attract certain customer groups and stand out from the competition. However, pricing is ultimately guided by the desired gross margin level. For it, all operational costs, including the efficiency of operational processes, have to be considered. Cost leadership as a competitive weapon requires streamlining of the whole value chain and eliminating inefficient work. At the same time, it enables a radically lower price level to consumers without harming the quality of operations or products. Cost efficiency is particularly true for value retailers that have enjoyed steady growth during the last decade. True price leadership cannot be achieved without cost leadership.

Continual assortment renewal

Most customers are seeking something new every time they shop. New products create excitement and keep the store interesting. Continual assortment renewal is strongly associated with certain categories; in cosmetics, for instance, new products form a considerable part of sales and are very important to customers. However, grocery retailers can also add excitement to the shopping visit by changing the assortment frequently. Renewing the assortment continuously maintains buyer interest and helps the retailer differentiate from the competition and enhance customer loyalty.

The best of Zara's customers know on which day new products come to the store and are there waiting for them. The best products run out quickly, so one has to be there in time. The buying frequencies of these customers are high and they are always waiting for something new. Dr Brian Harris cited Costco's Treasure Hunt as a good example of this kind of action. In Treasure Hunt, only a few items at store are offered with very good prices with the idea: 'you better buy it now, since you might not find it tomorrow'. Another example is Tchibo in Germany, which changes its non-food assortments regularly, sometimes weekly, and thus ensures that the concept is interesting to customers.

Retailers have many ways of being innovative. The traditional approach has been to find innovations made by suppliers, and global sourcing models have driven retailers to look for innovations from remote markets. Efficient purchasing of innovations is essential in gaining competitive advantage. It requires a good knowledge of potential purchasing sources and the ability to find new suppliers before the competition does. Indeed, the sourcing locations in the Far East continue to be trade secrets.

Naturally enough, continual assortment innovation requires a good knowledge of customers and their needs. Traditionally, innovation has been based on experience and the good intuition of the retailer. With the advent of loyalty programmes and shopper data, retailing has shifted more and more clearly into the experimentation business. An increasing number of products are given a chance in store assortments, and the product combination that is perceived as the best is taken into wider distribution. Multiformat retailers often use hypermarkets as pilots, and leverage the best selling products in other formats. Target is known for its innovations and the new product launches, as it often tests them in its web store before introducing them in brick and mortar stores. A web store has been found to be a cheap and easy means of piloting to identify successful products before starting wide-scale distribution.

The ability of retailers to recognize the success of new innovations has improved significantly during the past decade, and this has also changed the power relationships in the retail value chain. Retailers have responded to many new products by introducing private label products. Little by little, retailers have enhanced their product development expertise, and the focus of private label development has shifted from the replacement of 'B brands' into profitable premium segments. Target, for example, invests in original product development and emphasizes the role of design in its products. The company continually creates innovations and improves existing products. Some value retailers are skilful in identifying and imitating successful products with cheap import versions within the bounds allowed by patents and trademarks.

Particularly within speciality retailing there are many chains demonstrating product development that is truly creative and helps in differentiating the chain. Product development in these companies is run by retailers, albeit manufacturing can still be outsourced. Excellent examples include IKEA, Zara and H&M. The product development process at Zara enables the introduction of new products to stores in a very short time frame. Trend sniffers observe street fashion, and the best ideas are immediately taken to implementation. An efficient process enables rapid new product development and manufacturing, then the introduction of new products to stores within a few weeks.

Besides product assortment, the retail format itself may be innovative, always creating experiences for the customer. That said, it is not only what you serve, but how you serve it. As an example, a retailer may offer the best recipes and always have new, interesting combinations at the store, but the basic assortment and menu ingredients can still remain largely the same. The role of service as part of the customer experience can be significant.

The renewal of retail concepts always has two sides: innovation and execution capability. New ideas without the capability to execute them do not bear fruit, whereas a good execution without anything much to execute induces unnecessary costs. All continual change in assortments, business models and concepts causes significant costs. Stores with a fast rate of renewal need extremely efficient and clear procedures for in-store changes. In our experience, the execution of new ideas and efficiency of chains in this area vary to a great extent.

Grocery retailing with its low margins and slow renewal is not leading the field of continuous renewals, and examples of best practice are found in fashion products and high-tech electronics where products have higher margins and short lifecycles. Speed and agility carry costs, and these have to be balanced with customer expectations. In food retail, some customers may even oppose change; repeated planogram changes in particular may make customers irritated because they want to find the products they need in the same place as usual. Innovations and variety need to be implemented in a way that creates experiences and variety but does not complicate the customer's purchasing experience. Retail execution capabilities are examined in greater detail in Chapter 5.

Alternative retail strategies

At the beginning of this chapter we discussed the key retail success factors and differentiation options available to retailers. All means of differentiation incur costs, some more than others. Retailing is a price-sensitive business, and most activities augment costs, which cannot be passed on to consumers. It is critical to identify the factors valued by target customer segments, and to prioritize development efforts accordingly. At the same time, it is important to identify activities where savings are possible to improve cost efficiency.

To illustrate these options, a 'value innovation' approach may be used. Figure 2.4 describes the competitive factors of three formats: a hard discounter, a convenience store and a premium supermarket. The weightings of different factors are indicative and may vary from one chain to another. Even so, they illustrate the primary differences among retail formats.

A convenience store has its competitive advantage in good location, access and the ease of purchasing, whereas a hard discounter relies more on low prices and a limited assortment. A premium supermarket mainly competes on wide assortments and service, and loyalty programmes might also be important for many retailers. It is essential to see that the efforts of hard discounters are minimal in most aspects or at least clearly lower than among competing store types. This also means lower operational costs, which enables prices lower than the competition's. These key concepts and their differences will be discussed in more detail later in this chapter.

Retail formats and evolving competition

Retailing is typically classified into a few basic store formats to monitor structural changes in various statistics. The formats vary by size, assort-

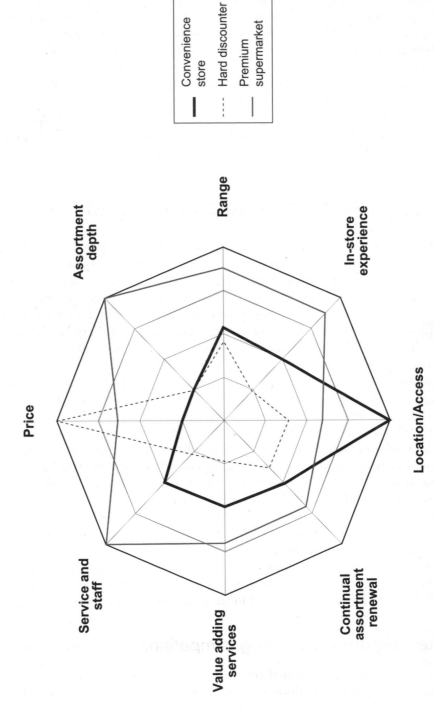

Figure 2.4 Examples of differentiators of key store formats

ment, pricing and location. They often have different target segments; for example, a warehouse club attracts large families, whereas a convenience store in a city centre appeals to singles. This section presents the most common store formats and rising trends in concept development. The central features of each type are presented, together with a few examples. For some, assortment depth is also estimated, but the figures are only indicative, and the actual figures may vary a lot in individual cases.

A *department store* carries many categories without focusing on any in particular. Selling floor space is at least 2,500 square metres, and no category exceeds half of the selling area. Different departments, such as cosmetics, clothing, furniture and electronics correspond to speciality store assortments. Assortment depth is usually more than 20,000 items. Stores may be freestanding or part of a mall. A department store features a high degree of service, and checkouts are located in departments. A department store usually offers many kinds of additional services.

Department stores can be mainly divided into three classes: upscale department stores, mid-range department stores and discount department stores. Upscale department stores include, for example, NK in Sweden, Saks Fifth Avenue, Bloomingdale's, Takashimaya, Neiman Marcus, and Galeries Lafayette in France. The mid-range includes, among others, JCPenney and Kohl's.

Some can be classified as *discount department stores*, where the degree of service is not as high as in upscale or mid-range department stores, and checkouts are usually not situated in departments, but near the exit. Also, they attract a different customer base than department stores. Discount department stores are usually strongly linked with larger retailers than department stores. Discount department stores are especially popular in the United States, with Wal-Mart, Target and Kmart as the biggest players. Price competition is common, but Target has also made an effort to underline quality and design.

A *hypermarket* is a retail establishment mainly based on self-service and offering a broad range of products, with a selling floor space of more than 2,500 square metres. The share of food products is less than half of the total floor space, but sales are focused on fast-moving consumer goods (FMCG). Assortment depth is usually more than 20,000 items, and might exceed 100,000 in some cases. The pioneer of hypermarkets is French Carrefour, which founded its first store in 1962. Likewise, US-based Meijer and Jewel-Osco also set up hypermarkets as early as the 1960s. Today, most multi-format retailers have a hypermarket chain.

A *supermarket* is a grocery store mainly based on self-service and focusing on food sales with a selling floor space of at least 1,000 square metres. The share of food is more than half of the floor space, and typical assortment depth is approximately 10,000 to 20,000 items, but might also be much larger. Examples include Carrefour's Champion and Tesco's Superstore.

In *small supermarkets* assortment is narrower than at a supermarket (with around 2,000 to 10,000 items) and selling floor space is approximately 400 to 1,000 square metres. In small communities, a small supermarket may be the only store, or in big cities they often operate more like a convenience store. Supermarket retailing is still very regional, and there are few global or even European-level supermarket chains.

A *convenience store* is a small store or kiosk with a selling floor space of less than 400 square metres. A convenience store is often situated at a petrol station. It can also be situated at a railway station, in densely populated suburbs or in other places with high consumer traffic. Assortment usually includes basic foodstuff and groceries, newspapers and magazines, cigarettes and alcohol. The number of items varies between 500 and 2,000. Some stores may also have a café and deli selling sandwiches, salads and snacks. 7-Eleven and Wawa are examples of convenience store chains.

In *hard discounters*, the number of items is limited (approximately 600 to 1,200) and the share of private labels is often high. They are self-service establishments with few services, and always carry groceries. Non-food products are used especially for promotional purposes. Prices are very inexpensive. This business type is particularly popular in Germany, but the format is internationalizing fast. Example chains are Aldi and Lidl.

A *warehouse club* is a membership store resembling a hypermarket. However, it differs from hypermarkets with its bare interior decoration, tight membership policy and different assortments. Products are often sold straight from pallets, and the layout resembles a warehouse. Selling floor space is large, for example an average Sam's Club total floor space is 12,000 square metres. Wide (but not deep) assortments help maximize inventory turnover and, for example, Costco reports to carry about 4,000 stock keeping units (SKUs) in normal assortment. Warehouse clubs are especially popular in the United States. The biggest players include Sam's Club (Wal-Mart's wholesale club), Costco and BJ's Wholesale Club. Clubs are for members only, though Sam's Club also offers one-time day passes. Prices for customers using these passes are, however, higher than for members. The price of membership starts from about US~$50. Most of the members are large families and small companies.

Cash-and-carry stores serve wholesale clients (retailers, professional users, caterers, public services, etc). Products are sold from a wholesale warehouse either by self-service or through orders made on the basis of catalogues. Cash-and-carry purchasing differs from conventional wholesale in that products have to be paid by cash and not by credit. Also, transport has to be arranged by the customer. Many multi-format retailers (such as Carrefour and Metro) have a cash-and-carry chain.

'Category killer' is a term used for a company operating in one specific category with a very wide assortment. Such companies are the destination for consumers looking for products in that category, and other players might find it hard to operate profitably, as category killers can buy huge volumes compared with other players in the market. Entry of a category killer often affects many traditional retailers and may concentrate the market to a few players. Category killers can be found in many product areas, IKEA, ElGiganten and Home Depot being good examples. They offer a wide assortment in a certain category and the price level is low. The rise of category killers has made life difficult for many department stores. On the other hand, there have been signs that many category killers are being trampled by Wal-Mart and other similar chains, which gain ground for one product area at a time. Even the sales of the world's largest toy chain (Toys 'R' Us) have stalled, as toy sales have shifted into hypermarkets.

The current trend is for an increasing share of category killers to move into e-business. Over the internet, a category killer may combine large, geographically scattered communities to provide purchasing power and maintain wide assortments. Successful category killers have been born in the area of various hobby domains, such as Cabela's and Bass Pro Shops in the area of fishing and hunting. Amazon, of course, is the classic example and one of the most successful category killers operating over the web. However, Amazon cannot be classified as a true category killer anymore, as it provides services in several categories, and is expanding its category portfolio continuously.

Changing competition

As customers' behaviour and needs evolve, retailers will face competition from many directions. Food retailers need to evaluate the competitive positioning from a wide perspective, not only comparing themselves with traditional competitive chains and stores in different size classes. Figure 2.5 shows how different players, operating on different principles, are invading the field of conventional grocery retailing, trying to benefit from the changing trends in consumer behaviour.

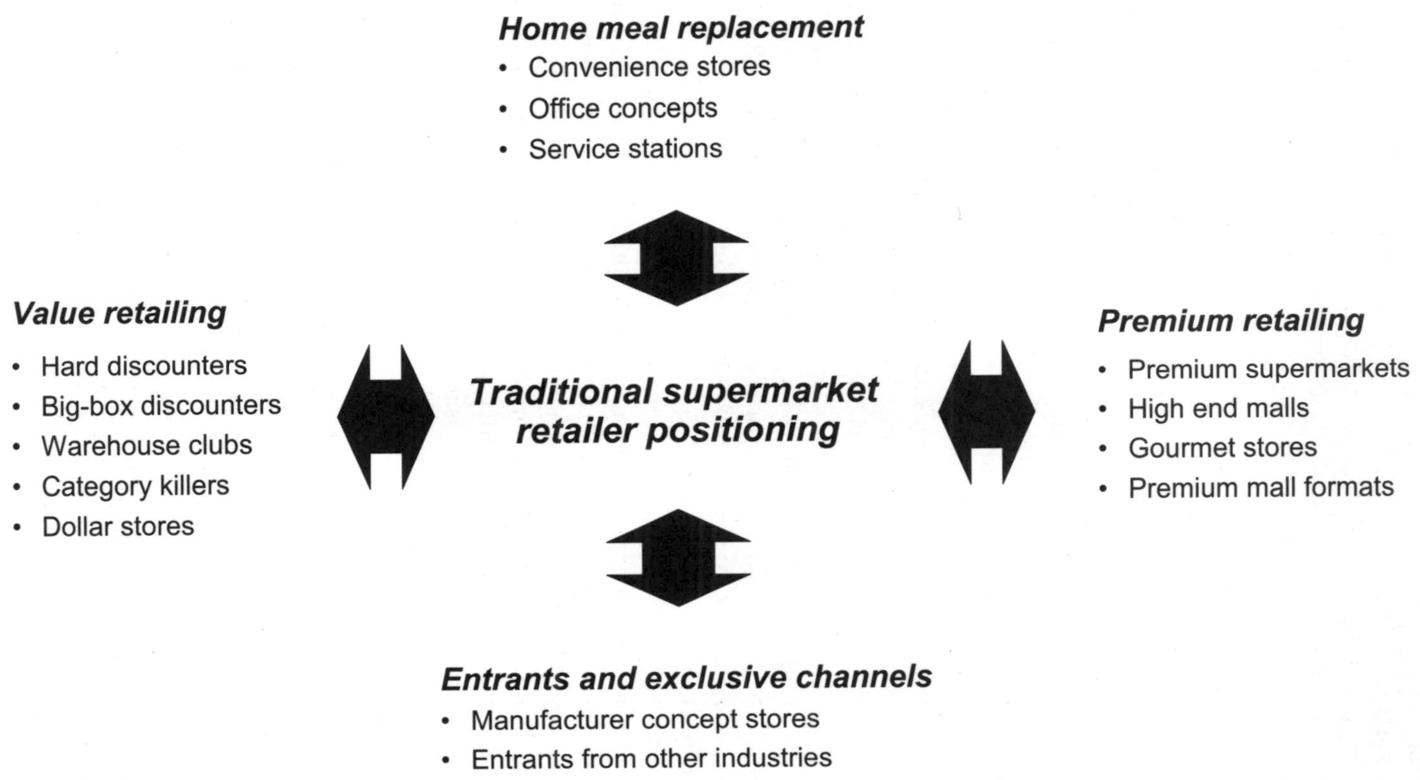

Home meal replacement
· Convenience stores
· Office concepts
· Service stations

Premium retailing
· Premium supermarkets
· High end malls
· Gourmet stores
· Premium mall formats

Traditional supermarket retailer positioning

Value retailing
· Hard discounters
· Big-box discounters
· Warehouse clubs
· Category killers
· Dollar stores

Entrants and exclusive channels
· Manufacturer concept stores
· Entrants from other industries

Figure 2.5 Conventional grocery retailing will face competition from many directions

Conventional grocery retailing will face competition from many directions and through a variety of means. Value retailers have been gaining ground in price-conscious customer segments. This area includes not only hard discounters but also other players such as category killers and dollar stores. As a partial countermove to value retailing, the markets have also seen the birth of a new premium and added-value retailing that has been growing rapidly during the past years. We can also see a steady growth of convenience stores. Experience gained by some European companies suggests that as they offer one-stop shopping convenience stores can charge premium prices in almost any product area. The customer is willing to pay for the ease of purchasing, and the price sensitivity for individual products decreases. Food services are also strongly entering the competitive field of retailing in many ways, as was discussed in Chapter 1.

Some of these new entrants will certainly be successful in gaining share from more traditional players. However, nothing prevents the traditional retailers from expanding into new areas to gain growth. Convergence is interactive and offers possibilities for all parties. We will next examine the key success concepts that have changed the dynamics of the retailing industry, and are likely to continue to do so in the near future. The concepts include value retailing, premium and added-value retailing, convenience stores and malls.

Value retailing

Value retailers have been very successful during the last five years or so. There are several value retailing formats in the market such as big-box discounters, hard discounters (especially in Europe), warehouse clubs, category killers and dollar stores. All of these formats have in common the low-price focus and extreme cost efficiency. Success can be seen from the world's largest retailer list, on which 4 out of 20 of the largest retailers are value retailers: Wal-Mart, Costco, Aldi and Schwartz group (Lidl). All of these retailers are also growing faster than the market.

Wal-Mart's growth during the last 10 years has been tremendous, affecting retailing in the United States in all sectors. Wal-Mart's revenue amounts to over US$350 billion, which is about the same as the world's four next largest retailers' revenue combined. The growth of Wal-Mart has been remarkable, with a compound annual growth rate of 11 per cent during 2002–06. The company's buying power is on a totally different level from others'; to many suppliers Wal-Mart is the biggest client, and it has very different requirements from other clients.

Wal-Mart and other big-box discounters are also key outsourcers of production to China, India and the third world. The massive volumes and price focus shifts production to the cheapest option in the world, and manufacturers have to lead or follow this development to be cost efficient and able to compete. However, Wal-Mart's effect to global retailing has been limited, as most of the business is still in the United States and nearby geographical areas. International operations have not been easy, and do not enjoy similar economies of scale as operations in the US market. However, Wal-Mart is investing heavily on emerging markets, and is likely to gain new growth, for example in China and India.

As outlined earlier, another format of value retailing that has been particularly successful in the United States is warehouse clubs and the biggest players are Sam's Club, Costco and BJ's Wholesale Club. Costco in particular has gained good growth during the last five years or so, both on the domestic field and internationally. Costco is now the world's ninth largest retailer, but with this growth it is likely to step up a couple of places by around 2010. A key challenge for warehouse club internationalization is the availability of large store spaces it needs.

In Europe the key concept for value retailing has been the hard discounter format. The market share of hard discounters in Europe adds up to about 20 per cent of the retail market. The biggest and best-known chains are Aldi and Lidl. The success of hard discounters has varied greatly from market to market. In Germany, the home market of successful hard discounter chains, their combined market share comes close to 50 per cent. But in the UK the market share is still under 10 per cent, and the hard discounter base has not grown significantly in the last 10 years.

Why have value retailers been so successful in many countries during the past decade? There are several reasons, and they can be illustrated well with an example of a hard discounter. Firstly, if we compare the cost structure of a hard discounter to a typical supermarket, a hard discounter can reach the same target profit with a gross margin that is smaller by about 10 percentage points than that of a conventional supermarket. It has been estimated in various studies (eg Brandes, 2005) that the sales margin of hard discounters is in the range of 12–14 per cent of net sales whereas a typical supermarket has a sales margin of about 21–24 per cent. This enables hard discounters to offer the cheapest prices.

What does the cost advantage of a value retailer consist of? The foundation is a simple business model where there is no room for extra activities beside core retail processes. The number of items for a hard discounter usually varies between 600 and 800, and only one version of each product type is usually offered. As the number of SKUs is small, only about 5–10 per cent of a conventional supermarket, the employees know almost all the products, which reduces complexity throughout the business model. Table 2.2 illustrates the sales and number of items in the hard discounter format compared with the traditional supermarket retailer, and emphasizes the importance of product-specific purchase volumes for a hard discounter. With only a small number of items, each item is sold at large volumes,

Table 2.2 Sales and number of items in a hard discounter and a supermarket – illustrative example

	Store level		Retail chain level	
	Hard discounter	**Supermarket**	**Hard discounter**	**Supermarket**
Number of SKUs	700	15,000	700	60,000
Sales €	1,000,000	5,000,000	1,000,000,000	1,000,000,000
Sales €/SKU	1,429	333	1,428,571	16,667

which gives the retailer negotiating power with suppliers. A conventional supermarket might stock approximately 15,000 items and have net sales of around 5 million euros, whereas the net sales of a hard discounter can reach 1 million euros but the number of items sold is only about 700. The difference in net sales per item is impressive even at a store level.

Traditional supermarket assortments consist of about 15,000–20,000 items, and may also consist of local products. When summing up local products purchased by different stores, the total number of SKUs in a retail chain might add up to 60,000. In reality, the figure may vary from 15,000 items in a tightly controlled chain to more than 100,000 items in a chain where the share of local sourcing is high. At the chain level, the volumes in sales per item for a hard discounter are large and give great negotiation power with suppliers.

Hard discounters are really a countermove against retailers with wide assortments that do not produce enough value to consumers. Category management and large store formats have widened the assortments radically, and added the complexity of retail operations. Hard discounters achieve large savings in supplier relations, as they have notably fewer suppliers, and thanks to the small number of items, time needed for supplier discussion is also low. Most value retailers also have a prohibited participation in supplier events. Not even lunches sponsored by suppliers are allowed.

Value retailers typically sell a lot of private labels, since most of them are not ready to pay for branded products. They can suggest reductions in marketing and sales costs to be able to grant lower prices, as the manufacturers do not need to market the private label products. The quality of products provided by hard discounters has improved considerably during the past 10 years. In fact, for instance in Germany, product quality has become the focal reason together with price for shopping at a hard discounter. With a small product portfolio and good inventory turn, good quality is easy to control and maintain. High sales per item is also helpful in this respect.

Some hard discounters also sell non-food items as traffic builders and change them as often as weekly. While this increases the number of total items at the annual level, the number of these products sold at the same time is limited. The share of non-food items of the margin is often higher than that of net sales. Most of these items are sold 'short', so the retailer doesn't need markdowns and shrink is minimal. If customers are interested in the items on sale on a particular day, they better buy them right away as they might not be available the day after. Some customers learn to visit the store often to check for new items, as the assortment changes often.

With a small number of items and large volumes, considerable savings are gained in logistics, as cross-docking is simple and most products can be picked in large lots. In the store, products are often displayed in transport packing or in shelf-ready packages, which reduces the amount of expensive manual work. Stores are often very similar in terms of layout, and cross-docking terminals follow the same arrangements. Picking can then be done in accordance with the shelf layout in the store. Transport comes nearly exclusively from the terminals owned by the hard discounter chain.

Sales at a value retailer are based completely on self-service. Customers do not expect service or service counters, and this naturally reduces the need for store employees. This is a key factor for cost efficiency as personnel costs are a major cost driver in retailing. The flexible use of store employees is also underlined at hard discounters, and a shop assistant stacking shelves may also work at the checkout if needed. Many other retailers have also adopted the same operational model after seeing its benefits. Some hard discounters have chosen to have specialized replenishment teams working in several stores.

Marketing communication costs are traditionally small in value retailing companies. They do not operate loyalty programmes, which often results in savings of a few per cent in selling price. In other chains, customers get back some of the price paid in the form of loyalty rebates, but all costs stemming from loyalty programmes are seen in selling prices and price comparison studies.

Store property solutions are another instrument for hard discounters to create competitive advantage. Stores built on the same format can be built fast and cheap. The building costs of hard discounters are estimated to be approximately a quarter of the building costs of a conventional supermarket. Even if the cost difference in reality were not this large, the total sums are still considerable.

Big-box discounters and warehouse clubs have been very successful in the United States and emerging markets, but not so successful in other mature markets. One of the key reasons for this is the availability of suitable retail properties. Setting up a large retail unit is restricted in many markets by the land use and building acts, which makes the situation favourable to the hard discounter format. This trend can be seen especially in Germany where hard discounters have enjoyed huge success. Building permits for large stores located out of town always require a long process and an exceptional permit, and these store sites are rarely available. The best business sites in busy city centres have been reserved a long time ago, and this also applies to smaller size stores. The 1,500 square metre stores with a selling floor space of about 1,000 square metres that hard discounters are looking for belong to the size class that the legislation in many markets restricts the least. Non-food stores do not have to face such strict laws and, for example, IKEA has very successfully penetrated many new markets around the globe. For destination shopping, as in IKEA's case, a central location in a city centre is not very important, so there are plenty of good building sites compared with the choice for food retailing.

The fast growth of value retailers is in some cases also enhanced by wealthy parent organizations. Most chains are private companies, some even family firms, which makes it possible to grow the chain at a rapid pace. The companies are not forced to focus on quarterly financial results in the way many others are. Also Wal-Mart, even though rated on the New York Stock Exchange (NYSE) and under quarterly investor pressure, has huge resources for entering new opportunities in the market.

The value retailing culture is tightly interwoven with extremely tight cost discipline, and management shows the way by example. Ingvar Kamprad of IKEA and Sam Walton of Wal-Mart have an almost legendary reputation for showing others how to be cost effective. Still, these chains have gained cost efficiency through different management tenets. Lidl and Aldi with their German origin have relatively hierarchical organization and management models, whereas Wal-Mart's culture has involved strong management by results combined with individual entrepreneurship. No wonder Wal-Mart faced a cultural crash in Germany and had to step back from the market after an unsuccessful experiment lasting several years. Another key reason for the retreat was that Wal-Mart was not prepared for the strong price focus of Aldi and Lidl and was unable clearly to differentiate on price as it has in most other markets.

Value retailing companies are typically secretive and tend to shy away from publicity. As an example, Aldi has for a long time owned Trader Joe's in the United States but did not release the news publicly. Some of the value retailers have been criticized by trades unions because of their several personnel scandals. Tight employee policies and internal control with secrecy around operations have not always received good publicity. Extreme cost efficiency has also sometimes led to use of unacceptable behaviour, such as use of illegal immigrants. Paying minimum wages and using government resources, for example on healthcare, has also been criticized. Some companies have also actively tried to prevent their employees from unionizing. One value retailing company is a fine exception to the rule. Category killer IKEA has been named on the *Fortune* list as one of the

100 best places to work, and its reputation as an employer is also good in its original home market of Scandinavia.

Value retailing seems to be healthy and here to stay, so traditional supermarket retailing needs to find ways and means of coexisting with it. Even though value retailers focus mainly on price-sensitive customer segments, these concepts still have a strong influence on the general price level in the market, and will provide a healthy benchmark for competitors. Some retailers have started to compete against hard discounters with their own weapons. These chains have a hybrid strategy, complementing conventional supermarket retailing with some characteristics of hard discounters. The prices of certain products have been cut to the level of hard discounters. For example, Carrefour's Maxi Dia format clearly shares characteristics with the operations of hard discounters. Separate hard discounter areas, such as price alleys, have sometimes been built inside stores. These have been implemented in many forms in hypermarkets, such as Citymarket in Finland and Auchan in France.

Premium retailing

At the other end of the market spectrum, premium retailers have also achieved success. This is a countermove to the success of value retailers, and can be especially seen in the United States and the UK. These retailers are positioned in upscale consumer segments well above conventional supermarket retailing. Some examples of the premium retailers include Wegmans, Waitrose, Whole Foods, Publix and Booths. Booths' philosophy describes premium retailing positioning well: 'Sell the best goods available, in attractive stores, staffed with first class assistants'.

Premium retailers often focus on some of the following differentiators:

- high-quality fresh products and wide assortments;
- exclusive products and premium own label product lines;
- local sourcing;
- cozy store design and in-store customer experience;
- excellent customer service and several in-store service desks;
- good employee satisfaction and retention;
- sustainability and ethical behaviour.

Price is, however, seldom an important differentiating factor for premium retailers, even if it cannot be totally neglected.

Premium retailers usually have a very wide product assortment, including several perishable categories. For example, Wegmans carries an average of 70,000 SKUs in their large supermarkets, whereas a typical average sized supermarket has 15–20 thousand SKUs. For instance, the number of cheese variants can be over 400 – a vast choice for the cheese shopper.

Focus in premium retailing is typically on fresh food selections, especially on fruit and vegetables, and healthy convenience food. Bakery, deli, meat and seafood departments are also typical points for differentiation. A wide wine selection is offered if the law allows. Wide assortments can enhance the element of surprise and exotic assortments augment the sense of adventure.

Most premium retailers also offer an extensive selection of own label products. There is one essential difference between their private labels and those of value retailers. While conventional private label products confront 'B brands' as price fighters, the own labels of premium retailers are usually similarly or even higher priced than manufacturer 'A brands' (better selling brands) in the category. These product lines often have some distinctly differentiating characteristics, which justify a higher price. For example, Whole Foods has a wide array of organic own label product lines. Premium retailers have become true product developers and also created exclusivity in this way. Some premium retailers have also integrated vertically in the value chain, and expanded into farming and manufacturing. An example is Leckford Farm in the UK, owned by Waitrose, that produces mushrooms, apples, pears, organic milk, eggs, free-range chicken and premium white flour for the shelves at Waitrose. Another example is Publix in the United States that operates several manufacturing plants for dairy, bakery, fresh foods and deli kitchen.

Organic and healthy products without preservatives are also important to a growing number of customers. Products manufactured ethically and naturally can be a reason to visit a premium store. In grocery retailing, some premium retailers have profiled themselves more towards gourmet food, whereas the profiles of others put more emphasis on organic and natural products. Whole Foods has been one of the pioneers in organic foods, and gives a promise to customers that all products in their stores are 'free of artificial preservatives, colors, flavors, sweeteners, and hydrogenated fats'. Waitrose has been one of the visionaries of organic products in Europe, introducing them in early 1980. Currently, the Waitrose organic products line exceeds 1,700 items. Marks & Spencer has also been very active in developing an organic own label line, and besides food has also introduced organic fashion products. The organic cotton comes from farmers using natural methods that encourage local wildlife, minimize impact on the environment and protect the health of farmers and farm workers.

Most premium retailers are forerunners in retail ethics. Besides selling Fair Trade products, premium retailers are included in many sustainability acts and certifications. As the global standards are lagging behind, these forerunners have set their own standards for the operations. Most conventional supermarkets provide choice in the assortment and leave the ethical decisions for the customers. Adding ethical options to assortment is often considered to be enough. Some premium retailers have set much higher ethical standards, and do not leave all ethical decisions to consumers. As an example, Waitrose was one of the first supermarkets to refuse to sell fresh eggs laid by hens kept in cages in 2001. Also, in the DIY sector several retailers have stopped selling wood from tropical rainforests.

A local touch may have a big impact on the success of a retailer. Most premium retailers invest heavily in local sourcing. Value retailers and tightly managed chains have little resources to integrate into the local community, and local assortments can really differentiate a store. Most premium retailers have supplier support programmes that help new suppliers to integrate to their operational model. Local products are typically visibly placed in some perimeter categories, especially in perishables like fruit and vegetables, meat and seafood. Pictures of local farmers might be found on the walls next to their products. Stores can also have special occasions to promote local suppliers, such as the farmer's market hosted by Whole Foods. Local suppliers have opportunity to sell their products in the parking area of certain Whole Foods stores every Sunday. This enables customers to meet the producers and ask questions about the products. Premium retailers can bring alive the traditional downtown market places in a new format, where people can shop for fresh food directly from suppliers.

Premium retailers can arouse customers' interest with value-adding elements of the product offering. The best retailers inform customers of the products and educate them about their characteristics and use in an appealing way. One of the reasons customers visit premium retailers is the sense of adventure, the possibility to learn something new. A good story sells the product, and can raise it to another level on Maslow's hierarchy of needs. Local products are usually important, as many of them have a relevant story to tell, justifying a higher price. For exotic items the story is also a vital part of the total offering. For example, a little brief of the origin of a foreign cheese, or the tender and well-marbled Kobe beef raised using traditional Japanese methods may add a new experience to shopping, and an interesting story for the customer to tell the people he or she will cook the beef for. Today's consumer trends for health and wellness also set high requirements for retailers' ability to communicate with consumers. Customer dialogue capabilities will be one of the future core competences of the retailer.

However, even for the premium retailers, all products and categories cannot be only 'premium' to be able to reach enough consumer segments in the market and gain the required sales volumes. Many of the 'only premium' food stores will turn into small gourmet boutiques if they focus just on high-end consumers. Because of this, many premium retailers use consistently low pricing in selected known value items that some customers are price conscious about, and create basic volume for the operations with these core products of the food basket. For example, Wegmans, which is considered a great place for good customer service and a great shopping experience, still promotes EDLP pricing heavily in in-store customer communication to attract wider audiences.

Service counters with wide and high-quality assortments are an important part of many premium retail formats. Good customer service is an essential competitive factor for most premium retailers. As shown by external studies (eg ACSI – the American Customer Satisfaction Index), these retailers have performed well in terms of customer satisfaction. Customer service is offered at many service counters, including the confectioner's and bakery, deli, meat and seafood, and at a wine information desk.

Furthermore, many of the premium retailers have also built successful gourmet restaurants or cafés. Customer comfort has been ensured with many complementary services. For example, the Wegman's stores have childcare centres, where children can play while the adults shop. Besides food retailing, upscale department stores also have a tradition of good customer service. Spanish department store chain El Corte Inglés has invested heavily in customer service and quality of operations. Interestingly, El Corte Inglés has succeeded in extending excellent customer service and quality from its department stores to other fields such as insurance, travel agencies and convenience stores. All operate by the same principles: products are of a high quality; service is personalized and takes the customer into account.

Good and high-level customer service naturally costs, and requires higher margins than self-service establishments. Premium retailers enjoy a margin level that is quite different from the industry average. Whereas a hard discounter can operate at a gross margin of 12–14 per cent and a conventional supermarket at the level of 21–24 per cent, Whole Foods, for example, reports in its investor communications (2005) a gross margin level of 35.1 per cent. The difference is vast. On the other hand, a higher margin is required to cover the personnel costs resulting from managing large assortments and customer service in particular. Retailers putting an emphasis on service and wide assortments always have to find a balance between the additional sales achieved through added costs. Customer service as a competitive factor of a store is discussed in more detail in Chapter 5.

Employee satisfaction is generally at a good level in premium retail chains, contributing to employee quality and retention, which naturally have an influence on the quality of customer service, as discussed earlier in this chapter. Premium retailers are often desirable employers. Attracting the best people and ensuring their retention can be a true source of competitive advantage, as is shown, for example, by Mercadona in Spain.

The market share of premium retailing is still small in many markets, but growth percentages are promising. These players may lead the shift in food-purchasing practices from an obligatory weekly routine into a genuine enjoyable shopping experience. At its best, food shopping may well become an enjoyable pastime, or hedonistic activity competing genuinely for the consumer's time with other forms of relaxation. It will also be interesting to see what conventional retailing will do in competition against premium retailers. In many markets we can already see a clear trend where traditional supermarkets step up to a new positioning by adding elements of premium retailing to their formats.

Even though premium retailers grow heavily around the world, we are not likely to see sky-rocketed growth figures. Premium retailer corporate culture can seldom be easily transferred in merger and acquisition activities, and it limits growth opportunities mainly to organic growth that is based on like-for-like sales development and opening new stores. The capability to open new stores depends heavily on retailers' ability to recruit and train people who can operate with the service and quality standards of the retailer. Training quality employees, for instance with long store training in other stores, is not a quick path, but will be beneficial in the long run. Assortments and new innovations are fairly easy to copy, but employee satisfaction and a good service level require operational models that cannot be easily copied. An extra smile for a customer from a motivated and competent employee can be a long lasting differentiation factor.

One interesting aspect of premium retailers is their ownership structure. Most of them are owned by interest groups that have a long-term involvement in the company. Mercadona and Wegmans are family-owned companies. Publix and Waitrose are employee-owned companies, which makes the staff very much involved with company matters and decisions. Whole Foods is rated on the NYSE, but has an extensive stock option plan, in which a large part of the options were given to non-executives. This type of ownership structure gives a lot of continuity for the operation, but also limits to some extent more radical solutions like mergers and acquisitions. However, the ownership structures and corporate culture form an excellent basis for committed staff and organic growth.

Independent, very high-quality stores appear as individual shopping paradises in many countries and cities, but few of them have grown into a global retail premium chain. Yet, these exclusive companies may exert a strong influence on retail innovation, as many major retailers visit these players constantly for inspiration. Best ideas are likely to be borrowed with care to nationwide assortments of large retailers. Interesting places to visit include, among hundreds of others, Zabar's and Dean & de Luca in New York, KaDeWe in Berlin, Di Bruno Bros in Philadelphia and Harrods in London. Similar dynamics and developments can be identified in other sectors; Michelin-star restaurant chains operating in several countries and with more than 100 locations are non-existent, but still Michelin star restaurants are often visited for pleasure and as a reference for ideas by others.

Convenience stores

Have stores become too complicated? When buying a snack or lunch, do you want to walk hundreds of metres in a large hypermarket? The basic idea of a convenience store is to be close to the customer and to offer the basic items easily. Small stores that are easy to approach are situated in central locations in the vicinity of customer flows, and opening hours are usually longer than in supermarkets. On the other hand, prices are higher. Pedestrians are reached by small downtown concepts, whereas consumers who drive are reached by stores close to high-traffic flows. A convenience store serves the customer's sudden need to make top-up purchases or the desire to pop in to get lunch or a snack.

In certain markets, convenience store operations are chain dominated. The biggest global player is 7-Eleven with convenience stores in 18 countries. It has operated using the same name since the 1940s. The chain operates by the franchising or licensing principle, as do many other convenience store chains. Besides the US market, 7-Eleven is highly popular in Asia, particularly in Japan and Taiwan, and is a market leader in many other markets too. Japan has the largest total number of 7-Eleven stores (around 11,700), and Taiwan has the largest number of 7-Eleven stores per capita, about one store for every 6,000 inhabitants. 7-Eleven is now under Japanese ownership, although it is still an important player in the United States, known as the synonym for a convenience store.

A convenience store can be styled as a mini-market grocery, off licence or pharmacy. A common type of convenience store is the one located at a petrol station. Customer flow is created through fuel sales, and people also buy something extra. During the past few years, these chains have gained ground in many markets from chains focusing on traditional fuel sales. A convenience store rarely earns a high margin on fuel sales, but attracts customers with low prices. Profits usually come from convenience store or the foodservice business operations. One interesting concept is BP Connect, which recently set up a joint venture collaboration with the M&S Simply Food chain. Together these players can create an interesting convenience store offering high-quality food products. A similar solution has been reached by El Corte Inglés and Repsol in Spain. Repsol offers fuel sales, whereas El Corte Inglés offers high-quality products and customer service.

The growth of fuel dispensers where customers pay at the pump has decreased customer flows at convenience stores located at petrol stations as customer do not need to enter the store in order to pay for the fuel. Sales flop as customers are not exposed to impulse purchases. Station operators have, however, found ways to attract customers into the store. At some stations, customers are shown advertisements while they fill up their tank, thereby enticing them to enter the store. Convenience stores not situated at petrol stations use many ways and means to attract customers. Lottery tickets, an evening paper, cigarettes, train tickets, or a coffee shop or post office may act as destination categories to customers.

Convenience store types and the services offered by them vary from country to country. In some countries, a convenience store is mainly a place for the replenishment purchases of basic foodstuffs or a place where snacks and soft drinks are bought when needed. While the United States is the home country of convenience stores, the Japanese, among others, have developed many practices and concepts into greater perfection, and affected the whole Asian market. In Asia, convenience stores have a wider offering than in the West, and they have larger importance to customers. Stores may stock video games, DVDs, music, office supplies, cosmetics and many kinds of convenience food. Convenience stores also provide several services, such as slot machine, postal services, and copying and faxing services. You can also take out insurance policies (for example, pension, sickness and traffic insurance) and buy basic housing-related services like telephone, electricity and water. In Taiwan, convenience stores also attend to many matters related to financial services and public agencies.

In certain markets, a convenience store is strongly based on pharmacy operations. In the UK Boots has for a long time used a pharmacy concept combined with a convenience store. This is common in the United States too, where the CVS chain, for example, has grown strongly both organically and through acquisitions. CVS has recently merged with Caremark, which led to a huge growth of the retailer. Many CVS stores today carry a range of food items similar to those in a more typical convenience store.

A convenience store can also offer luxury products and services to busy city dwellers. Harrods, famous as an upscale department store, has opened its first convenience store, Harrods 102. It focuses on luxury, well-being and health. In addition to the usual grocery products, the store carries items like champagne, sushi, Chinese herbs and gourmet meals. Besides products, the store also offers different kinds of indulgence services, like foot massage and manicure. The store also features a laundry service and home deliveries to nearby areas. Those living farther away may call the store and place an order, and the products are waiting for them when they come to fetch them.

Assortment planning is challenging in convenience stores since the selling space can be very limited. Customer needs have to be considered very carefully to enable convenience stores to have an optimal product assortment. Assortment management is highly developed, especially in Japanese convenience stores. Assortments are refreshed daily based on point of sale (POS) data and other demand data. Customer demographics are analysed closely, and even weather forecasts for the next day may have an influence on assortments. Accurate analyses aim at having an optimal assortment in the small space available. Stores receive deliveries two to five times a day. It is customary to have several convenience stores close to each other to enable an efficient total replenishment system.

Convenience retail includes considerable staff costs coupled with long working hours. An interesting concept that avoids these costs is Shop24, an automated convenience store system, providing about 200 SKUs for the customers. Beverages are mainly topping the sales and, for example, in the Netherlands milk is the best-selling item. The automated sales unit measures only 11 square metres and can be installed into most high traffic environments. It can be open when other stores are closed, and several retailers and convenience store operators like Casino and Shell have used it to complement their service hours. Because of low personnel costs the concept can target environments traditional convenience stores would consider as too low demand, and open new markets. Currently the concept is expanding with franchising, and is used already in several countries. In the near future it is likely that automated solutions like this will boost the convenience store sector, as several others start following the path of the pioneers.

Convenience stores cannot aim at as big a share of wallet of grocery purchases as stores with a wider offering, but they can have the target of a good share of top-up purchases. Some convenience stores, especially located at petrol stations, have loyalty programmes aimed at concentrating customers' fuel and convenience store purchases. Convenience stores can meet some of the customers' needs, but they cannot totally override traditional grocery shopping. It is likely that convenience stores will continue to be the favourite place for replenishment purchases. On the other hand, the convenience store market will grow in some markets more rapidly than conventional retailing. Stores specializing in certain target groups may conquer niche markets. Traditional retailing may compete against convenience stores by paying attention to store location and by designing alternative shopping paths for top-up shoppers. For example, lunch portions and evening papers can be sold in entrance halls so that a busy person having a lunch break has no need to enter the store itself.

Malls

In many areas, malls have surpassed town centres as shopping places. A mall is a convenient and practical place for shopping, as customers do not have to worry about weather or traffic. Unlike town centre locations, there are usually enough parking spaces. Also, thanks to abundant signs in most malls, it is easy to see what stores and services are available. With children, it is a lot easier to go shopping in a mall as there is no need to watch out for traffic or to bundle the children up during cold weather. A mall may be a preferable shopping place for the elderly as well because it is easier to move there than on cobblestone pavements that, for example, most old European cities have. A mall can also be a place for social get-togethers, especially for young people. Standing and strolling around mall aisles is socially acceptable, whereas in the street people usually hurry on.

On the other hand, mall shopping is made difficult with malls having remote locations outside the city, or even being in the middle of a field. In the United States, mall shopping nearly always requires a car, but in Europe there are a lot of malls in city centres and close to public transport routes. In the UK, many malls are situated downtown in big cities, where they have grown around old shopping streets. On the other hand, big malls can evolve into transport hubs. To give an example, Mall of America is a public transport junction with buses and light rail to the airport. Shopping by car enables larger purchases, and especially for food purchases a car is often a necessity.

Malls can be of many different types. A traditional mall is usually enclosed and has a few anchor stores, typically a department store or in some countries a grocery store. Besides traditional malls, open-air malls are popular today. In them, stores are not situated under the same roof, but in the same easily accessed area with common parking facilities. Open-air malls usually do not have an anchor store, but there are more restaurants, cinemas and possibly a few upscale boutiques. They are also called lifestyle malls. The purpose of a lifestyle mall is to offer not only shopping but also other entertainment. There are open-air malls nowadays even in countries where the winter is cold.

Open-air malls have also proliferated because of the competition created by big-box retailers like Wal-Mart and Target. Big-box stores are usually not likely to be part of an enclosed mall, but they may be situated close by. An area consisting of a couple of big-box stores and smaller stores is called a power centre or retail park. Category killers, such as IKEA, have also often been built close to malls. A new mall model is a hybrid combining a traditional enclosed mall and an open-air mall. These solutions have often been based around an old enclosed mall.

Malls can offer everything to everybody or focus on particular customer needs. To give an example, malls related to interior decoration are popular. Future malls may focus on the needs of a certain age group or people having a particular ethnic background. Theme malls, dedicated to, say, luxury products, shoes, children's supplies or golf, will also proliferate in the future.

On the other hand, what is important is an abundance of pastime possibilities in the area. Malls have to compete for customers' time with other forms of recreation. Lifestyle malls in particular seek to offer multiple options for leisure activities to attract customers. It may be difficult for an individual store to compete against a mall, which has a much wider service portfolio. Customers come to a mall to enjoy and to spend time; buying is just a pastime among others. Non-retail space will most likely increase in malls in the future and many value-added services attract customers and make them spend more time in the mall. Typical services include medical centres, gyms, libraries, cinemas, public services and agencies, chapels and various well-being services like hairdressers, beauticians and spas. Malls usually also feature a food court with a wide selection of meal options. In addition to fast-food restaurants, many malls, especially open malls, also have a restaurant. Efforts will also be made to make the life of customers easier with child care and checkroom services, for example.

Mall sizes vary considerably. The smallest malls have a dozen stores or so and possibly no anchor store. The largest malls can be up to 1,000,000 square metres and house hundreds or thousands of stores. Surprisingly, the largest malls by floor area are not in the United States but in countries such as China, Thailand, Canada and India. The Mall of America is, however, the mall with the biggest annual number of customers. The largest mall for the time being is South China Mall in China. Its area is 600,000 square metres and it has space for 1,500 stores. It was opened in 2005 but some of its store sites are still not leased. However, South China will soon lose its position as the largest mall, when the Mall of Arabia with an area of 1,000,000 square metres opens in Dubai.

The largest malls have many forms of entertainment to attract customers, and are attractions in themselves. Customers spending time at malls are at the same time susceptible to impulse purchases. As an example, the Mall of America includes the largest indoor theme park in the United States. The idea has been to make the park seem natural, for example by adding a wide variance of floor heights inside it. The park includes two roller coasters and numerous additional attractions. Besides the amusement park, there is an underwater adventure aquarium. There are plans to expand the Mall of America in the near future, new attractions including a dinner theatre, ice rink, three hotels and a water park. There are amusement parks, or at least individual roller coasters and merry-go-rounds in many more malls. The Mall of Emirates in Dubai houses Ski Center, which is covered with snow all year round.

For any retailer, operating in malls is an important strategic choice. A mall offers steady customer flows, and the retailer is left only with the task of window dressing and attracting the customer inside the store. Considerable savings can be realized on marketing aimed at customer traffic creation when the mall does it on behalf of the retailer. This is of vital importance in particular to small stores or formats entering a new market. The mall concept also simplifies a retailer's store site acquisition. It is easy to chart potential store sites, and renting store space is a fairly simple process compared with traditional store site search and building. When the site is empty, all that is needed is a small renovation and store set-up team knowing how to furnish a store. Building contractors and other cooperation partners are then needed to a considerably smaller extent. A mall also offers retailers many services for running the business, and besides normal facility management services, retailers can often buy, for instance, cleaning and security services from the mall.

Focusing on space profitability is important for any retailer operating in malls. A good rent-paying capacity guarantees the best locations. Space is basically always available if you can afford to pay a high enough rent. With a good rent-paying capacity, a retailer can also ensure a relatively fast growth. Stores in a mall change constantly, some close down and new players come in. Especially in smaller store size classes, it's easy to find the required selling space. Many speciality retailing chains have become international through efficient use of malls, especially in the fashion sector. Establishing operations in a new country is possible with minor organization as many activities have been outsourced to external players in the mall. The Body Shop and Footlocker are good examples of concepts operating mainly in malls.

Also, the efficiency targets monitored by the stock markets drive an increasing share of stores into malls or rented business premises. This makes it possible to move business premises from the balance sheet to variable expenses. For capital investors, malls represent a stable long-term investment offering foreseeable risks and income flow. The rent level stays the same or rises evenly if no similar competitors enter the market. However, an entry of a large new competitor, mall or large hypermarket may cause a radical change in the situation.

An extreme situation following new competition is dead malls. These malls are frequented by few customers, and anchor stores have usually left. There are hundreds of dead malls in the United States alone. Death has usually been caused by socio-economic change in the environment or by the rise of new, competing malls in the neighbourhood, especially when big-box discounters absorb part of the demand. Efforts are often made to save dead malls by renewing their architecture or other aspects. Another solution is to build an open mall around the old mall. Sometimes the decision is made to convert the whole mall to another use, such as office space, or to leave the property empty.

For an individual retailer, malls entail a major strategic choice: should we go fully along, compete against them or find a site close to them? All these options have great influence on getting customer flows into a store, the retail format's business logic and required support activities.

Summary

This chapter looked at various retail formats and their ways to differentiate and gain competitive advantage. The key format types and their core features were presented. In addition, this chapter looked in more detail at some of the growing retail concepts such as hard discounters, premium and added-value retailing, convenience stores and malls.

The business model of a retailer is often illustrated in a retail format description. It provides guidelines for differentiation and the attainment of competitive advantage in relation to major competitors. The concept should give answers at least to the following key questions:

- To whom do we sell? What customer groups or segments does the chain target?
- What are the needs of the target segments? What are their concerns?
- How can the chain differentiate in the eyes of customers?
- What is the unique value proposition of the retailer?
- What kind of assortments and service levels enable this to be implemented?
- What is the retailer's communication and marketing strategy?
- What is the retailer's pricing strategy?
- What kind of locations and properties are suitable for the retail format?
- What is the personnel strategy and how can the retailer acquire and retain motivated staff?
- What is the role of innovations and surprises to customers in the format?
- How fast and cost efficiently can the retailer renew itself in the market?

Retailers may use a host of different competitive tools and will have differences in cost structures, but many formats can still succeed in the market. In an interview with us, Dr. Brian Harris summarized it well: 'A booming retail format succeeds in three things: differentiation, collaboration with manufacturers and organizational excellence'. To be competitive, a retail concept needs to ensure the best long-term space profitability for the store site. In fulfilling the customer proposition, many elements of the marketing mix from location to assortments and services can be used. Chapter 4 examines retail demand management on a more precise level. Also, partnerships with suppliers may play a significant role in retail success. The next chapter focuses on collaboration models in the retail value chain and retail partnership levels.

3 Collaboration in the retail value chain

Competitive and structural changes in the retail industry have also reflected the relationships and collaboration in the value chain. With consolidation and the growth of retailers, power in the value chain has increasingly shifted from large suppliers to retailers and further on to consumers. Intensified price competition and the steadily growing number of private labels (own labels) have in some situations created tensions between trading partners, and global retail giants have sometimes been accused of dictatorial policies and pressure on suppliers. Generally, however, there has been a shift from confrontation and short-term transactions to close and long-term partnerships among the members of the retail value chain. The aim is to understand and manage the value chain as a uniform whole to create value for the shared final customer, the consumer. At the same time, competition is changing from a competition between individual players to one between extended value chains.

The idea of managing and improving the value chain as a whole is not new. For a long time, marketing literature has discussed the management and coordination of distribution channels, whereas logistics professionals widely use the term supply chain management. Despite the differences in terms, the fundamental question remains more or less the same: How could companies collaborate to improve the performance of the value chain so that the desired products and services are available to consumers as efficiently as possible? The fast-moving consumer goods (FMCG) industry has responded to this call with efficient consumer response (ECR). This chapter sets out to examine the basics and origin of ECR. Before that, however, let us have a look at the background and the fundamentals of collaboration within the value chain.

Collaboration and supply chain management

The key questions in managing the value chain are: 1) which principles and rules are used to control the value chain?; 2) who makes the decision about the steering model? Steering models can be traced back to the history of the industry and the companies operating in it, and they often are a trade-off between the hopes and collaboration skills of the various parties. Sometimes just one or a few sufficiently influential companies are able to steer operations in those companies' desired direction. In the extreme case, a company owns such a large part of the supply chain that it can manage the chain completely by its own standards and key performance indicators (KPIs). The more common case, however, is that control is exerted through contracts or general practices and standards.

One of the central concepts in the channel management literature is power, referring to the ability of a company to make the other party act in a way the company wants. Within the value chain, power enables a company to coordinate and steer how the distribution channel works. Power may be based on many different factors, but academic literature often discusses five sources of power: reward, coercive, referent, legitimate and expert power. Use of power does not necessarily mean forcing others to do certain things, but it can be subtle by nature and thus may be easily acceptable to the other parties. Companies may have power without using it, and often this approach may yield even better results than the direct use of power.

Trust is often seen as an alternative to the use of power. In practice, it is also a necessary prerequisite for intercompany collaboration. A genuine partnership can only be achieved with mutual trust, openness and sharing of risks and rewards between collaboration partners. Partnerships should offer competitive advantage and performance that the companies could not achieve on their own. A partnership does not mean a joint venture, which normally implies shared ownership. Furthermore, it does not involve the extension of ownership upstream or downstream in the supply chain – in other words, vertical integration. A well-managed partnership may provide similar benefits to a joint venture or vertical integration. Other common terms used for partnership include strategic partnership or strategic alliance.

Supply chain management

Discussion of supply chain management has been going on for quite some time, particularly in logistics literature. Demand chain or supply/demand chain management are also sometimes used in the same context, but in practice they all refer to the same activity. The focus is on the whole value chain used to deliver products and services to consumers. Supply chain management is not an industry-specific term: it is widely used in different industries.

In supply chain management emphasis is placed on process thinking, and the aim is to look at the supply chain as a whole, especially from the end customer perspective. The concept of supply chain management is fairly old, and its focus has undergone many changes during the years. When the concept was first developed, its main novelty was the idea of a value chain formed by all firms participating in the distribution channel as well as the identification of links and connections among these firms. Close and extensive collaboration among companies was seen as an alternative to vertical integration where sharing information and agreeing upon operating models would lead to as great efficiency as in a centrally owned and controlled supply chain. Later, focus in the discussion of supply chain management shifted to the importance of information and information systems in managing the operations, and then to the importance of processes.

Supply chain management and the partnership philosophy have also been applied in retailing. The two most important discussions are quick response (QR), introduced in the context of speciality retailing, and efficient consumer response (ECR), developed in the FMCG sector. The history and focus of these and related management disciplines will now be examined in greater detail.

Quick response (QR)

QR is one of the first partnership trends to have spread widely and attracted great attention in the retail industry. It originated in the United States in

1985 when a number of apparel manufacturers and retailers started to find ways to compete against growing imports.

The work was facilitated by Kurt Salmon Associates and the company also documented a summary report on the project. One of the most important observations in the report was that the average lead time in the apparel industry from raw material to consumer was 66 weeks, but only 11 weeks were taken up with processing – everything else was pure waste. With this observation, it was concluded that retaining competitiveness called for a radical redesign of operating practices.

A focal part of the QR approach was to rely on information systems to renew processes and create shared practices. The main thrust was to improve demand forecasting and follow-up in orders to reduce product stockouts and obsolescence costs. The QR report gave the apparel industry the impetus to introduce uniform barcodes, container labels and electronic data interchange messages. Attention was also paid to contractual matters, and the aim was to decrease risks for buyer and seller equally.

The success of the QR initiatives was largely due to a few determined leaders. They saw the considerable role collaboration throughout the supply chain plays in improving the competitiveness of firms and their ability to serve consumers. Technology as such was not the solution to the industry challenges, but getting it to a sufficient level was necessary to make collaboration work. Yet, the role of technology was remarkable as it enabled efficient information exchange among the members of the supply chain. However, changes in business practices and in the internal targets and culture of the companies was paramount.

As a result of the outlining of the QR approach, an association called VICS (Voluntary Interindustry Commerce Solutions) was established. VICS later participated in developing the collaborative planning, forecasting and replenishment (CPFR) model. QR efforts were also closely interconnected with a campaign aimed at raising the appreciation for and sales of US clothing production. The slogan of the campaign was 'crafted with pride'. Ironically, QR did not succeed in rescuing the US clothing industry, and the share of imports continued to grow. This is partly because many foreign competitors and large chains that had their private label clothes manufactured in the Far East also adopted the principles of QR as part of their operating practices.

Zara, as well as H&M, The Limited and Gap, are good examples of vertically integrated chains following QR principles. They are able to launch a new collection in an astonishingly short time. Responding quickly to market trends and consumer demand gives a clear competitive edge in the fashion clothing business where collections have a truly short lifecycle.

The process in the apparel industry starts with clothes design, which involves representatives from various business units. Ideas are collected from a variety of sources: trend sniffers, exhibitions, competitors and consumers. POS data from stores is also used in tracking consumer prefer-ences and demand. When models for new clothes have been agreed, negotiations are started with suppliers to reach agreement on prices, man-ufacturing volumes and shipping schedules, even though some of the com-panies have reserved the production capacity already with annual agreements. Most production is outsourced to contract manufacturers in low-cost countries (mostly in the Far East), but some of the products are manufactured close to home markets. For example, Inditex has its own highly automated plants in Spain, where some of the key work phases like dyeing, cutting, labelling and packaging can be done. Most companies use a network of subcontractors, each specializing in a part of the production process. The subcontractor network gives flexibility to cope with sudden fluctuations in demand.

In apparel retailing most companies can launch thousands of new items each year, testing them in selected stores before wider distribution. The products are shipped by road or air to the stores, in Zara's case to over 1,100 stores all over the world in 68 countries. The whole process from product design to store delivery takes less than a month, whereas the tra-ditional lead time in the clothing industry spans several months. Thanks to the QR operating model, the share of items manufactured to stock before the selling season is remarkably low, and a major part of the products can be manufactured during the season when demand is more accurately known. The clothing industry prefers out-of-stock situations to overstock-ing and the ensuing clearance sales. This solution is suitable for companies such as H&M and Zara that must continually attract fashion-conscious cus-tomers with new products. Fashion-oriented customers know on which days the new models arrive at the store. If the customer does not come shopping in time, the products have sold out.

Efficient consumer response (ECR)

In 1992, leading US grocery retailers and manufacturers founded a working group to study the supply chain and the principles of trade in the retail sector. The aim was to find alternative approaches for achieving cost savings and improving competitiveness in the industry. Kurt Salmon Associates, which had been active in outlining the principles of QR in the clothing industry, was also involved in the working group. One of the main themes of the project was to seek inspiration and good examples from other industries.

The observations of the working group were compiled into a report published at the beginning of 1993 entitled *Efficient Consumer Response: Enhancing consumer value in the grocery industry*. The report severely criticized many prevalent practices in the retail industry and identified considerable cost savings potential in changing them. The report received extensive attention both among retailers and manufacturers. It became a seminal work, and a wide-scale development of grocery operations started in line with the principles presented in the report. The abbreviation 'ECR' quickly came into standard use and started to appear in an increasing number of articles and seminar presentations. The first seminar focusing solely on ECR was held in the United States as early as 1993.

While the ECR report and principles had been prepared in the United States from the perspective of local grocery retailing, the concept of ECR was very soon and eagerly adopted in Europe as well. The idea was to adopt the US model to European circumstances, and to expand intercompany collaboration beyond national boundaries within the European Union. Consequently, ECR Europe was established for this purpose. It acts as a shared forum for organizations in different countries and coordinates collaboration projects that are underway. Since 1996, ECR Europe has held seminars, which in recent years have been attended by about 3,000 participants. Attendance has varied by country, also depending on seminar location, but a large number of retail and consumer packaged goods experts and top management come back year after year. In addition, national ECR initiatives have been founded in many countries. As an example, ECR Finland was established in 1996, and it has organized annual seminars and national ECR projects in Finland ever since.

The popularity enjoyed by the ECR model is explained by the fact that ECR for the first time provided a concrete framework for retailers and manufacturers willing to jointly develop their operating practices in a mutually beneficial way. So the premise is not traditional confrontation, but a 'win-win-win' situation for suppliers, retailers and consumers. Following the original report, ECR-related publications and articles appeared at frequent intervals. Beside Kurt Salmon Associates, many other consultants started to develop models and methods for ECR implementation. This has contributed greatly to expanded scope of the ECR concept. At the same time, ECR emerged as a popular topic of discussion at many retail events and in industry publications.

However, ECR has not been a success everywhere. Despite the success of ECR in Europe, the United States never gained the same benefits from ECR collaboration, and the initiatives were pushed forward with other collaborative forums like FMI and GMA under different banners. ECR was also criticized in the United States for growing so complex that it failed to achieve the real tangible benefits. Hence, the rest of the discussion of ECR in this chapter will concentrate mostly on the situation in Europe.

Basics of ECR

Views on the content and focus areas of ECR vary somewhat depending on company and individuals in different roles. To some, ECR stands for efforts to streamline logistics, whereas others see it as a way to perform assortment planning in an increasingly consumer-oriented manner. To some, ECR is foremost a shared development forum for the whole industry in order to unify standards and practices, whereas some firms regard ECR projects as purely bilateral development activities. One reason for the wide range of interpretations is the scope of the concept: ECR is not a rigid doctrine, but rather a combination of different management disciplines, adapted to retailing and combined into an integrated framework. Another reason for the variance in views is that the concept of ECR has significantly changed and developed during its existence.

According to the original definition, the ECR approach is a strategy for the grocery retail industry, involving close collaboration between retailers and suppliers in order to add value to the consumer. In line with this definition, ECR activities typically share the following characteristics:

- Operating principles have been designed to suit grocery retailing.
- Focus is on the whole retail value chain, not on internal operations of individual firms.
- The parties in the value chain work in close collaboration instead of conventional confrontation.
- Planning starts from the needs and behaviour of the final consumer.

The aim of ECR initiatives is a responsive, consumer-oriented operation where retailers and manufacturers work together to maximize customer value and to minimize costs. In an ideal situation, high-quality products flow through a paperless and largely automated supply chain from the production line up to the checkout with minimal disturbance. The goal is to integrate and optimize supply chain, where inventories are as low as possible and product availability is high. The integrated view enables the reduction of extra time and costs from the chain, while maintaining good product and operational quality.

ECR collaboration partners look at the activities in the supply chain one by one, analysing whether each one adds value to the consumer. If the answer is no, the parties work out whether the activity could be performed in another way and possibly with lower costs, or whether it should be eliminated. Consumer-perceived value consists of better products, wider assortment, increased product availability, shopping convenience and lower prices. These objectives can be achieved through a quicker, more flexible and more efficient supply chain.

ECR initiatives are guided by the following principles:

- Consumer needs have to be fulfilled better and faster all the time. This enables offering increasingly high-quality products, wider assortments, better service levels and more convenience at lower prices.
- ECR implementation requires committed leaders who strive to eliminate traditional barriers of interaction and are involved in win-win-win partnerships.
- Marketing, production and logistics need accurate and up-to-date information, which is exchanged electronically between partners.
- The product should flow from the production line to the consumer in the most efficient way possible, ensuring that the right product is in the right place at the right time.
- The whole value chain needs common and uniform metrics and reward systems that support key improvement areas and ensure a fair distribution of the savings and wins achieved.

In the original report, Kurt Salmon Associates estimated that ECR could benefit the US grocery industry with total annual savings of around US\$30 billion and a 41 per cent reduction of inventory. The savings to be achieved by suppliers and retailers would almost be equal. As the industry is very competitive, it was noted that most of the savings would probably be passed on to the consumer in the form of lower prices. However, it has been argued that in reality the consumers never saw the lower prices in the United States. According to a similar study conducted by Coopers & Lybrand in Europe in 1996, ECR could lower the costs of the retail value chain by 5.7 per cent, calculated in terms of consumer prices. Of this amount, most was estimated to come from decreasing operational costs.

As ECR initiatives have advanced, the savings estimates have been specified and fairly accurate information has been received of the collaboration projects implemented. In the calculations published by ECR Europe in 2005, savings can add up to approximately 3.3 per cent of net sales, that is, about 28 billion euros in Europe. The savings consists of decreases in operational costs (2.9 per cent) and lowered inventories, which would cut capital costs by 28 per cent, compared with the current level. In addition, it has been found that implementing the Demand Management concepts of ECR may increase sales by about 4.9 per cent. Our recent research (Finne and Kokkonen, 2005) on the benefits of ECR in Finland, conducted in collaboration with ECR Finland, indicated similar and, in some cases, even higher savings.

According to research by ECR Europe, suppliers who are advanced users of the ECR model have increased sales and profitability in the whole product category. Advanced retailers have succeeded in increasing customer loyalty. Consumer-oriented implementation ensures high consumer satisfaction, which increases the sales of companies participating in ECR initiatives, and enhances their image in the eyes of the consumers. Additional benefits include an increasingly open information sharing and ever-closer partnership relationships. Assessing their monetary value is still a challenge.

Key ECR development areas

The original report by Kurt Salmon Associates identified four areas or basic strategies to improve the efficiency of the supply chain in grocery retailing. These areas are product replenishment, promotional planning, assortment management and new product introduction. The first area focuses on the logistical product replenishment process, which is usually regarded as the main source of savings. The other three areas aim at improved consideration of consumer needs and product offering planning. Each basic strategy comprises a certain value-adding process.

Coopers & Lybrand refined the ECR model in 1996 by grouping the improvement areas of ECR into three main categories: demand management, supply management and enabling technologies. This classification has gained a strong group of followers; nowadays demand and supply management in particular are standard concepts in ECR discussions. Enabling technologies and methods have recently been divided into one or more sub-areas. The only established sub-area in terms of content has been standards and identification methods in the supply chain. The latest ECR framework includes a fourth entity, 'integrators'. It comprises collaborative planning and forecasting as well as cost, profit and value measurement. These are elements that support other key areas of ECR. Figure 3.1 illustrates the ECR framework.

Key areas of ECR will now be presented briefly. The focus of this book is demand management, and this area will also be widely discussed in later chapters.

Demand management

A central element of demand management and ECR as a whole is category management, which means dividing and managing the assortment in separate product categories as own business units. The goal is to plan assortments to match customer needs as closely as possible. Category management as a concept dates back to the 1980s, but it did not receive much attention among retailers and manufacturers until the 1990s, when it was adopted as part of the ECR discussion. Over the years the concept of category management has developed further both in terms of content and implementation methods, and it is still a developing approach. New areas like shopper information analysis and collaborative customer relationship management (CCRM) are continually linked to category management, as it offers both retailers and manufacturers a framework and terminology to assess, plan and improve retail assortments collaboratively.

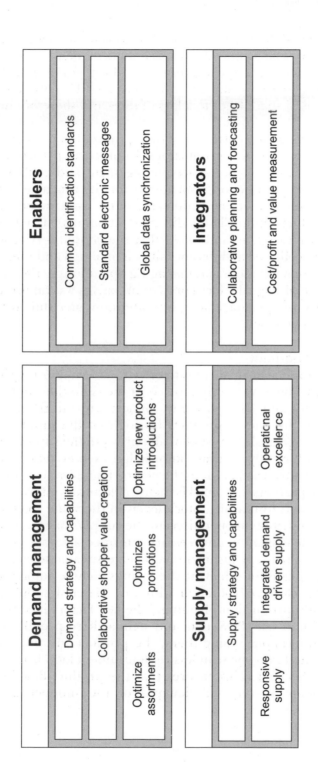

Figure 3.1 Framework of the ECR scorecard (Source: ECR Europe, 2004)

In the original ECR report, one key tool for demand management besides category management was space management, which means allocating store space efficiently to products and categories to maximize total revenue. Store space is limited and consequently a valuable resource. Inefficiently used space leads to a loss of sales and therefore involves considerable opportunity costs.

Demand management also covers the optimization of assortments, promotions and new product introductions. In practice, all these elements are interrelated via assortments, space management and product replenishment: The aim is to develop assortments for the available store space to meet the customers' needs and add value to the assortments; to place and price the products optimally for different situations, taking into account the competitive situation; and to see that the chosen service level is realized. The data collected at different stages is analysed and used continually when making new decisions and managing operations in the desired direction. In the initial stage the focus of ECR initiatives was on product replenishment and supply management, but attention later shifted to key areas of demand management.

Supply management

The aim of supply management is to offer the consumer the right amount of the right products, in the right place, at the right time and as efficiently as possible. This aim is supported by an accurate and timely information flow, linked to the flow of products throughout the supply chain. In an ideal product replenishment system all parties in the supply chain have at any time a sufficiently accurate knowledge of how many products are moving or stored at each point in the chain. Therefore it is important that collaboration partners can quickly deliver accurate information to each other for demand forecasting. Stock levels in the value chain can then be reduced and distribution operations in the supply chain can be simplified so that less time is spent in unnecessary intermediate stages.

Efficient product replenishment has been estimated to yield most of the ECR savings. Means for achieving the savings include automatic ordering, cross-docking, close collaboration with raw material suppliers, demand forecasting and production planning. The key factors in supply management are point of sale (POS) data and standardized product and delivery package identifications. Using them, the product and information flows can be integrated into one seamless replenishment loop from manufacturers to retail checkout. This ensures that the product flow in the supply chain can adapt to the real demand of the shopper and the final consumer.

Enabling technologies and methods

Several technological enablers form the basis of ECR and new efficient operations. When a customer buys a product in a retail store, the barcode is read at the checkout to identify the product. Information collected includes the name, brand and price of the product, as well as shopping baskets and shopping times. Customer loyalty programmes, offering a practical way of gathering information about shoppers, have become more common. When consumers register as club members, they often share information about address, life situation, characteristics and other behavioural qualities. This information together with purchase history can be used in analysing the customer's behaviour and trends to support operations in several key retail processes. For example, as real sales of products are known, stores are able to forecast demand quite accurately and therefore can plan order volumes appropriately.

The sales data can also be used to create local assortments in line with consumer needs and in planning customer-oriented marketing campaigns. Information about consumers and their behaviour can also be acquired by other means, such as market and consumer research. The methods are often not new, but thanks to modern technology, collecting, handling and analysing the information can be done today more easily and accurately than ever.

The information gathered by retailers and from other sources is typically distributed to the other members of the value chain in an electronic format. The partners use this information when planning production volumes or deliveries. Information on consumer behaviour and views is also valuable in new product planning and in many marketing activities. In recent years, collecting and analysing shopper and sales data have aroused considerable attention, and the topic has been closely integrated into ECR. Another key area of ECR enablers is standardization, which is closely linked with data sharing. ECR efforts focus on harmonizing the identification and communication standards in the retail industry internationally to reduce costs. The future improvement areas include radio frequency identification (RFID) and more advanced standard format messages that can be used for expanding e-business.

Information systems also enable increasingly accurate cost accounting. Activity-based costing facilitates the modelling of actual costs at all retail value chain process stages and thereby helps in identifying improvement areas or defining new metrics for operational efficiency. Extending activity-based costing beyond traditional company boundaries enables companies to get new information about the value chain cost structure as well as key factors affecting it. This approach is often called value chain analysis, and the trading partners can use it jointly to plan improvement actions and quantify the benefits to be gained.

As shown above, the ECR enablers consist of a wide and varied number of technologies, standards and operational patterns that support key areas of demand and supply management. With technology and standards development the enablers will also change, but their objective to support a more efficient retail value chain will remain the same.

Scorecards

The ECR global scorecard has over the years acted as a sort of guideline and trend setter for ECR initiatives by offering a framework for common improvement efforts. The scorecard helps companies to discover the key areas covered by ECR, the aspects included and the level each company has in different areas. However, this scorecard should not be confused with the balanced scorecard developed by Norton and Kaplan, though there are similarities between them. The scorecards have improved along with the ECR approach over the years. The content of each version has changed somewhat, new areas have been introduced and the ambition level has been raised in some areas as appropriate. The three current ECR scorecards are the global scorecard, intermediate-level scorecard and entry-level scorecard. The scorecards vary in content and accuracy, as described below.

The global scorecard is one of the best known and probably the most widely used ECR scorecard. It is extremely well suited for pilot use and for identification of improvement areas. Today it consists of four main sections: demand management, supply management, integrators and enablers. These sections are further divided into more than 40 areas where the quality and progress of collaboration can be assessed. The global scorecard has clearly improved over the years, which makes it more difficult to make long-term comparisons. On the other hand, few companies use the scorecard regularly, so this might not be considered a big problem in practice.

A scorecard can be created as an internal exercise, as 'homework', and the results can be used later for improving collaboration in prioritized areas. The most fruitful results, however, are achieved when the scorecard is used with a trading partner for joint assessment of key operational areas of collaboration. The global scorecard session takes time because the terminology and concepts used must be expanded and clarified for all participants. Therefore, it is advisable to include a fairly extensive training session, at least when the scorecard is filled in for the first time. Experience shows that a typical well-executed scorecard session tends to take 9–13 hours: a full-day, tough job.

A key benefit of scorecard process is in having people discuss operational practices and goals at the same table. For some consumer product companies, this may be one of the few occasions where production meets sales and marketing and the retail client. Discussions in scorecard workshops about such things as promotions are rewarding and beneficial because sales, production, marketing and field sales may have differing views on the topics. It is common, though, that those areas that arouse the most controversy typically also have the most development potential.

The major challenge with the global scorecard is that it is laborious to complete and vague. It has been developed for a wide user group to be used all over the world. Because of this, it is not necessarily suited to an individual company or even country. It is still a good tool for identifying development areas in collaboration, but needs more concrete metrics for the measurement of the continuous collaboration model. For the same reason, the global scorecard is rather inappropriate for regular annual use because it is not a proper operational metric. The best benefits are probably reaped by using it at an interval of a few years. Within a few years, the content of the scorecard is typically developed fairly extensively, and there will be new people or responsibilities in companies, which is why a little recap might be in order.

There is also a simpler, intermediate-level ECR scorecard. It is intended to make the review easier and more practical. Indeed, the intermediate-level scorecard is a good tool for regular planning and follow-up of operations. An example of one of the intermediate scorecard assessment areas, Promotions, is shown in Table 3.1.

The most uncomplicated ECR scorecard is the entry-level scorecard. Compared with the other scorecards, it is simple and straightforward, and filling it in is quick and easy. The entry-level scorecard uses illustrative 'traffic lights' instead of numeric metrics. If the light is yellow or red, justification of the answer is required. The entry-level metrics are concrete and easily understandable, but the scorecard can also be complemented with retailer-specific instructions. Most often it is used in a retailer's extranet solution, where both trading partners can access the results. An entry-level scorecard is especially well suited for retail-led operations, but does not work so well for identifying new development areas. At its best it can be a great tool for a retailer to manage a large number of small suppliers systematically, objectively and cost efficiently.

ECR – a chameleon?

Though ECR was born in the 1990s, it is basically not a completely new idea or approach, but rather a retail industry application of many other business management models. While many ECR principles, models and areas have been developed within grocery retailing, insights have been adopted from elsewhere, including the QR efforts, speciality retailing and quality management in the manufacturing sector.

The principles of total quality management (TQM) and lean management, originally based on Japanese tenets, and the related ambition to

Table 3.1 Promotional management section in the intermediate-level scorecard (Source: ECR Europe/Global Commerce Initiative)

		Red	Orange	Yellow	Green	Comments
D3 Promotions	Do both partners understand the category pricing strategy?	No	Need substantial clarification	Need minor clarification	Yes	
	Is there an agreed rolling promotional plan which matches your trading partner's planning lead times?	No	Plan to	Planning underway	Yes	
	Are promotion plans communicated effectively with the trading partner?	No	Plan to	Just started	Yes	
	Is there an agreed consumer rationale established for all promotions?	No	Rarely	Mostly	Yes	
	Are there clear commercial objectives for all promotions?	No	Some	Most	All	
	Are all supply chain partners actively involved in promotion planning, where appropriate?	No	Sometimes	Mostly	Yes	
	Is promotion execution monitored throughout the total supply chain?	No	Rarely	Frequently	Always	
	Are all promotions evaluated against objectives?	No	Rarely	Mostly	Yes	
	Are post-promotion learnings shared, and used for improving future performance?	No	Sometimes	Mostly	Yes	

eliminate all non-value-adding 'waste' from practices have had a strong impact on the basics of ECR efforts. Also, ECR has drawn some inspiration from business process re-engineering (BPR). In line with this, changing the existing approaches is often seen as a requisite for successful ECR initiatives. An important tool in ECR efforts is the earlier mentioned activity-based costing approach. It has led to activity-based management (ABM), which largely relies on process thinking. It is therefore justified to state that ECR initiatives comprise a collection of principles adopted from several 'three-letter abbreviations'.

However, ECR differs from these other models in two important ways: it is clearly wider in terms of content and is focused on a particular industry. The ECR model aims at improving the efficiency of the whole industry and is not concerned just with individual companies and their mutual relationships. Taking the consumer into consideration adds affinity to the marketing activities of companies, which differentiates ECR efforts from many other value-chain development strategies focused on logistics. An important new focus is collaboration in all operational areas. Saliha Barlatey, Co-Chair of ECR Europe's Operating Board, crystallized the key principles of ECR well in our interview – ECR is all about trust, collaboration and leadership.

While the ECR approach has adopted elements from elsewhere, it has also had a strong impact on many related models and trends. In the area of demand management, the methods of space management and category management in particular have developed considerably as the ECR approach has become more common, and an increasing number of firms have adopted space management and category management methods as part of their daily operations. Furthermore, customer relationship management (CRM) methods have found special forms in retail, especially with the introduction of customer loyalty programmes; and collaborative CRM, referring to CRM carried out by retailers and suppliers in collaboration, is an increasingly common topic. The ECR model has also contributed to the practice of measuring marketing and trade promotions efficiency, more accurately and extensively. All in all, the planning of operations is increasingly based on facts and collected data; new data warehouses and advanced analytics make it possible to have information in a variety of forms, easy to use and within the reach of business users.

In many contexts, there have been efforts to link price management and retail format strategies to the ECR model and to collaboration between trading partners. These aspects, however, entail both competitive and legal challenges. As a result, it is difficult to incorporate them fully into a shared operational model. This is, indeed, one of the paradoxes in ECR activities: there is a desire to continue the deepening of intercompany collaboration at industry level, but openly exchanging ideas about the most central competitive weapons will never be possible and would not even be appropriate within the essence of the market economy.

In the area of supply management, several new logistics models have been developed under the ECR umbrella. These include, for example, continuous replenishment programme (CRP) and vendor-managed inventory (VMI). The ECR movement has also actively participated in developing methods of CPFR and testing them in practice. The CPFR model is in many contexts seen to represent the 'second generation' of ECR efforts. It is seen as a practical way to connect the various elements closely together.

Retail partnership levels

All retail value chain models, for example ECR and QR, emphasize the importance of partnerships. However, they seldom identify the levels of partnership, and the partnership relationships in the retail value chain may vary considerably in terms of depth, ranging from a simple buyer–seller relationship to a deep and open strategic partnership. In this section we describe the key levels of retail partnerships, and analyse the opportunities for ECR collaboration in different levels.

The number of suppliers can vary significantly by retailer. Hard discounters with narrow assortments might be able to work with fewer than 100 suppliers, but a major supermarket chain with a wide assortment may have several hundred suppliers, and in some chains relying on local sourcing, the number of suppliers might amount to thousands. If the retailer has enabled local sourcing on the store level, the number of suppliers may add up to several thousand. Obviously, if a retailer has many suppliers, there is little time to collaborate with each supplier when the relationship is working efficiently. Supplier relationships need to be prioritized according to their importance to the retailer. Figure 3.2 illustrates key retail partnership levels.

Company size is measured by both net sales and market share, and is a natural factor to be taken into account when thinking about partnership levels. For example, to be able to practise category management collaboration efficiently enough, a supplier needs to have a sufficiently large market share and a vision for the development of the whole category. Small companies often do not have enough resources to implement long-term and complex category management projects. Other criteria for finding a suitable collaboration level include the supplier's interest in collaboration, strategic fit, the supplier's expertise and capabilities, as well as the potential to allocate resources for collaboration.

Measured by number, most suppliers have a transactional relationship with retailers, though their share of net sales may be small. With thousands of relationships, efficiency and systematic supplier relationship management are of utmost importance. Retailers who seek cost efficiency simply

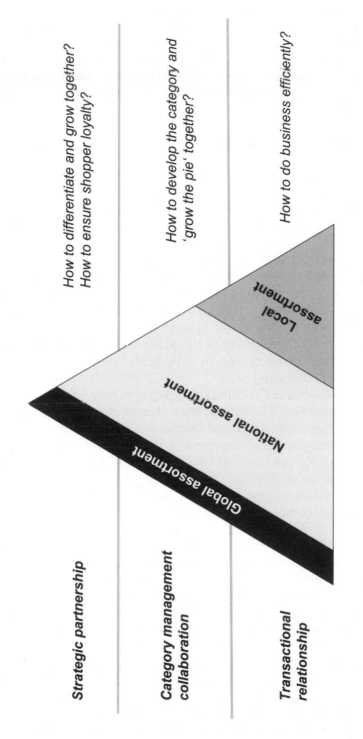

How to differentiate and grow together?
How to ensure shopper loyalty?

How to develop the category and
'grow the pie' together?

How to do business efficiently?

Strategic partnership

Category management
collaboration

Transactional
relationship

Global assortment

National assortment

Local
assortment

Figure 3.2   Key levels of retail partnerships

don't have time to talk to everyone, at least not many times a year. For these cost-efficiency reasons retailers might be resistant to start discussions with new small manufacturers, which unfortunately in some cases has led to discussions of growing retailer dominance and arrogance.

Some advanced retailers have created clear-cut standard processes for small suppliers and demand the suppliers to follow them in interactions with the chain. As an example, if a product is offered to the assortment, the standard product data needs to be recorded on a new product introduction card in electronic form before the retailer's category manager will process it. In addition to product information, the standards of orders, delivery time, transportation and billing need to be agreed upon to ensure the efficiency of the fundamental retailing processes. Standardized operational models help to minimize transaction costs and enable retailers to include small suppliers' products in the assortments. As a simplified and slightly generalized model for supplier management, the ECR entry-level scorecard developed with Sainsbury's might be used. This scorecard is publicly available from the Global Commerce Initiative (GCI) website.

A transactional relationship may also include large suppliers that sell rather simple commodities, such as sugar and basic canned foods, with a long lifecycle and a small need for fast assortment planning cycles. A wider and deeper collaboration would not guarantee sales growth, in which case it makes no sense for the retailer or supplier to spend resources on excessive planning of these categories.

Category management collaboration partners help retailers develop the category in question. These suppliers should have a sufficiently large market share and expertise in the category in order to be able to support the retailer in integrated development. The aim in collaboration is to 'grow the pie' and develop the category in accordance with the retailer's category management process. The supplier must have a deep understanding of consumers and their buying behaviour concerning all products in the category, including competitors' products. The retailer's task is to identify and clearly describe the target shopper segments, category role and resources available (for example shelf space, promotional areas, and marketing resources) for which the supplier should plan the offerings.

A so-called category captain may sometimes manage the category in a very autonomous manner. This is applicable especially in some categories that are relatively unimportant to the retailer or where the supplier has superior competences in the category. Usually, the retailer cannot allocate a lot of resources for developing these areas, and the manufacturer can best support the retailer with a holistic approach. Typical examples include necessity categories such as cleaning supplies or batteries. A retailer may even outsource category management to a competent partner. In pick'n mix confectionery, this kind of model has been in existence for a long time. The supplier may create assortments and manage the category as a whole very independently. Fresh fish is another category that requires special expertise as well as efficient sourcing and logistics. Consequently, some retailers have outsourced seafood departments to external partners using shop-in-shop service concepts. Likewise, bakery products, magazines and records are examples of categories that large stores have often outsourced to partners to some extent, and they are also good examples of widely spread shop-in-shop approaches. An extreme case of outsourcing of different departments is a mall, where all shops are operated by different retail operators.

Deepening a partnership generally results in costs because shared development projects and joint planning need resources. Consequently, a key decision facing manufacturers is to balance the collaboration costs with the benefits. The question is also about how to allocate promotional efforts for building the brand in mass media versus investing in retail channel activities. Building a well-known brand is in any case vital for all products, regardless of whether the partnership is on a local, national or global level. New in-store technologies and consumer media will shift many brand-building activities to the shop floor. In the cultivation of collaboration, choosing the correct relationship depth means seeking a balance between resource costs and sales benefits.

A strategic partnership means that the manufacturer and the retailer create shared long-term business goals collaboratively and develop business operations together. The significant difference from category management cooperation is the relationship scope, which in a strategic partnership often goes beyond the supplier's own category. A strategic partner helps the retailer to differentiate and may support the retailer in category definition, role identification and even concept design. The objective of collaboration is usually to ensure retail shopper loyalty in core segments, and increase the total net sales and profit generated by the categories.

The best strategic partners help retailers differentiate and increase new customer flow into the store. For example, monopolistic liquor stores are often preferred collaboration partners in Scandinavian countries because they can make a remarkable impact on customer flows. Likewise, suppliers can help retailers by making a certain category a destination that attracts consumers from far away, such as a special cheese counter or bakery with exclusive products. In the ideal case for the retailer, the product is proprietary, and is not even offered through other channels or competitors. Furthermore, auxiliary service providers such as ATMs and fast-food outlets may help a store to increase customer flow.

A national or regional retailer rarely has major international suppliers as genuine strategic partners, and many of them do not even pursue such a position. The focus of international manufacturers often lies in creating consumer demand and building a brand. Based on our experience, they often have less interest in participation in other development projects with retailers compared with local competitors. One reason for this is that global manufacturers carry out key development initiatives with major, big name global retailers, and are able to leverage those learnings in other relationships. It might be hard for an international manufacturer to help a retailer in differentiation and produce exclusive products, because the mega brands that companies are focusing on are typically sold through almost all channels. It might also be difficult to come to an agreement on exclusive product tailoring options with a manufacturing plant located in another country or continent, as more and more production is done centrally and in the most efficient location. The resources at local sales offices focus on implementation of sales and marketing strategy, and most decisions regarding areas like product development and new service concepts are made by the head office.

For national suppliers, the situation is different. The local market share is typically high, and in order to retain their market position they have been more or less compelled to deepen collaboration with retailers. Private labels gain market share from conventional sales, mainly 'B brands', and many companies want to retain this volume in own production. Strategic partners help retailers differentiate, and it is natural that they have multiple roles in also supplying private labels, co-branded products or exclusive products. If a supplier is not interested in retailer-specific operations, the lack of exclusivity may become an obstacle for a deep partnership.

For local manufacturers, collaboration with local retailers is often easy, and retailers open for collaboration can achieve differentiation opportunities. On the other hand, as whole value chains start to compete with each other, strategic partnerships may prove a hindrance to collaboration with other retailers. However, this might balance power in the value chain because good suppliers are preferred partners, and retailers may well be obliged to compete for them. Openness and deep collaboration with suppliers, which are necessary elements in partnerships, are new things for many retail buyers, and it may also be necessary to modify the traditional metrics used. International collaboration partners are increasing their role as strategic partners in retailing, compared with traditional suppliers and vertical partners. Horizontal partnering is also gaining share. Through shared sourcing and product development, retailers collaborating can achieve differentiation benefits such as products designed and made for exclusive sale. International sourcing pools and collaboration in areas like product development will become more important throughout the industry.

It is also evident that some retail groups have learned to tap into suppliers as skilful resources by sharing information with them and letting them conduct analyses that the retailer would otherwise do itself or buy from outside. Thus, retailers have achieved cost savings, but the suppliers have also acquired valuable new information and lessons learned. Openness has created mutual competitive advantage, fulfilling the requirements of good partnership.

The position of local suppliers, operating in a limited geographical area, as retailing partners will become increasingly challenging. They are usually bakeries or manufacturers of perishables, often focusing on local specialties. In practice, they must adapt to chain assortments and create close contacts with a local purchasing body. On the other hand, many retail chains have increased local purchasing over the last few years. As an example, Tesco recently opened regional buying offices. Also, Whole Foods has supported local – even store-level – purchasing and has strongly emphasized local suppliers in its operations. The focus is also visibly communicated to customers in the stores.

Brand management and brand awareness are critical success factors for manufacturers of consumer products. In principle, even a local supplier may be accepted as a strategic partner if it is strong in its area and has sufficient resources and expertise. However, as global sourcing and various collaboration models become more common, the probability that this will happen gets smaller. Through active networking, regional suppliers can, however, increase their status as trading partners. Good examples of this are alliances formed by regional bakeries or small farms that have pooled their selling power to retailers.

ECR as an industry community

From the beginning, ECR has been an industry-wide movement, though ECR as such is largely based on collaboration and partnership between individual retailers and manufacturers. The ECR movement has spread in different ways depending on country and continent. ECR Europe has gained a significant role as a discussion forum for collaboration between retailers and manufacturers. Besides annual seminars, it sponsors many development initiatives in order to promote retailer–manufacturer collaboration within the ECR framework. There are already more than 20 national ECR organizations closely linked to this effort.

As mentioned earlier, ECR has not gained as much ground as a community in the United States, where it was born. This is partly because there are many other established associations that have taken ECR principles as part of their agendas and have done so to such an extent that there has been no space for a separate movement to be born. Important forums in the United States include the Food Marketing Institute (FMI), Grocery Manufacturers Association (GMA) and VICS. Europe did not have a similar supranational discussion forum, and ECR has been a suitable umbrella concept to fill this deficiency. Whereas CIES – The Food Business Forum – has done remarkable work as a retail top management forum, it doesn't have a strong role in establishing industry standards or development of best practice collaboration models in the retail value chain as the focus has been more on retailing than retailer–manufacturer collaboration. In Asia, ECR has gained a foothold somewhat more slowly and has remained scattered. National ECR associations have been established in Thailand, Singapore, Taiwan and the Philippines, but their activities are still relatively new compared with their European counterparts.

Globalization of retailing presents new challenges for global data standards. As many retailers have expanded their activities to several continents over the last few years, retailing is becoming a truly global business. More than 45 major international companies operating in the retail and consumer products markets comprise the Global Commerce Initiative (GCI), with the aim of improving international supply chains through efficient practices and joint standards. The goals are similar to ECR initiatives, but the practical activities are more focused on data and communication standardization. Furthermore, new areas such as electronic product codes (EPC) are being developed. To some extent the establishment of GCI may be seen to make up for the lack of a strong ECR community in the United States.

GCI has borrowed a major part of its content directly from the ECR concept, and the same presentations are often used at both GCI and ECR forums. The ECR scorecard and many other methods have been introduced under the new concept as such. Though GCI has so far been a distant organization to many small-market companies, it may have a significant indirect impact for them in the future. Part of the European ECR discussion and decision making may shift to the global level, where GCI is an influential player. The merging of the EAN and UPC organizations into the GS1 community acts as a catalyst for a similar trend. With the world's biggest retailers and FMCG manufacturers on board, the standards formed within GCI will be introduced all over the world. These standards slowly make their way to small companies and markets, whether they are actively involved in the work or not.

An important feature of the ECR community is its independence. The events are organized by retailers and manufacturers, and in most cases system vendors and other service providers have not dictated or supported the operations too visibly, as in many other forums. Participants in ECR forums widely represent company executive levels, including sales, category management, product management, logistics and information management. Though the topics have always focused on consumer benefit, throughout ECR history there have been fewer participants from the marketing field for one reason or another. However, brands are key competitive differentiators to retailers and manufacturers. Brands are increasingly built together, so there will be plenty of opportunities for collaboration in marketing.

ECR Europe also aims at bridging the gap between academia and businesses. Important instruments include ECR Academic Partnership seminars, training programmes organized in collaboration with leading universities, for example the Progressive Management Program – Building leadership in the consumer goods industry and the publication *ECR Journal*, started a few years ago. In addition, ECR Europe annually grants student awards for ECR-related papers, and many local ECR forums have followed suit. The last five years or so have in many ways marked a boom in European retail research. This has been caused not only by the popularity of ECR initiatives but also by the internationalization of retailing, increasing price wars, and convergence of retail industry. Loyalty programmes, shopper data use and category management have also gained a lot of attention in the research community. New phenomena and research areas have induced retailers to seek ideas from the academic world, and also encouraged new students and scholars to study and research retailing.

It seems likely that ECR will exist as a collaboration forum in the future for retailers and manufacturers. New participants such as non-food retailing, foodservice and other service areas that come with retail expansion into new areas might join the ECR forum. ECR is a chameleon, and the content and key development areas within the framework will change over the years, but the objectives will remain: *working together to fulfil consumer wishes better, faster and at less cost.*

4 Demand management

The foundation of ECR collaboration, and successful retailing as well, is building profitable business based on consumer needs. The aim is to provide real value to the consumer and thereby to improve customer satisfaction, sales and profitability. Demand management is a broad topic, covering all activities related to management of the retail product and service offering as well as communicating it to consumers. Consequently, demand management comprises areas like new product development, assortment management and marketing communications in its various forms. The main goal is 'to grow the pie' to increase benefits for all parties – retailers, manufacturers and consumers.

As retailers form the ultimate interface between consumer demand and product or service delivery, demand management is often a retailer-led activity. Manufacturers' role is mainly to support retailers by sharing their category expertise. As experts in their own categories, manufacturers can provide valuable insights into the market situation and current trends as well as consumer behaviour. Manufacturers also actively drive new product development initiatives based on changing consumer needs.

Over the years demand management has become more and more a collaborative activity between suppliers and retailers, and ECR efforts have been a key accelerator in this process. A central part of this collaboration is category management, regarded unofficially as the core of demand management. The term category management refers to managing retail product categories as own business units to meet consumer needs. The main difference from traditional approaches is the focus on consumer needs instead of traditional production- or product-centred approaches. Category management aims at defining an optimal assortment for various kinds of stores based on actual consumer demand.

Originally the need for category management rose from the explosive growth of product varieties and number of stock keeping units (SKUs) that caused challenges for assortment management. The second key factor was the growing interest in space management, which aims at utilizing scarce square footage in stores as efficiently as possible according to consumer demand. The number of items on offer is often manifold considering the space available, and new products are launched at a rapid pace. High-selling products need reasonable space, and non-sellers should be eliminated from the assortments. The goal is that the customer always finds the desired product in the store. Space management also facilitates and speeds up store operations, reducing workload in the store.

There are several category management models, but the most famous one is the eight-step category management process model created by The Partnering Group and Roland Berger for ECR Europe in 1997, also called the Brian Harris model, after one of the developers. The model has been widely adopted globally, but often heavily adapted. According to the original definition, the category management process is a structured, measured set of activities designed to produce a specified output for the trading partners and their consumers.

Category management has been around already for about 20 years, which is a very respectable time for any operational model. In our interview, Dr Brian Harris summarized the key success factors of category management, and defined the key reasons for its existence. Category management:

- forced consumer focus for retail decisions;
- provided a strategic foundation for differentiation and competitive advantage;
- provided an effective model for collaboration;
- improved decision making through better information sharing;

- developed organizational capabilities;
- provided strategic logic for tactical decisions;
- established clearer priorities for asset allocation;
- clarified responsibilities and accountabilities;
- provided a platform for more advanced methods;
- delivered superior results.

Category management has been and still is one of the key development areas for most retailers, and provides the collaboration platform for retailers and manufacturers in demand management. Category management is here to stay.

Beside its great success, category management has also faced challenges. The biggest challenge with all off-the-shelf category management models is that they often are considered as projects and not as a continuous process. They tend to portray category management as a set of discrete projects instead of permanently integrating the new approach into the everyday processes of both the retailer and collaboration partners. The category management process model is primarily meant for pilot projects, to be carried out at the starting stages of collaboration, in which it has been tried and tested. For continuous use, the original model often needs to be heavily simplified, as only some of the actions are part of seasonal or even annual planning. In terms of retailer–manufacturer collaboration, the key is to make category management an ongoing collaborative process where procedures and expertise are continually developed. The lessons learned from a one-off exercise are too easily forgotten.

Increasingly, category management is seen as a core competency of retailers. This is understandable because it is ultimately up to retailers to decide which products and services to offer consumers in their stores. The category management process should be guided by the retailer's business strategy and the needs of the key target segments. Without a clear retail format description and value proposition, it is impossible to achieve uniform procedures, especially as most categories are managed more or less independently. On the other hand, category management competences have quickly increased in both retailing and manufacturing, and we are now in a situation where retailers need to link category management more closely to retail format development.

Though this may at first sound as if power has shifted solely to retailers, it is likely that collaboration between the parties will increase. Most retailers cannot just passively choose the best alternatives among the products manufacturers offer them – instead, they need to communicate the needs of the target consumers to manufacturers, who can then design products and procedures to fit the requirements. In the future, suppliers and retailers can focus more on their own special areas and support each other with knowledge and expertise. However, the traditional collaboration roles will also evolve as retailers become product developers with private labels, while at the same time manufacturers build concept stores and shop-in-shop solutions to serve the consumer interface directly.

Based on the challenges identified in the traditional category management process, a shopper-oriented demand management process was developed by Finne and Kokkonen (2005), introduced in Figure 4.1. Compared with traditional models, the new model is oriented more towards retail positioning and format development, and also includes store-level implementation. It describes one way of responding to consumer needs and behaviour in all key levels of retail demand management.

The shopper-oriented demand management process model starts with identifying and describing the retailers' target segments that provide the foundation for retail strategy formulation. Format development and cate-

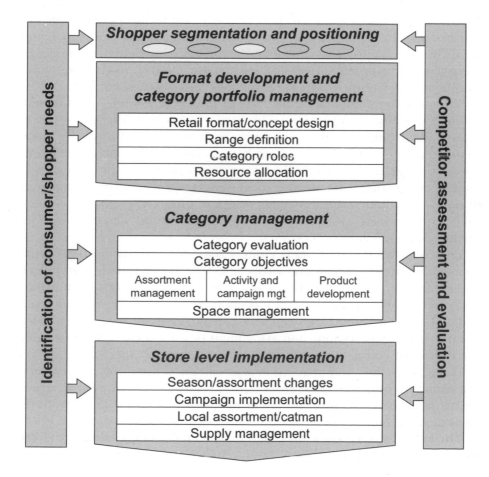

Figure 4.1   Shopper-oriented demand management process model

gory portfolio management mainly comprise the planning carried out by the retailer, though strategic supplier partners can sometimes support the retailer. This is the time to look at some fundamental questions: What value do retailers create for target consumer segments? Which categories and services must retailers have in order to fulfil the needs of target segments? How is competitive advantage created compared with key competitors? The retail format description including retailer value proposition can be thought as the foundation of chain operations, and they should be solid from the very beginning, so that there will be no need for revisions except during significant changes in the operating context, perhaps once or twice a decade.

Category management involves developing individual categories and services in accordance with the retail format. The effort is divided into three focal areas: assortment management, activity and campaign management, as well as product development including new product introductions (NPIs). Category management creates the necessary basis for collaboration between suppliers and retailers, targeting to meet customer needs better and promoting profitable category growth. Activity management aims at bringing variety and excitement for the selected segments, leading in an increase in average purchases and consumer loyalty.

Store-level implementation puts the actions planned into practice with efficient operational processes. This stage focuses on the execution of assortment changes and various activities in stores. Both assortment changes and particularly campaigns have significant impact on workforce needs in stores, so they need to be taken into account in employee management. Local assortments are also addressed at this stage. An essential part of store operations is the management of the store replenishment process to ensure on-shelf availability. Store-level operations are examined in further detail in Chapter 5.

Consumer and market data guide each phase in the process, from concept development to local assortment design. Operations are supported by continuous piloting, measurement and tracking of consumer behaviour, and the best practices and lessons learned can be leveraged chain wide. Market and competitor tracking helps to keep an eye on retail positioning, pricing, marketing and assortment development, and to evaluate the impact of competitors' actions on the company's operations. Market tracking can be referred to as business intelligence, involving the systematical collection and analysis of information related to the competitive field and customers. Efficient information processing is a prerequisite of efficient demand management.

The following sections will focus in more detail on the main areas of the shopper-oriented demand management process model.

Format development and category portfolio management

The retail format describes the retailer's business idea as a clear business model, and its value proposition to consumers. Customers should be able to trust that they receive uniform service and the same basic assortment at all the chain's stores. The retail format description also indicates how a product or service offering is delivered to the customer. In other words, it describes the processes that are the best for meeting consumer needs and that should therefore be adopted throughout the chain.

While there are several strategy and positioning possibilities for retailers, many chains are astonishingly similar to each other, trying to attract the same type of customers and operate in similar ways. One of the main reasons for the similarity among retailers is the great significance of competitor information in today's assortment decisions. Where the measurement of actual customer needs has been challenging, the retailers have at the same time easily received information on the operations of their competitors from syndicated data sources, such as IRI and ACNielsen ScanTrack that can be called almost an industry standard in some markets. All players in the market, both retailers and manufacturers, quickly identify high-selling products and bring them into assortments or try to imitate them. As a result, assortments become more and more alike. The winners in this game have been the retailers with the most cost-effective business model because it has been difficult to differentiate with assortments in this environment. However, in recent years many retailers have resigned their contracts with syndicated data providers, and do not openly share data, which helps to protect the points of differentiation.

Despite the similarity of many retail formats, there are many examples of well-differentiated ones, including for instance IKEA, Trader Joe's, Sephora, Whole Foods, Lidl and Nordstrom, which all have a clear and unique profile among customers. Awareness among target customers is certainly one characteristic of a successful retail format. It is desirable that the shopper identifies the retailer on the basis of the product assortment, display and service. If the shopper were taken into a store blindfolded and the blindfold were taken off at some point in the store, the shopper would be able to tell immediately which chain he or she was in. Retailers fight for space and position in the mind of the shopper. Just as suppliers create product brands in the minds of consumers, retailers need to brand their formats.

Retailer target segments form the majority of the regular shoppers, whose needs and expectations are used as the basis for designing the retail offering. Secondary customer segments are also important, but because of their size, profitability or buying frequency, they are not as attractive as the target segments. The preferences of all major segments should be taken into consideration in planning from retail format design to assortment management. Furthermore, it may be beneficial to identify other occasional and potential customer segments and take their needs into account, provided they are not contradictory with the needs of target segments. An example of such a segment is tourists, who may create new needs for a store during a holiday season.

The shopping process in format development

In store format planning, the whole shopping process of the consumer is taken into consideration, starting from the arousal of shopping needs and continuing all the way down to the use of products. This process consists of several interconnected phases, which all have an impact on the shopping experience. An illustrative example of the shopping process is outlined in Figure 4.2.

A consumer's shopping process might vary significantly by customer type and situation. For a habitual buyer who stops at a newsagent's to buy something to read on the way to work, the length of the whole process from impulse to buying decision and consumption may last only a minute or two. On the other hand, a young couple planning the renovation of their first home may spend several hours in a DIY store. During the same shopping trip, they might stop to have lunch and buy groceries at a nearby store. An online shopping experience might work differently, but is also more and more important for retailers in a multi-channel environment.

It is vital for a retailer to understand the shopping mission types to be able to focus on activities and touch points that create value for customers. It is also important to trim down activities that do not create value. Shopping mission types may have significant impact on retail format and store layout design. As an example, the charting of a shopping process often reveals that the drive to and from the store is actually a key part of shopping, especially relative to the time spent by the consumer. The average consumer visiting a store four times a week, and driving just 15 minutes one way (which includes finding a parking space and walking to the store entrance) uses over 100 hours annually just to access the store. No wonder location is such an important factor in choosing a grocery store, even though consumers don't often consider the matter this rationally.

Failure in just one customer touch point during a shopping trip may cause disappointment and in the worst case lead to the end of the relationship between that customer and the retailer. It is important for retailers to have internal touch points in order, but sometimes external touch points also create challenges. As an example, frequent traffic jams or unpleasant

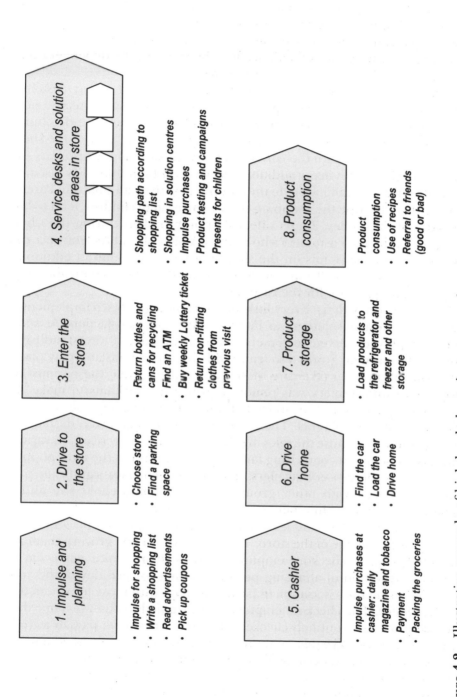

Figure 4.2 Illustrative example of high-level phases in a grocery shopping process

1. Impulse and planning
· Impulse for shopping
· Write a shopping list
· Read advertisements
· Pick up coupons

2. Drive to the store
· Choose store
· Find a parking space

3. Enter the store
· Return bottles and cans for recycling
· Find an ATM
· Buy weekly Lottery ticket
· Return non-fitting clothes from previous visit

4. Service desks and solution areas in store
· Shopping path according to shopping list
· Shopping in solution centres
· Impulse purchases
· Product testing and campaigns
· Presents for children

5. Cashier
· Impulse purchases at cashier: daily magazine and tobacco
· Payment
· Packing the groceries

6. Drive home
· Find the car
· Load the car
· Drive home

7. Product storage
· Load products to the refrigerator and freezer and other storage

8. Product consumption
· Product consumption
· Use of recipes
· Referral to friends (good or bad)

parking lots may cause dissatisfaction. Other customers may also have an effect on the shopping experience. A crowded store with noisy children or impatient shoppers trying to jump the queue can make the shopping trip quite unpleasant. Mail-order selling and online stores form a different type of example – the service experience may be significantly dependent on a third party, such as a delivery service provider.

It is also possible to surprise the shopper pleasantly at any customer touch point. Easy access and a pleasant entrance to the store create a positive start for the shopping trip. Easy-to-find service desks and solution areas that meet the needs of the customer are a critical part of the shopping process, as they are the core of the buying situation. Customers can also be delighted with many additional services and solutions. For instance, Shoprite offers cleaning wipes to the customers with small children. Parents can use them to wipe the shopping trolley since small children tend to bite the sides of the trolley. Target offers shopping baskets during the whole shopping path, and customers who didn't take a basket at the entrance can find one at several points on the shopping trip. This kind of additional service might seem small, but can be an essential factor in making the shopping easy and pleasant for the customer.

In connection with its 'Every little helps' campaign, Tesco implemented many store design solutions to improve customer satisfaction. At some stores, employees served customers in a non-traditional way, standing in front of the counter. Stores also featured baby-care rooms and play places with babysitters, who take care of young children while the parents are shopping. Confectionery was removed from the checkouts to make the area more spacious and to prevent children from making a scene to the annoyance of their parents. These measures have been taken despite the fact that some may cause the sales in some categories to decrease. In various markets the segment comprising families with children is the most popular target group for grocery retailers. This segment makes significant purchases compared with other groups because of household size and is usually very attractive to retailers.

Paying at the cashier and leaving the store are important places for creating a positive image of the store. The customers of one grocery chain are delighted when a checkout employee wishes them a nice name day (a European tradition of attaching personal names to each day of the year, and celebrating the association of particular days with those for whom that day is named). The checkout employees are trained to observe name days because names are routinely checked whenever a customer pays by a credit card. Good service like this causes no extra costs but leaves a good impression on the customer, perhaps about the whole shopping trip.

Customers can also be delighted by taking the product storage and consumption phases into account. These phases are often neglected in planning, since the customer is no longer in the store. However, there shouldn't be any unpleasant surprises for the customer, since malfunctioning products or other difficulties create a bad image of the store and the shopping trip as a whole. An interesting example of creating a better storage and consumption experience comes from Japan, where a selection of upscale stores sell square watermelons. Before, the consumers struggled to fit and keep the round fruit in their refrigerators and had difficulty trying to cut the fruit because it kept rolling around. The new square watermelon does not have these challenges, but instead, a premium price.

Providing information to customers at different stages of the shopping process may have a positive impact on customer satisfaction and purchasing behaviour. Information can be subtle, such as guiding the movement of the customer with the help of fixtures, or very clear, such as clear signs indicating sale prices hanging above mass displays. The purpose is to use various kinds of adverts and signs to drive impulse purchases, but the goal may also be to attract the customer into the store with window displays, signs or easy-to-find free parking places during peak hours. In-store solutions are discussed in more detail later, in the section 'Activity management and stores as advertising media'.

Store layout design

Retailers also need to focus on the physical architecture in the store. The objective is to design a layout that is easy and natural for shopping, and also enables the retailer to display products and categories to be able to influence purchasing behaviour and customer experience. According to Dr Brian Harris, a key trend in format development is making stores more 'shoppable' and logical to the customer. The grocery store layout has remained largely the same during the past 20 years in spite of the changes in shopping behaviour and the growth of customer information available for retailers. Future store layouts should be designed around customer needs.

In grocery retailing, it is common to place perishables at the beginning of the shopper's path, but completely different solutions are also possible. Stores can choose 'multiple shopping path' solutions, enabling shoppers to choose path length and categories according to their needs. As an example, a different shopping path may be arranged in a hypermarket for those interested in speciality products and grocery shoppers can choose another path. Smaller stores can also design a path for those who just pop in to buy some snacks. In Best Buy customers can go directly to one of the solution centres that are highly visible, and the route for shoppers might be quite different depending on the needs.

The customer's shopping route is closely related to the store's fixture layout and the physical setting of the building often narrows down options.

The use of store fixtures and decorative solutions can have a great impact on the shopper's perception of the store. As an example, a heavy warehouse-type shelf fixture may not be aesthetically pleasing but it can create an image of low prices. Fine wooden surfaces and decor may increase the warm atmosphere of the store but may also create some preconceptions about assortments and prices. Grocery stores often have fairly uniform fixtures based on standard-size modules and shelves. This solution is justifiable from the perspective of purchasing costs, adaptability and store logistics, but it results in stores that are very much alike, with only fixture colours and signs varying from one chain to another.

Some stores have been systematically designed with the customer relationship process in mind. A classic, but good, example is IKEA, where the shopping process has been taken into account in many ways. Table 4.1 lists some observations.

Store formats may sometimes involve solutions that clearly stand out from the competition. As an example, the Nordic DIY chain K-Rauta has a type of cash-and-carry concept: customers can drive into the warehouse yard and load the products themselves or ask for help if needed. Hence, K-Rauta can serve commercial and private customers using the same concept. As many DIY retailers have focused on only one or the other of these target groups, its unique approach offers K-Rauta a competitive advantage as it can use the same space to sell products to several segments. The owner of the chain, Rautakesko, has grown to become the fifth biggest DIY seller in Europe, and continues to expand rapidly. In the United States both Home Depot and Lowe's use a similar approach serving consumers and commercial builders in some stores.

Service counters, including in-store bakeries, can also be used to stand out from competitors and to increase the attractiveness of the store. The general layout of a store may sometimes clearly differ from the conventional solutions. One example is Coop Forum, the flagship store of Coop Norden in Stockholm, where the FMCG categories have been placed in a round market-type space in the centre of the store, whereas speciality products are placed along the outer walls, in separate sections.

Customers increasingly seek a personalized shopping experience and wish to get ideas for grocery purchases. Those going to New York should visit Zabar's, a former coffee shop that has over the years turned into a gourmet store. The store has brought the market hall atmosphere back to life, with temptations including a variety of smoked fish and speciality coffees. Even though the facilities are not as fancy as in other gourmet stores in the area (such as Balducci's or Dean & de Luca), there is a true romance in shopping with several delicacies and the smell of coffee beans around.

In speciality stores, the store layout, fixtures and the use of colours play an even greater role than in food retailing. The general appearance should

Table 4.1 Examples of in-store solutions supporting the shopping process at IKEA

Shopping path	• Shopping path 'forces' the shopper to visit many departments and to meet many buying impulses.
Food service	• Restaurants and other food services are visible in the shopping path and also after cashiers. Shoppers using food services also spend an average of 25–30 minutes more in store than other consumers.
Bags and other carriage aids	• IKEA's large bags (carried on the shoulder) are available in many places during the shopping path. This makes the shopping more pleasant, frees up the hands of the shopper and enables the consumer to buy and carry more.
Playground	• Playing centres make the shopping experience interesting for kids and more pleasant for parents. Playing centres are located in several places during the shopping path.
Product displays and model rooms	• Several model rooms and examples, built with IKEA's products, give ideas and stimulation for buying, and shows possibilities for product combinations.
Self-service warehouse	• Self-service warehouse is located at the end of the shopping path. Shoppers do not need to carry the products long and that enables buying of large quantities. A separate warehouse section keeps the store buying section clean. Self-service is a very cost efficient process for this retailer.
Integrated customer communication	• Product catalogue and assortment in stores are well integrated, and complement the shopping experience both in store and at home.
Impulse purchases	• Products for impulse purchases are found in several places during the shopping path, often the same product in multiple placings. Mainly daily products with high sales volume, and products on sale change regularly to keep up the interest of regular shoppers.
Shopping aids	• Many aids for shopping are provided. Typical examples include measurement tools, pencils and paper for notes.

support the retailer's brand image, complement the products sold and, if possible, emphasize them with the help of displays and different sorts of stands. This is especially important in high-profile speciality stores, where there may be relatively few products on display and the aim is to give a luxurious impression. Haute couture fashion stores in, for example, Paris and Milan are seldom filled with products, but display carefully selected pieces of the collection. Service plays an important role in speciality retailing and separate areas are often reserved for it. Music and lights can also be used to create a particular atmosphere and shopping experience. For example, clothes retailer Hollister uses loud music and a dark store environment to create a very different feeling in the store from what is happening outside the door in the mall.

In malls, the key is to attract the customer into the store as the great majority of buyers are impulse shoppers. This underlines the importance of the entrance solutions and window displays in creating customer flows. Imagination can be used in the selection of influence methods, and the store can appeal to any one (or more) of the five senses to attract customers inside. Colourful and imaginative window dressing can be used to display products and services in many ways; for instance, many department stores build spectacular displays before Christmas. These often attract customers with children, in particular. Music and fragrances can also be important factors for certain chains, and some clothing chains trying to attract young people use loud music to arouse interest. Fragrances are important to beauty and cosmetics chains such as The Body Shop and Sephora, as well as to speciality food retailers, selling, for example, chocolate or coffee. Cigar shops might also catch the attention of customers with a fragrance.

The entrance is a challenging area for stores in other respects as well. Retail anthropologist and consultant Paco Underhill has discovered that stores have a kind of 'decompression zone' right after the entrance. When shoppers enter a store, they get used to lighting, temperature and conditions, at the same time slowing down their walking speed. In the parking area, shoppers usually walk faster, but as soon as they walk into the store, they slow down and assume the normal 'shopping pace'. As the circumstances change, the observation zone of the shopper remains narrow. In line with this, it has been observed that products that are on sale in this zone do not sell very well, if at all. In a grocery store, the fruit and vegetable department has often been placed at the beginning of the shopping path to attract shoppers and to give a good impression. In rational terms, however, this department should be situated toward the end of the shopping path so that soft fruits could be carefully put in the shopping basket or cart on top of other products. However, the first impression of freshness and abundance often takes the upper hand.

Beside shelves, stores have several other kinds of spaces and fixtures for displaying and selling products. Some of the most important are mass display areas, which facilitate the implementation of campaigns and adaptation to seasonal fluctuations. Mass display areas are usually not allocated for any fixed category; on the contrary, continual change is typical. Mass display areas can house large amounts of seasonal products, such as chocolate boxes at Christmas time or backpacks and other school supplies just before the start of school. Some best practice retailers change assortments in these areas as often as weekly, and ensure continuous change and excitement to consumers without having to interfere with the store's basic assortment and planograms. If there is no special season or campaign going on, mass displays can be used to promote new products or surplus products from the previous season. However, this still needs good planning and discipline, since these high selling places might easily turn into a mess of leftover products, if not managed well. It is also possible to locate mass display areas in the middle of aisles, especially on store centre floor, where they guide shoppers not only to the main aisles but also to other areas.

A special case of mass display areas are end caps. Like mass display areas, they are often used to display high-selling or topical products. End caps face heavy customer traffic, and they are highly visible for most shoppers and key opportunities to enhance store image (for example price image, category range, quality level) and impulse sales. Compared to the usual mass display areas, end caps are relatively small, having space for one or two pallets and a few shelves on top of them. Shelves are particularly useful in the case of product adjacencies and impulse purchasing. As an example, the end cap in a Scandinavian store including spiced wine for Christmas (glow wine) may also be used to display raisins and almonds (as these are often added to the hot wine), alongside products used when setting the table, such as Christmas-themed napkins and stirring sticks. End caps are important for impulse shopping especially in large stores – small stores often have very few end caps because of limited space. End caps are also used for products prone to being shoplifted, such as batteries, to stock them in a visible place. Reduced shrink pays back quickly.

Though end caps are excellent in attracting customer attention, based on our experience they still are seldom used systematically to their full potential. They are often managed from category management (commercial) organizations, and not from chain management with a holistic perspective of the shopper experience. Consumer flows around them are great, and these places should be key basket fillers, but also have a consistent message for the shoppers.

Too often they are used for manufacturer-driven promotions not linked to the retailer's value proposition, and many retailers have also developed a systematic process for selling the spaces. This enables the retailer to gain marketing support from manufacturers, which helps the retailer's short-term marketing budget, but often does not support retail differentiation. Best retailers have a clear plan for using the end caps for enhancing customer experience and store image, and use them for manufacturers' promotions very selectively – slotting allowances paid by suppliers are not the main selection criteria.

End caps as key retail selling spaces should always have clear sales and image targets with a systematic follow-up process. In this area most retailers have a lot of development potential, which can also be achieved relatively quickly. The tricky part of achieving the benefits is cross-category coordination.

End caps are excellent in promoting new products and innovations. Beside selling and displaying products, they can also be used to provide customer information material that can educate the consumer or tell the story of a product. The use of end caps can be intensified in the future by incorporating more customer information with tools such as personal digital assistants (PDAs) and videos on flat screens.

In addition to mass displays, checkouts are also efficient sales areas. They usually include products from many categories that aim at generating additional sales through impulse purchases as customers stand in the checkout queue. Many chains use 'price baskets' near the checkouts, displaying products on sale. Checkouts can also be used to display necessities that customers often forget to buy. For instance, cosmetics retailer Sephora has a selection of basic beauty care products, such as nail scissors, next to the checkout, and customers are guided past them with ropes leading to checkouts. Furthermore, the checkout area can be used for products that otherwise would be difficult to control or have high shrink, and careful placement can decrease shoplifting significantly. A typical example is cigarettes. Checkout areas typically are space-efficient because a small area contains a lot of items, with a higher-than-average margin. This makes them a focal point of retail space planning. However, most retailers could benefit more from checkout areas by using them to introduce new products and services.

Destination categories can also be located in the store to guide the shopper's path. Typical examples are nappies and baby food, which stores do not necessarily want to place in the best impulse-buying locations. Both items are purchased when needed, and the shopper will walk through the whole store to get them if they are on the shopping list. These categories also require a lot of space and are usually some of the least profitable categories in a store, but they must be stocked – families with children are a very sought-after target group as their total purchases are well above average. Because of this, the margins of key destination products have declined in many markets due to heavy competition, and are in extreme cases on minus margins, if allowed by local legislation.

Dairy products are placed at the back of the store in many store formats, where the shelves can be replenished continuously at the rear directly from the cold storage room without having to interfere with customers, which is pragmatic as dairy shelves are typically under heavy traffic. Dairy products can be found in most shopping baskets, and positioning them at the back of the store forces shoppers to walk through most of the store. At the same time, however, this has opened the door for convenience stores where the shopper can get small purchases without a long walk through a large supermarket. However, supermarkets can play the same game, and establish double positioning for certain items. For example, Wegmans has built a convenience case – located close to the cashiers, where customers can grab key dairy products without having to take a long shopping path.

Different areas in retail stores have very different customer flows and sales. Most retailers measure average purchases, but far fewer chains measure the purchase penetration of different departments. This measure refers to the share of customers who make purchases in the specific category or department. The quantitative metrics are relatively easy to form, if the retailer is collecting receipt-level data of shopper purchases. It is important to inform customers about the store's services and get them to use the services to their full potential. And as the old CRM cliché says, selling more to old customers is easier than acquiring new customers. Understanding the shopping paths in the store, and making a clear communication and product placement plan based on them, are the keys to filling up the consumer's shopping basket with additional purchases. Measuring category and end cap purchase penetration (in comparison to total store customer flows) constantly will give retailers great insight for selecting appropriate store marketing actions.

Store service can also affect customer loyalty. Certain customer segments expect personal service and are sometimes willing to pay a price that is higher than usual. Service desks are labour intensive so the need for personal service (especially by key target segments) should be considered carefully. How much are customers really prepared to pay for the service? On the other hand, a high level of service may provide a way for the retailer to stand out from the competition, in which case a single category profitability is not the primary factor guiding the decision, as service is considered as more of a marketing or differentiation cost. Another form of service is to offer extended opening hours.

Local adaptation of the store format

Only in a few cases can stores be designed from a clean slate, fully in accordance with pre-defined principles and manuals. It's more likely that a retailer has a group of properties of different sizes and shapes that cannot be modified to any significant extent but to which the retail format must be adapted. The retailer's premises may consist of buildings that have been built at different times, and they may be very different in terms of layout scheme. It is not always possible to place related categories beside one another, and sometimes a shortage of space makes it necessary to allocate significantly less than average space to some products. In addition, certain fixtures, especially refrigeration equipment and some points of service, are fixed by nature, and changing them may require an extensive and expensive renovation.

The competitive situation may vary greatly from location to location, and each store should take into account its competitive environment. One store may be the only store in the neighbourhood whereas the other is squeezed by competition from several hypermarkets, and still they have the same format. Stores too close to each other may also cannibalize sales. Also, the customer portfolio in the catchment area should be reflected in space allocation among categories and in assortment decisions.

To sum up, retail format development needs to take into account factors that ensure a similar purchasing experience for the consumer and uniform procedures in all stores, and, at the same time, take the local market situation and consumer portfolio into account. The retail concept is the 'playbook' that should spell out rules and guidelines for all categories to keep the retail format integrated. A good retail format is easy to describe to personnel and collaboration partners, and will be remembered by consumers, but is still hard to copy.

Range definition

The needs of customer segments are the key for determining product offerings. The primary question concerns the scope of the assortment: which categories do customers expect to find in the store, and which products should these categories include? Besides assortment, the character of the products needs to be addressed: what is the quality level demanded by customers, and how do we attend to quality criteria? Expectations about product and service quality may vary widely among different segments.

Range management is category management at the macro level, and it defines space and resource allocation among categories and various services. Range management calls for close attention to new, growing and shrinking categories as well as to the profitability of each category. One way to differentiate is to emphasize certain categories, thereby linking the store brand with specific consumer needs. These goals need to be communicated to suppliers as well, who can then plan their operations and products to meet the needs of retailers. However, changing the balance in different categories is often not enough to achieve true differentiation. Retailers should carefully evaluate which categories they want to keep in their range.

The development of store range should always begin with the consumer, focusing on the needs of the primary and secondary customer segments. The key questions related to range decisions include:

- What categories and services do the target consumer segments need?
- What are the destination categories and services that make target consumer segments decide where to shop?

- What product offerings attract secondary customer segments who would not otherwise come to the store?
- Would the total sales and profits of the store increase if the weighting of resources allocated to certain categories were changed?
- Should new and growing categories be given more space and current categories removed or decreased?
- What categories and services can be used to create impulse purchases and increase the size of the average shopping basket?
- What is the role of non-food and seasonal items in profiling the retail format and in growing the shopping basket?

No category should be included in the assortment just because it has always been sold. For example, the share of non-food items has been increasing significantly in many retailers' assortments. These categories often affect retailer positioning and, naturally, the changes have also been taken into account in space allocation. It is sometimes healthy for a retailer to conduct an exercise about the entry of a new competitor to the market. When an ideal retail format is built from scratch without any limitations and using actual consumer information, the result may be a totally new kind of store format, or at least a list of good development ideas for current concepts.

Range definition aims at forming a category portfolio that the target customers find appealing and that provides the retailer with the maximum long-term profit. A central part of this goal is to maximize space profitability. Selling space should be allocated to categories efficiently to optimize total profit. The allocation is affected by the law of diminishing returns; adding space for a certain category results in less additional profit. At some point, it is more profitable to add a new category instead of continuing to increase space for an existing category. Also the number of items in some categories is limited and only a certain amount of selling space is required, after which added space only means more facings given to the same products.

Space efficiency can be measured in many ways. Net sales or gross margin are key metrics, and can be often measured on store, product area, category or even an individual product level. Modern CAD-solutions used for store design (such as Store Designer) enable measurement typically on macro-level, from subcategory level upwards. Item-level space efficiency is measured with category management and space management solutions that are used also for drawing planograms. In most advanced chains that have loyalty programmes, space efficiency metrics are used that are specific to consumer segments.

However, it is sometimes worthwhile putting an emphasis on less profitable categories and store services if they enable the store to better serve key target segments. Good examples of services that do not generate additional sales as such, but may be essential for customer comfort, include children's play places. Another example is sanitary facilities, which are often very important, for example in convenience stores at fuel stations. All these solutions should still have a clear business case that supports their existence.

Range planning involves a host of factors, such as the category profitability, available space and layout solutions, local customer structure and competitive situation as well as qualitative factors related to customer comfort. In choosing categories for the assortment and making decisions on their relative weighting, it is always vital to start with the needs of target consumer segments. This is not an easy task, but at this stage even some consideration of the consumer may help the retailer to differentiate from competitors.

Category definition

In category definition retailers make decisions about which products to include in each category. As these decisions have an essential impact on all subsequent planning phases, sufficient time and care should be devoted to them. It is especially important to gain a clear 'big picture' of the category and its scope for all the parties involved.

Product decisions are very much linked to pricing; high-quality products generally require a higher price level. The quality and price positioning is also closely associated with the decision about whether to incorporate branded products into the assortments: should we create a high-quality image by relying on strong brands, or do we want to create an image of a low price level by focusing on generic products or price fighter private labels? The assortment image can be enhanced also by actively displaying new products, preferably in highly visible locations.

In many areas, category definition is relatively simple. In practice, products have been grouped in a certain way in statistics and store displays, and consumers have got used to the order. Cheese, dairy and meat products are examples of this kind of traditional product grouping. A standard traditional grouping may be of great help, but it should not always be accepted as such. Many categories were born out of production-related, distribution-linked or legal aspects. Furthermore, if the division of products was decided long ago it will no longer be easy to add new products to the category. One sign of this is that the group 'Others' makes up an increasing part of the category sales.

A category can be understood as a wide or a narrow whole. For example, snack products may in the strictest sense include only potato crisps, but in a wider sense also include biscuits and dried fruits. There is no official guide for determining the scope of a category, but in practice the number of products in a category sets some limitations. It is not practical to create a category that is so extensive that it becomes unmanageable. Also, a standardized product grouping used by a supplier or a third party may guide the definition of category, as gathering all the data needed in category management may become unduly burdensome if it is necessary to combine data from different sources.

Categories should be formed based on how the consumer finds them, and how they best serve the target consumer's shopping trips. If the consumer sees crackers as similar snack products to potato crisps, and looks for them in the same place in a store, it seems justifiable to place them in the same category instead of the traditional biscuits category. If the decision is made to change categories, it must be ensured that the new arrangement can be managed in a more consumer-driven and efficient manner than before. The changes almost always affect not only an individual category but also the structure of other categories. Changing product categories in systems, procedures and responsibility areas is always a labour-intensive action.

A category tree can be used to help in defining categories in a consumer-driven manner. The tree illustrates the whole category structure composed of products as seen from the consumer's perspective. A category can be further divided into subcategories reflecting attributes that are essential for the consumer. Examples of subcategories in hot drinks include tea, coffee and hot chocolate. Market research or other consumer data should support consumers seeing these groups as essential in buying decisions. The product hierarchy is further defined in segments and subsegments. For instance, in the subcategory of coffee, segment-level division can be made based on the brand, as that might be the central decision-making criteria for the consumer. After this, different ways of making coffee (for example filter coffee, instant coffee) can form nodes or subsegments in the category tree and include individual products. All products find their place in the hierarchical category structure. However, at this stage, it is sufficient to determine the category tree down to the segment level and no further. Individual products will be allocated in the category tree at a later phase in assortment management. Figure 4.3 illustrates examples of category hierarchy levels.

The structure and contents of the category tree vary depending on the category. In some cases product types (filter or instant coffee) or use (everyday, celebration) may be important to the consumer. In other categories, decision making is based on price, quality, brand, image, material or colour. For instance, in napkins and cigarettes, colours are an important element in the product placing. Therefore, the category tree needs to be planned for each category separately. In building a category, the product characteristics also need to be taken into account. Though dips and crème fraiche are easily recognized to be adjacent products, there is seldom cold storage near crisps, for instance. It is often wise to avoid double placing, as it easily leads to inefficiencies in store logistics.

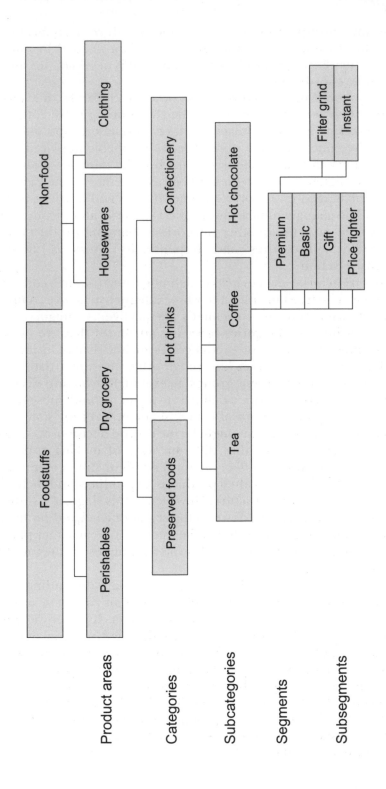

Figure 4.3 Examples of category hierarchy levels

Though those responsible for assortment planning may have a clear picture of the products and segments included in the categories, and the key criteria for division, the consumer's perspective is not necessarily that well known. Consumer insight is, indeed, one of the main reasons for collaboration between retailers and manufacturers in category management. Manufacturers have traditionally invested significantly more than retailers in consumer research, and they usually have a clear understanding of the needs and behaviour of consumers in their own categories. Collaboration enables the parties to get an extensive view of the category under review, where retailers have insight of their own customers and their profiles, and suppliers can support this with a deep knowledge of consumer behaviour.

In defining the category tree, it is often worthwhile to rely on separate market and consumer studies, which examine the thinking of the consumer in greater detail. This is necessary especially in situations where the new category structure does not conform with traditional thinking. Readily available studies conducted by manufacturers are typically based on a traditional, production-driven grouping, which might reveal little of the actual behaviour of consumers in this sense.

When category definition is planned, a tree-like, purely hierarchical structure is not the only alternative, and not necessarily the best either, but a structure is needed for business management. However, products have several common attributes or parameters, which can be tracked throughout the category or even across categories. The category may be analysed from many perspectives that complement each other. Examples of product attributes include country of origin, organic content, material or information concerning suitability for consumer groups (lactose-free, gluten-free or sugar-free composition). Moreover, products can be accompanied by information on brand levels and classifications (premium, standard or value) or brand family. The best retailers have defined a variety of product attributes that help track broader consumer trends.

Category roles

In defining category role retailers need to describe what the category means to both the consumer and the companies implementing category management. Therefore, categories are assigned certain roles that indicate the position in the minds of the consumers and in relation to other categories. Roles help retailers to organize store layouts and allocate resources among categories. It is recommended that roles for all or most categories are defined at once to avoid overemphasizing certain roles. The aim is to create a balanced and consistent category portfolio, highlighting the categories desired by target customer segments, of course in line with the retail format positioning.

People shop in different types of stores in various ways and for different reasons. Some tend to visit convenience stores fairly often for daily convenience goods. Others shop at hypermarkets for basic products and expect convenience stores to offer a more delicatessen-type experience. On the other hand, a convenience store may be the primary shopping place for those living in a town centre without any nearby supermarkets. Consequently, their needs should also be taken into account. Consumers also visit large supermarkets for more unusual products and for adventure, and the role of exotic and speciality categories is on the rise. Price sensitivity of consumers also differs a lot according to consumer segment and category.

Category roles should also include a competitor perspective, and a comparison with key competitors may reveal interesting differences in assortment priorities. Identifying the focus areas of other retailers may require research, and use of educated guesses. Competitor analysis is an important part of retail positioning development, so integrating it into the annual processes is essential.

According to the original category management model, developed by The Partnering Group and Roland Berger for ECR Europe (1997), four category roles were established:

- destination category;
- preferred category;
- occasional or seasonal category;
- convenience category.

Destination categories include items that are essential to the needs of some or all of the retailer's core target consumer segments. Consumers should perceive the retailer as the leading provider of the category. Typically only a few per cent of categories have a destination role. Categories with a preferred role account for the largest proportion of the product range, comprising more than 50 per cent of categories. These are the typical everyday consumables, such as dairy and bakery, which all customers need, and often this role is also called the 'routine' role. Convenience categories are not at the forefront but complement the range and therefore ensure that customers can cover their daily needs with one-stop shopping. These categories are not part of the store's core focus, but beside encouraging customer traffic, they may create additional sales. Some examples are plants and hair accessories in grocery stores. Seasonal categories are available in the store for a specific period. Some seasonal products are in a convenience role, whereas others have a destination role.

Best practice retailers have defined clear roles for all categories, and often also developed new roles that suit the retail format. For example, the seasonal role has been removed in some chains, and the preferred role can be divided into two parts: impulse products and repeatedly purchased basic products. The implementation of category roles is very important for the uniformity of the chain concept. If the defined roles do not work, it's likely that there will be additional challenges further on in the category management process.

Continuous competitor assessment is important for categories in the destination role, because they are the keys to attract the customer to the store. However, for categories in other roles, the retailer should invest relatively more time in tracking the shopper and not as much on the competitor. Focusing on the shopper may lead to new innovations and opportunities to create added value and margins through impulse purchases and creating a truly differentiated offering.

The boxed section on p154, using the example of paint, illustrates how this one category has different category roles.

Futhermore, a role might not always be suitable to the category as a whole, but might apply well to an individual subcategory or segment, with the rest of the category belonging to another role. For example, the hot drinks category includes gift packages and cut-price coffee packages, which play very different roles in the same category. To compensate for these limitations in category roles, the original category management process model incorporates category strategies and tactics, which will be discussed later in this chapter.

Retailers should always include a sufficient amount of destination categories that draw target customers into the store. At the same time, retailers should have products in other roles as well to ensure the profitability of the store. Category roles may also be defined by consumer segments which may clarify the roles of each category and service. Roles other than destination can also benefit from having a definition for each consumer segment.

In best practice, each category has clear goals for each customer segment, including well-defined quantitative metrics for setting targets and tracking the success of the category. The customer relationship process often still focuses on marketing and customer communications, although the greatest benefits could be gained in the area of category management. The needs of the consumer segments and the roles of the products may vary greatly among categories. Whereas nappies may play a destination role for a family with a baby or young child, other children's products may be routine or service products. As seen in the paint example above, the role of the category can also vary greatly by retail format.

The seasonal character and the role of a category need to be identified in assortment planning, particularly in space management. Some categories sell evenly throughout the year, whereas others vary widely according to season. In produce, seasonal variation is usually less pronounced than in speciality goods, but also has exceptions to the rule. Examples include many traditional New Year, Thanksgiving or Christmas foods. Speciality

Paint as a category – three different roles

The paint category comprises not only paints but also paint brushes, rollers and other associated supplies. The role of this category varies significantly by store type. In the destination role, paints represent the foundation of the business. The assortment is wide, including decorative, exterior and industrial paints. The product knowledge of salespeople is very high, which enables them to serve the demanding customer groups such as professional painters and builders, in addition to the usual DIY consumers.

At another extreme, the complementary role is represented by hypermarkets, which often offer only the basic assortment of decorative paints with a focus on environmentally friendly interior paints. The product knowledge of salespeople is often scant, because they work in many departments and have no special training for paints. The most typical role in Europe, routine, falls in between these extremes, and it exists, for instance, in DIY and hardware stores.

These roles should be the starting point in creation of the optimal layout and service concept for the shop. In hypermarkets, for instance, everything should be designed to be based on self-service. For the colouring process this means all phases, including paint and colour selection, colourant dispensing, and mixing of paint and colourant should be so self-explanatory and simple that the usual DIY customer can run the whole process by himself or herself without any assistance. The three rules are illustrated in Table 4.2.

This example of the three different category roles of paint was provided by Dr. Anton Helander, Business development manager, CPS Color Group Oy.

Table 4.2 Example of the paint category – three category roles

Role of paint	Customer's view	Shop's view	Share of paints of total sales	Paint assortment	Example
Destination	Paints are the reason for visiting the shop	Paints are the core business	over 70%	Extensive	Sherwin-Williams store (USA)
Routine	Paints are bought along with other construction items	Paints belong to main categories	10–20%	Rather broad, flexible	Gamma (Netherlands)
Complementary	Customer comes mainly to buy groceries	Paints are an add-on sales item	below 5%	Very limited	Prisma hypermarket (Finland)

stores also include a continuous basic assortment, such as white shirts, which rarely change. By contrast, most of their assortments are naturally seasonal, especially in clothing, and particularly fashion, retail. Gardening supplies in many markets are also seasonal. The seasonal role is often not a means of achieving competitive advantage, but rather a general factor to be taken into account in category and space management.

Resource allocation to categories

The allocation of a retailer's limited resources to categories forms a central part of the demand management process. Attention needs to be paid to the profitability of each category, but also to the roles of categories in different segments. Resource allocation should start with an evaluation of the impact on the most important segments. Can certain efforts bring in more customers, and what impact would it have on the profitability of the store and average purchase? Categories should also be analysed as individual entities. What is the actual space requirement and profitability, and how should they be located in the store, taking into consideration, for example, possible shrinkage and easy replenishment?

The most important resource in store is available selling space, which sets tight limits on assortments, especially in small store formats. Space is usually measured by square metres (or square feet), shelf metre (or foot) or the number of shelf modules. The starting point for space allocation is provided by average product size and total category sales. Small-size products naturally require less space than large ones, even though unit sales may be equal. As an example, the whole condiment assortment may fit into a space that would barely be enough for a few paper towel brands. On the other hand, large sales volumes require more space to avoid constant replenishment need and out-of-stock (OOS) situations.

Space allocation based on product size and sales does not necessarily lead to an optimal situation, as the net sales and margin levels may vary to a great extent. If a category carries an unusually low margin and needs a large space in the store because of large size or unit sales, the retailer needs to consider whether it is more profitable to allocate the space to another category. One guiding factor in this decision is category profitability, but as has already been noted, the needs of the target customers and the retail positioning should guide the decision.

Placing categories along the shopping path is closely connected with allocation of selling space. Where allocating a certain amount of space reflects the scope of assortment and service level, location-related decisions can have an impact on category awareness. In practice, most stores have a main shopping path, which the majority of shoppers follow. Categories positioned near this route get more attention than others and are therefore more prone to impulse purchases. One of the most visible and attractive places in a store is often the checkout area. Correspondingly, categories located on the edges or corners easily go unnoticed by at least occasional shoppers. When a category is placed by the main shopping path, its sales are likely to increase. Furthermore, these categories are essential in creating an image of the store, so the category roles are important in guiding placement decisions.

Long-range planning also needs to address the service resource allocation to categories. Some categories may benefit from personal service, and some even require it. As an example, the assortment image of a store's perishable categories may become quite different depending on whether customers are provided with personal service. Some electronics products or watches may require a service counter because of the risk of shoplifting, or because consumers need expert advice in choosing products from many models. In certain categories, such as cosmetics, personal selling may have a considerable impact on sales. Even though personnel resources are often scarce, service can be used to highlight a category and create an image of the retailer. A full-service cheese, seafood, bakery, deli or meat counter helps to create a high-quality image of a grocery store. Product availability level can also be thought of as a resource, and the allocation translates into increasing the safety stock (in-store or backroom space) of selected important categories to ensure sufficient service level.

Marketing investment is also one key retail resource. A considerable amount of money is allocated to various marketing actions annually, and retailers should link category roles and target segments to marketing communications. All marketing resources are more or less variable by nature, and the costs directly affect the company's profit. It is therefore important to identify clear benefit logic for all marketing efforts both in the short and long term.

Category management

Category management is the second main stage in the shopper-oriented demand management process. Attention is on individual categories with an aim to optimize the assortments, space usage and marketing activities based on the needs of the defined target segments. In this section, we will discuss category assessment, category objective setting, assortment and space management, activity management and stores as advertising media, as well as product development and new product introductions.

Category assessment

In category management, category assessment is a collaborative effort between retailers and manufacturers. To gain an integrated view, many different data sources are used, and the best view is reached by combining the data of both parties. Key areas to be analysed include category assortment scope and contents, pricing, promotions, space usage and new product introductions.

The retailer's customer relationships can be divided into three sub-areas as illustrated in Figure 4.4: the total market, shoppers (people who shop at the retailers' stores but cannot be identified), and identified shoppers (for example those with a loyalty card). The behaviour and needs of all of these segments can be examined, but the means are different. The information about identified shoppers can be tracked on a very detailed and precise level when observing what happens in the retailer's stores. The total market information tends to be more general in nature, but gives also a picture of what is happening elsewhere. In the following section we discuss key market research types in retailing.

Syndicated data

A key resource for consumer and market data are syndicated data sources. Research companies gather data from a variety of sources, modify it and sell it to retailers and suppliers. Consumer panels are one key type of these studies, and an example is the Consumer Panel study conducted by ACNielsen, based on households keeping a record of their purchases. The study measures purchases of several product areas like foodstuffs, household goods, health and beauty, durables, confectionery and beverage products. The panel includes nearly 125,000 households from 24 countries,

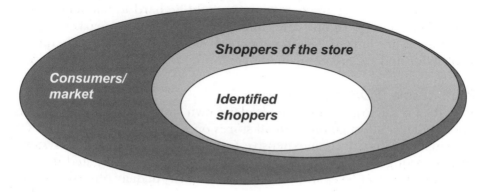

Figure 4.4 Focal target groups of customer and market research in retailing

and the study offers quite an extensive view of consumer behaviour around the world. Other key syndicated data providers are IRI and NPD, which provide data by market.

Consumer panels help to identify demographical characteristics or loyalty among various segments. For category management, the panel provides valuable insight on how many households buy the products as well as on how often and how much they purchase at a time. A weakness in consumer panels is the dependence on the activity and attentiveness of the consumer households participating. Some purchases may be unrecorded, accidentally or for a reason. Because of manual recording, the results are received relatively slowly, and most panel research is updated three to four times a year.

Another important syndicated information source is scanner data studies, of which the best known might be ACNielsen's ScanTrack. Many retailers send item-level sales data weekly to ACNielsen, which classifies the material and delivers it in an easy-to-interpret format. Data is gathered currently from 80 countries, and they cover various retail channels from hypermarkets to kiosks. Despite an extensive sample, some retailers are missing; for example, most value retailers do not provide their data for the study.

Scanner data can be analysed at many different levels, for example the total market or sales in certain store sizes, and enable comparisons among retailers and their market shares. Region-specific analyses are also possible with certain limitations, and chain-level information is also available to suppliers in many markets.

The only option for speciality stores is usually to analyse their own sales data, as there are no syndicated data sources available. Trade associations gather some data about the market, and companies can also buy external reports and market studies, but there is no regular and extensive data on consumer demand in the same way as in food retailing. Also, the share of private labels and exclusive products is huge, especially in clothing retailing, and items change frequently, so it would be hard to maintain syndicated data sources. In any case, opportunities to gather market data in many areas are limited, so assortment development needs to rely on the knowledge and experience gained by piloting new products and services.

Point of sale (POS) information

POS data is sales data from the retailer's own stores, and covers typically the item-level information from all stores on a daily or hourly level. POS information is relatively inexpensive to produce if modern POS systems and reporting tools are in place. The data is usually aggregated on day-store- and product-level, which covers the majority of daily reporting needs for core retail processes.

If a deeper insight is sought, more detailed information is needed. For example, the analysis of shopping basket contents requires transaction records at receipt level. This analysis can be used to identify auxiliary products, for example for promotion planning and product placement decisions. Replenishment often benefits from analysis of hourly data, especially for fresh products such as bakery and seafood.

POS information is internal data and does not provide a big picture of the whole market situation. It is very efficient in fine tuning existing assortment and use of space, but does not give any insight on new products and categories not yet sold by the retailer. However, continuous piloting with NPIs and activities can reduce these limitations significantly.

Shopper information

Loyalty programmes have enabled customer identification as well as the collection of shopper demand data that provides valuable insights in shopper behaviour. Monitoring how various actions affect actual consumer behaviour gives a solid foundation for fact-based management. Shopper data can be used for segmentation, which enables retailers to track development of their customer portfolio and profitability. The analysis may reveal many insights in customer behaviour, such as products purchased, buying frequencies, basket sizes and even product-specific price elasticity. The analysis can also be complemented with descriptive information from external data sources.

Shopper information also enables new analyses such as measuring purchase frequencies and brand loyalty in different segments. Repeat purchase frequencies can be calculated, which is an important metric, for example in assessing the vitality of new product introductions. Particularly when compared with category benchmarks, it provides a relatively reliable view of a product's future performance.

The key benefit of shopper data analysis is the ability to measure the success of activities in different segments almost real time. The success of any activity in a segment can be measured against the control group, which lays a foundation for efficient fact-based management. Daily and easily accessible data on the actual behaviour of the target shopper segments enable a cultural change. Experience shows that once this path is taken there is no return, as facts speak for themselves. Shopper analysis and loyalty programmes are discussed in more detail in Chapters 6 and 7.

Surveys

A survey is a fairly expensive method of getting insight into consumer behaviour, especially if samples are large. Surveys can, however, be used to elucidate perspectives that cannot be determined on the basis of POS or loyalty data. A survey is a very quick method as the results are ready to be analysed immediately after the interview, and can be carried out also at the point of purchase in the stores.

Surveys can give insight in several key questions, such as:

- What was the reason for buying the product or choosing the store?
- Had a decision been made in advance about the brand?
- What was the reason for choosing a certain brand?
- Had a decision been made in advance about the category?
- Was the customer aware of the price of the product?
- Was it an impulse buy?
- How often is the product bought?
- Did the customer find the desired product in the store?
- Who made the decision to buy the product?
- Did the customer pay attention to promotions and campaigns?
- Did advertising impact the purchase decision?

Furthermore, surveys offer an opportunity to ask customers about their expectations and suggestions. Listening to customers is vital for the success of the retailer and manufacturer. This is an old truth, which has been repeated time and time again, but still few retail chains systematically walk the talk. Mercadona, a Spanish supermarket retailer, is one of the examples of best practice in listening to the 'Boss' as they refer to customers, with over 180,000 meetings in 2006.

The recording of customer complaints is another form of customer research that is worth mentioning. Amazingly, few retail companies collect consumer feedback systematically at all key customer touch points. However, if a consumer has taken the trouble to give feedback, it is usually a matter of great importance to him. Consumer feedback should always be recorded and evaluated, and necessary action should then be taken to develop operations. Also, consumers should be thanked for their activity and informed about corrective actions. This enhances customer satisfaction and encourages the customer to give feedback in the future as well. Unfortunately, experience has shown that those giving feedback are often not the best customers, or do not represent the target segment. Customer surveys can be conducted also by retailers' own category management or merchandising departments, which will give fresh insight and a pragmatic approach in category development.

Complaints and other customer feedback should be enabled through as many channels as possible. A feedback box after the checkout is not always the easiest option for the customer carrying many bags and perhaps with no pen or writing pad available. The internet can be used as a vehicle for collecting feedback, but retailers need to have clear customer service processes and sufficient resourcing, as the customers in the online world expect rapid reply to their feedback. Most of the feedback can also be handled centrally cost efficiently, and only a fraction of all feedback will be handled directly by the store staff. Stores may get monthly or bi-monthly customer feedback summary reports that are handled as part of the normal store development routines.

Customer satisfaction surveys have a long tradition in other industries such as banking, insurance and automotive. Most car manufacturers require their dealers to conduct certain customer feedback measurements or to buy them from external players. Customer feedback may also have an impact on the bonuses of car salesmen. 'We listen to our clients' is a nice-sounding cliché, but there is still a lot to do for retailers in listening to customers and acting on the feedback in a systematic manner.

Observation studies

Surveys can be complemented by customer observation studies, where consumer behaviour is observed quietly and unnoticed. Observation studies may reveal many things, such as:

- What is the customer's shopping path in the store?
- How does the customer approach the shelf or display?
- In which categories does the customer purchase?
- How does the customer behave by the shelf?
- How much time does the customer spend in choosing products?
- How many products does he choose from?
- What draws the customer's attention to a product or shelf?
- How easily is the desired product found?
- How much time does the consumer spend in choosing products?
- What is the impact of special displays or promotions on behaviour?

Studies conducted with a camera (video or web cam) can show customer flows in the store. This information can be exploited, for example, in the planning of category placement, shopping path design and development of end cap use. It shows how long the customer stays in the store and to which offers or messages in the store he or she responds. In addition to a camera, devices attached to the shopping carts and positioning technology can help track customer movements. However, these methods may also cause resistance among customers. Wal-Mart, Kroger, Walgreens, Procter & Gamble, Coca-Cola, Disney, Kellogg's and Miller Brewing have a joint development programme, where a less intrusive infrared camera is used. Movement in front of the shelf is compared with the POS data in order to analyse purchasing behaviour. Infrared does not, however, make it possible to identify the shopper or to track the time spent in front of a shelf, as it only measures traffic.

Observation can also be made by the retailer's own personnel, but we have seen so far only few category managers using this practice systematically and proactively. Spending half a day observing customers in front of a shelf offers significant insights for assortment improvements. Some retail employees have an eye for these things, but this great insight is seldom collected and used in chain-wide operations, as there are no processes and measures in place. For a good assortment manager regular store visits and direct observation of customer behaviour are a must for success. For those interested in this topic, we recommend the books by Paco Underhill: *Why We Buy?* and *Call of the Mall*, which are full of concrete examples of retail customer behaviour as well as hints for carrying out observation studies.

One form of observation is mystery shopping, where an outside observer shops in a store playing the role of a customer, making detailed observations. This shows how the service concept of the retailer comes alive and how the staff treats customers. Mystery shopping is a relatively difficult but thorough method, so it is typically used at regular intervals, such as once every year or two. Some chains, especially department stores and speciality stores, use the method systematically to monitor and improve service quality.

Category management has many options available for identifying and understanding consumer behaviour and needs. Those presented here are just some of the methods. Some are very narrow, focusing on a certain area, whereas others are extensive market reviews. Bearing in mind that research is usually quite an investment, it pays off to plan it carefully. In the future, retailers will most likely set the target groups to be interviewed themselves to be able to link the information to behavioural segmentation and the retailer's own core segments.

Category objective setting

Categories need to be assigned objectives and strategies in line with category roles. Category management needs hard financial metrics for performance evaluation. Traditional metrics include sales, gross margin, shrinkage, number of products, market share, number of NPIs and sales of NPIs, as well as trends of these metrics and benchmarks to the previous period or the competition. These metrics will be richer in content when defined per segment, and at the same time they provide a foundation for a uniform business model for serving the retailer's target segments. Though the objective setting is guided by the retailer's format and category roles, this task is done in collaboration with suppliers. Typically, objectives are set annually, and are further detailed in periodical category planning.

In defining and setting goals for each segment, the category strategies defined in the category management process can be used as an entry point for idea generation. Category strategy refers to a general action plan, which guides the planning of categories and is used to improve category performance to the desired level. Aided by Roland Berger and The Partnering Group, in 1997 ECR Europe defined seven general strategies for guiding the planning of category marketing. These strategies have been established in the ECR community and category management all over the world. The original category strategies can also be exploited in category goal setting at segment level or by type of shopping visit, as illustrated by the following examples:

- *Traffic building.* The aim is to increase the customer flow, especially with destination categories. In other words, the category is intended to be an attraction in the store. Products suitable for this purpose generally include those with a price that plays a large role in purchase decisions, and products bought by most households and relatively frequently.

  A shopping basket analysis can be used to choose products for this role that encourage customers to make large total purchases. This is especially important in chains that operate using high-low pricing. As an example, taco shells or fajitas may even be sold at a loss when the customer at the same time buys a large amount of higher-margin products. It is important in high-low pricing to choose the correct products for campaigns, and this is typically an area with large differences among cultures and consumer segments. Hence, good customer knowledge is a must for a retailer with a high-low price strategy. Customer flow can also be increased through services. The lottery, for example, brings in customers to a convenience store chain. A bank branch, an ATM or an alcoholic beverages department may also attract additional consumers.

- *Transaction building.* The aim is to increase shopping basket size by getting customers to buy products they do not usually buy. This emphasizes product and category displays and various promotional activities. A case in point is confectionery. Sweets are not necessarily on the shopping list, but if they are placed near the shopping path, they might end up in the shopping cart. Key placements for these products are near the checkout, with magazines and at gondola ends and promotion displays where they are visible and passed by a large number of customers.

- *Cash generating.* The goal is to increase the company's revenues by increasing the cash flow generated by the category. In practice, this means trying to decrease the amount of capital tied up in the category, for example, by emphasizing fast-moving products, negotiating better terms of delivery and decreasing the number of products held in stock. This strategy is especially important in speciality stores, which have often resorted to advance purchases to balance the level of risk in the value chain, and the value chain may include a large amount of capital costs.

- *Profit generating.* This involves increasing the returns from a category, thereby improving the profitability of the store as a whole. This is usually done by choosing high-margin products or products that are purchased with high-margin products. The same outcome can sometimes be reached indirectly by increasing customer loyalty in the category.

- *Turf defending*. Using this strategy, efforts are made to retain current customers to defend the market position achieved in the category. This usually applies to categories where competition is tough and price is used as a differentiator to attract customers. This strategy option differs from the others in that it does not aim at improvement but rather at maintaining the status quo. The active efforts of competitors are nullified by taking counter measures. Turf defending is not a dynamic strategy, but it may be the only practical alternative in a situation where gaining share is no longer possible. This strategy is often used for product areas where customers are very price sensitive. As an example, families with babies are often well aware of the price of nappies. A store may need to sell products at a loss (if allowed by local legislation) in order to get the consumer segment into the store. When a new entrant comes to a market where a turf-defending strategy is in place, there is a strong likelihood of an ensuing price war. For example, prices for large yoghurt packs were low for years after Arla entered the Finnish market and other key players responded to the new threat by lowering their prices. The consumer was the only winner in this war.

- *Excitement creating*. Some categories are used to add variation and thus arouse the interest of shoppers in the store rather than to achieve significant financial results. This may be an instrument for maintaining customer loyalty and it may also appeal to the increasing number of consumers who want to get not only products but also excitement and adventure. Excitement and variation can be achieved in categories by regularly adding new products or seasonal products to assortments or by putting emphasis on products that have traditionally been in a marginal position. A good example of an excitement creating strategy is Tchibo's continually-changing non-food assortment.

- *Image enhancing*. Some categories are suitable for building customer perceptions of the store by underlining certain special characteristics. A category may be in the assortment to strengthen a certain image. For example, ethnic food may be added to create a perception of an international retail chain. Similarly, perceptions can be built inside categories through products. Pro-environmental image can be enhanced to emphasize eco products in particular categories and displays. In a similar vein, assortment perception can be built by adding more items or facings than would be needed to cover the actual demand. Image creation can be considered as a support strategy; and may be adopted in some categories as an additional strategy.

A comparison of category strategies and roles reveals that some strategies are especially well suited to certain roles. For example, the destination role and the traffic-building strategy are a matching couple. As the roles are more general and longer term by nature than strategies, they must guide strategy definition. Some categories may pose limitations on strategy definition by nature. If products are included in 90 per cent of all baskets, it is hardly worthwhile to consider as a strategy. Similarly, some categories have a low margin because of competition and the profit-generating strategy might not be possible.

Category strategies also involve challenges. They tend to vary greatly within a category, which is why it is often wise to define strategies for subcategories or segments. Category strategies also vary to a large extent depending on target segments. Strategies should be derived from the retail format and positioning, and from category roles. If not, categories will be managed as separate entities. In the extreme case, separately managed categories rely on the customer flow generation of the other categories, and all categories only optimize their own returns. Little by little, prices in all categories are raised, and as the total price level rises, customers churn.

Assortment management

Assortment management starts with the evaluation of the category situation. Category evaluation aims at acquiring, modifying and analysing data that helps in understanding the category and its parts (subcategories, segments and subsegments) as well as their importance to the customer. Another aim is to identify improvement areas to 'grow the pie', improve the financial profitability of the category and to make it more customer driven. The category's current situation needs to be analysed using sufficiently varied metrics, taking into account not only the consumer perspective, but the perspective of the retailer and supplier. The retailer's objectives are ultimately derived from the category roles and strategies.

In a study that was recently conducted in Finland, assortment management was found to be the most beneficial of all ECR development areas. It was also stated that the category management process has made the retailer–manufacturer collaboration process and methods more systematic and has moved the focus from buying and selling to joint consumer-driven sales growth and integrated development of the category.

The retail format and the needs of the target customer segments form the guidelines for category management. It is important that collaboration partners understand the main characteristics of the retail format as well as the key consumer segments for differentiation. Unless target consumer segments have been defined accurately enough, there is the risk that each category manager drives the categories in the manager's own direction, and chain operations will not be consistent. Hence, although many customers may still consider service appropriate, no consumer group is completely satisfied with service. This creates space for competitors.

As noted earlier, the primary and secondary customer segments are defined in the retailer's strategy. These consumers should be able to meet their needs at the store, and find the products they require in all categories. As the loyalty of these consumer groups is vital for the success of the chain, they also have to be given appropriate service. This is why each category should contain product options that these segments find pleasant and relevant. Serving these consumer groups is the starting point of good assortment management.

Assortment planning should also take into account consumer segments that may increase sales. These can be consumers who are not regulars or targeted customers but who may occasionally visit the stores and bring in additional returns. It is worth considering the needs of these groups as well if there are free resources left after serving the primary and secondary customers.

One risk in category management is that manufacturers use the same model and assortment in all chains. This is not just the manufacturers' fault – often the information provided by the retailer about the retail format and target consumer segments is not enough to enable good differentiation. As a result, manufacturers might use standard category management measures 'to one average consumer', based on the aggregated data from syndicated data providers instead of the real target groups of the different chains. This is an easy path for manufacturers to follow, and it is cost efficient, as all retailer-specific analysis raises costs.

The power in assortment management has moved from wholesalers and sourcing companies to retailer chains. This is a major change in the retail value chain, where assortment management is brought closer to the end customer. Separate buying activities carried out by sourcing companies are merged with chain operations, and some have even outsourced logistics services. Assortment management by chains promotes differentiation from the main competitors. In multi-format retailing extensive splitting of assortment management operations to many chain units can, however, also entail additional costs, and the benefits of central assortment planning and joint sourcing are lost. National or regional retail groups typically have many relatively small chains, where it is worth utilizing shared resources in assortment and space planning, even though they still operate according to targets set by the chains.

Assortment periods

Assortment periods (also called assortment pulses) give a rhythm to assortment changes and the introduction of new products to assortments. The length of periods varies. For example in Finland, most retailers and manufacturers use the practice of three annual category periods. The standard update rhythm in most categories has been to review assortments at four-month intervals. This offers clear advantages as it would be very difficult for both chain management and the store to change assortments continually and maintain the related data. Uniform assortment periods also give clarity to the operations as the majority of categories can be managed according to the same model.

The practice of three assortment periods also brings challenges, of which the biggest is the increased workload in stores at the start of the assortment period, when all categories are changed at the same time. Planogram changes may require a huge number of person hours. Some categories have different natural update cycles; for ice cream and barbecue sausages, for example, assortment needs mainly change according to season and weather. Similarly, certain holidays like Christmas and Easter disturb the normal rhythm of assortment periods and are in a way seasons of their own for many categories. Overall, for some categories the update frequency of the assortment periods is too low; for others, it is too high. For instance, fresh products need more assortment periods since, for instance, fruit and vegetables have a considerably faster assortment cycle.

It is justified to use different assortment cycles for different categories. In some categories it is sufficient to update the assortment once a year, whereas in others, up to 10 or 12 periods per year are suitable. Campaign and seasonal display areas as well as gondola ends can be changed even more frequently, on a weekly or even daily basis. Certain convenience store chains also change assortments during the day; they have morning, lunch, afternoon, evening and night assortments according to the hour and the needs of the customers.

Quick assortment changes and innovation can spur impulse purchases and create variation. At the same time, challenges and costs are created:

- Assortment changes take up a lot of resources in the store. Even a small increase in products may change the display of the whole category.
- The complexity of assortment management grows – including, among other things, the numbers of items, the selling of remaining stock, product cannibalization and new displays.
- Assortment management and sourcing require significantly greater resources to enable the continual change.
- Demand forecasting becomes more difficult, leading to overstocking, outdated products and OOS situations.

For these reasons, innovation and seasonality have often been focused on separate areas, such as gondola ends, mass display areas or some other place where they do not 'disturb' the core assortment of the category. Implementing campaigns and changing assortment periods at stores are discussed in more detail in Chapter 5.

In speciality retailing, seasonal assortment periods are part of normal daily operations. In certain categories, such as mobile phones and computers, products have a short lifecycle and assortments are continually renewed. In clothing retailing, seasons in practice guide assortment management, and assortments are also strongly guided by fashions and trends. Continual renewing of assortments can offer a true competitive advantage, as is shown by clothing chains that may update assortment on a weekly basis.

Assortment management levels

Just as in sourcing, assortment management decisions can also be made at different levels. Some retailers plan assortments over national borders on a global level, because of cooperative agreements or sourcing consortia. National or regional assortment planning is, however, more common. For example, in Europe national food cultures differ quite a lot, and it is natural to carry out planning on this level.

Assortments can also be planned regionally or even at store level. In the latter case, the store manager or staff may decide which products to include in the assortment to some extent. The share of store-level assortments and sales volume is often small or negligible, but a few products are used to provide special services for key shoppers to ensure their overall store loyalty. The customers can be demanding consumers or local entrepreneurs (eg pizzeria owners) who need special products not included in a basic assortment, and if the store has these products available, they do not need to drive to a competitor's store. The cost of the special service needs to be linked to the consumer's total purchases. Unfortunately, many category-specific ABC projects have killed several of this kind of product assortment, as the importance to store loyalty has not been thoroughly examined.

Whatever the level of assortment planning, updates should also be based on responding to changes in demand and customer needs. The most obvious cases are season changes or other 'external' demand periods, or the discontinuation of certain products. The next phase is to analyse the performance of all SKUs in the category. There are usually no clear instructions for approving new product introductions, so the final decision often needs to be made by the category manager. Suppliers also seek to have a say in the decisions, either directly through the category manager or indirectly through consumer marketing.

With category management, many retailers have adopted a category captain model, where the retailer develops assortments collaboratively with a chosen supplier. In some cases, retailers have almost outsourced the assortment assessments of certain categories to suppliers. The aim of retailers is to optimize returns, and the supplier may sometimes have better expertise in that area. However, showing the margins of competitors' products is not only ethically, but also legally challenging, so margin information is often provided only on an aggregated level. Because of this, amazingly often retailers and manufacturers are just optimizing the sales, not margins.

An extreme case of the category captain model is shop-in-shop solutions, where suppliers manage assortments relatively independently, including fixture solutions. It is typical in these cases that the supplier has some special competences (eg strong brand, customer communication elements supporting the shopping process) or efficiency that the retailer does not have. For example, in cosmetics and pick 'n' mix confectionery, shop-in-shop solutions are common. Similarly, in some categories that complement the basic assortments (eg batteries), it may be easiest for the retailer to trade with a single supplier, in which case a shop-in-shop is the natural solution.

Planning and implementation of local assortments

Local assortments and local sourcing offer one option for differentiation. Whole Foods in the United States and Système U in France have long used local products as a competitive differentiator. In the British market, both Tesco and Sainsbury's have lately started to focus on local products. The business models of value retailers and tightly controlled chains, trimmed to be extremely cost effective, often cannot be adapted to use local products and suppliers. At the same time, stores operated by entrepreneurs are used to local sourcing, even to such an extent that they have sought tighter chain operations to achieve cost efficiency. The modern winners are likely to exist somewhere in between, using economies of scale with a local touch.

The products of local producers can be important to the retailer for reasons other than just the money. Support for local suppliers demonstrates that the retailer is socially responsible, and strengthens the retailer's role in the community. The importance of these matters varies by community and consumer group, but, for example, among young people, the origin of products has been found to play a big role in the purchase decision of certain categories. Local products also often carry a 'story', which may justify their higher prices. Narrative marketing is growing in importance with exclusive and local products leading the way. Even very basic products, like water, can add value for consumers with a good story, as is shown by the example of Voss water from mountains of Norway that is served in top restaurants all over the world.

Local assortment management may contain several layers. As a wide concept, it may refer to assortments at regional cooperatives that differ from the nationwide assortments. Big international players also use local assortments; for instance Asda, owned by Wal-Mart, has a local version of assortments for its stores in Wales. Tesco has also increased local sourcing by establishing many local sourcing units. Separate local sourcing teams are responsible for trading with local suppliers and for adding local products to assortments. Whole Foods, with a strong focus on organic items, has purchased a large portion of its products from local suppliers for over 25 years. Local farmers also have a good opportunity to sell their products directly to consumers at Sunday markets, held in Whole Foods' parking areas.

However, regional assortment management needs to be integrated into the chain's process to be able to reap the benefits of centralized operations. In space management, it is often wise to have separate rooms for local products so the chain assortments can be implemented in accordance with shelf planograms. Another option is to 'stretch' the shelf planogram and place local products next to the main product segment, but this often requires some adaptation. One solution is to set up a separate department or display for local products, which might emphasize the local focus, and is easy to use in in-store marketing.

The success of the local assortment should be measured in the same way as that of other products. POS systems create a good basis and enable the tracking of the main metrics of success (sales, profits, loss and turnover). These analyses can also be delivered through centralized reporting tools, which should help the retailer both in eliminating products and in evaluating the success of new products. In entrepreneurial retailing with store-level sourcing, a lot of local products have traditionally been sold. The sales at different stores should be systematically benchmarked to enable continual assortment innovation and the leveraging of the best products to other stores. Product sales in proportion to store penetration is a very useful metric in item chain-level evaluation. Data on regionally and locally successful items are also often available from syndicated data sources. Tracking them accurately and regularly shows the successful products and product segments that are gaining share. Nowadays the data is available, and often the success of the retailer depends more on execution capability than in-depth analysis of the category.

Choosing new products for local assortments can take place in many ways. As an example, Tesco organizes roadshow events, where buyers meet local suppliers and acquaint themselves with their products. Suppliers can also contact stores themselves to market new products. Tesco and Sainsbury's provide websites where suppliers can enter details of new products and ask the retailer to contact them. Many stores also take into account customers' desire for new products, and this information is gathered at service counters or on customer feedback forms. It has, however, been observed that when feedback is given on paper, suppliers have also sometimes given 'customer feedback', expressing hopes for their product to be included in the assortment.

It has often been noted that the margin for local products is not necessarily high enough if they are sold at the same gross margin level as is used for chain-level assortments. When assessing product profitability, sourcing-related HR costs are rarely taken into account, but they should be. Situations may also arise where the products are not profitable as such, but are important for a certain consumer group. For some local products, selling on commission with short delivery time is an option worth considering. The customer may regard it as good service, whereas selling the same slow-selling product off the shelf could even deteriorate a store's image because of challenges with best-before dates and a small range.

As previously noted, assortment management tools also streamline the planning of local assortments. In centrally planned local assortments, mass customization takes place in accordance with the consumer portfolio and local demand of the store. However, these automated analyses can use considerably smaller assortments for local sourcing because tightly controlled chains do not have any local sourcing organization for small local suppliers. However, automated analyses are a big help in dealing with mid-size suppliers and especially in planning of optimal shelf space.

The local assortments of large, centrally controlled chains will hardly ever apply to small suppliers as their volumes simply are not big enough. It may also be difficult for a small supplier to respond to the requested procedures and quality requirements. Sainsbury's is helping local suppliers develop their operations with the Supplier Development programme to ensure that suppliers' procedures and product quality meet Sainsbury's requirements. Participating in the operations of big retailers is for many suppliers a double-or-nothing solution, for they quickly become dependent on the volumes sold to the retailers. The up to 40–60 per cent drop in sales caused by being eliminated from the chain assortments presents great challenges to any supplier. A small but well-known supplier is in a clearly better situation than other companies, because the consumers' trust in the products is an asset in negotiations with the retailer.

Automated category management solutions

Assortment planning and drawing planograms have traditionally required many people, and the planning of store-specific assortments centrally with manual methods has been too costly. Shopper data and efficient new solutions have enabled the automation of assortment planning. Based on local demand and customer portfolio, both assortments and required shelf volumes may be optimized with centralized solutions. These solutions revolutionize assortment management especially in tightly controlled chains, which may in the future also compete with mass-customized assortments based on local demand. Even though the systems are not fully automatic, they can still create a good foundation for the manual assortment work, thereby saving a considerable amount of resources. The dynamics and roles of assortment work change, as illustrated in Figure 4.5.

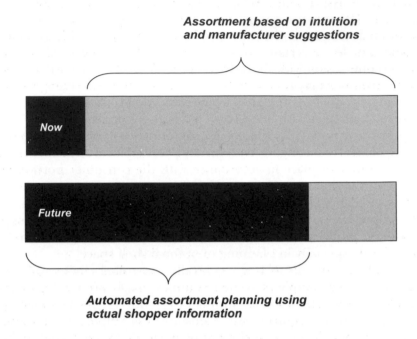

*Assortment based on intuition
and manufacturer suggestions*

Now

Future

*Automated assortment planning using
actual shopper information*

Figure 4.5   Automated solutions improve assortment planning

One of the key changes in the assortment management process will be the diminishing role of assortment recommendations made by suppliers, with the exception of new products and product innovations. The role of objective POS and shopper data, based on actual consumer behaviour, in decision making is growing. Together with automated solutions, this data systematically guides retailers towards fact-based management where the importance of marketing subsidies and personal relationships in assortment decisions will become history.

The role of intuition hardly disappears or even significantly decreases; it will merely be directed towards new areas. Automated solutions are always based on historical data, and the ability to use it in new product planning and introduction is relatively small. When automated solutions can decrease manual effort with assortment period planning, there will be more time for creating real added value for the customer.

Catalogue retailing and products sold on commission are an interesting area of assortment management, worth more attention. If one of these products sells remarkably well, incorporating it into the basic assortment can be considered. Similarly, it may be justified to demote standard products that sell poorly to commission products if they do not earn their place on the shelf. Consequently, it does not pay to track commission products as a separate category or business unit, but they should be compared continually with the permanent off-the-shelf assortment. This may also give good information on which type of products are increasing in demand. Tested tools and models are found in traditional mail-order companies, where large stocks have been a challenge and efficient demand forecasting is well integrated into assortment management. Also, the online sales enable a quick and cheap testing ground to determine the success of new products.

Space management

Space management is an approach started back in the mid-1980s in retailing, with the aim of using retail selling space as efficiently and effectively as possible. Space management solutions are used to draw planograms, which represent products intended for a certain location in the store, given their correct dimensions. Using planograms makes it possible to estimate how well products fit in the fixture and whether limited space makes it necessary to eliminate some products altogether. Live product images help show products and packages in a planogram accurately and in true dimensions. When drawing planograms, one should also consider the aesthetics of display: it is perhaps possible to place products efficiently into the space available, but the consumer should also be able to find them. Moreover, a good looking and clear shelf layout most likely improves the store image among consumers.

There are a host of solutions for the implementation of space management, such as ACNielsen Spaceman, Storeplan, SAS Marketmax, JDA's Intactix and Aldata Spacemaker. Of these, Spaceman has achieved a dominant position in many countries and is widely used among both retailers and suppliers. However, the others are gaining share.

Planograms facilitate the display of products in the store and enable a distinct and uniform appearance. Even more importantly, the assortment manager can use planograms to optimize the products' fit in the shelf space reserved for the category. Planograms have become a central instrument for category management store-level implementation.

Planograms have been used in the FMCG industry for a long time and have established their position, but they are increasingly also being used in speciality retailing. Black and white planograms can be printed easily and quickly in stores. A good planogram is clear and illustrative, taking into account both vertical and horizontal dimensions. For example, baby foods have often been placed horizontally by age group, whereas brands have perhaps been placed vertically according to the same division. There may be different colours in the planogram for subcategories and segments, which illustrate the perspective of the consumer in the category.

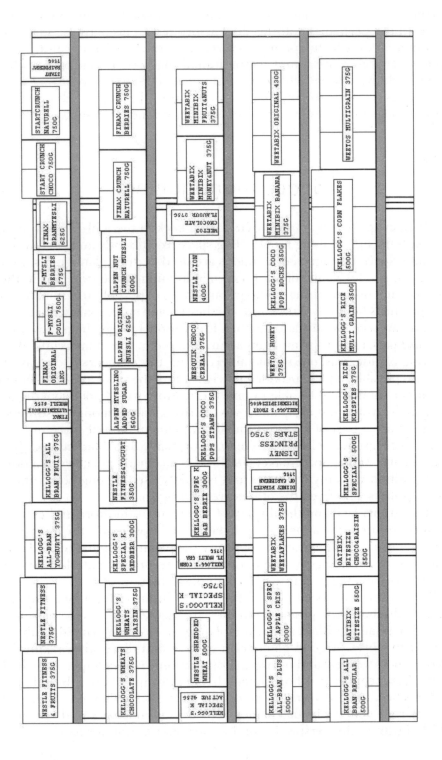

Figure 4.6 Example of a planogram

The shelf must house at least one delivery consignment at a time so that there will not be extra packages under or above the shelf and to avoid having to transport products between the store backroom and the shelf. Space allotted to products is often measured by facings. They indicate how many packages of the same products are displayed side by side at the same time. Planograms should also take into account the direction in which customers move through the store and can be changed if store layout is different. Often there are several versions of the planograms depending on the space available, for example three-, four- and five-module versions.

Using planograms leads to several benefits:

- Chain operations can guide stores to follow a shared process.
- Assortments and allocated space respond better to actual demand and the needs of the chosen customer segments.
- Products are in a logical order and therefore easy for the customer to find.
- Product shortages decrease as the sales and delivery rhythm is taken into account in space allocation.
- Demand can be guided towards premium products or private labels.
- Innovations are clearly displayed and accessible to customers.

Manufacturers used to have a key role in space management and drawing planograms, drawing even store-specific planograms, especially when retailers did not yet have the necessary knowledge. Nowadays, space management is a retailer's core competence, but suppliers still have roles as commentators and consultants in terms of assortments and planograms, especially in strategic collaboration. Suppliers may also play a focal role in categories that are non-core for retailers, but can be managed as a separate whole, including several speciality product areas, such as magazines, greeting cards, cosmetic supplies, batteries or CDs.

Activity management and stores as advertising media

Activities refer to anything special taking place in a store that is done to attract consumers' attention. Activities can have many different purposes, such as creating impulse purchases, introducing new products, creating a price image or just offering consumers variation and surprise. The adventurous nature of shopping can be augmented by various means. Traditional means in grocery stores have included product demonstrations and tastings. They have been particularly important for new product introductions but also in developing customer dialogue. Particularly during weekends, people have time to walk around the store and take a closer than usual look at products. This is a good time for getting them interested in the benefits offered by new products, and several tastings and product demonstrations take place. A store can also organize events independently to support business. Examples abound, from fashion shows to DIY nights. Other possible means are private parties organized for loyalty club members, or established events such as 'Crazy Days' at Stockmann and the farmer's market at Whole Foods.

With operations in Finland, Russia and the Baltic countries, Stockmann department stores are a good example of implementing integrated campaign themes over departmental boundaries. Themes vary from the miracles of the Far East to various seasonal offerings. The same message is shown in catalogues and in-store merchandising, and assortments are often complemented with special products sold only during the campaign. The placing and display of products in the store also create a suitable atmosphere and increase impulse buying.

Hard discounters such as Lidl often use non-food items to create a surprise element. Variation is added to the otherwise fairly stable assortment of daily consumer goods by offering weekly changing non-food items, often grouped according to a certain theme. These products are usually sold 'short' – in other words, the product might not be available unless you go to the store straight away. Product shortages are not felt to be a problem in the same way as in traditional supermarkets. The non-food items are stocked to attract customers into the store and to increase the average purchase and margin. Additionally, they are used to maintain a price image by offering standard products at very low prices. Curiously enough, Lidl has become Germany's biggest television retailer.

Surprise and variation are essential in fashion retailing, and assortments continually change. Food retailing could draw some lessons from this. In fashion retailing, a new product may reach stores in a few months or even weeks after the start of its design, whereas in daily consumer goods the time line is much longer. Surprise can be a good foundation for a concept. A store where the customer comes to find bargains has an easier job keeping the customer value promise than a one-stop shopping store, where even one missing product may cause disappointment. Surprise is an important factor in the marketing and assortment planning of many value retailers, but ensuring it requires creative sourcing. Implementing surprise elements includes several factors from planning end caps to price promotions and campaign demand forecasting, so it is not only about finding suitable products. Campaigns link category management and supply management processes closely together, as it will also be necessary to deliver products to stores in a timely and cost-efficient manner.

Nike has a particularly systematic and integrated approach to activity management. It has moved from one sport to another, making each of them a success. In each new sport area, shoes are always introduced first with heavy sponsoring by a leading athlete. Then the assortment is expanded through activity management to clothes and sporting equipment. How many of us would have believed 10 years ago that Nike will be a success also in golf?

The use of space is one of the key challenges in activity management. Large supermarkets nearly always have several gondola ends where advertised products can be placed on pallets if needed, but in small town-centre stores placing additional products not included in the daily assortment may be hard. The retailer's head office needs to plan carefully which products to display and how to schedule promotions. Often the only practical solution is to have a separate promotion space used within categories, if end caps and other large promotional spaces do not exist.

Additional sales achieved with a campaign naturally look good on paper, but not many retailers evaluate how much additional work the campaign caused in the store, and how much cannibalization aroused in the same category or other categories. It is also important to know whether the promotion did truly attract new customers to the store, or they would have come in any case. Campaigns are too often implemented without clear connection to the strategy of the retail format and category management, with objectives that are too tactical, mainly due to manufacturer-driven marketing subsidies.

Stores as advertising media

More than 70 per cent of product purchase decisions are made in the store. Yet, only a few per cent of the total investment in advertising and merchandising is directed at in-store communications and activities. Suppliers would often be willing to have a greater impact on in-store marketing, and they have always tried to get their promotional material into stores. During the last few years, retailers have effectively eliminated suppliers' separate advertising materials and in many cases have prohibited their use altogether.

Inspirational retail concepts include, among others, Starbucks, Wegmans and Publix, where shoppers can come to have a good time. To Starbucks, its own coffee shops are the chain's primary medium, and other marketing is carried out to a very limited extent. In the United States, for example, new Starbucks coffee shops have appeared at a fast pace, often very close to an existing outlet. Many industrial companies have created own concept store solutions to replace traditional marketing and to strengthen the brand image, such as Apple Retail and Niketown (described in Chapter 1).

In-store merchandising is growing as it is beneficial for both the retailer and supplier to have an impact on the consumer at the decision-making moment. The retailer can standardize the store as a medium into a comprehensive marketing concept and sell advertising space and time to suppliers. With a well-standardized store as a medium, most of the suppliers' merchandising efforts can be moved to the store. A good example is Wal-

Mart, which sells advertising time in stores for televisions that are sold at the stores. As in the case of Wal-Mart, part of in-store communications will be based on the traditional push model. Examples of other means available include written material in stores, such as customer magazines, recipes and instructions. For a long time, customer communications have also included in-store television, and in the current era of broadband networks, the contents of television advertising can be controlled centrally from the head office, and no additional work in stores is needed.

On the other hand, the interactive model also provides many opportunities for developing a dialogue between the store and the customer. The most typical examples of interaction in stores are price-checking devices. If the screen size were expanded, the same product identification could be exploited to show considerably more information about the products. This information may be important, for example, to people suffering from allergies or other groups who want to know more about the products.

Touch screens make the dialogue interactive as the consumer can surf for additional information on whatever interests him or her. The data about products can be largely similar as that available over the internet, but at the store it reaches the consumer at the moment of purchase. Additional information on products can be sought by the consumer, as needed, with many kinds of search criteria. One example of making use of such new technologies is offering recipe banks. Also the rapid growth of the internet as an information channel has considerably changed the relationship between the consumer and the retailer. Particularly in speciality retailing, it might be easier for the consumer to get information on products on the sofa at home than in the store. Retailers need to respond to this trend by offering at least internet-level interactive services at the store unless they want to become pure logistics operators and warehouse outlets.

Instead of traditional information kiosks, a PDA device in the shopping trolley can also bring the dialogue closer to the consumer. Communications then become more personal, and if desired, can be personalized in accordance with the customer profile. In many US chains, the consumer can load a shopping list created over the internet into a PDA device (a 'shopping buddy') in the trolley. According to the customer profile, the screen may also show a few messages to arouse interest in new products. Tools like this also enable the retailer to apply personalized pricing and focused real-time offers in the store.

NCR and Excentus have together developed interesting personalized marketing solutions for fuel stations located by a supermarket. The customer is identified with the club card before filling up the fuel tank, and during the fill-up sees personalized offers on the screen. The timing is excellent as filling up is typically an activity where the customer has time, and is not focused on any other activity. In this environment, advertisements have a considerable potential to be viewed.

Changes in in-store merchandising have a large impact on mass media, at least in the long run. More and more marketing efforts are focused on direct communications and personalized services as well as on other store-level activities, which can improve the total sales and profitability of the store. The share of traditional mass media of all activities will decrease considerably over the long run though it will continue to have a role in new customer acquisition and customer activation.

Promotional activities today are so widespread that the impact on the major consumer segments may remain sporadic. In many cases focusing on the simple key elements and allocating resources to them would yield the best results. In the future, retail sales and marketing activities will be targeted ever-more closely to certain segments. Communication tools include mass marketing, store promotions and focused customer dialogue, but the impact of all these measures on the major consumer segments will be measured. Examples of personalized customer communication will discussed in Chapter 7.

Measuring the effectiveness of campaigns

Measuring the success of campaigns has traditionally been limited among both retailers and suppliers. The experience gained from using the ECR scorecards has shown that the skill to plan campaigns exists, and partly also the skill to implement them, but few retailers systematically measure how well campaigns succeed. Typically, when the time for analysis comes, all available resources are spent on planning new campaigns. Collaborative planning, forecasting and replenishment (CPFR) projects have, however, made logistics and production people pay attention to the impact of campaigns on sales, and the results of these projects have served to wake up marketing and sales management as well.

New technologies enable quick and easy measurement of the campaigns and bring added value to the follow-up. Tracking the success of a campaign at the segment level gives plenty of input for improving sales. This also enables new business models to be applied in collaboration with advertising agencies, for example 'success fee' contracts, tied for instance on increasing the average purchase or buying frequency in a certain target segment.

Measuring marketing efficiency is a rising trend in both retailing and manufacturing with marketing return on investment (ROI) as a central metric. The new, sophisticated campaign management solutions support constant measurement in daily retailing environments, but it is worth noting that these tools will not eliminate failed campaigns. However, as activities are learned from, the same mistake should not be made twice.

Efficient measurement does not eliminate the need for intuition and creativity in marketing, but allocates it better and more accurately to the areas needed. An efficient and continual measurement of activities also creates cultural change in retailing, towards more and more fact-based management. There will be more piloting, everything will be measured and the best working solutions will be spread to the field. The change in business model is enabled by new IT-solutions, the most important of which are campaign management tools. These solutions will be examined in greater detail in Chapter 6.

Product development and new product introductions

Product development has been largely a process carried out by consumer product companies, with retailers having had little involvement. Manufacturers have developed and made products, and retailers have sold them. With the growth of private labels, retailers have also adopted a role in product development. The move is from product imitations to more innovative, genuinely differentiating products. In a study on new products (Ernst & Young and ACNielsen, 1999), items were divided into six groups according to how 'genuine' the innovations were and how much innovativeness their development took.

According to this division:

- Classically innovative products are truly new products and may introduce a totally new category. Examples might be iPods and MP3 players.
- Equity transfer products are new to the category but are recognized by consumers. An example might be the use of xylitol not only in bubblegum but also in sweets.
- Line extensions are a new version of a product within an existing category, such as a new flavour.
- Me-too products are identical to a product already in the market, but generally with a new brand.
- Seasonal or temporary products have a short lifecycle. They include, for example, clothes made for a certain time of year or campaign products.
- Substitutes mainly refer to a new EAN code because package size or the place of manufacture has changed.

Product development covers a lot of options, and few new products are true innovations. Both manufacturers and retailers continue to carry out some product development independently. To some extent, product development may, however, be conducted jointly by manufacturers and retailers. This arrangement comes close to the business model of strategic partnership. Manufacturers can help retailers in developing products that enable them to stand out in the markets.

Consumers too can increasingly play a role in product development and innovation. Most manufacturers of consumer products test their products with consumers extensively before launch, but they can also take the consumers to the process earlier. For example, Lego has build active communities around the Lego Mindstorms robotics kit. Lego lets consumers design and order their own models, and selected consumer-designed models go into production and into the stores with Lego facilitating this process, including production, packaging and distribution. 'Most often, innovation comes from the core community of users', said Søren Lund, director of Lego Mindstorms (source: *2016 The Future Value Chain* by GCI, Capgemini and Intel).

An important metric for the long-term success of a supplier is the market share of new products launched during the last year. It may also indicate the trend in the company's future sales. However, as stated before, the transparency of the sales data in syndicated data sources ensures that the success of products will not remain a secret, and the competitive advantage is often temporary.

Private labels

There is a risk that retailers' product development efforts will decline on the whole. Though the sales of private labels are continually increasing, retailers now spend a significantly smaller part of their net sales on product development than manufacturers have traditionally done. Unlike the pharmaceutical industry where patents protect innovations, retail products are quickly open to plagiarism. Getting true innovations to market is increasingly difficult and expensive and the quarterly economy does not favour long-range product development among manufacturers either. Few CEOs are willing to invest in costly R&D programmes where benefits won't be realized for many years.

So far, private labels have mainly won market share from weak brands, the 'B brands' in the category. But in some cases traditional strong brands are also under attack. For example, in CVS or Target, the private label products next to Kleenex use similar packaging and even similar colours to the original product. New products are launched at a steady rate, and the exit of private labels is very low in many markets. Private label share of total sales varies greatly by market, from a few per cent to over 40 per cent on average. Typically, private labels have an extremely high share (80–90 per cent) in hard discounter chains like Aldi and Lidl, but premium retailers have also invested heavily in private labels. For example, Marks & Spencer has a tradition of high private label share in sales. The share of private labels also differs by category. In frozen foods share is very high, whereas private label share in cosmetics and beer, for example, is generally low. Perishable categories have fewer private labels, but the share is slowly gaining in these categories.

If we look at some of the best differentiated retailers in the world, we can see that most of them are selling only or largely private label products.

IKEA, H&M, The Body Shop – you cannot buy the same products anywhere else. As Kenneth Bengtsson (President and CEO of ICA) put it, the most successful private labels are the ones that are really innovative and new, filling the gaps in the market instead of copying branded products. Product development is one of their core competences, and constant innovation is the way to survive. We can see the same shift happening in food retailing, but the share of private labels varies considerably by category. Interestingly, Wal-Mart, with its estimated 40 per cent private label share, has become one of the leading contract manufacturers in the FMCG industry.

Retailers have introduced private labels for different price classes to attract various consumer groups and buying situations. At Sainsbury's, besides the standard line, products are also available with 'Basic' or 'Taste the difference' labels. Tesco also uses three classes: 'Tesco Finest,' 'Tesco Standard' and 'Value.' International buying associations have also introduced private labels. Their focus is most often bulk products, where they introduce 'price fighters' (like Euroshopper) that can enhance the price image of the store. New private label lines are often introduced as consumer solutions. In Sweden ICA's healthy eating private labels have been a success, and Sainsbury's carries a similar line called 'Be good to yourself'. Another good example is 'Tesco Free From' a range of products that are gluten- and wheat-free for people with allergies or food intolerances.

Continual innovation is the only way for manufacturers to succeed. Private labels are here to stay, and only brands that add value for consumers will get shelf space in the store. Some manufacturers have also systematically changed their offering to new areas that are less prone to private label competition. This trend can also be seen on a macro level, for example Procter & Gamble acquired Gillette and Wella, and is focusing on health and beauty, not so much on food. Health and beauty is a category of constant change and innovation, large marketing budgets and consumer branding, and few supermarket retailers have competences and resources to compete against global manufacturers in this area. However, large pharmacy retailers like Walgreens have wide assortments of private labels in these categories too.

It is clear that most consumers do not constantly favour innovations in their purchasing habits. The choice of store is more dependent on other factors, and follower chains selling high-volume basic products may succeed better in the market than real innovators. There is, indeed, the risk of assortments getting narrower as consumers only look at the price. On the other hand, a backlash can be seen. For example, Whole Foods sells many private labels and functional foods, and underlines ethics and social responsibility in its operations. The wide assortments include specialties as well, but the price is not always the lowest in the market. The sales per square foot and gross profit margin of the chain are among the best in the market.

Consumers trust branded products, which will make up most of the shopping basket. Brands will survive, but it is not as obvious who will own them. Beside own labels, retailers might also buy brands from manufacturers or from each other. Wal-Mart has already purchased the White Cloud brand from Procter & Gamble. It will be interesting to see whether exclusive products will be more common through ownership arrangements. Certain small brand houses with a relatively small value but a solid clientele may become potential acquisition targets, as they could be used as exclusive brands to attract new customer flows to stores. Lumene, a Scandinavian cosmetics brand, has chosen different strategies for different markets. In Finland it is a common and well-known brand, but in the United States it was at first the exclusive brand of the CVS chain, and is now gradually expanding to other carefully chosen chains such as Target.

Department stores have used exclusive products for a long time. The Finnish Sokos department stores collaborate closely with the German Karlstadt-Quelle and UK-based Boots, and have exclusive rights to sell their products in Finland. According to interviews, European or global purchasing may also grow through purchasing alliances or other collaboration agreements, and these cases are often related to exclusive products, designs or private labels.

Furniture manufacturer Natuzzi has implemented exclusive distribution in an interesting way. The company has an extensive product assortment, of which it has given selected products to different chains for exclusive sale. This means the stores are not competing with each other unless the customer is ready to consider choosing between different products. Cloth and leather options on the furniture are, however, the same at all stores, so synergies are still gained.

On a smaller scale, manufacturers can produce exclusive products for retailers. Cornetto Soft ice cream has an exclusive flavour for the Hema chain, and Coca-Cola has made a special 3 × 1.5-litre package for buyers of light drinks in the French Monoprix chain. Many markets have relatively small volumes for exclusive products, but as manufacturing technologies evolve, smaller and smaller production runs can be produced cost efficiently. For example, Nokia can make a very small quantity of its mobile phones for chosen operators and customers. Another alternative is to offer a product for exclusive sale for a certain period, after which other chains can have it in their assortments. However, manufacturers face difficult political issues when giving exclusive products for a retailer, and most manufacturers have decided to stick with their own products and timetables.

However, small suppliers might gain competitive advantage with exclusive products. Global companies producing consumer products build mega brands that have a natural place on the shelf of a retail store, and their product development and production are largely centralized. When a local retailing company wants to use exclusive products, the natural partner is a local supplier with existing good relations. The ability to respond flexibly to the needs of the retailer and customers by producing sufficiently small differentiated batches cost effectively may arise as a central competitive advantage for some small suppliers.

High-quality product development requires precise knowledge on the part of retailers and manufacturers. The role of quality assurance is extremely important as even one faulty product may spoil the reputation of the whole private-label product line. When an umbrella brand may comprise thousands of different products, this risk must be handled by the retailer, and a certain caution is required. It is already clear that not all quality requirements are met in certain price-fighter private labels, which has made consumers move to other, better-quality products.

A retailer can have the product and laboratory tests for quality assurance in-house or outsource testing services to an external service provider. However, it cannot avoid the responsibility. Package design is also a central part of product development, and in the case of retailers' private labels, it is necessary to think about who will plan the packages. Here, the expertise of both manufacturers and external experts can be used.

Retailers' private labels also pose additional challenges in terms of purchasing expertise and practical implementation. For production planning, demand should be forecasted accurately enough, but retailers cannot require manufacturers to take the risk of overstocking private labels to the same extent as with branded products. Retailers themselves usually have to bear the responsibility of the demand forecasting for manufacturing plants. Another alternative is to make service-level agreements with manufacturers, transferring the risk to the manufacturer against a suitable premium.

Product introductions

ECR Europe has developed a new product introduction scorecard, which can be used to evaluate the efficiency of product launches and the factors having an impact on it. Using the scorecard, the product's success can be analysed early, during its planning, but currently only some companies systematically use the scorecard. It is likely that most retailers will define an own NPI scorecard as a foundation for all new products for their assortments, if they do not have one in place already. This is a way to systematize procedures within categories and in collaboration with trading partners.

It has been interesting to see that the most active users of the product launch scorecard have been manufacturers and not retailers. The measures required for the NPI scorecard should, however, be set by retailers for their own assortments. It can be assumed that in the next few years most retailers will clarify their business practices and will require a certain rationale in due form for all products taken into the assortment. This is a central part of a fact-based business model, where the role of marketing subsidies and 'free lunches' in assortment decisions decreases.

Promotional funds connected with product launches have aroused a lot of discussion within retailing. According to a study conducted in the United States (Sudhir and Rao, 2004), the slotting allowances paid by suppliers for new products increase the efficiency of operations. As space must be paid for, no unnecessary products are included in the assortments, and only products that sell will be allotted space. Suppliers do not pay for shelf space unless they themselves believe in the product. Slotting allowances also balance the new-product-related risk in the value chain. The study did not, however, take into account the time spent by both parties in 'slot allowance negotiations'. This means that one of the biggest cost items (which does not even create value to the final consumer) has been ignored.

The key metrics for product introductions include:

- sales and gross margin on sales;
- store penetration;
- shopper penetration, that is, market share in the target group;
- cannibalization and impact on the sales of the whole category;
- repeat purchases.

Nowadays, competitors can detect the success of innovations quite easily and quickly using syndicated data sources. With retailer private labels, the situation is somewhat different as manufacturers cannot sell them to other retail groups. Product development also takes time, which may guarantee a temporary competitive advantage. Innovation management might offer a retailer a way to stand out from the competition, especially if the target groups consist of trend-conscious consumers or variation seekers.

Sadly for the consumer, category management and more efficient data analysis have led to a situation where an ever-greater part of product development efforts has been directed to the tracking of competition and to imitation instead of new innovations. This leads to quick profits as required by the market. Real product innovations have a payback period of many years, and management at many listed companies does not have the time to wait. Better competitor tracking also ensures that all innovations are quickly recognized and imitated, be they brands of competitors or private brands. On the other hand, it is delightful to see that there are also genuinely different companies in the market, who do it their way and also show good results. Maybe a grocery store could get inspiration from successful non-food formats like Best Buy, H&M and Home Depot?

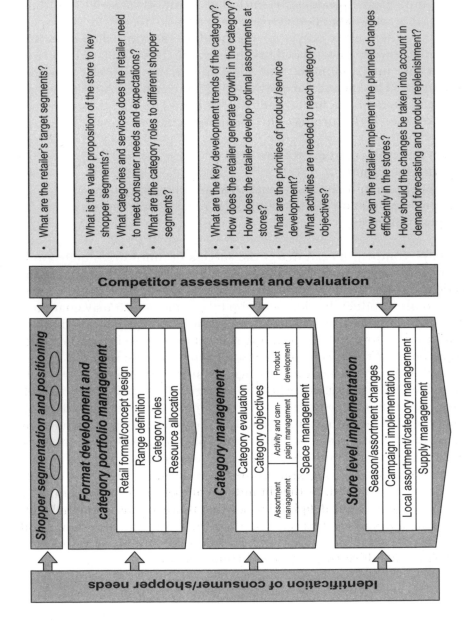

Figure 4.7 Summary of the key areas of the shopper-oriented demand management process

Summary and some insights into the future

Demand management is a broad area, including elements related to retail format development, assortment management and new product development. Category management is an essential part of this total process. However, the focus is shifting from individual categories to wider ensembles, and solution centres for consumers. Many categories will be redefined, and category definitions will differ from chain to chain. Figure 4.7 captures the essential questions of retail demand management.

Category management is becoming more strategic, optimizing the whole shelf, gondolas and solution centres for consumers instead of small categories, which enables greater flexibility in space allocation. The focus of the assortment management shifts from basic assortments towards impulse purchases and enhancing shopping experiences. Even one additional euro, pound or dollar in the shopping basket may result in a significant increase in space profitability, and systematic changes in assortments and themes add necessary variation to shopping.

Using stores as advertising media is also very important for retailers. Consumers cannot keep up with all new product introductions, and retailers need to find efficient ways to make shopping easy, but at the same time informative. Consumers need to be able to find at least similar information about the products from the store as they could on their sofa at home. As more and more products come in to the market, it is very important for retailers to learn to educate consumers to try to use them, also with self-service methods.

The speed of change will be an essential competitive differentiator. This is divided into two elements: reaction time and the time needed for implementation. Reaction time is getting shorter since information systems enable automation for recognizing changes both in consumer behaviour and competitor actions. There will also be a significant development in terms of implementation time. Implementation efficiency and store-level category management are discussed in Chapter 5. The length of assortment periods will become category specific and the number of seasons is likely to increase. Success finally will be measured on the store shelf, which shifts attention to the efficiency of implementation.

Global sourcing as well as local assortments will increase in importance and share in retailing, and there will be distinct levels in assortments that differ significantly by retailer. In addition to national chain assortments, the roles of global, regional and store-level sourcing will be clarified, and category management procedures will vary substantially by chain. Local assortments based on customer structure and competitive situation will no longer be a differentiating factor, but a requirement for efficient operations. There will, however, be many means of implementation.

5 Store operations

Efficient store operations are vital for all retailers, since a large part of a retailer's variable costs are store employee expenses. Even the time taken to implement small operational or concept changes multiplies easily to hundreds of work days as tasks are spread out to hundreds or thousands of stores. Store operations require a considerable workforce. Retailers have optimized product flows and logistics for a long time, but store-level task management and optimization of the workforce are often still taken care of by local store management without efficient optimization tools and systematic planning.

Retail workforce management faces several challenges, including for example managing a workforce with high attrition, a large number of part-time employees and employees with a low overall education level. As in other low-pay industries, motivation and employee morale may pose challenges for efficient workforce management. Training is challenging as not all sales employees can be freed from their work at the same time. Moreover, training in large numbers incurs high costs. However, as employees have a large impact on customer satisfaction, this is an area that needs attention. Good employee satisfaction is often a key to high customer satisfaction.

Efficient management of store operations can create sustainable competitive advantage for retailers. In-store processes such as assortment updates, sales promotion activities and product replenishment to ensure product availability are labour-intensive tasks, but will ultimately determine the success of the retail format. Store operations include a large number of processes. This book concentrates mainly on store activities related to demand management, such as assortment changes, campaign implementation, ordering and product replenishment, and customer service. In addition, the last part of this chapter focuses on centralization and chain-level execution of store operations as well as the role of manufacturers in store operations.

Store ordering

In modern retailing several successful retail formats are based on self-service concepts, where a key task of store operations is to ensure on-shelf availability. If a customer does not find the desired product, sales may be lost and in the worst case the customer may be lost as well. Product shortages should be managed and measured expressly from the customer perspective. A product may well exist at the store, in backroom storage, for example, but if the customer does not find it, the situation can be interpreted as product shortage.

If not centralized, product ordering is one of the daily store-level core processes, ensuring a sufficient product availability to customers. It can usually be divided into three main categories:

- manual ordering;
- automated ordering;
- advance purchases and seasonal ordering.

Traditionally, retailers have ordered their products manually by checking the inventory situation and forwarding the order to the manufacturer through channels like fax, e-mail, electronic data interchange (EDI) or the web. Manual ordering requires a considerable amount of time, which is why retailers try to avoid it. The first phase in the streamlining of operations has been to move ordering from supplier representatives to store employees, leading to savings in personnel and travel expenses. The next step was to automate ordering practices by using handheld scanners. They enabled retailers to give up manual order forms and speed up the ordering process. This phase still requires substantial manual work and may be inefficient, as ordering the right quantities requires knowledge and optimization skills that the store employees might not have. However, store-level manual ordering is still surprisingly widespread, particularly in non-food retailing.

Many retailers have moved into using automatic ordering systems, which are also called automatic replenishment programmes (ARPs). ARP is a general abbreviation given to all solutions in which restocking is based on actual sales data and not on long-term forecasts or safety stocks. Instead of using store employees for ordering, the orders are generated with the help of actual sales data and sales forecasts. Several retailers have automated over 90 per cent of their ordering. A slightly adapted version that enables store-level control of automatic ordering involves an order proposal built by the point of sale (POS) system, but it requires approval of store employees before the order is sent.

Automatic ordering brings many benefits of which the reduction of manual work is the most important. In most cases the workload at stores decreases, on-shelf availability improves and order accuracy gets better. Furthermore, automatic ordering is not dependent on the attentiveness of the store employees. There are no products left unordered even if a shelf edge label is missing or the space reserved for the item has been replaced with another product. Automatic ordering also takes into account products stored in the backroom, which can otherwise be forgotten when checking shelf inventories. Automatic ordering also supports chain operations, as it typically covers the products belonging to the retailer's core assortment. Consequently, automatic ordering prevents unnecessary out-of-stock (OOS) situations and also helps ensure assortment integrity.

As retailers launch automatic ordering and continuous replenishment, the number of order lines typically grows and deliveries take place more often and in smaller lots. In this context, it is reasonable to look at an appropriate order size and order line level because too frequent orders cause additional costs. This may happen at both ends of the value chain. Manufacturers' picking robots or manual pickers need to do a lot of extra work as the number of order lines grows. Order quantities that are too small also cause a lot of extra work on the shop floor and, in our experience, optimizing the order quantities for store replenishment can yield significant savings. In addition, the use of trays and other replenishment techniques are important elements for achieving the right order quantities and efficient operations. Demand forecasting for automatic ordering will be discussed in more detail in Chapter 6.

With automatic ordering, the role of store employees has often been limited to in-store product replenishment and regular product inventory counting, performed to support automatic ordering. Actual ordering activities have been centralized, with some exceptions in, for example, situations where local demand fluctuates.

However, not all ordering can be automated. For instance, some products have to be bought as advance purchases. Typical advance purchase situations include the following:

- time-consuming manufacturing process;
- long distance (transportation time);
- disturbances in demand (eg campaigns, competitor activities);
- limited demand period (short season).

For various products, such as wines, cheese and clothing, the manufacturing or delivery process may take many months. As production is planned significantly ahead of the selling season, production plans must be based on speculative sales forecasts, which are rarely completely correct. Miscalculations backfire in the form of high shortage costs or overstocks and obsolescence costs.

Strong demand for fashion products cannot always be fully exploited as there are usually only a fixed number of products available. In addition, with production capacity reserved for the products of the following season, replenishment ordering is only possible to a limited extent. In the clothing industry, this leads to loss of potential sales that may translate into the loss of sales margin of up to 40–50 per cent. Lost potential sales are called OOS costs. These costs are usually best detected by mail-order companies, which have an accurate knowledge of customer demand, also for products not delivered due to stockouts.

Shortage costs and product obsolescence costs are typical challenges for products with a short lifecycle and demand that is hard to forecast. Short seasons also result in stockouts or unsold products. The season for Easter eggs or Christmas foods is, in practice, very short, and it may be difficult to sell them outside the season, even at discounted prices.

Campaigns also disturb product replenishment cycles by creating order peaks, and often having an impact on the demand of substitutes. These need to be taken into account not only in order quantities but also in space allocation in stores. As customers constantly wish to see something new and entertaining in the store, the share of various activities is growing in many retail formats. Efficient demand forecasting and simulation are requirements for efficient store-level operations. On the other hand, campaigns can also be used in reverse, as tactical actions to even out fluctuations in demand.

Few retailers have automated tools supporting the management of demand fluctuations. Meetings with suppliers, as well as time used for demand forecasting, cause considerable costs. Yet, these personnel costs are rarely allocated to campaigns. Even retailers following an everyday low pricing (EDLP) strategy are not totally free from the challenges of demand fluctuations. This is because demand is affected by many external factors, such as the weather and various local circumstances. Also, competitor campaigns may influence the demand for certain products, even though the retailer itself uses EDLP pricing.

Increasingly, demand forecasting, product ordering and sourcing are handled centrally by the retailer's commercial teams in the head office, and conventional ordering activities are moving out of stores. In many chains, store employees are only involved with ordering in terms of continuous stock counting, carried out to maintain efficient automatic ordering. The cost advantages brought by central ordering are huge. Put simply, a small team centrally may do it more efficiently than a thousand people spread around different stores, when supported with highly automated optimization tools. With these cost savings in store-level manual work, small shortages would be acceptable every now and then. However, centrally operated automatic ordering usually also improves on-shelf availability.

Product replenishment process

A significant amount of distribution-related work is completed at stores, and logistics costs often take place at store level. The product replenishment process at a store resembles the stocking process. Indeed, stores can be seen as pick-up warehouses for consumers. The next section describes an overview of key areas in the store-level product replenishment process.

As a delivery arrives at the store's back door, it is received, and often the load is inspected. Any deficiencies or damage caused during transportation are recorded on the consignment note. At the same time, products are accepted from the electronic data interchange message or entered into the store inventory accounting system if one is in use. To save time, inspection can sometimes be omitted, and in practice it may be impossible to carry out the examination when the delivery occurs, for example, early in the morning or during the night. Because of this, stores may make claims afterwards. Some retailers have dropped regular inspection of loads coming from their own terminals as the costs exceed the received benefits. Random spot checks may, however, be done for monitoring and shrink management purposes.

Store backrooms are, in practice, an additional storage level in the supply chain and as such a non-value-adding phase as customers cannot buy the products but the items still tie up capital. With continuous replenishment and similar practices, it is becoming more common to decrease store-level intermediate warehousing. New stores have less space reserved for backrooms or in some cases these areas are totally absent from store layouts. Experience has shown that all the space there is in the backrooms will be filled, one way or the other.

The next replenishment phase at a store is moving products to the sales space and display fixtures. Products often need to be removed from transport packages for shelving and displays need to be built. Sometimes it is necessary also to price the products, though it is more common today to use shelf edge labels. The aim is to deliver products to the store in a condition that makes them as ready to sell as possible and in a form enabling the items to be placed in the sales space. Ideally, products coming in the same shelf location are picked up and delivered together, in accordance with the display. Retailers that have arranged terminals, warehouses and store layouts similarly have noticed notable savings in hours spent on store-level replenishment.

Product package design has a significant impact on how efficiently products can be shelved at stores. Unpacking transport packages and placing products on display consumes time and resources. Shelving is sometimes dependent on small details; for example, a wrong-sized package or holes that are too small in the backing board of a product cause a significant amount of additional work to the store employees. Many kinds of trays can be used to decrease the time needed for shelving. Shelf-ready packaging (SRP) is currently one of the hot topics, both retailers and manufacturers driving the development initiatives. According to the definition by ECR Europe, SRP is a product that comes in a ready merchandised unit that is easy to identify, easy to open and can easily be put onto the shelf and disposed of, allowing an optimization of shelf replenishment and enhanced visibility. In addition, it should not cause any difficulties for the customer. SRP brings many benefits, especially in replenishment. For example, it is considerably easier and quicker to lift 12 cans on a cardboard tray to the shelf than to lift each can separately. Also, manufacturers and consumers can benefit from SRP that displays more information about the products and enhances brand visibility.

If a product is sold in large quantities, a special pallet or a 'dolly' (a wheeled platform) may be justified for display. Products displayed like this take a lot of space but are easy to handle at the store. Hard discounters, in particular, gain economies of scale by focusing on certain products and save in replenishment costs by displaying most products in full transport packages. A small number of stock keeping units (SKUs) guarantees high volumes for an individual product. This justifies the use of large selling lots and pallets for display. This is a way of further reducing costs compared with the competition.

There are large differences in product displays not only among retailers but also among countries. In many countries in Europe where labour is expensive, the cost of stacking apples in an impressive pyramid in the fruit and vegetable department is excessive. In Scandinavia, where personnel costs are undoubtedly higher than, for example, in the United States, it is common practice to put full shipping pallets at gondola ends. By contrast, many markets require products to be shelved or the pallets to be covered in order not to be visible to customers. Premium retailers often have products arranged neatly in rows with the labels facing the same direction. This significantly adds to personnel costs but also helps to create an elegant store environment. SRP can also support this approach significantly, and beside premium retailers particularly in more traditional supermarkets, where replenishment resources are scarcer, can benefit from them.

Efficient store operations require that sufficient personnel resources are reserved and allocated to relevant tasks. However, challenges vary according to store size. Small neighbourhood stores may have one salesperson working at a time, taking care of all in-store tasks. One practical model is to make orders and carry out most product replenishment tasks in the morning before the store is opened. During store hours, most of the time is spent at the checkout, but the employee can occasionally also work with displays or in customer service. In large hypermarkets, the main challenge is to optimize the number of checkout personnel as the number of customers varies greatly during the day and a considerable amount of resources need to be reserved for the afternoon rush. These periods only last for a few hours, so employees can be assigned additional tasks at other times. This is one reason why product replenishment is often done during the store hours in hypermarkets, and in addition employees can guide customers at the same time.

One way to reduce the number of store employees and even out resource needs is to use replenishment teams for basic shelving activities and implementing assortment changes. As an example, Zara has reduced non-commercial activities at store level with replenishment teams. Clothes are put on their places early on while staff are fully dedicated to sales. Many retailers also use these teams for attaching price or security tags, and for other tasks related to the preparation of products for sale, if these tasks are not prepared centrally in the warehouse. To avoid disturbing daily store operations, some tasks may be accomplished at night. On the other hand, irregular working hours, low pay, the difficulty of the work and in some markets collective employment agreements may hinder the hiring of competent workers for replenishment teams. In addition, travel costs and time needs to be taken into account, and these teams are most often used only in small formats. Large stores have their own replenishment teams who work across several categories, but mainly still work in the same store.

Implementation of assortment changes

There are continual assortment changes at stores: new products are added and old ones are removed from the assortment. Fast-moving products may be given more space and slow-moving items less space. In grocery retailing assortment changes are usually managed through regular assortment changes in certain intervals known as assortment periods or assortment pulses. A year may be divided into, for example, three four-month periods, and most category changes are implemented in these periods. This kind of timing also has its challenges, as periodical assortment changes done simultaneously in several categories have often been seen to cause too much work at the same time, and a slight hiccup in sales may be seen during assortment changes. Some categories also require a slightly different assortment development rhythm, and they may be managed according to a different schedule. In many complementary categories, an annual update might be enough, whereas others need changes as often as each week. Varying assortment pulses help to even out the workload at the store, with changes made little by little and only for relevant product categories at a time.

Seasonality and special events such as holidays also set requirements for assortment changes. For instance, New Year, Easter and the start of school have a considerable impact on assortments in many markets. Fashion retailers are usually masters of assortment changes; they make continual changes, with seasons changing each month or week. Seasonal changes are particularly important in fashion retailing, but they also have an effect on grocery retailers.

Most store assortment changes are implemented with the help of planograms. There are many versions of planograms. In practice, a 'block diagram' showing product names and the numbers of facings has proved practical for most categories, whereas a photo-accurate 'live image' is, in spite of its impressiveness, difficult to use because product variants do not always clearly differ from each other. A planogram should be complemented with a separate change report, detailing new products, products to be removed as well as other potential changes in product quantities or facings. This report makes practical work among shelves considerably easier as work can be focused on the right tasks. The role of change reports is emphasized in fresh product categories where no detailed planograms are used. The situation is similar in many non-food categories where product sizes and shapes vary to a great extent.

If a retailer uses electronic planograms, the stores can independently choose suitable planograms from the intranet. It is common to draw several versions of the planogram for the same category, for example three-, four- and five-module solutions. For each of them, there should be solutions for both customer flow directions as the store layouts vary. If electronic planograms are not used, it is of utmost importance that the retailer's head office has good knowledge of the actual fixtures at each store to be able to send correct versions of the planograms for implementation. Typically, advanced chains have up-to-date CAD images and fixture libraries of all stores, which can be relied upon to determine the number of modules and flow directions for planograms. In practice, planograms need to be adapted for most stores, as there are different types of store fixtures that have been acquired over a long period of time and not all of them follow the same standards. Often, the property also limits the implementation of the planogram; as an example, the bearing joists may cut the space allocated to a shelf module. It is therefore important to provide clear instructions about how store employees may adapt a planogram in a situation deviating from the norm. Without good instructions, employees in each store will make decisions about the adjustments themselves, making uniform assortment layout in the chain hard to maintain.

When new planograms enter stores in the beginning of an assortment pulse, many changes are to be expected. New products need to be placed on the allocated shelf space, which requires that other products are moved somewhere else or removed. Best-selling products are given more space, whereas non-performers are removed or moved to less attractive places. Seasonal products also require their share of the space available. Often, moving one product also affects several others.

The amount of work involved in assortment changes varies by category. Large, standard-shaped products such as nappies are relatively easy to move on the shelf, whereas small products that need a special place, such as cosmetics, often require more time and effort, especially if SRP is not used. Products that require particular shelf fixture may also make it necessary to change shelf structures during assortment changes. In the worst case fixture changes might require emptying the whole fixture prior to the changes.

When assortment changes are made, prices might also change, which requires changing the shelf edge labels. Products being eliminated should be sold out before new products take their place on the shelf. It is often wise to start selling them off and cancel further orders a few weeks prior to the turn of the assortment pulse to get most of them sold. Seasonal product categories, and categories with a lot of new products and rapid product obsolescence, include a large amount of products to be removed. Clothing, cosmetics and magazines are examples of challenging product categories where a large amount of obsolete products and new products are on sale during each period.

In a surprisingly large number of retail formats, selling out old stock is left to the consideration and implementation of store employees. According to our experience, most retailers focus on providing guidelines for the new assortment; only rarely does the head office offer support and clear concepts for selling old products. Typically, this works best in chains where assortments keep changing and obsolete products have to be sold at discounted prices. For instance, in sports categories, it is typical to see discounts of 30–70 per cent after the season. Many retailers have separate clearance sale areas where remaining stock can be disposed of without disturbing the core assortment. Premium retailers often avoid giving large discounts, and in these cases, products are withdrawn and sold in separate discount outlet chains or destroyed.

Assortment pulse changes take a lot of time and personnel resources. Designing a planogram on a computer screen is fairly easy compared with moving hundreds or thousands of SKUs on store shelves. Best practice retailers involve category managers and space management experts in practising the implementation of an assortment change before sending the new planograms to stores. It is still regrettably unusual to have a dedicated person responsible for both planogram design and implementation resource planning. Only best practice retailers estimate the time consumed for each assortment change systematically and make necessary adjustments based on this analysis. However, it would be worthwhile for many others as well, as good planning and instructions may easily save hundreds or thousands of person hours in every assortment pulse. It is recommended to implement all changes during quiet hours when customer flows are small. Employees have more time to make the changes without interference and there is minimal disturbance to customers. Retailers can also even out the changes in different categories and activities over a longer time period, with good planning to balance the workforce needs in stores.

Though assortment changes can in many cases be implemented separately for different product categories, major space changes across categories should always be implemented at the same time. This is because changing the space allocated to one category often initiates a chain reaction, necessitating changes in the space for several other categories as well. As mentioned, space solutions and allocation vary by store, and the same change may cause different overall changes in other stores.

If assortments are renewed significantly and the whole structure of the category is altered, a lot of work is required to implement the change. Implementing a whole category planogram takes time, ranging from a few hours to dozens of hours, so compared with normal daily operations, additional helping hands are needed. In these cases, it is possible to rely on the retailers' own merchandising or new store set-up teams, who will have thorough experience in changing and building up the assortment in different categories. In some categories, supplier representatives can also be used for this task.

Campaign implementation

In addition to assortment changes, campaigns also create the need for changes in stores. Campaigns can be selling or marketing activities of a very different nature, ranging from a short-term price cut to broad events related to all product areas. At its simplest, a campaign can be implemented by changing the price tag, but often implementation involves several other actions. A campaign may have supplementary marketing or display material, and products can be placed in multiple locations at the store. Examples of campaigns requiring major arrangements are fashion shows, tastings, special night events or different artists visiting the store.

Regardless of the type, campaigns usually result in a lot of work for the store employees. Efforts are needed before, during and after a campaign. Achieving a uniform atmosphere at all stores requires good instructions from chain operations. Proper instructions enable efficient display and minimize the use of personnel time in campaigns. Good instructions also ensure that each store has an attractive campaign display. The best retailers provide a picture or planogram of the finished campaign display to make installation easier and set the expectation level for the store employees. Often there are a few display opportunities depending on the space available, and the campaign may be supported with a few photos of examples of best practice.

Campaigns require work from the store employees even before a campaign starts. Prior to the campaign, the relevant products are ordered for the store. This phase may be handled centrally; if that is the case, products arrive at the store automatically. In some chains, store employees need to make orders and forecast demand themselves. With campaigns altering the demand, forecasting of accurate order quantities requires effort even if automatic ordering is in use. Besides the products used in the campaign, cannibalization effects on the sales of substitute products should also be considered. This is especially important in fresh produce where demand forecasting errors may increase shrink significantly. Key characteristics of an advanced retailer are that all campaigns provide clear instructions for store employees about product display and demand forecasting including key substitute products.

Many retailers use local newspapers as part of their marketing programme in addition to central marketing activities. Many advertising campaigns are designed and produced centrally, but practical cooperation with a local paper may be handled by stores or the regional retail organization. In these cases, it is important that the campaign material is received early enough to enable local implementation. Sometimes a store has the opportunity to change products or prices in accordance with the local competitive situation. Furthermore, campaigning with local suppliers is often the responsibility of store-level or regional teams.

Campaigns are usually associated with price changes, which need to be updated on the shelves and systems before the start of the campaign. To facilitate this process, price tags can be printed and sent to stores. If prices are not updated at checkouts automatically, guided by the retailer's ERP system, the changes will have to be made in the store POS system. As the campaign starts, the stores change the price tags, but not until the morning the campaign starts, so that products always have an up-to-date, correct price.

Store employees are also responsible for displaying products in the store to stand out from the rest of the assortment. It is often justified to display products in two or more places, thus avoiding the need for changing the basic shelf layout. Campaign products may also be items that are not included in the normal assortment. Many stores have separate areas for campaign products including, for example, various mass displays and gondola ends that can house whole pallets or other transport packages, which are well suited for high-volume campaign products. For example, hard discounters often campaign continually changing hard-line items in separate campaign areas. In cosmetics, shop-in-shop concepts commonly have own areas reserved for SRP displays that are used for campaigns and new product introductions.

Campaigns may also require the display of marketing material or fixtures. Customers make most of their buying decisions at the store, so visible campaign materials attracting consumers' attention are important. With the store as a media trend, the amount of campaign material in stores has risen. When centralized chain operations and tight retail formats became popular in retailing, supplier-specific marketing materials in stores were reduced, but now they are coming back, though most often in the format defined by the retailer. The campaign material is usually sent to the store a few days before the campaign starts, often together with the products. The material may also be in an electronic form, if it is meant to be used on store TV or radio.

Retailers' chain operations usually do not have extra resources for campaign implementation, so stores have to take care of the preparations on their own, in addition to the normal work. Building attractive campaign displays that will sell products well requires clear instructions and possibly even training at store level. In our experience, a surprisingly large amount of campaign materials sent to stores are not used properly, in time, or at all, as the store employees have no time, motivation or competence to display them.

The input of store employees is needed during the campaign as well. Shelves have to be replenished more often and additional orders might be needed. Furthermore, the marketing equipment has to be kept clean and replaced or fixed when needed. When the campaign comes to an end, the remaining stock is usually sold, possibly at a discounted price and sometimes at a totally different store or at a separate area in the store. All campaign materials and fixtures are removed and potentially returned or stored for future use.

In addition to store employees, some retailers also use specialized campaign set-up teams that serve several stores. For example, in mall retail formats window displays are a major marketing media, and building them might require special skills and equipment that justify the use of specialized resources such as window dressers. Also, suppliers may participate in the physical implementation of campaigns at stores. The role of suppliers in store-level implementation is highly dependent on the retail format and the nature of the campaign. In tightly controlled retail chains, suppliers are usually not encouraged to take part in the store implementation of campaigns. An exception to this are various product demonstrations, when a supplier or a promotion marketing agency can work at stores and thereby free the store's employee resources from implementing the campaign. Furthermore, a retailer's strategic partners may have a role in producing campaign-related instructions and other information for store employees in their category.

Customer service

Although many retail formats are largely based on self-service, customers meet many store employees during a shopping visit. A customer service situation is always an important moment of truth, leading either to the success or failure of the shopping experience. The level of customers' expectations for service may vary considerably according to a retailer's format and image. At hard discounters, customer service has been cut down to a minimum, whereas department stores and many speciality stores focus strongly on customer service. Customer service needs personnel resources, and is one of the biggest single cost factors for a premium retailer. It is, however, a tool for differentiation, and when well managed, it may increase sales considerably. On the other hand, friendly gestures cost nothing, so every employee is in the position to improve the shopping experience, in any retail format.

There are several customer service roles in a store. Some retailers have a store greeter who stands by the door welcoming customers, and different departments have service personnel to whom customers can turn and ask for help in finding products or getting product information. At service counters customers can ask for recipes or, at a DIY store, for refurbishment instructions, and the attendant may also give tips and recommendations. Moreover, demonstrators from suppliers often come to stores to inform customers of new products and promotions. A store may have a separate information and service desk for returns, complaints and often for services related to its loyalty programme. These desks may also sell lottery tickets or the services offered by the retailer's partners, such as insurance. Finally, a customer meets the checkout personnel and possibly a packer, and may stop at the store café or restaurant before going home. A consumer may have dozens of customer service contacts during a shopping trip, and each contact contributes to the overall impression and image of the retailer.

As discussed in Chapter 2, a retailer's positioning is a key factor determining the level of customer service. Customer needs and service requirements, competition, retailer target positioning and a clear business case should be considered in this decision. The customer service level also varies by the market and to some extent by employee wage level. In countries with low minimum wages a large number of customer service employees may be considered whereas, for example, in Nordic countries many retailers have been obliged to focus on self-service due to high workforce costs.

The amount and quality of customer service might have a considerable impact on a customer's buying process. According to some customer behaviour studies, customers who are greeted buy more often than those who are not greeted. The conversion rate goes up even more if customers receive personal service, and the service has a particularly big impact when customers do not know what they would like to buy or when the purchasing situation is new to them. Service may also influence browsers who might not otherwise buy anything. However, selling style also has to be taken into account because too aggressive selling may annoy customers. The reaction also varies largely by culture: in the United States greeting and small talk are necessary, whereas customers in some other markets (for example, Finland) may find this intrusive. The conversion rate is also affected by peak hours, which remains a challenge to many retailers. Experience shows that many retailers do not allocate customer service personnel resources in proportion to the number of customers. Hence, at peak hours, the conversion rate may be lower.

Customer conversion is important to retailers. Many retailers lose sales because customers buy nothing or buy only from single category, and neglect the other departments. Not buying usually indicates customer dissatisfaction during some phase of the buying process, or it simply shows that the customer has not received an impulse to buy. The challenge is that the retail management rarely has information available on non-buying shoppers, and the reasons for non-buying remain unanalysed. What is not measured is often not managed in daily operations.

Customer conversion is not a significant challenge for all companies. In an online store, the conversion rate is usually very low, whereas in food retailing nearly all customers buy something. But grocery stores may have challenges with certain departments. Therefore, it is worthwhile to monitor conversion rates by departments. The best retailers continually track department-specific conversion rates, but this is not yet a common practice in all chains. If customers use several channels in speciality retailing, the conversion rate is usually higher than in cases where only one channel is used. For example, a customer may study products over the internet and enter a store only after having compared products and made an initial decision about the purchase. Automotive retailing is actively monitoring each phase of the customer's buying process from information search in the internet to test drive and to the final sale. Even though the role of the internet has grown a lot during recent years, personal service in stores is still very important in closing the sale, and there are huge differences between different salespeople in results and customer satisfaction.

The level of customer service is often dependent on personality and also rests on the personal chemistry between the employee and the customer. A high-quality customer service employee can cope without extensive product knowledge as long as the attitude towards the customer is correct. Even such a famous premium retailer as Harrods in London has ambulatory salesperson substitutes filling in for absent employees in various departments. If this succeeds at Harrods, it should be possible for most supermarkets, where customers do not expect quite the same level of service. What counts is the style and impression of service experience, not the thorough product knowledge. Some of the basic properties of good customer service are listening to the customer and supporting the customer in the buying process. These are areas where a suitable 'eye for the game' counts. Relationship skills are much more important to focus on during recruitment than the acquired expertise. Necessary product knowledge can be learned fairly quickly in the work, whereas relationship skills are more a question of personality and can be influenced only to a limited extent with the retailer's induction training.

On the other hand, some salespeople can be expected to have significant product knowledge. This is especially true in non-food stores. For instance, in a DIY store a salesperson may advise customers on how to prepare the foundation of a house or how to carry out a thorough refurbishment. This kind of advice involves a significant amount of responsibility and requires professional expertise. On the other hand, a competent service desk attendant at a grocery store may reap high additional sales with cooking knowledge in helping customers to plan gourmet menus. And a salesperson at a cheese counter may have stories to tell, giving content to the purchases and justifying a higher price. Especially in higher-priced consumer goods such as boat sales, storytelling competence together with the ability to listen to customers may increase sales significantly.

Not all people working in retailing are able to provide good customer service, and for a high-quality customer service concept to be successful, an excellent personnel strategy is required to attract and retain capable people. We have seen numerous cases where the best salespeople and customer service employees move to other industries where they can get significantly better compensation, and the current pricing models of services prevent retailers from competing for the best people. Unfortunately, most customers have not become used to paying for good service, and they are not always demanding it either. A low-paying industry and expert work are a difficult combination, which may explain why many successful retailers are largely based on a self-service concept.

For some retailers, customer service is a conscious differentiation-related decision. In these chains, service counters and customer service desks are not separate profit centres, but instead are treated as marketing expenses. For instance, a service meat department may provide a positive service atmosphere even though customers mainly buy industrially packaged meat. A service counter may be used for delicatessen items not available at other stores, but would not be profitable as such. An extreme case is a service counter where customers cannot buy anything but can get advice or some other type of service.

A sad but rational habit of customers is to get a service at one shop and buy products at another where they are sold at a cheaper price. This happens especially with more expensive purchases such as home electronics or DIY items. Customers, who do their shopping in big self-service value retailing companies, may be accused of being responsible for the decreasing service level in many product areas. Retailers cannot compete both on service and on price, especially if some customers get service at one shop and the product at another. Only the retailers selling the products will survive.

Customer service has rarely been assigned a price tag because customers have become used to not having to pay for service due to prevailing trade practices in the retail industry. Retailers differentiating on customer service usually rely on a one-stop principle, getting all of a customer's purchases under one roof. They may use slightly higher pricing than self-service stores. But there are also some areas where retailers are able to charge a legitimate price for services. For example, in DIY retailing, kitchen designs have often been priced at almost market prices, though a customer may usually deduct some of the design expenses from the final purchase price of the kitchen. The pricing policy helps to focus service on those customers who actually buy, and can considerably save additional work that would be caused if all customers were given the service free of charge.

In the home electronics field, after-sales services and product support are important services that come with a price tag. Some of the products are no longer bought in the traditional way but are leased including support services. After-sales services are offered, for instance, by Apple with its Genius Bar and by Best Buy with its Geek Squad concept. With Genius Bar, Mac Geniuses, as the service staff is called, provide face-to-face tips and advice, answer product questions relating to Mac or iPod, and do repairs when necessary. Customers are supported in areas such as how to download music to the iPod, or how to update software, or are helped with technical difficulties. The Geek Squad covers an even more challenging area, as products offered by Best Buy represent a number of manufacturers in the computer and home entertainment field.

Service operations in retailing are expected to grow significantly in the future due to retailers' diversification into new fields, such as insurance, financial services and mobile operator products. New services result in new requirements for retail training programmes and competence building, as store employees need deep knowledge, especially in technical services such as the Geek Squad concept mentioned above. The competences also need to be continually upgraded in line with the development. In addition, recruiting standards in many areas may need to be redefined.

Customer complaints are a special area of customer service worth mentioning separately. There are numerous reasons for complaints, but the most typical are related to product quality, product deficiencies, pricing or retail personnel. If a customer takes the trouble to come to the customer service counter, the matter is certainly important to that person. It is essential to listen to the customer and to handle the situation systematically and fairly taking the customer's situation into account. A well-handled complaint situation can often be transformed from disappointment to a positive experience, and the customer may even become the retailer's advocate after the process. In the worst case, a poorly handled complaint may lead to disappointment, with the customer sharing his or her disappointment with others. The ensuing negative word of mouth may cause the loss of many customers.

Some retailers have centralized customer feedback operations in stores, while others have decentralized them to different departments. The key is to have time and tools for serving the customer and solving the situation, if possible in peace from other customers. Also, employees need to be empowered to make necessary decisions so the matter can be handled quickly. It is important always to record the feedback received from customers. The information needs to be forwarded to the right people for corrective action but also for the development of chain-level operations. In true customer-oriented retail organizations, top management reads customer feedback regularly – if not weekly, at least on a monthly basis – and acts on the feedback received.

The service level is also a key topic for consumer product companies to achieve the desired brand image. It takes some character to sell products in just a few selected channels providing good service while other channels might momentarily offer big sales volumes, but without adequate service level. Starbucks is a good example of a company with a disciplined approach, as it has first ensured the brand experience with its own café and retail network prior to leveraging extra sales in supermarkets. Another example is premium cosmetics, such as Christian Dior, Gucci or YSL, which are seldom sold anywhere but at the finest department stores, and even then are backed with a good service concept. However, it is also vital to recognize that not all customers like being approached or serviced at a store. For example, cosmetics retailer Sephora has made this a differentiator, and has established a sales practice where employees only approach customers who ask for help. Service is always available, but customers may just prowl the store to test and experience products at their leisure. This approach differs from many cosmetics stores, where it is almost impossible to get acquainted with products without the help of salespeople or demonstrators.

Customer service can be replaced by certain self-service options to streamline operations. Sometimes customers prefer self-service for efficiency and speed. For example, online banks have made the daily bank transactions much quicker and easier than before. Technology solutions at stores, such as kiosks and touch screens, enable the sharing of information without a salesperson. These can also be used to ensure that customers have similar information to that they would get over the internet. Touch screens can also be used for ordering products at the service counter. For instance, at service stations operated by the Wawa chain and at Shoprite stores, customers can order a sandwich using a touch screen, choosing bread type, fillings and condiments. After the order, store employees prepare the sandwich and the customer can pick it up using the order number. In some cases, checkout employees can be substituted for self-service checkouts. New technology continually offers more cost-efficient possibilities for service automation in retailing that can be used for reducing employment costs and also for providing new services for customers.

Store management and key performance indicators (KPIs)

Store management is an integral part of the success of a store and the retailer as a whole. Different retail formats require different management models and approach. Where a store manager working for a tightly managed hard discounter should act as 'a tough cop', a store manager at a local premium retailer needs to act as a coach for a creative team, providing not only goals but also a degree of freedom and motivating his or her team to work as experts. At a small novelty shop, a store manager should preferably be a 'jack of all trades'. The manager's talent in merchandising and window dressing, for example, may add significantly to sales.

Not all store managers are the same. Why do some store managers always succeed, no matter where the store is situated? A good manager may make a store successful even if it is in an unfavourable location, but others fail to succeed even if the store is in a premium location. Store management involves many practices but, generally, major differences in performance can be detected among different units, as well as in comparison to the market potential in each area. From the perspective of a retail chain, it is important to identify successful management practices and to leverage the lessons learned and best practices to other units whenever possible.

Today an increasing part of a store manager's time is spent in the store, close to the customer interface. Many back-office activities have been centralized, and the main tasks at a store include taking care of product replenishment, checkout functions and customer service. The majority of in-store activities are related to these well-documented processes, but it is often an integral part of a store manager's job to perform safety and HR tasks, though some of these tasks can be efficiently handled centrally. In chains with small stores, many store management operations are often centralized to regional management. For example, a regional manager may do recruiting whereas in hypermarkets it may be done directly by store management.

In a retail chain, there are standard operating procedures (SOPs) for almost all tasks included in key processes. When materials supporting the operational processes are easily accessible to employees, they can usually quicken and streamline the leveraging of best practices within the chain. It is especially important for new employees to have clear SOPs and examples of best practice to rely on. They can make starting the job easier and decrease the 'fumbling costs'.

Tight SOPs are common in franchising, where the brand owner needs to secure the customer experience with certain concept elements and service operations. For example, in the automotive industry the sales and service processes have detailed instructions and requirements for retailers, but the employees are also offered (or more often require) training in these areas. Fast-food restaurants are another example of rigorous franchising contracts. There is a clear need for this: if the store operations are not clearly mentioned in the franchising contract, it is very hard for the brand owner to secure uniformity of the format and provide a similar customer experience in all stores. What is not mentioned in the contract will be tailored by the store.

Still, retail management has increasingly shifted from strict SOPs and control to management by results. A store is given distinct goals and all employees strive to achieve them. Many retailers have introduced simple store-level scorecards, enabling the tracking of a store's performance against targets in agreed areas. Perhaps the most famous of these is the Steering Wheel used by Tesco. The wheel is divided into five areas: customer, operations, people, community and finance. Each area includes several sub-areas, which performance can be indicated with simple traffic lights, green when everything goes on in line with targets and red in challenging cases. It is a good practice in retail to have a store scorecard clearly visible to the employees, for example as a wall chart, so all employees know the performance of the store. In many chains, scorecards have been implemented in retailers' intranet solutions, and most figures end up there automatically.

Perhaps the most important benefits of scorecards are in making employees committed for joint results and empowered to achieve them. Where a retailer's regional manager has earlier visited a store and listed corrective actions, the regional manager now may start the discussion with the store manager by going through the store's metrics. It is primarily a question of how to help a store to succeed in terms of chosen metrics and share best practices from other stores. The role of regional manager has changed from a strict concept guard into an active facilitator and provider of best practices. Concrete metrics encourage all employees to achieve shared targets. Table 5.1 lists examples of typical store-level KPIs.

Examples of traditional financial measures are sales development against the previous year, benchmarked with other stores in the chain or against the budget. Some of the best retailers know how to calculate the market potential of a store site, and assign a clear target based on store size, competitive situation and customer portfolio in the area. Good sales per square metre in a certain location may look good in comparison with other stores of the chain, but seen against the regional situation and competition, the measure alone does not always tell the whole truth about the store's success. It is usually a good idea also to measure sales and sales development by department or by category, supporting store-level organization and operating models.

In many centrally managed chains, measuring store margin is not an important metric, and usually a store does not even need to know its margin. On the other hand, this is an important measure in the management model for chains where pricing is managed at least partly at store level, adapting to local competitive situation. Pricing must be managed locally, at least to a certain extent, if the retailer's approach involves local sourcing. Store margin reporting can easily be automated in a retailer's POS system, but the competitor information needed for pricing often requires visiting nearby stores.

A typical figure measuring the total efficiency of a store is sales per personnel hour, which may vary greatly even within a chain. This figure also can be analysed by department, and analysing the best-performing units in the chain generally reveals best practices that can be leveraged across the whole chain. When benchmarked by category to other stores, this is one of

Table 5.1 Examples of store-level KPIs

Performance measure	Metric	Key notes about usage
Store sales development	€, %	• Against target or benchmarked to other stores in chain
Store margin development	€, %	• Key measure, if any pricing or assortment decisions done locally
Sales/working hours	€	• Important measure for store operations efficiency
Expenses controlled by store	€	• Typically measured against budget
Products out of stock (OOS)	#, %	• Automated, if possible to report from POS systems, otherwise manually from selected categories
Shrink	%, €	• Drill down from department and category level up to SKUs, as needed
New products/ campaign penetration	Penetration %	• Daily measurement of new/focus areas of the store
Number of customers	#	• Compared to last year/similar units in chain
Loyalty card usage	%	• As % of customers and sales
Share of key segments	%, €	• Sales to key target customer segments of the retailer (per segment)
Average sales basket	€	• As overall average figure or number of baskets in different sizes (eg number of baskets over €50)
Mystery shopper	Varies by study	• Updated often quarterly or annually. Benchmarking to other units
Customer penetration	%, #	• Measured by department, how many customers bought from the category/department
Conversion rate	%	• Number of customers that purchased after contacted
Employee retention	%	• Often measured separately for new (<12 months) employees and old employees
Absences	Hours, %	• Measured against target and other stores
Development project 1, 2, 3, …	Defined by project	• Measures for implementation and success of selected development projects of the retailer

the most beneficial measures in identifying opportunities to improve store profitability.

Examples of more accurate operational measures include the number of out-of-stock (OOS) situations or shrink percentage. Of these, OOS measurements can be automated if POS systems also have inventory accounting. Unfortunately, there are still retailers, especially in the grocery category, that do not have inventory accounting in place. In non-food retailing the situation is typically better. To get useful figures for this measure requires continuous inventory counts as the systems are not capable of recognizing shrinkage. Manual OOS tracking is also worthwhile in selected categories, at least every now and then. Suppliers also buy continuous OOS measurements from external service providers. Some retailers use scanners to read all empty shelf spaces every night to record OOS situations, which can then be acted on, and information passed to other players in the retail value chain for corrective actions.

Shrink is one of the big cost factors and store measures in retailing. Shrink refers to products disappearing, getting obsolete, going bad, and getting broken or becoming in another way unsaleable. The reasons for shrink may vary from annoying accidents to pure theft and negligence. Shrink can be divided into known and unknown shrink. Known shrink is detected and can be entered in company records or statistics. Examples include unsold and therefore spoiled fresh products, or transport packages torn by a forklift. These matters can usually be addressed to a certain extent with efficient practices and by measuring them. Similarly, it is wise to track expenses controlled by the store, recording them and monitoring how they develop.

Unknown shrink usually takes place unnoticed by employees, and the reasons for it often remain obscure. According to ECR Europe reports (2005), only 27 per cent of unknown shrink is caused by process failures. The major part, approximately 66 per cent, of unknown shrink is caused by theft and fraud. Shoplifting can be prevented by attaching alarm tags to items and by placing valuable products in locked glass cabinets or in places where they are easily seen by salespeople and other customers. Unfortunately, many of these actions make buying more difficult, which may be reflected in sales figures. Thefts by staff are harder to prevent, yet their share of shrink may be considerable. Shrink has a direct impact on the bottom line, and as the results are easy to measure, they have in many companies gone all the way to the top management agenda. Thereby, they have naturally been included in the group of store-level measures that are actively tracked.

Advanced companies have built automated POS controls, capable of identifying shrink in different categories and zeroing in on individual products if needed. The key is to identify which products and categories are especially vulnerable to shrink, and the root causes for shrinkage. After this, the retailer has to delve into the processes and models that are behind shrink. Tools for decreasing shrink include simple methods like improving transport packages, locked storage rooms, changes in product packages and regular inventories.

New products and campaign penetration measurement may speed up execution in many chains. There are usually a limited number of new products and campaigns, and taking them separately under ongoing monitoring may support quick execution. It is relatively easy to build automatic reporting in POS systems, indicating how the store performs in terms of campaigns or new products launched. When store employees know that these matters are actively tracked, they will usually give a higher priority to practical implementation as well. Ongoing tracking of key activities is one way to contribute to the efficient execution of chain operations.

Customer relationships can also be measured at store level from several points of view. Typical indicators include loyalty card usage and the number of customers visiting the store. Of these, the use of loyalty cards is mainly used as a metric for checkout and other service points; the aim is to offer loyalty cards to new customers and to remind customers that if they have a loyalty card, it pays to use it. Tracking the number of customers is interesting and it is an important indicator especially for stores that carry out local marketing activities. The number of customers is usually a good metric indicating how well these activities succeed. For retailers that manage marketing centrally the same indicator is rarely useful at store level as store employees have little chance to affect activities taking place outside the store.

Measuring sales development and buying frequencies in target consumer segments can be used to encourage store employees to focus on club members, their needs and to make sure they come back to the store over and over again. Tracking can be automated in the retailer's loyalty systems, and the store may get reporting on a monthly basis or more frequently if needed about the development of the most important consumer segments. However, it is not always worthwhile to track these metrics with systems, but rather to motivate employees with concrete measures, such as the number of customers they can greet by name. It is important that employees remember to treat a shopper as a customer, not as a factor disturbing the product replenishment process.

Service quality can be measured, for example, with mystery shopper studies. They are typically carried out in the stores quarterly or annually. The results often have a good correlation with a store's bottom line results, and mystery shopper results can be used in many ways both at the store and chain level to improve operations. Incidentally, the customer conversion percentage can also be measured at the store or department level, but it usually requires manual actions, which would be too expensive for measuring operations on a daily basis. However, customer purchase penetration percentage in different departments can be automated with analysis of POS data at receipt level.

One of the key store-level management objectives is to ensure employee job satisfaction. Good leaders can generally be measured not only on direct results-oriented targets but also on employee retention and satisfaction. It is always reasonable to evaluate these results on a regional basis as workforce availability may vary greatly among different places. It is up to the store manager to motivate a high-performance team and to provide a good working environment for employees. Retailers in many places suffer from acute workforce shortages, which may get even worse in the future, with employees having real chances to choose where to work. Raising employee retention average from 200 days to two years, for example, has a dramatic effect on training costs and cuts down 'hassle' costs, not to mention the growth of employee expertise. Levels of employee expertise and satisfaction have a strong correlation with customer satisfaction. It is typically worthwhile for retailers to measure separately the retention of more experienced employees, such as those who have been employed for more than a year, and that of new employees. Number of employee absences also have an impact on the efficiency of store operations and may also indicate employees' job satisfaction. A good indicator reflecting retailers' investments in retention is the number of training days per employee, which have an impact on retail operations' continual improvement.

The management culture, reputation and values of the retailer also have an effect on employee retention. The public reputation of a retailer has a strong impact on recruitment and personnel availability. For an individual employee, status afforded by the job is important: how proud employees can be of their employer, its accomplishments and its reputation. Naturally, the reputation of a retailer must be protected for the sake of customers as well. It is also important to employees that top management communicates the company's future both internally and externally and openly discusses the development views of the company. It is vital for employees to feel confident about the stability of their jobs.

Basically, good store management usually means managing in the frontline, both at store level and at chain management. A good store manager can demonstrate high-quality leadership by acting as an example to others, for instance by taking care of store cleanliness and picking up litter or package waste. Small actions may have a large impact on the general wellbeing and culture in the workplace. Everybody can contribute to the wellbeing of the employees and customers. Retail management should also lead by example, thus raising the appreciation for in-store work. Wegmans is known for top management participation in daily operations at stores. Top management representatives visit stores weekly to keep up to date with employee and customer needs. A similar model where management continually understands the challenges faced at stores can also be recommended for other retailers, regardless of the concept.

Centralized store operations

Traditionally, several store operations from sourcing to the ordering of products have been done at stores. However, at a modern store, more and more operations can be performed centrally. This may lead to significant efficiency advantages as well as improvements in the quality of operations. Examples of centralized store operations include demand forecasting, sourcing, pricing and value-added logistics.

Demand forecasting and product ordering can be executed centrally, supported by automatic replenishment programmes. At store level, sufficiently frequent inventory counting is needed, and product flows can be optimized centrally by using statistical forecasting algorithms and information on factors affecting future demand. No manual work is necessary at store level, and ordering is much less labour intensive than in a decentralized operating model. The same is true for sourcing, which often is at least regionally or fully centralized. As item quantities have risen, store-level space management and category management would be too challenging a task for store employees, and training in advanced tools too expensive.

Often, retail pricing can also be managed centrally. Many retailers have identical prices at all stores, but some large retailers, even Wal-Mart, empower store employees with significant freedom to price products in accordance with local demand and competition. A certain degree of flexibility enables adaptation to the local competitive situation and clearly can improve margins, but at the same time it takes resources and may have an impact on how much consumers trust the retailer if they visit several stores of the same chain. However, retailers with at least some regional or store-level pricing flexibility are typically more aware of the local competitive situation, and this can have other positive effects like entrepreneurial spirit in the company culture.

One of the recent trends is mass customization of prices based on the competitive situation and the structure of the local customer base, using the retailer's shopper data. The local pricing can be optimized centrally with support of new dynamic pricing solutions. Some advanced retailers in this area have even learned to identify regional price elasticities for single products. Price optimization is one of the most challenging but also the most useful areas of scientific retailing as even small changes may have a huge impact on total retail profitability. This area is likely to develop fast during the coming years.

Centralized value-added logistics services can be used to get products to stores in as sellable a condition as possible, by increasing the degree of processing and decreasing the work left to be done at the store. Performing the tasks centrally often brings significant economies of scale. Value-added services are often based on the postponement principle. In other words, products are stored 'half-made' and finalized when the final customer's needs are specifically identified. A good example is Dell, which assembles computers according to customer order. Value-added logistics services related to products and displays are often implemented during the storage phase and warehouses are, indeed, becoming 'factories' – all-purpose service centres. Examples of value-added services performed in warehouses are attaching price tags, labels or alarm tags to products; adding local instructions to packages; small-scale assembly of products; pre-installing software in computers; assembling display stands and other campaign material for stores; and storing bananas that are not yet ripe.

Particularly in clothing retailing, value-added services are widely used, for example in preparing products for sale. This is especially necessary as garments are often imported from the Far East folded and packed in a small space to minimize costs. For the items to look attractive in a store, folds and wrinkles need to be ironed or steamed away and the clothing hung on hangers for transport. Steam mannequins and tunnels help do the work efficiently. Other value-added services in the clothing industry include stain removal, label fixing and repair sewing. Garment dyeing by Benetton is another example. These kinds of services can be implemented by the retailer itself or provided by an external logistics operator.

Chain-level execution

Chain-wide implementation of plans and new operational models at store level is a key challenge in retailing. Centrally planned changes need to be implemented in every store and consume a lot of valuable personnel resources. The efficiency of executing new approaches is of vital importance to a retailer's transformation ability and therefore long-term success.

Store-level execution involves several challenges. The implementation of new operational practices is surprisingly often left to the store alone, without sufficient supporting resources or guidelines. Therefore, many development projects have been implemented only halfway. The measurement of the development project outcomes may have been neglected. As there are no verified results, the project might not be allocated the necessary resources, leading again to insufficient implementation. Many improvement projects have not been realistic in estimating the implementation time in stores, which also affect the quality and time line of the implementation. Because there are a lot of development projects and limited resources in stores, it is vital for retailers to be able to prioritize projects carried out at stores.

There are many ways and tools to support implementation and communication of the chain and stores. Planograms, campaign guidelines and other written material are part of the retailer's normal communication with its stores. With developments in electronic communication, an increasing share of guidelines has shifted to intranets or is sent to stores via e-mail. This is remarkably faster and more cost-efficient than conventional ways of communication. Execution can also rest on regional organizations or separate execution resources, such as experts on a particular product area or display.

One retailer studied the items mailed and e-mailed from the chain and commercial units to the stores. The results showed that reading all the material that arrived during one week would have taken almost half of the working time of the store manager. One can only imagine the extent to which instructions sent were implemented at stores. It is also important to note that not everything needs to be communicated to everybody. It is far too easy to send an e-mail message to a large mailing list 'just in case', and it is an unfortunate fact that the amount of unnecessary information has increased at many companies. These observations underline the need for a clear coordination model for store communication. All significant changes should also be carefully planned from the stores' point of view, workloads estimated in advance, and recorded in a workforce management solution.

Retailers can check their internal store-level communication with a few easy metrics such as: time per day spent on total communications (paper mail, voice mail, telephone calls, e-mail), hits on the intranet site, number of e-mails stores receive per week and the percentage of e-mails not opened. In best practice companies, head office communication to stores arrives during certain times of the week, when it can be easily linked to store staff meetings.

However, as stores are open for long hours and most people cannot be taken away from the customer frontline, retailers do not hold a lot of internal meetings in the stores. Instead, small meeting like 'huddles' with three to eight people are relatively easy to arrange on the shop floor for short briefings. Beside head office messages discussion may concern, for example, immediate issues, customer service feedback, or upcoming activities and promotions. According to our experience, the retail chain units still have a lot of untapped development potential with the briefing materials to make them more suitable and simple enough to be used in meetings on the shop floor.

In efficient chain operations, communication has been divided into clear priority groups for communicating necessary things efficiently but without disturbing the store operations too much. Store routines may include the receipt of new tasks via e-mail on a few mornings per week. One e-mail message to be printed may contain a long list of changes instead of dozens of separate e-mail messages. It is necessary to print to-do lists at stores as it is often the most convenient way of working between shelves. This operating model requires that the retailer has defined a clear role and responsibility for implementation in chain management. The role works as a funnel for store-level implementations and also handles prioritization as needed. In fact, this is one of the key management roles in retailing, but is often not regarded as such because of its operational nature.

Tasks set by the chain unit need to be integrated with store workforce management. In retail, the workforce is one of the main controllable variable costs. This is why optimal workforce allocation is a focal part of cost-efficient operations. Successful workforce management also affects employee satisfaction. New solutions enable efficient workforce management, taking into account factors such as demand per store and hour, transportation rhythms, employee wishes and working in a multi-store environment. These solutions will be discussed in more detail in Chapter 6.

It is increasingly common in chain-level execution to rely on collaborative piloting with stores. A project group involving the chain and pilot stores tests new ideas in practice and measures the results. Store employees participate actively through their own work and give feedback for the piloted actions and implementation material. In collaborative piloting the concept or approach might possibly be just a rough version when the pilot starts. Through experimentation it is developed into a viable model for wide-scale implementation. During testing, some ideas will fail and will not be implemented, but the successful experiments provide a good basis for execution in other stores. A real piloting environment and the comments of store employees usually guarantee a practical approach for the implementation and training materials for other stores.

Generally, the work of central chain units will increasingly shift to implementing plans at stores. At the same time, improvement projects will be more clearly prioritized and scheduled with understanding of stores' execution capability. It is also natural that the retail execution units will grow in relation to other central functions, to ensure the continual renewal and development of the concept. The tools for change execution will become more varied, more illustrative and advanced to support store level work. Suppliers may also have a significant role in developing store-level operations in their own product categories.

One possibility is to shift retail commercial category management organizations beside a real store where assortment managers themselves could practise all implementations and if needed monitor customer behaviour at the store with their own eyes on a daily basis. This would add content and real experiences to the planning of assortments and various activities. Many retailers use separate pilot stores or display rooms where product displays and store fixture solutions can be tested before spreading them to the whole chain. Some tasks related to assortment or space management planning can also be delegated to field personnel, thus ensuring the practical perspective in decision making.

In the best chains, all store-level changes have been recorded in a clear action plan, which enables store-level evaluation of the resource needs. Special resources travelling from store to store can be scheduled efficiently months in advance, and the stores will also be aware of future changes in good time. Key changes can be scheduled to take place during quiet periods to cause minimal disturbance for customers. For example, Inditex Group has reported a 42 per cent decrease in start-up costs by adjusting the calendar of openings and refurbishing activities. A suitable timing for operations may bring huge savings.

Best practice retailers have designed systematic 'pulses' for introducing new approaches to stores. There may be, for example, three or four pulses per year, and they are scheduled outside high sales seasons. Store employees know that procedures will change during these periods, but what will change varies every time. It may be a new subconcept, introduction of a new order system, customer service training or developing operations in line with the retailer's new strategy. Retailers need to create a systematic culture of continual development, an approach known to all store employees, to ensure capability to renew the concept and operational practices efficiently.

Store refurbishment

Setting up a new store and undertaking refurbishments are situations where a retailer temporarily needs a significant amount of resources in one sales location. If several stores are to be opened at the same time, a retailer may have to rely on external resources. To ensure flexibility, many retailers have outsourced some functions related to the setting up of stores. In many markets, new store buildings are rare as most retail sites have already been reserved. However, stores sometimes change owners and store concepts are refreshed at certain intervals, requiring changes in stores. Changes may be smaller, such as refreshing individual departments and implementing new subconcepts. These may be used to prolong the lifetime of old retail formats and properties without major refurbishments. In these cases, there is usually no need to close a store during the renovation. Major refreshes, in contrast, may require the closing of the whole store or at least may cause considerable disturbance to customers and daily in-store processes.

The time spent is critical if the store is closed during the refurbishment as the lost sales and shrink may be considerable. Therefore, over-resourcing and step-by-step actions are opportunities used whenever possible. Customer communication is also important, as store refurbishments may influence the attitudes and behaviour of customers both during and after the changes. A refurbishment may be given a positive flavour by telling customers about the improvements as well as their impact on the shopping experience. On the other hand, poor communication or lack of communication may easily lead to a situation where customers consider it an unnecessary impediment and do their shopping elsewhere. At worst, they can be totally lost to the competition as a new routine of visiting other stores develops during the refurbishment.

Store refurbishment is often one of the core competences of the retailer, closely related to such things as shopping path management. Particularly in fashion retailing and many other speciality retail formats, refurbishing is very important, as the store might be the only marketing media of the chain. Surprisingly often, however, many activities related to refurbishment and store buildings are outsourced. Certain functions such as planning and concept development should always be kept under the retailer's control. With the exception of emerging markets, refurbishments are most often carried out in existing properties that vary in size, structure and layout. Adapting the concept requires solid competences and a holistic understanding of the retailing format and its adaptability. Capable project managers for refurbishments and new store openings are one of the scarcest resources in retailing. Macro-level category management competence is also needed in this phase to be able to plan and schedule the changes on category level.

Actual refurbishments often demand special competences such as wiring, decoration and model building. Many retailers use specialized store set up teams to ensure quality. These teams move from place to place, which incurs travel costs, but the approach is often still feasible as the team typically quickly gathers a significant competence that can be leveraged across units. Some of the team experts might specialize in certain product categories such as fruit and vegetables. These experts may also be used for training store employees. However, this will change the competences required from the team.

Internal changes in the store are often related to the change of fixtures. It is often not justified to change fixtures one by one, with the exception of broken ones. It is also not necessarily worthwhile to implement small changes at once; instead many retailers wait until critical mass is reached and a sufficiently large number of fixtures can be changed at the same time. Fixture change is a major investment and continual renewal of fixtures may cost too much. Major fixture changes ensure fixture uniformity and large purchases enable the use of competitive bidding. On the other hand, old fixtures can make the store look outdated and reduce customer satisfaction, so a balance in fixture renewal needs to be found.

Special fixtures such as refrigeration equipment and various shop-in-shop fixtures are expensive, and often require special expertise in assembly or electrical installations. Continuity in fixture shape and size is important in terms of planogram implementation. Fixture formats cannot be changed annually; or if they are, procedures and planograms lag behind. Static fixture design is often a challenge for the impulsive marketing departments with a responsibility for the visual appearance and graphical guidelines of fixture solutions.

Refurbishment competence is also relevant to suppliers if they operate shop-in-shop solutions. Shop-in-shops are often used for cosmetics and apparel. The fixtures may be owned and maintained by the supplier. A major supplier may have tens of thousands of store fixtures in its ownership and control at stores all over the world. Their value on the balance sheet may rise to dozens or even hundreds of millions and it goes down fairly fast as the fixtures wear. Typical renewal time depends on category but most fixtures need to be totally renewed every two to four years. However, with good modular structure and changeable elements the lifespan of the concept can be increased significantly.

Continual maintenance of the fixtures may be troublesome, especially if there is a large number of fixtures and if they are located in different countries. As the support processes may require a lot of work, clear standards and self-service routines are important to ensure that a store can attend to maintenance tasks primarily on its own. Fixture storage functions and installation can be mostly outsourced, but the challenge often lies in the fact that not many installation companies operate as chains, especially across different markets. Therefore, they cannot offer a sufficient service level in every place where the retailer has fixtures. For this reason, many companies have hired set-up teams of their own. Another alternative is to take care of installations in a decentralized way with local players. Beside regional coordination, this requires good guidelines, simple structures and good control of the installation process to assure a uniform appearance. The efficiency and quality of execution are keys to success here too.

The best method for ongoing retail fixture service is to make the fixtures sufficiently simple, so that store employees can carry out the required service actions on their own. The cost of set-up teams generally forms the biggest part of the total fixture service costs, so if store employees can do part of the work themselves, cost savings can be gained. The retailer may include buying of spare parts in its normal ordering system, in which case the ordering processes are familiar to store employees. Simplicity and standard basic formats are keys for self-service success; it is difficult for store employees to find correct and suitable parts if there are thousands of variations available. Ongoing service of the property and fixtures extends the life of fixtures and postpones expensive refurbishments.

Interestingly, many retailers have different budgets for refurbishments and the maintenance of fixtures. Unfortunately, this has in several cases led to a situation where new fixtures are purchased during refurbishments, sometimes without thinking through the investment needed, whereas property and fixture maintenance might be handled on an extremely tight budget as these costs directly translate to the bottom line of an individual store. To find a proper balance, retailers need clear rules and guidelines in terms of both fixture renewals and service activities. The same naturally also applies to suppliers who use shop-in-shop concepts and need to give these guidelines to retailers or conclude a service-level agreement for fixture maintenance.

Facility management services have been outsourced in many industries and, as far as basic property services are concerned, this is a possible route for retailing as well. At the same time, it is worthwhile observing that in matters related to fixtures and the retail format the retailer is its own 'facility manager', and purchasing and maintaining fixtures is one of the retailer's core processes.

Supplier role in store operations

During the past decade, the role of suppliers in store-level functions has changed considerably. Most retailers, especially value-retailing companies, no longer meet supplier representatives in stores as all assortment decisions are made centrally and shelving is more efficient when carried out by the store. In stores where suppliers are still welcome, their role has changed considerably from conventional sales representative work. Orders are no longer taken, and suppliers are rarely allowed to handle products at stores. Long gone are the days when suppliers moved competitive products away to get space for their own products. Sales representatives have become local experts on category management. Besides product training, they can provide consultancy to store managers or other store-level staff in category management and store operations development relating to a category. The trend of diminishing field organizations might change in the future, as local assortments and different local events gain more share in customer experience development.

On the other hand, in product categories requiring good expertise the role of sales representatives has been and will be important. This applies to many DIY categories, for example, and domestic appliances. In some cases a retailer may even outsource a certain department to a supplier. With pick 'n' mix confectionery, for example, a supplier may have a role in product ordering, shelving and sometimes also in product-level assortment design within the agreed spatial and pricing framework. Service counters such as local meat, fish, restaurant or bakery departments may be outsourced, with the supplier bearing the total responsibility. These are often areas that do not belong to the retailer's core competences, or cannot be handled relying on the basic store processes. Moreover, it is typical in cosmetics for suppliers to pay partly or wholly the salary of a demonstrator or salesperson who displays products. Similar practices are used in department stores in clothing shop-in-shop departments where brand manufacturers may compensate part of a salesperson's pay.

However, store-level operations are often expensive. Not even the best manufacturer representatives can visit several stores a day since moving between stores takes time. If a representative can make, say, 500 store visits per year and the real costs incurred, with pay and travel costs included, are divided per visit, an individual visit may become relatively expensive. A supplier needs to consider these costs in relation to the benefits achieved; in other words, a clear business case for store-level operations is needed. Because of the high costs of sales representatives, many retailers have prohibited supplier participation in store-level operations, with the exception of special cases, and have demanded that suppliers shift the costs previously caused by representatives as discounts to product prices. In some cases, organization of whole field sales and store-level activation has gradually been dropped.

In emerging markets, however, the conventional sales representative still has an important role. Employee costs there are relatively low, chain operations are just beginning and stores are in need of product training. Also, ordering systems are often not near the level in Western countries, and to ensure sufficient availability and product coverage, a supplier may need to implement continual sales promotion activities. In these markets, efficient field operation management and sales force automation solutions are integral parts of a supplier's field sales organization.

The organizing of local events is becoming increasingly important as it is a good way of creating variety and a sense of adventure in a store. Events also offer an opportunity to demonstrate new products. The role of suppliers in the field may well be focused towards the organization of various events. Demonstration activities can be given an extra touch with famous chefs or experts. Suppliers may have a group of touring 'performers' who can be used at various promotional events, but also at other occasions held outside stores such as fairs or sports events. Typically, DIY stores organize customer events, attended by top experts of suppliers who offer advice on how to use the products or install them. These events can be organized by a store, but most often they are chain-wide agreements designed to require as little extra effort on the part of store employees as possible. Good examples of chain-wide customer events include cooking courses arranged by Williams-Sonoma for its customers. The courses are modified regularly, thus giving something new to long-established customers as well.

The more suppliers integrate into retail operations, the more store operations capabilities are needed. Shop-in-shop solutions, for instance, require significant competences in fixture design and maintenance, installation support, store-level employee training and several other areas.

Concept stores make an extreme case, as manufacturers become retailers selling products straight to the end customers and, hence, need to take care of all store operations themselves.

It is also vital for suppliers to be integrated with retailers' store operations development practice, supporting the training of store employees centrally. This usually leads to a good input–output ratio because an individual action may reach a large number of people. A natural way of developing central guidelines is to participate in the writing of retail manuals and other instructions. Suppliers may exert a significant role in developing the retail concept in their own category, and can prepare not only planograms and layout drawings, but also operating procedures for stores. It is a good goal for a supplier to be considered a pioneer in its own area. If the supplier succeeds in this, the retailer may automatically ask for the supplier's involvement when considering new solutions, knowing that the supplier's competence brings significant added value. Additionally, suppliers may offer to participate in retailers' competence building, for instance training for new employees, experienced employees or store managers. It is also typical that suppliers provide the product information materials used in the retailer's intranet solutions, where store employees can seek more precise data as needed. With good retailer–supplier collaboration, the efficiency and quality of store execution can be improved considerably.

In our experience suppliers have significant unused potential in store operations. In many cases, suppliers mostly contact retailers through the category management and commercial organization. The people setting up stores, and working on store-level execution, concept development, marketing and training are seldom in direct communication with suppliers. However, the most integrated suppliers, acting often as strategic partners to retailers, are strongly incorporated into chain operations at many organizational levels. Plans are made together, and both play clear roles in the setting up of stores and executing procedures, with necessary resourcing included.

Summary

Store-level efficiency largely determines the competitiveness of retailers, and staying at a certain level is a prerequisite for staying in business. There are many retailers that succeed fairly well with an average strategy but good execution. A good strategy combined with poor execution seldom leads to any significant results, and the retailer's business will quickly fade away. Retailing is a business with large volumes where the retail format strategy and processes need to be executed efficiently by thousands, or even hundreds of thousands, of people. The efficiency of training to the masses where a large number of people have received a low-level education is a true challenge to any retailer. As in any good implementation, simple is beautiful.

Store-level execution also defines the retailer's transformation ability, that is, the cost efficiency of a retailer in executing new ideas and concepts. This is a natural prerequisite for innovative operations. Superb display solutions and planograms are of little use if they cannot be efficiently implemented in terms of time and cost. The continual development and transformation of the retail concept is a core process, which needs efficient set-up and maintenance operations to support it. These functions can be implemented with a retailer's own resources or through a competent partner network – however, in the retailer's firm control.

Store management models will differ largely from each other in the future, and will be key differentiators for retailers. How many people want to work as robots bound by strict processes year in and year out? How can a retailer ensure a good work environment, where employees have the energy and incentive to give customers a genuine smile as part of good service? The well-being of employees is largely dependent on the management and leadership model used by the company and on the self-development opportunities provided for the staff. These factors also have a large impact on a retailer's attractiveness as an employer. Retailers compete not only for customers but also for the best workforce.

6 Information technology trends in the retail value chain

Transparency of information in the value chain is a fundamental element in efficient retail operations. Information sharing and joint processes require new solutions that enable automating and streamlining many activities in the value chain. One of the key areas is to reduce manual work at store level, which is one of the biggest cost drivers in retailing. Information gathered from point of sale (POS) and shoppers enables truly fact-based management, and the most successful retailers have developed many ways to use it, from assortment planning to measuring marketing efficiency. Information management has become a core competency in retailing.

During the past decade, many retailers have focused their ICT development on improving infrastructure, and the main focus has been on enterprise resource planning (ERP) solutions supporting wholesale and centralized chain operations. Supply chain management solutions have developed fast, and many retail groups actively use, for instance, store-level automatic ordering. In addition, manufacturers and retail sourcing companies have adopted vendor managed inventory (VMI) or co-managed inventory (CMI) solutions for joint inventory management. Most information technology (IT) development projects have, however, still taken place within companies, but the focus is slowly shifting to solutions serving the entire value chain.

This chapter looks at the key IT trends development in the retail value chain, including their major impacts. The chapter is divided into three parts. The first part focuses on trends affecting IT development in general, such as outsourcing. The second part explores key technological developments in both chain- and store-level operations. To end the chapter, the framework for fact-based management with shopper information and its key components are introduced.

Main trends

The following sections include a selection of the primary technological trends affecting IT development within retailing. Subjects discussed include, among others, how the India phenomenon and the internationalization of retailing impact the development. Key trends in the area of identification standards are also examined.

Offshoring and purchasing IT as a service

Offshoring is one of the main IT trends currently both in general and among those businesses affecting retailing. During the past few years, the growth of IT services in India has been tremendous. Global giants like IBM, Accenture and Capgemini have raced to enlarge their businesses in India, and in many system integration projects, over 50 per cent of full-time equivalents (FTEs) come from India or some other offshoring country. At the same time, new competition has been provided through fast-growing Indian 'pure' players, such as Tata, Infosys, Wipro and Satyam.

Offshoring has traditionally focused mainly on cost efficiency. The price level in India has been significantly lower than elsewhere, and there is good availability of talented people with technological education. Offshoring usually involves purchasing capacity, testing resources, configuration work of package implementation and system integration work. On the other hand, small markets can turn to India to purchase competences for new systems for which there would not otherwise be expertise available. This will extend the service offering of international system integrators on a local level significantly, also to customers such as retailers. In systems integration, the focus of offshoring has been on package solutions like SAP and Oracle, where the services are easier to standardize and industrialize than custom-designed application management services. Efficient offshoring requires well-standardized processes and procedures that enable seamlessly integrated teams working in multi-sites with different time zones and cultures. The clear description of procedures and processes required for the offshoring and shared services actions also enhance the internationalization of retailing.

The US market has clearly taken the lead in offshore operations development, but Europe is following suit, with the UK and the Netherlands leading the way. In the United States and the UK, one important enabler for offshoring has been the English language, which has facilitated development. In other markets, language may become an issue, as finding suitable people who speak languages other than English may be difficult in offshoring countries. Because of the offshore language issue, many companies have founded so-called near-shore or regional centres. It is more convenient to serve the customer base close to the home market in the same time zone and often in own languages. In Europe, Poland and many other Eastern European countries are important nearshore centres, and in the United States, Canada is often used. South America includes many Spanish and Portuguese-speaking centres and the French-speaking markets can be served efficiently from Northern Africa, for example Morocco. Originally inexpensive for offshoring, India has already started to become too expensive. First, work was shifted to new locations within India, such as Bangalore. Nowadays, work is moving to China, the Philippines and other countries where costs are still low.

In addition to IT services, business process outsourcing (BPO) is also a growing area in retailing. Many companies outsource non-core support processes, such as certain financial processes, payroll accounting and HR processes. For international suppliers, this is natural as they are already used to centralizing support functions when single country operations are relatively small. At the same time, support functions can be outsourced if desired. For example, Unilever outsourced its 600-person Indian support unit to Capgemini in 2006.

Another area of offshoring is product development and testing. For example, Sainsbury's has a sourcing centre specializing in private labels (own labels) in Krakow, Poland. Its tasks comprise searching and evaluating potential suppliers, assessing product quality, ensuring delivery times and controlling the meeting of technical and quality standards in the production process. The Krakow Sourcing Office is also involved with the brand management of Sainsbury's own label products. Locating the centre in Poland offers several benefits. The pay level is significantly lower than in the UK, which yields cost benefits. In addition, with many potential private label suppliers located in Eastern Europe, distances to potential collaboration partners remain short.

Retailing is relatively local by nature and needs more on-shore services than many other industries. On the other hand, it is also a low-margin industry where even small cost savings may have a significant impact on profitability. Retailing comprises many processes where activities such as information processing or analysis can in the future be handled to some extent offshore. These include, among others:

- demand forecasting;
- local assortment planning or automation (mass customization) into a standard proposal, which can be further amended locally;
- shopper data analysis (eg segmentation and predictive modelling);
- pricing follow-up and optimization models to support pricing decision making;
- data cleansing and maintenance.

For a store manager it does not make a difference whether a demand forecast or planogram comes from the chain's HQ or from remote markets, as long as it works. However, efficient offshoring requires disciplined definition of business requirements and constant collaboration. The mainstream of retail offshoring will still be in the non-core processes, related mainly to financial services and shared service centres, for example for HR.

IT expertise can also be regarded as a core competency in retailing. Hence, many retailers are not willing to outsource IT operations. For instance, Wal-Mart has in-house IT services, with good control over them. Another example is Tesco, which is one of the few major retailers with its own service centre in India. Tesco founded Hindustan Service Center (HSC) in 2004 as it wished to get cost savings in support functions, but was not keen to outsource business processes and solution development. The service centre has grown rapidly, today employing about 2,000 people, of which half work in IT and the other half in business services. HSC supports Tesco's current technologies, develops and implements new ones and offers IT services. The business service unit concentrates on supporting the finance and accounting functions, customer service and in-store help desk services. HSC also offers support services for Tesco's Clubcard and designs customer loyalty programmes for non-UK markets. Outsourcing has also led to countermoves like insourcing. For example, Sainsbury's migrated IT services back from Accenture, to whom it outsourced them in 2000.

International IT operations

Growing consolidation and globalization in retailing have had a significant impact on IT development. In today's retailing world, uniform IT is an important enabler for gaining synergy benefits. Shared master data management, data warehouses and processes, in addition to common sourcing applications, are major enablers for joint purchases. Likewise, the integration of logistics systems may bring benefits through network optimization. Other substantial benefits include lower application licence fees, as the number of users goes up.

In practice, IT often has an important catalyst role in business transformation, especially in mergers and acquisitions. It seldom leads the integration project following an acquisition, but defines the key post-merger milestones, even though this is not often openly stated. Marketing and knowledge of local markets are important, and from the perspective of synergy benefits, certainly also one of the last items to be integrated. IT harmonization slowly leads to harmonization of most support processes. The development becomes significantly easier if similar standard package solutions have been used in different markets.

Internationalization strategies define to some extent the requirements for different IT management competences. 'Copiers', or those duplicating their own standardized concept, such as Lidl and IKEA, can also largely replicate their solutions from one market to another. When a new market is entered, knowledge can be brought from other nearby markets. This usually means not only common IT systems, but also uniform processes and procedures. 'Acquirers' need strong knowledge of IT integration. Retailers that have carried out a lot of acquisitions have a pick 'n mix collection of systems from different chains, countries and periods. In order to gain synergy benefits, a strong systems transformation needs to be implemented after the acquisition. To be successful, IT management of an acquirer needs different knowledge and resources from that of a copier. However, in real life the situation is not as black and white, and might vary a lot by company.

Greenfield operations in new markets usually work in the same way as they do at copiers. Rarely does anyone reinvent the wheel when entering new markets. On the other hand, in emerging markets local systems support, or rather the lack of it, may have an impact on the choice of systems. Even though master data management, sourcing systems and other key solutions might be the same, often, for instance, POS systems might vary between markets. Sometimes acquisitions primarily focus on retail sites, and in these cases IT is usually replaced in predefined phases together with the concept renewal of the retail sites.

Operating in many countries and often also with variety of system environments presents major challenges for IT governance. The challenge is to work efficiently in a multicultural environment, accompanied by very different chains and IT requirements. In many regions, retailing has been relatively local, and language is another issue challenging successful collaboration. Many companies still have most process and IT documentation in local languages. Changing a language may be a greater cultural challenge than changing systems. Moreover, operating in different time zones together with cultural differences adds an interesting flavour to efficient collaboration. In extreme cases a new ERP project is used as a way to harmonize business processes after a merger or acquisition. This is a long and expensive route, but yields long-term benefits with synergies, achieving joint processes and commitment in participating countries.

IT service vendors are often required to offer support to retailers and manufacturers in several countries, or even globally. More and more, this development eliminates small local IT players, leaving the large players gaining market share. At the same time, especially Indian pure players buy these smaller companies for local front office services to handle customer interface, as well as to gain a new customer base for operations. Many companies are also acquired because of their perceived thought leadership position to strengthen the industry competences of the pure player. Consolidation also takes place among system integrators and service vendors.

In multinational companies, many IT services can be delivered from abroad. If a particular service is not available locally, the retail management often does not care whether the service comes from a neighbouring country or from farther away. The internationalization of retail promotes the harmonization of processes and IT. Furthermore, it enables more efficient implementation and outsourcing to offshore countries. A growing trend in this area is to have shared service centres, yielding cost advantages from service concentration. A centralized and efficient international shared service centre may also be a key enabler for the rapid internationalization of a company.

Development of identification standards

A significant number of consumer products companies and a growing number of retailers are international. The same products are produced for many different markets, and differing labelling and standards may result in additional costs. Challenges with data quality cause expensive mistakes in billing and the same applies for inter-company data synchronization standards, where practices have varied widely around the world. Developing uniform product and data sharing standards has always been a core area in development of efficient customer response. Synchronizing, for instance, product, price and location information may lead to significant cost advantages throughout the supply chain.

Product identification standards

Barcodes enable the unambiguous identification of a product, and thereby efficient control of the flow of goods in the various phases of the supply chain. The barcode system generally used in Europe has been EAN (European Article Number), and in the United States a corresponding code has been UPC (Universal Product Code). European and US businesses have merged their standardization organizations into GS1, and the new standard for product identification is a Global Trade Item Number (GTIN). This collaboration will significantly facilitate the international standardization of product codes.

The EAN-13 barcode is mostly used on individual product packages in Europe. As the name implies, it consists of 13 digits. The first two digits identify the country of origin (packaging country), the next four denote the manufacturing company, and the next six designate each product. The last digit is for validity check. An EAN-13 code is usually enough for identifying the product and price at the POS, but might not contain enough information for all logistical processes. For this reason, a more comprehensive GS1-128 code is also used for ordering and identifying transport units and pallets.

To be able to track individual shipping units throughout the supply chain, a special serial shipping container code (SSCC) based on GS1-128 standard has been introduced. With it, each pallet can be identified and the data collected into systems in all key phases of the supply chain. The SSCC code can be used with an electronic delivery note: the supplier sends the bill of lading information in advance in electronic format to the recipient, who at reception reads the SSCC code with, for example, a handheld terminal and gets the bill of lading information on the screen. This makes it possible automatically to acknowledge receipt of the shipment and enter the goods into the store stock figures.

In many cases where barcodes are used, no separate price markings are made on products. Instead, product price is indicated on the shelf edge labels, which also help customers and in-store employees to find the product location on the shelf. There are several exceptions in special goods, where price tags need to be attached either manually or preprinted by the manufacturer. In fashion retailing, for example, prices are often marked on product labels.

In some categories, it is necessary to be able to track an individual product down to the originating source. This applies particularly to perishables, where the retailer needs to know the producer farm. Avian influenza and gene-manipulated products, among others, have made consumers and authorities increasingly concerned about product safety and origin of groceries. This leads to new requirements in the development of product identification, and may accelerate the use of new standards.

Radio frequency identification (RFID) is expected to be the next technology that will revolutionize logistics and perhaps replace the barcode. An

RFID system consists of a transceiver equipped with an antenna, a tag and a reader acting as an intermediary between the identification and the background system. Electronic product code (EPC) is the key standard for RFID in retailing, driven by EPCglobal, which works in close collaboration with GS1. RFID is not exactly a new invention, and similar tags have been used for a long time, for example for marking cattle and pets. Antitheft alarms used in stores operating on radio frequency are also related to RFIDs. However, it has not been until the last few years that plans for an identification system encompassing the entire supply chain have emerged. Tags make it possible to identify each logistics unit or even each individual product, and track their way through the supply chain.

RFID tags may come in different shapes and sizes, and they are divided into two groups: active and passive. Active tags can usually be complemented with new information as they proceed in the supply chain, whereas passive tags are basically for one-time use and only send data originally stored in them. RFID offers numerous advantages over traditional identification methods, including:

- A large number of items can be read simultaneously.
- Data is read automatically without manual processing.
- The devices are always on and ready to read.
- Code reading does not require a visual line of sight, so it can take place even through the side of a truck without unloading.
- Tags may contain a large amount of information.

In spite of the benefits, RFID tags have not yet made a complete breakthrough, as there are also many obstacles to using them. Perhaps the main challenge is the price of reading devices, which can cost hundreds of euros per device. Full-scale adoption of RFID tags requires reading devices at each point in the supply chain, from the supplier to stores. This translates into a substantial investment. The price of tags has dropped significantly during the last few years, down to fractions of a euro depending on tag type. Still, everything over a few parts of a euro, pennies or cents in product marking costs can be considered expensive, compared with current EAN/UPC codes.

Another obstacle has been the lack of one global standard for the RFID technology. Instead, many different frequencies have been used, which again requires the acquisition of reading systems that identify many frequencies and are therefore more expensive. Only recently has an agreement been reached about the worldwide introduction of a common UHF frequency range and EPC product identification.

With the openness and transparency of the value chain, RFID enables significant benefits in the form of smaller shrinkage, especially during shipping and inventory handling – missing units can be identified easily and rapidly, and corrective action can be taken immediately. This may have a striking preventive impact on the number of products stolen by employees or suppliers, for example. In addition to logistics applications, RFID tags can also be used for several other applications. For instance, a loyalty card including an RFID tag enables many new applications, such as non-contact payment. Similar processes can also be implemented using other remote reading technologies, or fingerprint identification for that matter, but RFID has received more media time and attention than other technologies.

Some of the world's biggest retailers, including Wal-Mart, Tesco and Metro, have actively started to promote the adoption of RFID technology. Other active parties include the automotive industry, health care services and the US Department of Defense. Wal-Mart tried to commit its biggest suppliers to implement RFID technology for identification of shipping units as early as the beginning of 2005, but it had to compromise on the goal, as most suppliers did not have the necessary capabilities to adopt the technology. Also, not all were convinced of the benefits. However, in speciality stores there are already some successful examples of RFID implementation. For example, the Dutch book retailer Selexyz has implemented item-level RFID tagging for all products in pilot stores. The company has achieved better inventory control and is able to operate the stores with a smaller staff. With special customer orders, an automatic e-mail alert about book availability for pick up is sent to customers, as the products arrive at the store and cartons are passed through an RFID scan tunnel.

The use of RFID will most likely start to spread little by little. The first tagged items have been shipping tools, such as cartons and pallets. Furthermore, RFID tags will certainly be widely used for tracking valuable and courier consignments. However, it is still worth noting that many benefits promised by RFID in the delivery tracking could be attained with the EAN-128 code if it were used more widely.

The near field communication (NFC) standard related to RFID reading is less publicized but nevertheless is an important and rising standard, and it is already well established in the Asia Pacific area, with high penetration in mobile phones. It enables reading RFID tags through mobile phones as more and more terminal devices support this standard in addition to Bluetooth. This means that new information on products concerning, for example, allergies or other important matters, can be sent to the consumer's mobile phone, for instance when there is no room to print them on a shelf edge label or product package. Store employees can also be provided with handy terminal devices using this reading technology.

Albert Heijn and Capgemini are working together to add value and convenience for customers during their shopping experience using NFC. Currently, a pilot using the mobile phone as a self-scanning device is running in an Albert Heijn store in Amsterdam. The mobile phones are equipped with NFC, enabling the phones to read RFID tags embedded in shelf labels and wirelessly exchange the shopping list information with a dedicated point of sale to facilitate an express checkout. During the shopping trip, customers can monitor what they spend and save time by bypassing the queue at the checkout.

However, RFID tags are still relatively expensive compared with the price of most consumer products sold in retail, and a large-scale implementation at stock keeping unit (SKU) level would be expensive, both for retailers and manufacturers. In the near future, it is most likely that 2-D matrix symbology codes will be used instead for extending product information. The codes can be printed to packages with no additional costs, and consumers will receive the same benefits for additional product information with mobile phones as with RFID. Many mobile phones with camera are already embedded with 2-D symbology recognition, and this functionality will be available soon in most phones with camera.

In the future, mobile phones may include a personal trainer or weight-watching application that calculates the calories in the shopping basket and offers tips for choosing healthier products, such as products that contain less salt. Similarly, doctors may prescribe a certain diet for someone, who can use a mobile application warning of unsuitable products when shopping. Though these technologies are just visions of things to come, they may have a significant impact on retail development. New players bring content and communication to the store, and this information is not directly under the retailer's control and development. Still, it may exert a heavy influence on the customer's buying decisions at the point of purchase. As an example, cheaper or healthier substitutes can be suggested to the customer. If these are not found in the retailer's assortments, it may even drive consumers to other stores. In addition to general service providers, major suppliers can develop similar services in their own categories and expertise areas.

There are several other key standards that are relevant for retailers and manufacturers such as global location number (GLN) that gives every store a unique identification. Also, increasing use of pictures, videos and other multimedia in stores will drive standard development.

It is clear that new standards and technologies may cause significant, even revolutionary process changes in store-level operations. The most important of these activities include reception of goods in the store, speeding POS activities, ordering or product inventory in automatic ordering, as well as offering additional information about products to customers. The speed of change is strongly dependent on tag prices, but also on consumer adaptation of the new information services available. Retailing is a low-margin business, and few players adopt new technologies just for the sake of pioneering. Hence, real business advantages must be proved before large-scale adoption of these new technologies will take place.

Data interchange standards

Standards used in data transfer have developed quickly during the past few years. Traditional EDIfact has been expected to be replaced by messages based on XML (extensible markup language), which is a significantly more flexible and adaptable message format, but it exists in many different versions and 'dialects'. In other words, every integration often must be built or at least tested separately. Consequently, XML is not a proper standard, but more a way of presenting data to be transferred. Moreover, most XML messages have been largely built on traditional electronic data interchange (EDI) messages without changing their content.

Compared with the EDIfact form, XML represents a more than tenfold increase in the amount of data to be transferred. This in itself is not a problem with current capacities, but it should be taken into account in EDI contracts as they are often based on the amount of data. XML does not necessarily bring any essentially new content to inter-company data exchange but it does increase data volume and thereby causes additional costs. Furthermore, a majority of big retail companies already have point-to-point EDI connections with their key suppliers. Changing standards would cause new system development costs, possibly with a very long payback period. This is one of the key reasons for the slower than expected growth in the use of XML messages.

On the other hand, XML is not the only inter-company data interchange format. Other message formats, such as RosettaNet built by electronics manufacturers, and BizTalk by Microsoft, have been developed for other purposes. It remains to be seen which of these will become common. In any case, message formats that are common to all companies are still a long way ahead.

Global data synchronization (GDS) is a key movement in FMCG to synchronize the key data flows. It includes synchronization of information, for instance for trade items, catalogue items, location information and product price. This development is facilitated by the emergence of global data pools, such as Sinfos, 1SYNC and WWRE (World Wide Retail Exchange). A number of retailers and manufacturers have joined these, and also national data pools are in place in many markets such as Sweden and Norway. However, the number of attributes defined in global standards are few, because several compromises and a lot of information still need to be leveraged point to point between manufacturer and retailer. This is one key reason for growth of national data pools that can adapt better to these requirements. In non-food retailing, master data management and global data synchronization are still in their early phases, and there is significant efficiency potential to be gained.

Generally, standards development in the FMCG industry is concentrated in the hands of GS1, which has established its place as a global standardization organization. The harmonization of codes in the United States and Europe was an important step towards global standardization. It secured a critical mass, and now the rest of the world is following suit.

To conclude, standards develop and give new opportunities for even radical business process redesign, but most business benefits could already be gained with current technologies and standards; it is just a matter of implementation. Standards are especially important to global suppliers who otherwise have to fight in a different code jungle in each country. On the other hand, more attention will be paid to product safety and the transparency of the value chain, which both promote the establishment of standards. Product tracing is still in its early phases, but the demand for it is growing fast. Consumers are increasingly interested in the origin of products, and more and more retailers offer this information to their customers. In addition, the insecurity in today's world with terrorist attacks and other threats requires retailers to react quickly if certain products were to get polluted, for example. In certain markets the use of standards and better product tracking can be accelerated through legislation. Product tracing will be one of the key drivers for systems integration and development throughout the value chain.

Key development areas of retail IT

Many new technological solutions impact retail operations, either at the retailer's head office or at store level. This section deals with selected retail IT development areas, such as ERP, workforce management and POS systems, covering their current trends in retailing.

Development of ERP systems

In the 2000s, ERP systems have been a focal and visible systems development area in retailing, as well as in many other industries. The goal of ERP systems is to control and automate processes, and they cover the whole range of areas from the handling of customer orders to delivery and billing. ERP solutions offer on-time visibility to several functional areas, which have been traditionally handled with separate systems, each developed for a certain purpose. However, sometimes internal systems are integrated instead. This is done because no corresponding system is available or when a certain degree of flexibility is needed in systems development. The internal integration of systems is called enterprise application integration (EAI). In addition to internal systems, also external (for example manufacturers') systems may be integrated through firewall solutions.

Many applications have been developed on top of ERP solutions to streamline their functionality. Advanced planning systems (APS) and decision support systems (DSS) are some names used for sophisticated planning systems. The application areas of these expert systems is often narrower than in full-scale ERP solutions, but they are also easier to adapt and quicker to adopt. These functionalities have been actively integrated into ERP solutions that are continually expanding their portfolio of applications organically and with acquisitions. Therefore, it has become common to talk about second generation ERP solutions, which refers to solutions for managing ever-wider areas within the value chain. The aim is to manage data and processes, and distributing information at the right time to all parties in the retail value chain.

The biggest and probably best-known ERP vendor is SAP, which has gained a remarkable market share, and has become a more or less de facto standard, especially in large companies. The biggest competitor mainly in the United States is Oracle, which acquired two large US vendors of ERP systems, PeopleSoft and JD Edwards. The Siebel and Retek acquisitions by Oracle was also important to the FMCG industry, which has a large number of both implementations in place. In addition to these, there is a myriad of other systems, designed for particular industries. Microsoft, the world's largest software vendor, has also diversified to this area by acquiring Axapta and Navision. Of ERP companies specializing in the retail industry, we should mention JDA and Aldata. JDA is based on optimization systems for both category management and inventory management, and is known for its merchandising solutions, and has often been implemented on top of SAP solutions. Aldata has specialized in retail solutions, and it has a strong background in developing POS and ERP systems (eg Aldata GOLD software).

The advantage provided by large ERP systems is their wide customer base and consequently fairly secure long-term support. The disadvantages may include a certain rigidity and cost of adapting them to suit the needs of individual companies. The costs of version upgrades are significant, if a lot of customization has to be migrated to the new version. In any case, companies often have to make a choice between system adaptability and scope. Some companies have selected a clear best-of-breed strategy using several applications instead of ERP packages, and some of them have been successful with this approach. However, this sets high requirements for IT management, and requires very good architectural and sourcing competences within the IT department.

The purchasing of new ERP systems accelerated considerably prior to the millennium and the feared 'Y2K bug'. Since then, the implementation rate of new systems has been steadier. Thanks to the robust implementations during the past few years, the core ERP solutions are in good shape in many retail companies. The next phase is to adopt optimization applications, and integrate the different ERP systems in the value chain. To keep the costs of integration down, the industry relies on standardization, both on a global and national level.

In particular, it is a big challenge for multinational manufacturers to integrate their systems with key retail collaboration partners. Though the consumer products industry as such is fairly international, and solutions in different countries have been consolidated, retailers are still very local. In the worst case, a supplier may need to integrate with more than a thousand retail ERP solutions. On the other hand, the basic information in a value chain is relatively simple, consisting mainly of product, order, demand forecast or billing information. This data can be standardized, resulting in significant benefits. This is one of the main reasons for the existence of the Global Commerce Initiative (GCI), where large retailers and global consumer goods manufacturers are well represented.

Vertically integrated retailers are often furthest along in the integrated management of operations. To give an example, the clothing industry has fully integrated supply chains where the same demand information is leveraged in each phase of the value chain from retailer to production and subcontractors. These companies implement solutions efficiently on the basis of the same information (for example, product master data, demand forecasting), whereas other players need to deal with several interfaces and additional IT integration with other members in the value chain.

Analytics applications are a more and more integrated part of ERP solutions, and continue to gain ground from separate best-of-breed applications. The value of business intelligence also grows considerably when it is automatically incorporated into daily operational processes. Key focus areas for optimization and analytical applications in the retail industry include the following:

- trade promotion management;
- pricing optimization (including dynamic pricing);
- space management and optimization;
- markdown management;
- demand forecasting;
- workforce management;
- store design and layout planning;
- transport optimization;
- data mining (segmentation, optimization, predictive modelling).

ERP vendors have strengthened these competences considerably through acquisitions. Khimetrics, famous for its pricing optimization application, was acquired by SAP, as was Triversity. In addition, the Business Objects acquisition significantly strengthened SAP's business intelligence competences and customer portfolio. JDA has also been active on the market. It strengthened its already considerable knowledge of category management by acquiring Intactics, which is particularly known for the space management solutions. In addition, the Manugistics acquisition gave JDA strong credibility in the field of delivery optimization and demand forecasting.

Besides the ERP vendors, the market for analytics and optimization applications is also pursued by data warehouse and business intelligence vendors like Teradata, Greenplum, Neoview and SAS Institute. A few years ago, SAS Institute acquired Market Max and gained a strong position and competence in retail space management. The acquisition of Intrinsic gave SAS the platform for campaign management that is integrated with the SAS Enterprise Marketing Automation solution. After the Hyperion acquisition by Oracle and Cognos by IBM, SAS Institute is one of the only large independent business intelligence providers left.

In the future, manufacturers' operations planning will increasingly rely on the actual sales data received from retailers. Key areas for new operational applications include demand forecasting and optimization, trade promotion management, category management, and field sales applications. Moreover, vendors frequently offer ERP together with a customer relationship management (CRM) solution, typically including not only a sales force automation package, but also functions related to customer service. The ERP customer master data and billing data create the basic foundation for implementing a CRM system.

Many ERP vendors have favoured the optimization and analytical applications by integrating them into a total solution package, where customers do not need to pay new direct licence fees for their adoption. This means that in most companies adoption may happen through a different decision-making routine from a normal system investment. When a company uses more of the functionality of the ERP solution, the number of users typically grows, and with it grows loyalty towards the solution. However, the cost of system integration and implementation naturally also remain in concurrent development, although these costs are not always budgeted similarly as in other system investments.

A current focal development trend is towards packaged industry-specific processes. Where the processes of ERP solutions and their adaptability were previously criticized, the same aspect may in the future become a new competitive advantage. Retailers may buy the desired processes as a fully fledged package, meaning lower implementation costs. The same cost savings also apply to future version upgrades. System integrators also support this trend with their operations. In particular, non-core retail processes like HR, finance and payroll management can be efficiently purchased as a service, delivered from low-cost offshoring countries, such as India and China.

Whatever the development is, the consolidation and expansion of ERP products seems to go on. At the same time, the corporate ERP market has become fairly cemented, and the focus of ERP vendors has shifted to further developing existing customers and implementing light mid-market versions for medium-sized companies. Application development for new areas, especially for the optimization layer, continues and will help ERP vendors to grow. Acquisitions will play a big role in future growth, and we are likely to see more of them in the future. For a retailer, architecture and sourcing skills will be vital to ensure cost-efficient IT operations.

Workforce management (WFM)

In retail, the workforce is one of the biggest variable cost factors. This is why optimal workforce allocation is a focal part of cost-efficient operations. Effective labour scheduling ensures that the use of the workforce matches the needs of customers and the store operations in the best possible way. WFM development is currently one of the hottest retail development areas. New IT solutions enable improved labour scheduling, taking into account factors such as demand per outlet and hour, shipping rhythms and operations in a multi-store environment.

Efficient labour scheduling leads to increased net sales and profitability at stores. This is because an increasing part of each employee's time is spent on serving customers. The aim of a workforce management (WFM) application is to optimize work shifts to ensure the required customer service level and sufficient resources for in-store operations. A centralized WFM application enables constant KPI benchmarking between different stores and supports resource allocation for different operations.

WFM solutions cover many in-store processes. Figure 6.1 illustrates the areas of a WFM application. A typical WFM application comprises forecasting, labour scheduling and tracking. Resourcing needs can be forecasted on the basis of the history data from the previous period. Items related to workforce needs include the customer flows in store, logistics and product replenishment schedule, training, assortment and campaign changes, and several other activities using store resources. In solutions representing best practice, workforce needs can be forecasted with an accuracy of 15 minutes. Systems could also optimize on a more detailed level if needed, but store management cannot in practice make any actions with more detailed information.

Total work hours needed for store operations comprise selling, customer service and many other areas, as discussed in Chapter 5. While an optimal balance of selling and service is an important target, there are other activities to be carried out. Daily tasks such as ordering and product replenishment must be reckoned in the time forecasts. Special cases, such as big campaigns, seasonal changes or staff training, also take a significant amount of time. Moreover, time must be allowed for unexpected situations and sorting out potential daily issues. A time usage analysis at different retail operations at a task level typically reveals both time challenges and

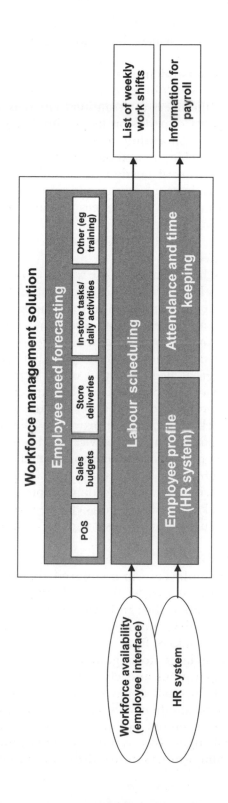

Figure 6.1 Key components and source information of a WFM solution

streamlining opportunities, which help to align the resources and operations.

Labour scheduling is dependent not only on workforce needs but also on workforce availability. Workforce competences need to be taken into consideration, as well as the necessary training to increase the competence level. Workforce availability depends on factors like the use of multi-store replenishment teams, the opportunity for employees to let the employer know when they are available, as well as the possibility of employees to work in more than one store if needed (in a multi-store environment). Preparing a labour schedule requires access to time budget data and local legislative rules and restrictions. Employees can also have access to the solution to enter their preferences and availability as the basis of labour scheduling. Based on the data, the WFM solution can create a suggestion of an optimal labour schedule.

A completed labour schedule needs to be tracked to ensure its functionality and effectiveness. A labour scheduling application tracks actual work hours and costs, and can issue an alarm in predefined situations, such as overtime accumulation or understaffing situations. An attendance and timekeeping solution provides input to payroll systems.

Labour scheduling usually brings benefits quickly in terms of checkout staffing but there is a great need for it in other departments, too. For example, customer service can benefit from labour scheduling that optimizes shifts by stores' customer flow and other department-specific parameters. The use of the workforce can be improved by eliminating non-value creating tasks and by maximizing the service level offered to customers. Operations improve when workforce needs can be met more precisely and resources are in the right place at the right time. Moreover, scheduling takes less time and the principles of scheduling become uniform and more visible for the staff. Workforce-related costs can be forecasted more accurately, and often some unnecessary costs can be eliminated during the process.

Effective labour scheduling is also beneficial to employees, as it leads to flexible planning, and employees can be offered chances to decide about their shifts. As an example, it is easier to grant holidays at times wanted, if employees may record their wishes and availability. Successful scheduling can also reduce overtime work, and prepare the company better for exceptional situations like outbreaks of flu.

In store-level planning, large stores gain most benefits from WFM, both for department-level operations and checkout work. But WFM can also yield significant benefits in small stores, especially if employees can move flexibly from one store to another within a specified area. Illnesses, holidays and other absences even out in large masses, and total optimization will balance many challenges. In a multi-store environment small stores may actually be the prime winners in workforce optimization.

Regardless of its benefits, labour scheduling is not always easy to implement. The solutions need to be integrated with, for instance, HR, POS and logistics solutions. The complexity of WFM solutions may also present challenges during the implementation. The solution requires training for tens or even hundreds of thousands of staff members, and retail employees typically have little time for studying new solutions. And as staff attrition is relatively high in retailing, this training needs to be continual. This means that ease of use is of vital importance to ensure successful implementation. In addition, resistance to change among employees and store managers may hinder implementation. Therefore, change management and training are an important part of the implementation of a WFM solution.

When considering a new WFM solution, it is good to remember that employment legislation varies considerably among different countries, even within the European Union. The solution should be flexible enough to accept the required local parameters like flexi-time and holidays. On the other hand, a good solution can also help to meet the requirements of legislation. However, in WFM the flexibility of employee roles is often very important. Also, the skills and availability of employees have to be known in labour scheduling. To get maximum flexibility and efficiency, checkout employees can be used in quieter hours for shelf replenishment, but at peak hours other store employees may be staffed at the checkout. Checkout work is often part of the training of all sales assistants in many chains.

In the current climate, the adoption of WFM and task management solutions will be the next big implementation projects for many retailers. The introduction of a WFM solution will be driven by a clear business case, which is easy to prove compared with many other retail systems. Employee work hours are expensive, hence the payback period of a system implementation will remain short. We have seen WFM business cases with much better payback times than in any other system implementation projects in retail. WFM is also a catalyst for modelling store-level processes and activities, specifying roles and responsibilities, and supporting the development of store management. Retail task management tools give retailers a better chance to develop and manage store-level operations, both at individual store and chain level.

Intranet solutions in the execution of chain operations

The wide-scale adoption of intranet systems within retail chains is one key factor that will strongly affect the speed and cost efficiency of chain operations. Intranet refers to a company's internal network, which can be accessed through a browser. Intranet solutions are a considerable help in streamlining the interaction and information exchange between the retailer's chain unit and the stores. A key advantage of intranet solutions is the interactivity, enabling an easy and flexible way of communicating among many different parties.

Another advantage of intranet solutions is the low price compared with that of conventional chain-wide communication methods. Retail instruction manuals and standard operating procedures (SOPs) can be updated online and are always available. Instructions may be in many different forms, such as retail handbooks, assortment instructions, planograms (and other display models), promotion instructions and many other materials related to the retailer's ongoing operations. E-learning solutions support self-learning in several tasks, especially the ones not carried out daily, and reduce the need for central support. As retailing is a very labour-oriented business with high attrition, quick and inexpensive store training and support is a must.

A major obstacle to intranet solutions is the utilization possibilities at the stores. The aim is to get store employees out of the back office, but there are often no computers between shelves to support working. Because of this, a large amount of material must still be either printed at stores or printed centrally and sent to the stores. A personal digital assistant (PDA) device might be one solution for this challenge and support store employees in, for example, the implementation of planograms, end cap set ups and in many other in-store tasks.

The significance of fast and efficient execution will grow, and with it the importance of tools supporting execution. Intranet systems will become increasingly important in operational management. PDAs can deliver the information required for task completion and also show examples of best practice that may be applicable to the task. Some solutions might offer a possibility for feedback comments, but these are still most often easiest to record in the store backroom with a computer.

Store staff can easily comment on centrally planned assortment decisions on the intranet, and make suggestions for improvement. Category-specific discussion forums enable knowledge sharing, for example of best practices in campaign management, such as product displays. Besides other stores that can leverage the experiences, this helps head office functions to better use the first-hand experiences and practical views gained at stores, for example in category management. However, discussion forums require a corporate culture that favours and supports the active sharing of ideas and best practices. These systems may also be used for many other purposes, such as collecting customer feedback and sending campaign instructions. Document management is often an integral part of the solution, and the discussions can also be linked with images, for example illustrating best practices in display implementations, end caps or planograms.

Using an intranet can also benefit retail internationalization because procedures become uniform and are therefore easier to replicate for new outlets or new operating areas. Thanks to a shared internal network, employees at stores operating in new market areas find it easy to become familiar with the chain concept. Also, it allows one method for keeping them up to date on all changes that will affect them. Making the chain concept accessible to employees also entails risks as it may leak to competitors more easily. On the other hand, if the retailer hesitates to communicate the concept openly to its own organization, the concept will collect dust in the desk drawer and there will be no uniform procedures and customer experience.

Point of sale (POS) systems

POS systems at stores become thinner as a larger share of activities is moved to centralized ERP solutions. The aim is to reduce labour-intensive in-store work and set employee focus from the back office closer to the customer. Examples of possible centralized functions are demand forecasting, ordering and category management.

The main task of POS systems is to identify sales price and collect money from customers at stores, and to do it efficiently. Solutions used for this purpose are very straightforward and cost efficient in most chains. In entrepreneur-run and franchising chains, POS systems may require considerably more functionality than in centrally managed chains, which makes the systems complex and more expensive. For example, additional functionalities may include ordering, inventory control and product data management functionalities for local products. In speciality retailing POS systems sometimes include billing systems and customer master data, and are actually small ERP systems. More functionality also means higher competence requirements for users and the system support.

One key development trend in POS systems is customer communication. Customer identification is a key functionality in POS systems, and this may happen with many standards from traditional club cards to barcodes, and more recently also including biometric scanning and RFID identification. Checkouts are one good area for personalized customer communication as customers are identified there for the purposes of recording payment and loyalty bonuses. Some retailers have adopted flat screens to display marketing messages, and some print personalized information on customers' receipts. Of course, this information does not always need to be personalized, and then the integration to POS systems is not a must either, as identification is not needed.

One important trend in POS systems is the growth of self-service checkouts. Their key benefits include small workforce costs, as the checkouts can be kept open 24/7 without big variable costs. They often also provide quicker customer service and level out peaks in customer flows – dozens of checkouts can be open even during quiet hours. Self-service checkouts have been tested with fairly good results. In stores that are using self-service checkouts, a noticeable amount of transactions take place through them, and the number continues to grow as customers get used to them. One of the forerunners has been DIY retailer Home Depot, which has installed self-service checkouts in well over a thousand stores already. These checkouts offer significant savings in employee costs because cashiers have traditionally accounted for a significant amount of personnel resources at most retail chains.

Self-service checkouts raise an interesting question about whether to accept cash at checkouts. With self-service checkouts, the acceptance of only card payments makes the POS solution significantly simpler, and also decreases the need for daily maintenance. If retailers refused to take cash, considerable savings would be achieved in checkout functions and security arrangements. It is true that certain target groups who pay by cash would be lost unless they were given a chance to pay at separate checkouts. It remains to be seen whether retailers will ever be prepared to charge a service fee from those who pay by cash, as banks already do. Interestingly, with other means of payment, traditionally there have been limitations. For instance, some retailers refuse to accept certain credit cards because of the high fees charged.

As RFID technology becomes more common, it will change POS functions because tags and readers can identify the contents of an entire shopping trolley or basket in a brief moment. The technology can be used at both self-service and staffed checkouts. It can be presumed that shopping trolleys will at that point include places for the customer's own bags, into which the goods can be packed straight at the store, as is done in some stores offering self-scanning. However, the adoption of RFID in checkout functions will take a long time because efficient utilization would require equipping all items with RFID tags.

Hard discounters and some speciality retailers are well equipped to be the first to adopt RFID technologies on a wide scale. Their relatively small number of items and centralized management model makes the execution essentially easier. As hard discounters sell most of their items as private labels and the number of suppliers is a fraction of those at a conventional supermarket, they could easily incorporate the tag requirements as part of a new product development and purchasing process instructions. The only challenge that hinders hard discounters from proceeding briskly in this field is the relatively low selling price of products, where the cost impact of the RFID tags is still high in relation to the advantages gained.

Ordering and demand forecasting

Automatic ordering is already common in many chains. Some successful grocery retailers have automated as much as 90 per cent or more of all order lines, including a large amount of seasonal and promotional products. This mirrors a general trend where the aim is to centralize and automate tasks requiring a lot of expensive manual work. Automatic ordering naturally significantly reduces the tasks at the store.

Sub-optimal orders lead to many direct and indirect costs, as for example too small order quantities lead to out of stock (OOS) situations that decrease sales and customer satisfaction. OOS situations are a challenge, especially in the case of perishables and during campaigns, so the main problems primarily apply to products that the customers come to the store for. On the other hand, depending on the category, stores may have three to five days of inventory, tying up a lot of capital and space. Besides OOS situations and overstocking, shrinkage also causes challenges. For instance, as much as a half of shrinkage in perishables is caused by sub-optimal ordering.

Forecasting the demand is a huge challenge, as a mid-sized supermarket has about 10,000 to 15,000 SKUs for sale. Department managers in non-food categories may have several thousands of items in their responsibility. Taking into account the space needed by products, actual demand and delivery package sizes, planning of optimal order size demands sophisticated optimization. Skilled demand forecasting decreases OOS situations, shrinkage and inventory management costs, but manual planning is usually too expensive in relation to the benefits. With good optimization solutions, product-specific alarm levels can be set for the majority of items for automatic ordering. In this case, employee time can be freed up for planning and execution in other areas, such as promotions and seasonal sales. However, automatic ordering does not save poorly working logistics and in-store operations. The latter must be in order before automatic ordering can be beneficial. Moreover, automatic ordering is not suitable for all categories. As an example, when demand varies strongly by weather conditions, manual ordering may still be able to react to a changed situation better than automated systems.

Automatic ordering needs to have inventory bookkeeping incorporated into the POS or ERP system, which is not used in all retail chains on store level. Getting reliable inventory balances also requires sufficiently frequent and systematic inventory counting as well as tracking sales, returns and deliveries. In this area, speciality retailing is many years ahead of grocery retailing, where inventory book-keeping is only used in some chains. In consumer electronics or DIY retailing, a salesperson has been able to check a product's inventory situation at his or her terminal for a long time, and sometimes the inventory levels at other stores as well. When inventory figures are in order, systems with real-time sales tracking can be used for generating automatic orders for products with low inventory balances to enable replenishment early enough and avoid OOS situations.

Automatic ordering is based at SKU-level inventory levels and sales forecasts made on the basis of sales data. Most categories are forecasted with day-level data, but for some fast-moving categories such as bakery products, best practice companies use hour-level forecasting. Based on the forecast, the system proposes orders or automatically makes them without employees' approval. Automatic ordering takes into account not only up-to-date inventory status and forecasted demand, but often also shelf capacity, ordering cycles, inventory minimum levels and promotions. Some also use external data such as weather forecasts. The system can also help in avoiding human errors, with logical rules issuing an alarm in predefined situations, and the solutions may ask the user for confirmation.

Key parameters needed for automatic ordering can usually be managed centrally. In certain product categories, suppliers may have the best competence in demand forecasting, and in a deep partnership the supplier may adopt the task of setting all demand forecasts for the entire category.

Based on inventory balances, it is possible to centralize ordering fully. In this case, one person may be responsible for product replenishment for hundreds or even thousands of stores. This model is typical for centrally managed clothing retailing where the purchasing department is responsible not only for buying products but also for selling them. Models for the entrepreneur retailer and for franchising may add legislative challenges to this solution. As a result, ordering will probably remain, at least to a certain extent, as a store-level function as long as products are owned by the store. However, central order proposals based on statistical demand forecasts can and should be used to support store-level decision making also in these cases.

Demand forecasting

Automatic ordering can be improved significantly through demand forecasting. Sophisticated solutions are available to support automatic ordering by forecasting demand per store and product at the daily or even hourly level. Demand forecasting supports optimizing inventory levels and maximizing customer service. Successful forecasting can lead to improved inventory turnover without increasing OOS situations.

Estimating demand for each product at store level is challenging, as the forecasts are based on enormous amounts of data and are updated continually. Demand forecasting solutions need to have a high automation level to be able to produce up to date and correct forecasts in a cost-efficient way. Forecasting relies on background information such as historical sales data. Good solutions automatically choose a suitable model out of many, even hundreds of forecasting models, for the data in question. Rules for using the models can also be set manually, for example based on special characteristics of the category. Besides historical data, the solutions are usually able to take into account manually entered data, such as promotions, special seasons and future price changes. Minimum order quantities also have to be taken into account.

Forecast reporting helps to track the accuracy of forecasts and tackle possible challenges in time. Automatic alarms support directing attention to exception management, and the solutions can also produce best- and worst-case scenarios to aid decision making. Sales forecasts are used, among other things, in planning product replenishments, assortment, product display, promotions and pricing. At its best, the efficient use of accurate sales forecasts may be a significant factor promoting competitive advantage.

Successful demand forecasting requires high-quality data over a long period of time, so the retail data warehouse needs to be in order. The limitations and potential errors in the data must be taken into account and, if possible, eliminated. The assessment of data accuracy can rely on applicable statistical measures. A sophisticated solution may help in improving the quality of forecasts by automatically observing outliers and demand fluctuations caused by OOS situations.

Data forecast suitability can be assessed by three statistical factors:

- data sufficiency;
- deviation;
- robustness.

Sufficiency refers to the number of observations, for example in this case the number of days for which sales data are available. Good sufficiency improves the accuracy of sales forecasts because the longer the time period covered, the more time-related dependencies (such as effects specific to the day, week, season, or long-term effects) the forecasting model can take into consideration.

Deviation refers to the amount of variation from one observation to another, such as the amount of daily sales of one day compared with another. Small deviation improves the accuracy of sales forecasts. Deviation is often measured by standard deviation. Using standard deviation as a measure of deviation may still be problematic, because it also entails factors (such as effects specific to the day, week, season, or long-term effects) that most statistical forecast models are able to allow within the bounds set by data sufficiency. The deviation-related challenge can be solved by filtering time effects away from total deviation and by looking at the remaining deviation. Based on this, one can assess how large a share of the total deviation reflects a variation typical to the product and the store, and how large a share is dependent on the day of week, season or longer-term trend.

Robustness in this case refers to the degree to which daily sales are independent of an individual consumer's daily purchase. Robustness also improves forecast accuracy. If the sales of an individual product are not robust at an individual store, it means that the purchase by an individual consumer has a significant impact on the daily level of sales. Data robustness can be assessed by the relationship between standard deviation and average, and by the shape of data distribution.

In addition to sufficiency, deviation and robustness, data forecasting suitability should also be examined through other statistical measures.

There are hundreds of forecasting models available for retail data to suit different situations. Seasonal and promotional products require different models from those in the same category with fairly even demand. In the case of demand for new products, forecasts often rely on demand curves of substitutes or marker products in the same category. Campaigns, both a retailer's own and competitors' as well as other factors having a large impact on momentary demand, can pose many challenges for demand forecasting. Though forecasting in these situations is not easy, even small improvements can lead to significant financial results.

Increasingly, demand forecasting is a core part of ERP systems, or has been integrated closely into them. Best-of-breed solutions in demand optimization usually include ready-made interfaces to the most common ERP systems. Efficient demand forecasting is one of the key areas of efficient retail processes, and is an area where solution development continues to proceed at a very fast rate.

Stores as advertising media

The importance of customer communication at the store level is growing. The store itself is an important form of advertising media for consumers, and more than 70 per cent of buying decisions are made at the store. However, only about 2 per cent of the marketing budget is spent on in-store advertising. Technological development enables the adoption of new customer communication tools in the customer interface. Figure 6.2 lists key technological enablers having an impact on solutions that involve stores as advertising media.

Wireless networks are one important enabler for efficient in-store communication as they do not need expensive and hard-to-change in-store cablings. They enable the sharing of content to practically all customer touch points for personalized and mass communication. Application areas include flat screens as well as interactive touch screens, which the customer can use to seek information. Wireless solutions also enable the use of electronic shelf labels (ESLs), an effective tool for a retailer to use in dynamic pricing.

Wireless networks and new cheap cameras revolutionize the store environment. Of course, cameras play a big role in controlling internal and

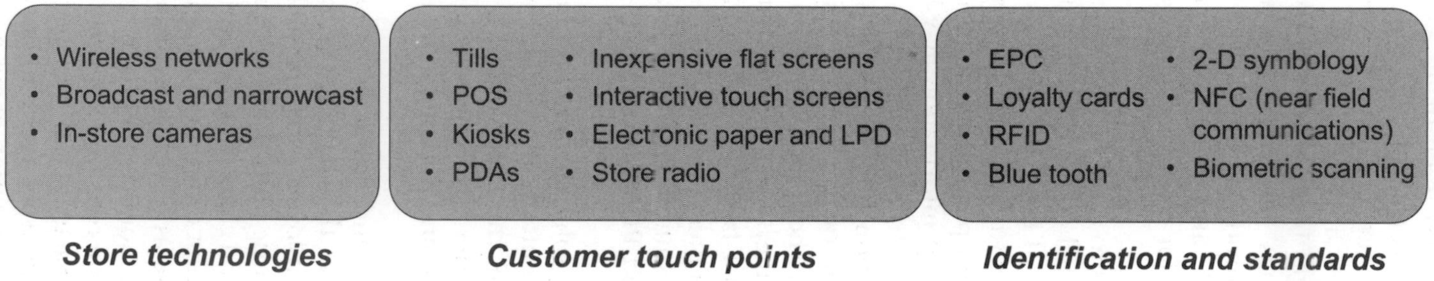

Store technologies

- Wireless networks
- Broadcast and narrowcast
- In-store cameras

Customer touch points

- Tills
- POS
- Kiosks
- PDAs
- Inexpensive flat screens
- Interactive touch screens
- Electronic paper and LPD
- Store radio

Identification and standards

- EPC
- Loyalty cards
- RFID
- Blue tooth
- 2-D symbology
- NFC (near field communications)
- Biometric scanning

Figure 6.2 Key technology enablers of stores as advertising media

customer-induced shrinkage and in ensuring security, but there are also other applications. One such is tracking and observing consumer behaviour, though local legislation may restrict opportunities to implement this approach. In some countries, filming customers is forbidden. With web cameras, real-time live images from stores can be shown at the retailer's assortment planning meetings, illustrating how customers behave by a certain shelf or particular products. Similarly, the degree of execution readiness may be observed, and as needed, store employees can be instructed without the need for a regional manager or equivalent to visit the store.

There are also other ways to observe customers' behaviour. In experiments made by the Wharton School, shopping trolleys were equipped with tags that allowed an analysis of how customers moved in stores. This has led to many interesting observations about different customer shopping routes, use of time in different parts of the store and customer behaviour in different aisles. This kind of information may be very useful for retail format development. Some advanced retailers have also experimented with linking the trolley location information to shopper information by using time and location at the cashier creating a link to transaction information, enabling them to see shopping paths per consumer segment.

Stores have several customer touch points that are used in campaign communication, new product launches and product information to the customers. Different kinds of media can be used for both mass and personalized communication. For example, in-store TVs and radios are used as a mass media, while kiosks and PDAs serve as both mass and personalized communication channels.

Conventional in-store TV solutions have gradually been replaced with flat-screen monitors where content can be driven directly from the chain's central unit. The central unit can even control a campaign shown on an individual screen. This provides an effective means to ensure that the customer material is always fresh and updated in an effort to keep customers interested.

The importance of music and customer announcements in stores is growing. Previously there was the challenge of difficult manual cassettes and separate devices that employees were compelled to use at each store, but with new technology, music and customer announcements can easily be transmitted from the central chain unit, also with better quality. Another option is centrally to implement different music and communication packages, which the store can use as it wishes according to the situation. The use of music and customer announcements is in its infancy in most chains, and this is an area where numerous new applications will be seen.

Touch screens enable interactivity with the customer. It may be difficult for a customer living in the internet age to understand that on the sofa at home he or she gets more information about a product than while shopping at the local grocery store. This situation cannot be sustained for long, and it is to be expected that product information services offered by retailers and suppliers will increase substantially. Applications can provide information on, for example, product use, health effects and allergies. The role of retailers is to act as content service integrators, but the required information is often provided by suppliers. It is possible that product information required will be standardized in many markets and brought into general distribution in the same way as in product data pools. A simple way to proceed is to provide customers with terminals that they can use to surf suppliers' web pages while shopping, for example.

Touch screens are also typically used in information kiosks. One of the most common applications for kiosks in grocery stores is recipe services. If a retailer also runs an online store, a kiosk can also operate as a remote terminal, offering the customer wider assortments. Moreover, terminals have been installed at tables in fast-food outlets. Customers may play games for a fee or search for information. A kiosk may also include an identification mechanism, in which case customers can be provided with personalized content. As an example, US grocery retailer Jewel-Osco has equipped its stores with information kiosks where customers can print out rebate coupons and recipes.

It is also possible to combine home and store use of internet services. Benjamin Moore Paints has developed a personal colour viewer service, allowing customers to choose paint hues from photographs, either the customer's own or models provided by the company. This may be a great help in designing home decor. When the desired hues have been found, the corresponding barcodes can be printed from the website and the paints can be picked up at a DIY store selling Benjamin Moore paints.

In the field of shelf information, electronic paper and liquid crystal display (LCD) screens are gaining ground from conventional shelf edge labels, for example at UPM Ella Store. Together with wireless networks, these technologies enable dynamic pricing, even according to the hour of the day if needed. Electronic labels can also be used to deliver new information to customers. Benefits are especially gained in store operations, where screens may be used for other information including, for example, a field indicating product location during shelf stocking. During a period of assortment change, the shelf labels for products to be removed can be made to blink, whereas changes to facings are indicated by another colour. These opportunities bring significant advantages at the store. Dynamic pricing also permits entirely new approaches in retailing. The principles of yield management (also called revenue management), used by hotels and airlines, may make inroads in retailing as well.

New technologies enable shelf communication to be partly sold directly to suppliers. The store offers the infrastructure – in other words, suitable methods for customer communication – and sells the service to suppliers, who push content directly to the store in accordance with their user rights. In the extreme case, a supplier can manage the effort as a shop-in-shop operation, where the supplier defines not only assortments and promotions but also product prices remotely. The store only takes care of in-store operations like ordering, shelf stocking and collecting money. Contracts for sharing risk and revenue, based on total return, are also possible.

In addition to mass communication, some stores might want to communicate personalized messages to individual customers. Solutions like PDAs and kiosks enable this type of communication, if the customer can be identified with, for instance, the help of a loyalty card. Push content can also be delivered easily to POS terminals, to be printed on the receipt. This also offers a good opportunity for content personalization, often in the form of coupons, as customers are usually identified at the checkout.

PDA devices designed for customers have been tested in many retail chains, and they have been used actively in, for example, self-scanning. In many pilots, the devices installed in shopping trolleys have proved relatively expensive compared to the benefits, and their use so far is fairly low. PDA devices are more likely to be used by store employees for many purposes ranging from inventory counting and ordering to display instructions. However, PDAs may be used for mass or personalized communication. For instance, Conad in Italy and Shoprite in the United States have piloted devices installed in shopping trolleys. When shopping, customers receive marketing messages via the terminal in the shopping trolley at intervals of a couple of minutes. Customers have reacted positively to the service, and campaigns have been successful.

Using mobile phones as a communication tool brings new opportunities for in-store marketing and expands its sphere of influence. Customers may be contacted before the shopping visit, during it or after it. For example, car dealers already use mobile services in customer communication in several ways, related to both sales and service. Mobile phones can also be used for receiving coupons (with or without barcodes), adverts and other communication. Moreover, mobile phones may be used as paying devices and loyalty cards. The future of in-store targeted communication is still very much open and in its infancy, but the opportunities seem promising. Experiments with using personalized communication at store level have been successful and promotions have reached significant pull percentages. This area is covered in more detail in Chapter 7.

Case study: Metro Future Store

Metro, the second largest retailer in Europe, has together with major IT vendors developed 'the store of the future': Metro Future Store, in Rheinberg, Germany. Metro has had dozens of companies as partners in the initiative, with the main sponsors being IBM, SAP, Intel and T-Systems. Planned solutions are tested in a real store environment with customers.

Here are some key examples of technological solutions that Metro Future Store has tested:

- Product data has been stored in remote RFID tags at the production stage. Signals sent by the tags allow the tracking of their route up to the checkout and theft alarm. These characteristics are in daily use only in some shipping packages.
- Smart shelves use RFID technology and detect whenever a product is taken from the shelf. This may invoke an order or a replenishment process from the back storage area of the store.
- An intelligent scale identifies the product to be weighed through pattern identification. If the scale cannot uniquely identify the product (for example, if the customer has bought tomatoes, of which there are many kinds for sale) the program offers a selection for the customer.
- ESL are always up to date, and they can be updated quickly and flexibly without manual work.
- Interactive information terminals offer consumers product information, recipes, etc.
- A personal shopping assistant is a PDA device equipped with a touch screen and mounted on the shopping trolley. An identified customer gets a purchase proposal based on his or her earlier purchases. The personal shopping assistant also comprises a scanner, which the customer may use to scan products in the trolley for self-service checkout. At the same time, the customer sees the total sum updated and the total remains on the screen throughout.
- At self-service checkouts the customer is charged for scanned products gathered during the shopping trip. Payment takes place either by cash or credit card.
- A PDA is a terminal device designed as a tool for store employees. It can be used to check store inventory and ordering data, and it also has e-mail connected to it.
- Wireless networks enable other in-store technologies, especially mobile solutions. Also, they significantly reduce store cabling costs.

• The store manager uses a 'workbench', or an electronic desk, where he or she can track in real time both sales and inventory levels. Transparency facilitates the management of the store's operational processes.

Source: based on 'Metro Future store in ECR Europe', www.future-store.org

Fact-based management with shopper information

Data on customer behaviour shapes the development of in-store information systems and offers many fact-based management opportunities for retailers' core planning processes. Loyalty programmes form an essential part of the gathering and use of shopper information. Loyalty programmes use increasingly sophisticated solutions but are also simpler for customers. Optimization algorithms help to define the right offerings for the right customers at the right time, and customers see a programme that is simpler and relevant for them. Figure 6.3 shows the key components of fact-based management with shopper information.

Solutions supporting the management of customer relationships and the use of shopper information have become a key development area. The solutions may be divided into five groups:

• Customer identification – how do retailers identify customers in different customer contact points in a multi-channel environment?
• Collect and store data – how can retailers gather, cleanse, transform, store and refine shopper information?
• Analyse and distribute – how can retailers track and analyse shopper information and distribute the information efficiently and in good time?
• Act in key processes – how do retailers use the insight in key retail processes and applications supporting them?
• Communicate with customers – how can IT solutions support customer dialogue and personalization in different channels?

Trends regarding these areas are discussed in greater detail in the following sections.

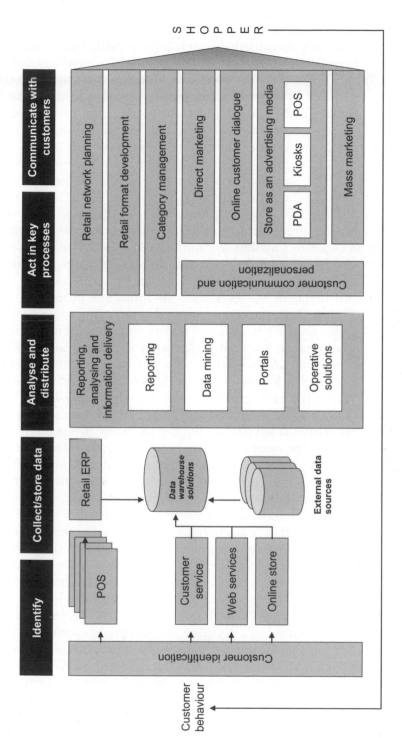

Figure 6.3 Key components of fact-based management with shopper information

Customer identification

Customers are usually identified through loyalty cards with a magnetic stripe. The relatively low unit price of the cards and the existing card base are strong supporting factors for their use. However, the customer often has several cards, and retail loyalty cards may have to compete for space in a customer's wallet. This is particularly challenging for small speciality retail chains, the services of which are used only occasionally.

Besides cards, stores also use other identification methods. Albert Heijn (part of Ahold group) in the Netherlands has used a barcode on a key ring for identification. The barcode is read the same way as the products, and the customer gets a rebate on products purchased. Albert Heijn's programme differs from other loyalty programmes in that most rebates are given to the customer immediately through reduced prices, so scoring procedures and an expensive mailing are not needed. There is some question though as to whether this kind of programme strongly commits the customer to concentrate purchases over the long term.

An interesting detail in the customer identification process used by Albert Heijn is that if the customer loses the key ring containing the barcode, he or she can get it back based on the customer identification. If a customer finds someone else's barcode, he or she can return it to any service desk of the chain and it will be sent to the owner. As the other customers do not get any information about the key owner apart from the barcode, the approach is also an efficient way to prevent abuse.

A customer may also be identified with other cards than the retailer's own loyalty card. This has led to the merging of loyalty programmes such as Nectar in the UK. The same idea is used with the cards of financial institutions, when a loyalty programme can be integrated as functionality on the card. This makes a customer's life easier by reducing the number of cards in the wallet. In addition, the bank might earn customer loyalty as more services are linked to the same customer relationship.

It remains to be seen how actively retail banks want to take part in this area, which, at least in the beginning, requires high system development costs and provides only marginal direct returns. Customer identification is closely linked with payment methods though, so there is an opportunity for retail banks to act as developers of a new approach. However, many retailers have their own banks and that often prevents collaboration with other retail banks. In other cases, retailers and retail banks have tight cooperation, and offer joint cards for customers. A good example is the collaboration between Kesko (retailer) and OP-Pohjola (retail bank) in Finland, where both parties have gained impressive results by offering joint cards.

EMV (the acronym comes from the initial letters of Europay, MasterCard and VISA, the three companies which originally cooperated to develop the standard) and chip cards are becoming a more common means of payment, and they may also get a role in customer identification. Their growth is based on security features compared with conventional cards with a magnetic stripe. The 'smartness' of the cards brings one important advantage over conventional cards: key data from the customer's profile can be stored on the card, and used in sales outlets in an offline state. In theory, customers could also edit their loyalty card profile themselves, if they were offered an option to do so that was easy to use. Key challenges to the growth of RFID in customer identification are the costs of reader devices for all checkouts in large-scale implementation.

Cardless identification

As loyalty programmes become more common, cardless identification methods have begun to increase because the battle for the share of wallet has grown too fierce. Cardless methods to identify customers include biometric identification, identification with a mobile phone, and some personal piece of information like car plate number, personal identity code or mobile phone number. These identification methods facilitate shopping and make it possible to join many loyalty programmes without having to carry the cards.

A customer can be identified with biometric identification (such as fingerprints). In the United States, this technology is already used by several chains. Examples of pioneers include Cub Foods and the Piggly Wiggly chain, which uses biometric identification in all its 120 stores. Payment takes place through fingerprint-based identification, which essentially speeds up the checkout process, so customers are happy with the new service. Interestingly, the chain's research shows that customers using biometric identification felt customer service was better than the other customers.

Credit card companies have woken up to the threat caused by biometric identification to their business: the retail channels might slowly take a large part of credit card companies' business as retailers carry out customer identification in stores anyway. Why not also use the identification information for retailers' own credit company or bank? Not surprisingly, credit card companies, retail banks and other companies offering card technology have started to develop cardless payment solutions. To give some examples, MasterCard uses PayPass, American Express offers ExpressPay service and Visa a solution called Visa Contactless. Other players like VeriFone, OTI and ViVOtech have also developed their own solutions. The customer just flashes the card in the reader and payment takes place without the traditional need to swipe the card through a magnetic stripe reader. For example Meijer has adopted this service in all its outlets. Meijer Platinum MasterCard is equipped with PayPass features including loyalty card functionalities.

RFID tags may have a future in customer identification. This was already piloted in Germany at Metro Future Store, where a loyalty card with an

RFID tag was distributed to more than 10,000 customers. However, the retailer did not inform customers sufficiently about the use of the tag, and the experiment had to be stopped because of opposition from consumer activists objecting to RFID identification. The card dispute received a lot of unwanted publicity in Germany as well as international attention.

Barcelona night club Baja Club has gone even further in the use of RFID technology. VIP clients can get an RFID tag implanted in the arm under the skin. Then the customer is granted access without having to queue and is able to pay for purchases at the night club without having to carry a wallet. The tag opens access to rooms reserved only for VIP members. Even though this is a very small-scale operation and primarily represents sensational marketing, it does illustrate the opportunities provided by RFID identification.

One of the newest customer identification methods is mobile phone identification complemented with standards like NFC, as discussed earlier in this chapter. To cite an example, Mobile Lime in the United States has developed a technology that enables the use of a mobile phone for customer identification, loyalty card use and payment. Customers may load several desired loyalty programmes into their mobile phone. Identification and payment take place by flashing the mobile phone in front of the reader. Though not yet widely used, this technology may have a large-scale impact in the future as a significant number of customers carry a mobile phone while shopping. The forerunners in this area will most likely be in Japan.

Data warehousing in retailing

Data warehouse solutions enable the storing of vast amounts of shopper data collected from stores, often enriched with other data for business analysis purposes. Most retailers with a loyalty programme have collected shopper data aggregated at the level of total receipt amount, especially in the early phases of the programme. However, the apparent trend is to gather more insightful data, down to receipt line level, which yields a wider understanding of the customer's purchase history and the products purchased. The amount of data is huge (often several terabytes) and sets high requirements for retail IT solutions. The key development needs are often in data warehousing and the solutions supporting business processes with the information.

Figure 6.4 provides a rough description of the dimensions of a retailer's shopper history data. Key dimensions and characteristics of shopper history data will now be examined in more detail.

The receipt header and receipt line data form the foundation of data collected from stores, and represent the large data masses in the data warehouses. The rest of the fields are classifying and explanatory by nature,

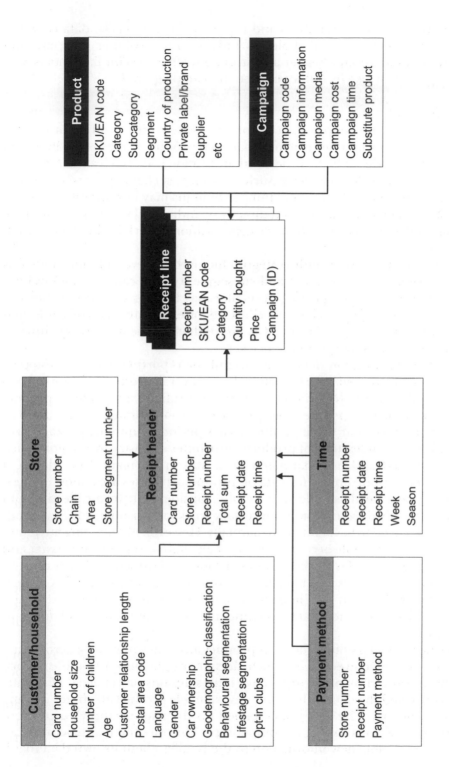

Figure 6.4 Key dimensions of shopper history data

and are used in data analyses and reporting. Traditionally, data collected from customers or households is linked with attributes like payment method, time, receipt header and store, but when receipt line data is analysed, the data also includes product and campaign data.

Product data

The analysis of shopper data is complemented with product attributes. The most important piece of information is product name, as the POS data typically includes only the product identification code (such as EAN), which says little about the product as such. The biggest challenges are presented by local products; though the number of items may be vast, sales may still be modest. Products purchased directly by individual stores have often the weakest data quality, which may cause additional work in the data analysis phase.

Product data also includes category hierarchies (levels often include category, subcategory, segment and subsegment). The category hierarchy is used particularly in reporting. A retailer may have several product groupings and, for example, chain-specific categories or categories of syndicated data providers (such as IRI or ACNielsen) that may be used in benchmarking the retailer's success in the market.

Other classification data is also useful for reporting and business purposes. Sophisticated retailers often have several product categorizations and product attributes to facilitate customer profiling. Examples of product attributes include private label products, various brand categorizations, green products, fair trade products, sales period identifiers, package sizes or other special features of products. Attributes also vary by category, such as marinated and non-marinated meat and bread made from different crops. The opportunities for data on product attributes are almost endless, but business needs should be carefully considered before collecting and analysing this data to avoid unnecessary work, as attributes for new products often need to be maintained manually. However, maintaining attributes is usually worthwhile because it makes data analysis significantly easier and provides new angles to the analysis. Properly classified and rich data on product attributes is one key characteristic of an advanced retailer in fact-based management. It is important that the business has ownership and cost responsibility for data updating to ensure efficiency and focus of operations.

Where retailers often focus on product attributes that work across categories, manufacturers need much deeper insight into a single category. Some advanced manufacturers have built solutions on retailers' POS data, and enriched the data with a lot of new valuable product attributes relating to the category. The data is maintained for the manufacturer's own products and also for those of its competitors. This way the manufacturer can provide valuable new information to the retailer about its own data that is not otherwise available. In addition, the manufacturer's internal operations such as category management, merchandising and product development can benefit significantly from this new data.

In speciality retailing, a product is often linked with additional data. Especially in clothing and shoe retailing, it is necessary to look at products in terms of models, sizes and colours. Every size and colour has its own identification code that is needed for operational logistics control. However, in other business use this level of accuracy often makes reports hard to read or downright useless. In many situations, model-level reporting provides a better idea of product demand and the sales situation. Similar classification and reporting levels may be used in grocery retailing in areas like brand and taste reporting for products such as yoghurts or packaged meats.

Customer data

A loyalty card number provides the link to the customer relationship and background variables. Customers can be linked with profile-building data, which can also be purchased from external sources, as will be discussed later, in the section 'External data sources'. The basic data of a club member mainly consists of the information provided in the loyalty card joining application. Unfortunately, updating this data is difficult, with the exception of address data, if there is no continuing dialogue with the customer that can be used to complement and validate the data. Besides the address, good background variables usually include only the customer's age and gender.

Customer segmentation or other categorization enables tracking sales at the retailer's core segments. Segment-specific reporting is important to the retailer to see the impact of activities on the target segments. Without easy-to-use and clear segment-specific reporting, the tracking of measures and marketing activities is done only for the average customers, and any real differentiation among target groups is difficult.

Though retailers talk about customers, actions are seldom aimed at individual consumers, but at the household linked to the loyalty card. The data is gathered at the individual level, but aggregated to household-specific figures. A key reason for this is the retail bonus systems, which are often specific to the household. Household-level analysis can also be justified with the cost efficiency of customer communication. However, retailers should also consider using individual-level customer classifications, especially when targeting in-store marketing. The factors affecting the behaviour of different household members might be very different, and the messages should also be targeted person by person. Would you like to receive targeted marketing from a store based on the purchases of some of your family members, such as your mother, spouse or child? It is likely that most retailers will run two (or more) customer segmentations in parallel, one for household-level customers and another for individual customers. This is also a common practice, for example, in retail banking.

Time

Time is one of the key dimensions of data warehouses, and there are many functions for it. Date and time can be used to combine key time attributes (such as weekdays and holidays) for reporting purposes. Similarly, time data is used as an aid for other important classifications, such as sales during morning or night time hours.

The presentation of time may also vary. Presenting data on a monthly or weekly level will reveal different things from a daily or hourly presentation. Longer time frames even out fluctuation and make it easier to interpret results. However, shorter time frames may reveal details that are not shown by the high-level analysis. As an example, presenting week-level results evens out fluctuations caused by weekdays during campaigns, which may make the results significantly easier to interpret. Similarly, it is sometimes useful to use hourly information for demand forecasting in product replenishment planning.

Time classifications are typical data modelling work, and only a few of the requirements are retailer specific. However, use of retailer-specific campaign and assortment periods together with control periods will support reporting and follow-up actions significantly. Number of sales days per month is also an important measure for reporting purposes.

Payment method

The payment method is recorded in the receipt data. Besides cash, different credit cards, use of bonus vouchers and other payment types such as retail accounts will be recorded. This data makes it possible to profile shopper payment behaviour.

Loyalty programmes are often linked with banking functions and payment cards, and this allows analysis of the payment method importance to customer loyalty. Many retailers, like Swedish ICA and French Carrefour, have integrated payment cards into their loyalty programmes. However, legislation in many countries limits the retailer's ability to use customers' financial information in marketing activities, as credit and retail banking have considerably tighter regulations, which most typical retailers do not need to comply with. To avoid this complexity many retailers have partnered or established joint ventures with financing companies instead of building their own operations.

Store location data

Store location data indicates the place of selling and even the checkout counter the customer used. It also includes data such as area codes and store attributes, which can enrich the analysis. Syndicated store directories provide additional information on the competitive situation in the area. In terms of retail success, it is important to analyse performance in various competitive environments, and the data may be of great help in the planning of local assortments, for example.

Address data reveals the catchment area of the store. This data can be used in the analysis of local marketing or in evaluating a certain regional manager's performance. Store location can also be defined in the form of map coordinates, which enables a wider use of the data in various GIS (geographic information system) solutions. They include a remarkable amount of information on the customer base, traffic solutions and customer flows within the catchment area of the store. The best retailers have determined the market potential of each store based on competitive pressure, customer portfolio and location of the store. This information can also be used when setting budgets for each unit. With this kind of analysis, several stores may be identified that do relatively well with other measures, but weakly compared with market potential, and vice versa.

A store location can also involve data about the store manager or the merchant running the store. These background variables can be used for identifying successful store managers, which provide guidelines for future recruitment and training. In addition, area managers or other geographical roles can be attached to store location data to enable easy reporting.

Store location data also contains some interesting risk management properties. As data can be received by the POS terminal, it is relatively easy to build algorithms for identifying deviations and special situations at checkout counters. Centralized and automated systems support can help in risk management, and even forecast and identify theft by employees. The same top data-mining gurus may at one time develop a predictive model for customer acquisition and next identify sources of shrinkage and then continue with credit risk analysis. Centralized analysis teams may operate as shared service resources, which helps to build up competences and secure critical mass for services compared with distributed and dedicated competences. This is a viable option particularly when the total amount of analysis is small.

Activities

There are two main types of activities: 1) campaigns targeted at individual customers, such as coupons sent with a direct mailing; 2) untargeted campaigns, including regional or national marketing campaigns. Targeted promotions are linked to individual customers, and the aim is to find out how the customer has reacted to the campaign. This data is a key part of the retailer's campaign management tool. With it, the effectiveness of marketing activities in various customer segments may be tracked efficiently.

For untargeted campaigns, measurement is conducted by combining product, time and store location data. The retailer knows at which stores, at what time and for which products the promotion has been implemented. This also works for testing most retail promotion activities, but it is critical to compare results with an equivalent control group, where the same marketing activities have not been implemented. Campaign management tools are discussed in detail later, in the section 'Campaign management and personalization of customer communication'.

Data warehouse solutions

Collecting data at the receipt line level requires efficient data warehouses. Data masses seem huge now, but the price of capacity is falling all the time. In 2010, a normal home computer's hard drive will perhaps be able to store a retail group's historical data for one year for all customers. Large data masses pose requirements for data transformation and cleansing. In practice, collecting data from stores at the receipt line level requires broadband connection, which will also be essential when retail outlets engage in an active customer dialogue and targeted offers.

The time span naturally affects significantly the required data capacity, but for business planning purposes, data is generally needed for a period of more than a year at least. Because of the seasonal nature of the business, the data of the previous similar period is important. To give an example, it is difficult to analyse and plan Easter sales without the data concerning the previous period, for it is no use planning assortment based on, for instance, the past month. Also, an analysis of several previous periods may yield a good indication of trends. Therefore, it is necessary to gather at least high-level sales data from earlier years.

Data processing speed has enabled the storing and analysing of very detailed data. Typically, the data warehouse and business intelligence solutions aggregate the data in accordance with predefined attributes, but with the falling price of capacity, storing data on a detailed level will provide significant benefits. For example, if product categories or product attributes are changed, the data for the previous period or year can be handled retroactively in line with the new classifications. This gives comparable data right from the beginning, only if the variables needed in the model are available from earlier periods too. Detailed data is also needed in analytical modelling where long time series can be used. Variables created from receipt line data may significantly improve the forecasting accuracy. Storing detailed data enables the development and rescoring of the model as accurate data is available from earlier periods too.

Collecting, storing and analysing large data masses are not necessarily part of the basic retailing business, so these activities can be outsourced.

Tesco has relied on a consulting firm dunnhumby to build data warehouses and analyse customer data for its loyalty programme. After many years' experience in developing the loyalty programme, Tesco bought in to dunnhumby to ensure the continuity of expertise and operations. Currently, Tesco already owns more than 80 per cent of dunnhumby. As small analytics companies have relative low net sales, one attractive option for retailers is to buy one of these analysts to get plenty of expertise at one go.

At the same time, it is necessary to ensure long-term retention of employees, since without competent people companies are worth next to nothing. There is one interesting, perhaps less known example of a big company that owns shares in an analytics company. Itella (formerly Finnish Post) owns a significant share of a marketing consulting company specializing in customer analytics and predictive modelling, which enhances targeted communication and direct mailings in many industries. Analytics can also be seen as essential strategic expertise, which cannot be outsourced. For example, Sainsbury's has stated that an internal customer analysis team is a more cost-efficient and a better solution than outsourcing.

Case study: Tradeka Loyalty Factory

Several retailers have made progress in the use of shopper data. To cite an example, Tradeka in Finland collects receipt line data about its customers and shopping baskets. The data is used on a segment level using statistical analysis, but not on an individual customer level. The information is used for business development purposes, ranging from local assortment development and services to measuring the efficiency of activities and marketing. The data warehouse solution and reporting tools are used as a Loyalty Factory service from Capgemini, and an external partner ensures customer data privacy. The service has also enabled the opening up of reporting at shopper segment level for selected partners, which supports the use of joint metrics and genuine partnership throughout the retail value chain.

External data sources

Retailers can also capitalize on external players for complementing the data. There are numerous companies and organizations specializing in information enrichment and the sale of analytical services. A large amount of external data is related to the profiling of the customer base. Profiles are created to give a more accurate explanation of the movement and changes in the customer portfolio. Geodemographic classifications may illustrate the structure of a company's customer base in relation to regions on average. Classifications include Mosaic, Acorn Star, RISC and Lifecycles. An interesting application area for geodemographic classifications is new customer acquisition, as service providers often sell direct-mailing lists covering segments that are not current customers of the company. Assortment management for a new store may also benefit from analysis of the customer structure of the catchment area.

In many markets, customer data can also be purchased from state-maintained services. Typical data includes name changes, address updates, records of births and deaths. In other words, it is mostly about the maintenance of basic customer master data, but, for example, childbirth may trigger an event-based marketing campaign.

External data sources can also be related to product sales, providing benchmarks of the total market. In grocery retailing, the primary sources are syndicated data sources, described in more detail in Chapter 4. Linked with retailers' own data, these provide a good comparison of market trends. A 10 per cent annual sales growth of a category may seem like a good figure as such, but it appears in a different light depending on whether the growth of the total market was 2 or 20 per cent during the same period. In grocery retailing, market data is generally in wide use, but the speciality retailers often need to rely on their own data for there are fewer syndicated data sources available.

Shopper information updating and cleansing

Shopper data can be updated from external data sources, but outsourcing its maintenance to the customer is also an option and, when properly implemented, can be an efficient way to make the customer committed to a particular retail outlet. An example is Amazon.com where customers can easily indicate interest in books bought. Similarly, customers browsing book recommendations may with a single click indicate that they own the book already, in which case they will not be offered it again. Based on the customer's buying history and self-disclosed preferences, more personalized recommendations and promotions are offered.

In retailing, interests indicated by customers have been actively used in various sorts of clubs, of which baby and wine clubs are common examples. Data maintained by the customer also has risks, particularly if the customer club involves significant and continuing customer-specific costs for the company. It may be difficult to identify and eliminate ex-customers and passive customers, and the quality of the customer register weakens over time. Club activities also create expectations among customers. A club cannot conduct just one campaign; it has to be active continually and use varied communication patterns, which genuinely benefit the customer. This is the only way to create a long-lasting programme. When operations slow down, customers stop maintaining their own data and the benefits are not reaped. Data has been collected in connection with a loyalty card application, but how many still remember what data has been given, and in addition, how often is the data updated?

The internet as a channel enables multi-directional communication and creates prerequisites for developing customer dialogue. In the best possible case, customers evolve into a community that serves the customer in a significantly wider area than a conventional retailer does. In 2001, Tesco received a prize from the *Mother and Baby* magazine because it had established a baby club on its website. It was the first time that this recognition, related to baby care, was awarded to a retailer. The baby club has prompted a vivid discussion forum and an active community on the website. The baby club is 'a temporary offering' – in other words, the club is relevant to parents only for a certain time, after which they direct their attention elsewhere.

Another interesting but less well-known example of customer communities over the internet is SmartClub in China. Community members earn benefits by participating actively in discussions about products and services they have bought and by filling in various questionnaires. Also, customers benefit every time a community member makes a purchase at a company belonging to the system. The community now has 100 million customers and more than 50 participating companies. SmartClub has collected an enormous customer database, which companies may use for direct marketing, among other activities.

Loyalty programmes and capitalizing on the data received through these programmes present a challenge for internationalization. Customer databases as well as data storage and usage are largely based on local legislation, which may vary considerably in different countries. Among companies specializing in customer analytics, only a few operate in several European markets, let alone globally. The data collected by the company itself is usually easier to unify and therefore quicker to exploit in new markets. On the other hand, loyalty programmes that genuinely cross borders are still few. Companies operating in many countries usually establish a separate programme for each country, for instance Carrefour has more than 20 different programmes. OnCard, offered by DCS operating in Asia, is one of the few loyalty cards that are valid in many countries. In new markets, gathering data about customers and their behaviour takes time, which may justify using a local service provider.

Data privacy

During the past few years, data privacy has been a burning issue in public debates. Loyalty programmes have met with criticism in the media since retail programmes are often used as examples when data privacy issues are discussed. In many other industries, an active and efficient use of customer data is already an integral part of operations. If a customer wants to buy spare parts for a bicycle he or she bought through mail order a few years ago, the contact centre agent can check the bicycle model from the buying history data during the call. Insurance companies know how their customers live, what car they drive, how old their family members are, if they have a summer cottage, boat, valuable art works and many more things. A bank knows details of its customers' income, properties, loans, home value, investments, service channels used, card use behaviour and many other personal details. It is no coincidence when one of these companies telephones a customer to offer a particular product. The choice is usually based on sophisticated mathematical algorithms and extensive customer data. And still, retailers analysing grocery purchases seem to face most resistance. One reason for this might be that other industries do not have a separate card that would be in daily use: the retail loyalty card has become the symbol for customer data collection, and customer privacy issues.

Industries that have used customer data actively for a long time have carefully considered their approaches and principles for data use. Companies that have proceeded furthest have established genuinely customer-centric operations. Back in early 2000 one of the authors helped a sophisticated company to define the ethical aspects of data mining in its business. The attitude of the company was advanced as it did not approach the subject based on what legislation allowed, but focused instead truly on customer benefits and ethically sustainable operations.

It is often forgotten in data privacy discussions that data collection and use also creates responsibility. In a traditional model, retailers have not known the buying behaviour of consumers and have thus not been responsible for them. An interesting example of the responsibility issues is found in the United States. BSE, or 'mad cow' disease, had been reported in the catchment area of the QFC supermarket chain, and it was possible that contaminated meat had been for sale at the chain's stores. The retailer had a loyalty programme, which would have enabled it to identify customers who had purchased meat that might have been contaminated. When the chain did not use this possibility to inform customers, the customers filed a class action against the chain. Like Albert Heijn in Holland, QFC also promises to return the customer's keys (identified with a barcode) if they are lost. The customer's attorney, Steve Berman, asked an interesting question: 'If a customer can be contacted because of lost car keys, why can't the retailer let him know that the steak he bought may kill him?'

It will be interesting to see how the responsibilities of a retailer evolve with regard to active customer relationship development and dialogue through various promotional campaigns and marketing activities. For example, can a retailer be held accountable for a customer overusing a product? Should a heavy beer drinker be encouraged through promotional campaigns to increase consumption? Should people who buy unhealthy food get heavy user promotions for confectionery and fast food? Retailers are increasingly expanding into health categories and pharmacies, especially in the United States, and they should have the competences in-house for evaluating the health effects of campaigns if needed. Of course, this would not be cheap and a retailer might end up cancelling certain traditionally profitable campaigns that are deemed unhealthy for consumers. The responsibilities and rules of the game in large-scale data use have not been set yet, and a societal debate on the subject is needed in the near future.

There is also increasing debate about what is the difference between marketing and normal customer communication. For instance, does a personalized customer magazine represent customer communication or marketing? And are the coupons sent with the bonus statement rewards given to a loyal customer, or marketing? The debate on these differences may lead to a more precise distinction between marketing and customer communication and, hence, also affect privacy issues.

Data privacy naturally aims at good consumer protection, and all consumers should be given the ability to opt out of marketing targeted at them. Many companies also provide the option to prevent only part of the marketing; the customer can, for instance, prohibit communication from partner companies but allow communication from the retailer. Retailers generally have a very cautious attitude towards data privacy issues, and the current approach does not imply any great risks from the consumer's point of view. The data is mainly handled per shopper segment, which means that the privacy of individual customers is secure. A retail customer's identification with name and address or customer history is accessible to very few people compared with the situation in industries like insurance, banking or telecommunications, where customer-specific data is open to almost all customer service employees.

If, in the future, customer-specific marketing and selling activities are conducted at store level, data privacy issues need to be thought through more carefully. This is a very different way of operating and sets high standards for store-level actions, so it should be included in training programmes. Examples and best practices are already available from other industries that handle individual-level customer information daily.

Reporting solutions

Operations management can be improved considerably with reporting tools that are efficient and easy to use processing up-to-date information. There are many viable business intelligence solutions in the market, including for example SAS, Business Objects (SAP), Cognos (IBM) and Hyperion (Oracle). Almost all retailers and suppliers use at least some kind of reporting tool; some buy package software and some develop their own systems. Either way, successful reporting enables better and faster decision making.

When it comes to reporting there are many user groups, whose needs differ. Some users need to be able to delve deep into the data and to choose variables and time spans flexibly. Dynamic and interactive reporting is increasingly popular since it drastically reduces the need to create numberless reports for every new need in the company. Many business users are willing to create their own reports, if the user interface is easy enough. Time is saved, since not all information needs to be requested from an analyst team or specialized resources. Ability to drill down to more detailed data is also important, since the reasons behind the high-level development trends may be discovered by analysing the more detailed level.

Static reports are also needed as some employees are pleased with standardized reports used for regular tracking of operations. These also help to keep the basic KPIs standardized and common in the company. In addition, management is often interested in the big picture and business trends to be able to tackle selected areas of interest. The majority of reporting tools are well suited to the basic needs of companies, but some of them do not provide the scalability needed for receipt line data analyses, especially with short response times. In these cases, the actual data processing may be carried out with a scalable data warehouse solution, whereas report distribution for the user interface may be placed in a familiar, generally used solution. The more advanced reporting solutions are then used only by analysts and report developers.

In many companies, however, reporting is not unified in all application areas, so users must rely on several tools to get the information they need. Moreover, a large part of reporting comes directly from operational systems, which further increases the number of systems used. There are signs that reporting tool harmonization will take place, at least with user interfaces. This will bring down licensing costs and make user support considerably easier.

Besides reporting sales figures, continuous benchmarking against business targets and budgets are the key reporting development needs for most retailers. In many companies, reporting only indicates the current state or development compared with the previous year. Only in some best practice companies, reporting generates automatic comparisons in relation to budgets and process targets, which is somewhat surprising. One reason for this is the fact that spreadsheet software packages like Microsoft Excel are still the most important budgeting tools, and actual scorecard solutions are not yet used by many companies, at least beyond the finance department. In the future, visual scorecard solutions that can be flexibly integrated into various data sources are likely to become increasingly popular.

Another common development area is user access rights management. When almost all reporting is received from the same consolidated reporting system, it is justified to restrict the access to data by user groups. Typically there is a need for limiting the access to detailed customer data for most users. Restrictions play a big role in terms of customer data privacy, especially in databases that include the names and identification data of individual customers.

Data mining

Data mining applications refer to systems used for segmentation, predictive modelling and various statistical analyses based on sophisticated mathematical algorithms. Analyses for predictive modelling may use, for instance, regression analyses, decision trees or neural networks. For example, analyses of customer attrition have led to excellent financial results in retailing. Predictive modelling for campaign targeting purposes is one of the key applications of data mining. The models may be used to calculate customer-level propensities of campaign success or product purchases, which can then be used in targeting marketing in different channels.

Retailing is in many countries clearly lacking behind many industries such as telecommunications, banking, media and insurance, where data mining tools have been in operative use for a long time. In the analytics operations within retailing, it is worthwhile using the expertise gained in other industries, and hiring experienced analysts from other industries pays off quickly. It is often necessary to recruit analysts as it is rare to find people with strong statistical knowledge among traditional retail employees. An exception to the rule is store location acquisition function where the use of statistical analyses has a long tradition.

Shopper segmentation is one of the most important features in data mining applications. Behavioural segmentation gives retailers a good chance to track the structure of the customer portfolio even at a daily level, thus forming the foundation for customer-centric operations. Methods used in shopper segmentation include, for example, SOM (self-organized maps) neural networks, k-means analysis and decision trees. Also, demand forecasting algorithms can be developed for seasonal products for automatic ordering. These algorithms can be used as the basis for order planning both at chain and store level.

Data mining tools are meant for a small and limited team of analysts, and they are of no use to people without a statistical degree even though the easy user interfaces would enable their use. Data preparation for analysis requires a set of tasks that may have disastrous consequences when done incorrectly. The results of the analysis carried out by analysts should, however, be offered to a wide forum, preferably using the normal reporting tools of the company. To attain results, seamless cooperation between the analyst team and key business functions is extremely important. The role of business knowledge is of the utmost importance in briefing, analysis variable selection, interpretation of results and, naturally, executing the results of the analysis. The analyst team supports business primarily through data transformation, and statistical skills and tool knowledge.

Usually more than 80 per cent of the time spent on data analysis is consumed by data collection and transformation. Therefore, it is useful to spend some time on the tool selection in this area, as manual work is a considerable cost factor. The automation of scoring and daily maintenance of models often also needs more attention in the tool selection.

The market for data mining tools is dominated by SAS Institute and its Enterprise Miner product, which is estimated to have a market share of about 80 per cent of the global data mining market. Another commonly used tool is SPSS, which after acquiring Clementine has focused on data mining. SAP has also started to develop a data mining product, which is tightly integrated into its own solutions. Recent acquisitions of analytical solution vendors (eg Khimetrics) are also likely to be seen in SAP's integrated offering in the near future. The data mining market still is relatively small, but because of its strategic character and high market visibility, it is extremely important for major solution providers.

GIS systems and retail network design

GIS refers to an information system combining the map and location data, which can be used in many ways. In retailing, GIS systems have many different functions. They can be used to model store locations on the map and to link them with demographic data on the inhabitants in the catchment area provided that such data is available. It is also possible to identify certain customer segments and locate them on the map, and outline store locations in relation to customer flows. Moreover, GIS systems are a key tool in store network development where, for example, catchment areas, customer flows and cannibalization of stores can be analysed.

GIS systems can also be used to model and describe the geographical coverage of campaigns and study the promotion sensitivity of customers within a certain coverage area. This provides practical information on campaign efficiency in different areas and customer segments. Also, the map can even be used to illustrate the retail outlets and consumption areas of a single product. This information is particularly interesting for the manufacturers in joint marketing planning and evaluation of the efficiency of promotions. Cross-running results with the circulation areas of newspapers sometimes yield interesting outcomes. However, as the number of customers may vary a lot geographically, GIS analysis should always be analysed carefully, as fancy maps may easily point business users to incorrect conclusions.

Category management solutions

Several solutions offer tools to support category management. Choosing products for assortments is supported by category management applications in ERP systems and of various reporting solutions (for example, ScanTrack and the retailer's own POS data). When products have been chosen for assortments, space management solutions are used to plan optimal order quantities and product location. In addition, space management is used at store level where the space is optimized among different product categories, an action often also called floor planning. These applications are used to examine category space profitability, shopping paths of various customer groups, the importance of end caps and promotional areas for different shopper segments, and fluctuations in customer shopping patterns at different hours.

The objective is to automate assortment management for each category whenever possible. Product selection and preparation of planograms take a lot of time when done manually, and also result in significant personnel costs. With new solutions, assortment management can be made easier. As an example, an automatic assortment proposal may be generated as the basis for work of category experts. Increasingly, category management work focuses on local or store-level assortments in accordance with local demand. It is in practice impossible to implement store-specific assortments and planograms manually, with the exception of the largest formats (eg hypermarkets), and using a business model like this demands robustly automated applications.

Automated assortment management applications and data openness have a big impact on traditional assortment work. Traditional assortment proposals are based on conclusions made with the store's own data, and decisions will be based not only on intuition and personal expertise, but increasingly on facts. In new product launches, facts are naturally not there, but even decisions made based on intuition can be evaluated afterwards with facts. This alters the business model in many areas and requires training and change management.

In automated solutions, strategic collaboration partners may in an ideal situation participate in planning the parameters used for assortment optimization in a particular category. It is clear that the importance of traditional assortment proposals in joint category management processes will reduce. Suppliers need to allocate resources for new solutions, or eliminate them, as the old way of working is not needed. This enhances the cost effectiveness in the retail value chain.

Campaign management and personalization of customer communication

Measuring the effectiveness of marketing and sales activities will be one of the key focus areas of retailers and suppliers in the next few years. A campaign management tool is an operational tool for managing marketing and sales activities, and should be the primary tool of a retailer's marketing director. Campaign management typically includes key information about the campaign such as target groups, media to be used, time periods, budget and control groups. A campaign management tool allows the tracking of the following items in marketing activities:

- actual campaign pull (with the data of the control group deducted);
- campaign sales (units and monetary value);
- campaign price/successful sales;
- campaign return on investment (ROI);
- campaign success in relation to budget (sales, margin, pull);
- campaign product repurchase rates.

A campaign management tool often supports the entire campaign process ranging from planning and budgeting to follow-up. Campaign management is traditionally divided into two different sub-areas: untargeted and targeted activities. In campaigns targeted at customers, follow-up can, if needed, be implemented at the level of an individual customer. This enables the measurement of campaigns in customer segments to see which campaign messages and channels work for each segment. Campaign follow-up may be carried out with campaign management solution, but it is often suggested to build campaign follow-up reports to the retailer's common reporting tools for wider distribution. This saves licensing costs, and the system support can also be narrowed down to the few active users.

Retail marketing is slowly changing to event-based marketing. Marketing activities are built as packages, which are sent to customers when the time is right. Classical examples include campaigns for those who have moved to a new house, and for the parents of a newborn baby. To identify these events, changes in customer behaviour need to be tracked continually and automatically. A data mining tool may support this with predictive modelling. The scoring runs need to be carried out daily or weekly, defining the campaign lists, and the information is sent to the campaign management solution, or external partner sending the actual campaign message to the customer.

With typical evolution, many retailers will have, at least to start with, two different campaign management solutions. One will be for their loyalty programme, enabling optimized targeted communications for customer segments or individual customers. Another solution is needed for promotion management, complementing category management and merchandising solutions for evaluating in-store marketing activities and more general mass marketing campaigns. These solutions are often based on conventional category management and product sales, and often bypass the customer relationship point of view and the optimization of the retailer's total marketing spend.

Separate campaign management solutions make it difficult to compare different campaign formats objectively, and it will also be expensive in the long term to maintain two overlapping systems. The challenge is that there are few packaged solutions on the market that are capable of meeting both requirements. In most cases, using two overlapping solutions may still be economically justifiable because customized solutions are not cheap either. However, we are likely to see development in this area, especially by large ERP vendors.

Efficient campaign measurement contributes to the adoption of new operational models in, for example, advertising agency collaboration. It is possible to shift from hourly charges to result-based pricing since accurate measurements are easily available. At briefing meetings, the retailer can provide a good description of the shopper target group, their behaviour and clear metrics for campaign success. The fee can be based on the success of the campaign, with measures like increasing the shopper segment's purchase frequency, growth of average basket size, new product penetration in the baskets, or other agreed measures that are essential in terms of the campaign.

Personalization solutions are used for managing customer communication content and targeting, also in real-time situations if needed. They can be used, for example, to define which banner the customer is shown over the internet, which campaign is printed on the back of the receipt and which personalized messages are printed on the bonus statement. With the enormous assortment of retailers, amounting to tens of thousands of items, and the number of customers rising to millions, it would be impossible to select personalized messages without the support of efficient information systems. Personalization solutions are not yet well known within retailing, because the targeted dialogue and the use of targeted media at stores are still in their infancy in comparison with some other industries. In practice, often the only fully personalized messages today are bonus account statements, customer magazines and some direct mailings.

Personalization tools use rules management solutions, which can be used to define campaign execution according to various criteria. They also enable the use of conditional statements, which include, for example, preventing a campaign for customers who have already participated in it, preventing marketing to underage consumers, or targeting the campaign to a certain restricted area. Conditional statements are also an easy way to automate time-specific campaigns such as sending birthday cards.

When the number of messages targeted at customers amounts to many hundreds and there are several communication channels, there is a need to coordinate customer communication as a whole. Personalization tools meet this need together with campaign management tools. The content offered to the customer is selected in the personalization tool from several alternatives aided by suitable criteria. The data have often been pre-scored to speed things up, which is needed particularly in online personalization. These applications will be obligatory for retailers at the latest when in-store targeted communication is started, as they are needed for selecting marketing messages for each shopper segment, and for determining the campaign priorities and order for each customer. This also enables personalized pricing based on shopper segment. There are dedicated personalization solutions like e.Piphany Personalization Engine or Teradata Relationship Optimizer, but a more general rules management solution can also be used. What counts is that they work seamlessly with the retailer's campaign management solution.

Campaigns displayed to the customer are recorded in the personalization tool, and are not shown to the customer again, except if expressly defined. Similarly, rules can be created that banners are changed after, for instance, every second loading on the website. Another example involves repeat purchasing – whenever a customer has bought a certain product for the fourth time, for example, the customer may receive a coupon with a free offer printed automatically on the bonus statement or, say, at the bottom of the receipt. In non-digital media, such as direct marketing or customer magazines, many different personalized messages are already used. Few customers even notice this as it has not been emphasized in advertising. As an example, a retail bank customer may get a brochure on investment opportunities or wealth management with his or her statement of accounts, whereas another customer may get an advertisement that focuses on the ease and flexibility of a particular consumer credit programme.

Operational direct mailing tasks have often been outsourced, and the personalization tool needs to be well integrated with the company's partners, such as printing shops and media agencies. Postage fees are a key driver impeding the growth of direct mailings, but their relative share of campaigns is still considerably high compared with additional sales for most consumer products and retail chains overall. Because of this, retailers try to pursue digital marketing whenever possible.

Summary

In the retail value chain, the transparency of information continues to grow and IT systems enable the automation of functions as well as cost efficiency. IT solutions will become increasingly real time and allow quicker decision making and operation of the key processes. New identification methods, such as RFID, 2-D symbology, NFC and biometric identification will significantly alter the main processes within retailing as soon as a critical mass is reached for execution.

'Retail is detail', so efficient solutions can take the retail operations management to a totally new level. Shopper information enables fact-based management in key demand management processes. Data collected through loyalty programmes will be used with easy-to-use reporting solutions and applications that are available to people and processes needing them. Little by little, pilot processes and manual reports will be incorporated into daily operations, and automated as part of ERP systems. Data sharing throughout the retail value chain will extend to the use of shopper segment-level data that provides joint tools for retail differentiation. Suppliers will start using the reporting solutions offered by retailers, or build their own systems for information processing, and several other players will emerge specializing in information analysis and exchange.

In the field of solution development, single-point best-of-breed applications in many different areas will be increasingly replaced with consolidated solutions to allow cost savings. More generally, systems integration will be speeded up by the international debate on standardization. Moreover, the outsourcing of information systems is on the rise, with the players of the retail value chain concentrating on developing their core activities. All non-core activities are likely to be outsourced to external, more efficient operators.

7 Loyalty programmes and shopper information sharing

Customer loyalty programmes have quickly become common practice and now form a key part of retail marketing and dialogue with customers. But are loyalty programmes really tools for strategic management and sources of true competitiveness, or merely automatic discount generators for best customers? There are many, often contradictory, views on what loyalty programmes are all about.

Loyalty programmes bring many benefits to the retailer. Several studies indicate a positive effect between loyalty programmes and customer retention. Because most loyalty programmes are based on rewarding customers' prior behaviour in the future, they may serve as a switching barrier for the customer. If the amount of rewards depends also on the length of the relationship, as is often true in the insurance industry, customers are less likely to switch since it would take time to get back similar rewards.

Loyalty programmes might be the answer for increasing customer retention and shopping frequency, but they also have other benefits. Loyalty programmes provide a means to capture transaction and customer information. This information can then be used to learn about the customer behaviour and hence deliver better value to them. However, the focus of retailers with loyalty programmes will increasingly shift from category management to communicating about new products and services, and their important features to customers. A retailer using shopper information can accurately target messages even when assortments keep becoming wider. Small micro-segments that have been inefficient targets in the mass media or at store-level communication may now be appealing and reached effectively through targeted communication.

Loyalty programmes are also one of the key factors that differentiate retailers. Simply – some players have a programme, others do not. Many premium retailers and supermarkets with wide assortments and good customer service invest significantly in loyalty programmes to gain competitive advantage. Loyalty programmes are also popular among cooperative retailers, where customers own the retailer. Traditionally customers in this form of retailing have collected receipts for rebates, so loyalty programmes are just a modern way of implementing the idea of the cooperative movement. This is a way of carrying out 'dividend distribution' according to rules of the cooperative. As a byproduct, the retailer gains customer insight to be used in different processes. Cooperatives with a loyalty programme exist in many markets. Some examples include Migros (Switzerland), Coop Italy, Coop Denmark, KF (Sweden) and S-Group (Finland). In cooperative retailing we can find the rare examples of companies that focus on cost leadership and have a loyalty programme, and this is largely due to cooperative traditions and company cultures.

The costs of a loyalty programme are often significant and not all retailers choose to have one. In Finland, for instance, the average bonus rebate of grocery loyalty programmes is between 2 per cent and 4 per cent, and taking into account the costs related to customer communication, cards and other operational costs, the total impact may account for several percentage points of retail net sales. The major part of loyalty programme costs consists of bonuses paid to customers. Hence, the programme should bring in significant add-on sales that justify higher base prices.

Some retailers have found loyalty programmes too expensive compared to the benefits; for example, most convenience store chains, where average purchases are low, do not have loyalty programmes. Also, hard discounters and most other value retailers do not have loyalty programmes because of their extremely pared-down approach. Among the large retailers that have chosen not to have a programme is Wal-Mart. In addition, many programmes have been ended. In 2000, Safeway in Britain ended its loyalty programme and shifted discounts to selected product prices instead. In 2002, the Domino customer loyalty programme in Norway, shared by six companies, was scrapped. Afterwards, one of the companies, Statoil, continued loyalty programme operations on its own with a new programme. Among the latest examples of companies having dropped loyalty programmes are Sentry Foods in 2005 and Albertsons in 2007. Two signs at Albertsons stores describe the reasons well: 'No card. No hassle' and 'With no card, saving money is a great deal easier'. Lidl has also promoted anti-loyalty card campaigns promising rebates for any card, even playing cards.

It has to be remembered, though, that not all retailers need to offer big bonuses to attract customers to programmes. To cite an example, Finnish department store retailer Stockmann does not pay any direct monetary bonuses but uses club member offers on a regular basis with its two-tiered loyalty programme. Still, customers actively use the cards. Stockmann has succeeded in creating an emotional customer relationship, and their Exclusive card with special benefits is a desirable membership card that can only be obtained by buying at least a certain amount during a year. Exclusive card members will get invitations to special nights and activities during the year. Loyalty programmes have a direct bearing on a company's image, but the image may also limit possibilities of the loyalty programme. Where Stockmann customers use the card without getting any direct bonus, most other retailers are compelled to reward customers with big bonuses. But when a customer can be bought with big rebates, how loyal will that customer be when a new cheaper offer is made?

Loyalty programmes lead to a strong polarization in retailing, with retailers relying on wide assortments and targeted customer communication competing against self-service value retailers focused on minimal assortments. This is a vital strategic choice for a retailer; a far more significant choice than is usually thought. It also has impact on the retailer's management approach with the information available for managing the business. In this chapter, loyalty programmes and the use of shopper data are introduced. We have also interviewed 16 retailers in 11 countries about shopper information sharing in the value chain, and results of this study are presented at the end of the chapter.

Loyalty concepts

Loyalty programmes exist in many different formats. The simplest concepts feature the collection of stamps or points in order to get, say, the tenth product for free. These programmes do not necessarily identify customers, and loyalty cannot be influenced after the free product has been redeemed unless the customer starts to collect stamps again. At the other extreme are loyalty programmes with complex bonus collection and reward models.

Many programmes are based on collecting a certain 'currency' and paying bonuses. Some programmes do not have the collection phase, but rewards rest on rebates and benefits right in the buying situation. Rewards may be based on monetary rewards (refunds and rebates) or on soft benefits. Most rewards are known to the customer when joining the programme, but surprise benefits may also be used to enhance customer loyalty. A programme may involve various levels achieved, for example, by buying a certain amount annually, or by paying a membership fee. A loyalty programme may also involve partners, both for point collection and rewarding customers. Moreover, it is possible to set up joint programmes.

This part of the chapter looks at the key areas of loyalty concepts. We will also examine opt-in clubs, a growing form of targeted customer communication in today's retailing. Whether they are true loyalty programmes is left to the consideration of the reader.

Joining a programme and programme tiers

Joining a customer loyalty programme is most often done at stores, but some retailers also offer the possibility to join on the web, via the retailer's contact centre or through partner organizations. Joining is often linked with the collection of customer information and the entry form is used for collecting personal details such as year of birth, family details like household size and children's ages, and interests like hobbies. The customer's contact information is also usually collected to enable customer communication later. However, in some cases such as stamp card programmes, very few details, if any, are collected about customers.

Most of the information in the entry application becomes out of date quickly and, in our experience, retailers should have well-defined information updating processes in place or leave the additional questions about customer details off the application form. Some retailers with significant loyalty programme experience have simplified joining applications, and more detailed information about the customer is collected later on during the customer relationship. Customer information collection is a continual process linked to the development of the customer relationship. A good example is provided by Amazon.com, which asks very little from the customer the first time, and ensures an easy first purchasing experience, but collects information about customer purchases, preferences and ratings during every visit from then on.

Joining may cost something or be free. Most charges associated with retail loyalty programmes are linked to a card payment function or other feature; loyalty cards as such are often free of charge. At many cooperatives, members pay a membership fee when joining the programme. However, the fee is often repaid if the customer leaves the programme. Other examples of programmes subject to a fee are warehouse clubs, and in some cases customers often cannot even enter the store without paying a membership fee. Some stores offer programmes where customers pay an annual fee, but receive discounts at the checkout with the card. This creates value for both the customer and retailer: true heavy users get better prices, and retailers get more loyal customers as they concentrate their purchases at that store.

A loyalty programme may have several tiers, which may be transparent or invisible to the customer. If the levels are visible, individual customers know the level they belong to and the benefits included. They may also be aware of the benefits received at the other levels, but in some programmes, the top-level benefits, such as special events arranged for the best customers, are not communicated to all customers. The top level is a challenge to attain and only some of the customers get there. These programmes are used particularly by department stores. In the invisible communication and rewards model, individual customers do not know whether they are rewarded according to the same rules as others. Selected offers and activities may be communicated only to the best customers. The same programme may include both visible and invisible levels. The customers know the levels and the related benefits but some benefits are based on a hidden model. These programmes are common in the airline and hotel industries, and customers have become used to them.

Moving from one loyalty programme tier to another can take place as a result of a particular payment made, or it may be earned through a certain volume of annual purchases or some other behaviour the retailer desires to reward, for example shopping frequency. If the upgrade to the next tier is based on collecting and earning, this may play an important role in committing the customer. On the other hand, for the target level to be attractive to the customer, it must offer significant benefits. Tiers may be based, for example, on purchases or points, and a level can also be lost if the requirements are no longer met. Customers may sometimes choose the level themselves and pay in order to get the benefits. As an example, Barnes & Noble's Readers' Advantage programme carries a fee (US~\$25 in 2006), but a customer belonging to the programme receives big discounts on product purchases.

Tiered programmes have been used by airlines and hotels where customer behaviour frequencies and profitability levels vary significantly among different customer groups. In grocery retailing, loyalty programme tiers have only been used to a relatively small extent, but many examples are found at department stores. Examples include the Stockmann's two-tier programme (Clubcard and Exclusive Card) or NK's three-tier programme in Sweden. There are also extreme examples like the highly differentiating and exclusive Saks Fifth Avenue Elite card. High-quality communication to add purchase frequency and cross-sales of different categories are of prime importance at these department stores running a loyalty programme.

Collecting benefits and rewarding customers

Many loyalty programmes are based on customers collecting a certain loyalty currency (points, bonuses, etc). The currency accumulates based on monetary purchase amounts, purchase occasions or product volumes. In retailing, more advanced models are usually based on the amount of money spent, whereas collecting stamps or points from product purchases is more commonly used by smaller companies. At most companies, customer rewards are based on percentage rebates. They are often progressive, encouraging the customer to concentrate purchases and enabling big discount percentages to be shown in marketing communication. Table 7.1 shows examples of different reward structures.

Loyalty programmes can offer monetary and non-monetary rewards, of which monetary rewards are more common. However, non-monetary rewards might be a more effective way to ensure customer loyalty. Some reward types, such as instant rewards, can be both monetary and non-monetary. These different kinds of rewards are discussed next.

Monetary rewards

Monetary rewards include several formats such as fixed or progressive rewards, different kinds of discounts and instant rewards. Most loyalty programmes with fixed or progressive reward structures are based on past purchase volumes. Customers may earn promotional currency, for example points or miles, from their purchases, which can be used for rewards or future purchases. For example, Kesko in Finland uses this approach. A progressive bonus based on the percentage of total purchases is the most common loyalty scheme in grocery retailing.

Special discounts are also a way to give monetary rewards to customers. They can be based on coupons where they are fairly invisible to other customers or on in-store campaigns where customers without the loyalty card can also see the benefits. At department stores and in fashion retailing,

Table 7.1 Examples of loyalty programme reward structures

Type		Description	Example
Monetary rewards	Fixed percentage	Customers get fixed percentage rebates.	Delhaize (Belgium) offers €5 rebate after every 5,000 points collected.
	Progressive rewards	Customers get rebates from purchases, and the percentage depends on the amount used. The more used, the bigger the percentage.	S-Group (Finland) has a loyalty programme with progressive rewards. The rebates vary from 1 to 5%.
	Discounts	Customers get discounts from specified or all products in store. Coupons may be used as vehicle.	Tesco (Britain) sends six discount coupons to its customers with all bonus statements.
	Chosen products	Customers can choose which products are discounted.	In Carrefour's (France) loyalty programme, customers can choose 25 products and get permanent discounts from those.
Non-monetary rewards	Instant rewards	Customers get instant rewards for the purchase. These can be monetary or non-monetary.	Albert Heijn (the Netherlands) has an instant rewards programme where customers get a discount on about 50 products, which continually change.
	Point based – selection of rewards	Customers get points from purchases and have options for redeeming points. These are usually non-monetary rewards, such as travel, electronics and sports.	Nectar (a joint programme in Britain) has a points-based programme. Customers can choose from a variety of different redeeming options such as travel, wines and entertainment.
	Special recognition and treatment	Special recognition and treatment programmes offer non-monetary rewards such as customers being recognized by name; own, fast checkout lines and personal service.	Nordstrom's (United States) customers have an ongoing access to the 'fashion emergency' hotline with personal service.

Table 7.1 cont.

Type		Description	Example
Non-monetary rewards	Customer community programme	Community programmes bring customers together in a club. Mothers of small children are especially popular targets of customer community programmes.	For example, Tesco (Britain) and Nordiconad (Italy) have baby clubs.
	Affinity group	In an affinity programme, customers feel a connection to the offering of the firm.	The most well-known example of affinity groups is Harley Davidson's *Harley owners Club* (United States).
	Knowledge building	Knowledge-building programmes help a company to know its customers and also customers to know the company. The offering may be tailored to fit customer needs.	Tesco (Britain) uses shopper information widely in its operations to create a better shopping environment for the customers.
Other	No rewards, only communication	The programmes are based on customer communication, and no direct rewards are given to customers.	Several mail-order retailers offer to send a catalogue without any other promises to the client.
	Hybrid	Hybrid programmes include several kinds of rewards. Most programmes are hybrids to some extent.	Carrefour's (France) programme contains chosen products, discounts, fixed percentage rewards and promotions in stores.

loyalty programme discounts are often 10 per cent or more. This naturally has a significant impact on the company's pricing strategy, leading to strong differentiation between club members and non-members. Big reward percentages are a double-edged sword. They are very visible and may be important to some customers, but at the same time may limit flexibility in other retailing activities and pricing. When a retailer provides attractive rewards, there might not be sufficient funds for other major activities. And once something has been given to the customer, it is hard to take back. In the worst case, most of a retailer's marketing budget may be tied to predefined loyalty programme bonuses, and there is little room to act when changes happen in the market.

For this reason, many retailers have redefined loyalty programme reward structures so that they are no longer based on conventional rebates. For example, Target uses a reward structure where after a certain amount of purchases customers may make purchases at a 10 per cent discount for one day. In this case, the discount is not focused on the customer's earlier purchases but on future additional sales. The 10 per cent discount will leave a decent margin in most cases, so every bonus used is likely to generate additional profit for the company.

There are programmes that do not use a collection phase but give benefits at the moment of purchase instead. In these programmes, the customer is not rewarded for concentrating purchases, so loyalty is based on other factors. A famous example of such a programme is Instant Rewards by Albert Heijn. Club members get a discount on about 50 products, which continually change. Carrefour uses an instant rewards programme with pre-chosen products. It rewards club members by letting them choose 25 products that they will get at a discounted price. Furthermore, stores have special offers and ongoing discounts. The instant rewards approach can also be used to surprise customers at the time of purchase. One way to provide instant rewards is to give a certain discount based on the purchase amount on a particular shopping visit.

Non-monetary rewards

Although monetary rewards are common, non-monetary rewards may sometimes create greater perceived value, and often are not as expensive to retailers. Non-monetary or soft rewards include product rewards, special recognition and treatment, affinity programmes, customer communities and knowledge building. Soft benefits, such as different services and special privileges, are used particularly at department stores, but other retailers are also starting to become more innovative in creating intangible and experiential rewards.

Customers can be rewarded with different products and services, for instance for a major goal like a holiday trip. Partner programmes, in particular, use product and service rewards, and often some programme partners focus entirely on customer rewards. As an example, Nectar, which is a joint loyalty programme including, for instance, Sainsbury's, BP and Debenhams, lets its customers choose anything from wines to holiday trips as rewards. The points earned can also be donated to charity. As a recent feature, there is an option to pay certain service fees, like movie tickets, directly on the Nectar card with earned points.

Special recognition and personalized services are also an important form of customer rewards. Examples of rewards include customers being recognized by name, faster checkout lines for best customers and personal service. The best customers often value these benefits more than extra offers or discounts, as the benefits may make the regular shopping visits more pleasant. These kinds of rewards are especially popular among department stores. Customers can also be offered free home delivery, fashion advice or other services designed to make the shopping experience easier. Some programmes provide special privileges for the best customers, and other customers may not be aware of them. Such service may include private shopping evenings when club members may make purchases with no other shoppers in the store. These shopping events often also involve discounts and new product demonstrations.

For the retailer, loyalty programme exclusive events offer a good way to create traffic at quiet store hours. Besides, with fewer customers in the store, they can also be offered better service. In addition, club members may be entitled to choose what they want to buy during a sale before other customers can get access to the products. For example, Nordstrom arranges private shopping parties at department stores for its top club members. Moreover, these customers have ongoing access to the 'fashion emergency' hotline. Nordstrom also organizes shopping trips for its customers.

Affinity groups are customers with shared interests. The key aspect of an affinity group is that the company's offering becomes an integral part of the customer relationship and the customer feels a connection with the brand. However, not all companies have products or services that can create this kind of strong interest or emotional link. The use of affinity groups might be extremely difficult in grocery retailing, since FMCG do not often invoke as strong feelings as other products. However, some companies have been creative and tapped into the customer community and customers' emotional connection.

Customer community programmes are closely related to affinity programmes. In an affinity programme, the customer feels a connection to the offering of the firm while in a community programme customers are connected. Often a customer community will exist along with an affinity programme, but many customer communities exist without affinity groups. A customer community can be created if customers see benefit from the connection to other customers. Customers' perceived cost of switching can be increased by creating the community. If a customer leaves the company, the person also leaves the community.

There are many examples of customer community programmes in retailing. Mothers of small children are an especially popular target of these programmes. Many retailers and suppliers (including Tesco, Heinz, Waldbaum's and Nordiconad) have baby clubs. Retailer-facilitated customer communities and affinity groups can also be considered opt-in clubs. These are covered in more detail later in this chapter. Affinity programmes and customer communities are most likely to exist in areas where customers need a lot of information about products and services, and are interested in searching for information beyond the basic needs during their free time. Some key areas for such clubs in grocery retail are health and wellness, wines, gourmet foods, cooking and allergies.

Emotional connection and particular interest in the product are not always required when non-monetary rewards are offered. Knowledge-building programmes can help a firm develop loyalty by creating trust. Every time a customer interacts with a retailer, both learn something about each other. A customer in a grocery store might learn, for instance, where certain items are located and the times when the store is busy, which makes shopping easier. The retailer learns about customer behaviour and purchasing patterns. This creates structural bonds between the retailer and the customer. The retailer can tailor its offering to fit the needs of the customer. Thus, it becomes more costly to switch to the competitor since recreating trust and learning from each other takes time.

Integration of a loyalty programme into the retailer's core business is particularly effective in situations where the retail brand is strong – for example, when its own labels can create prestige value for customers. Exclusive buying evenings at premium department stores have been effective in enhancing customer loyalty, but drive sales at the same time. Department stores do not always have loyalty programmes as such, but they ensure customer loyalty with credit cards. The card owners might receive benefits similar to those offered to members of loyalty programmes. Many popular department stores, such as Macy's, Bloomingdale's and Harrods, have their own credit cards. For example, the Harrods Card has several benefits, including exclusive cardholder 10 per cent days and invitations to events hosted by Harrods. In addition, before the start of any sale, Harrods cardholders are given the opportunity to pre-order selected sale items ahead of the crowd and save an extra 10 per cent. An extreme example of an exclusive department store credit card is Saks Fifth Avenue Elite Card, which was developed to attract cardholders with annual household incomes of at least US~$250,000 per year. It has no annual fee or pre-set spending limit. The benefits include, for instance, 24-hour personal concierge service, airport lounge access, travel insurance, a personal travel consultant and preferred rates and availability at over 650 hotels around the world.

Other types of reward

In reality, most of the loyalty programmes are hybrids with many different reward types. Fixed or progressive monetary rewards usually form the base of the programme and other benefits add attractiveness to the programme or surprise customers. There are several options for a retailer to optimize the reward structure depending on the targets of the programme. For instance, Carrefour uses several different kinds of rewards in its loyalty programme containing chosen products, discounts, fixed percentage rewards and in-store promotions.

The IKEA Family programme is a good example of a programme that is well integrated into the core business of the company. The customers get product discounts, special products available only for club members, a newsletter, *IKEA Family Lifestyle* magazine and special activities in the stores. Today IKEA Family has several million club members in Sweden alone. In IKEA's case we can see clearly the need for critical mass to make a good and profitable loyalty programme. IKEA Family is not running in most small and new markets, even though it is well established in the local Swedish home market.

Customer behaviour can be modified by different reward mechanisms. A typical example is to award double bonuses on purchases made on certain days or times that encourage shopping at non-peak hours. Extra bonuses can also be given for certain product categories that are selected for special attention. Awarding extra points can support other desired behaviour, such as using self-service checkouts. Giving bonuses may be a more politically acceptable way of guiding customer behaviour than direct price discrimination. Bonuses may also be given to customers in certain situations, for example when they join the programme or on their birthday. Retailers can use bonuses to reinforce desired customer behaviour, and also to encourage customers to try new products and services.

Sustainability makes its mark on loyalty programmes, and there are many ways to encourage environmentally-friendly behaviour among customers. Tesco, for instance, awards points to customers using their own shopping bags as a way to reduce the use of plastic bags. In the UK both Tesco and Sainsbury's reward customers for recycling old mobile phones. Nectar also donates the old phones to developing countries. At the beginning of 2007, Tesco rewarded customers for buying organic products. This was a way of encouraging people to try environmentally-friendly products. In the Wells Fargo loyalty programme customers are able to donate bonuses to development projects focusing, for example, on renewable energy. In a joint loyalty programme from Germany, called Payback, customers can donate rewards to Unicef. This is just the tip of the iceberg, and there is much more to come in the near future, as sustainability is a major trend driving the industry. Customer loyalty programmes are a key channel for customer dialogue, and bonuses or rebates are important tools in having an impact on shopping behaviour.

Value-based rewards can be used to communicate company values and social responsibility to customers. In addition to pro-environmental behaviour, the customer can be rewarded for a healthy way of living or studying. For example, Tesco offers an opportunity to pay for Open University study modules with Clubcard vouchers. For a more unusual example, consider the American uTANGO programme, where rewards are based not only on purchases but also on couples not divorcing. Hence, loyalty to the participating companies as well as your partner is encouraged. Rewards are based on long-term saving, during which married couples have to spend a certain amount at companies belonging to the programme, such as drugstore.com and homedepot.com, and stay married.

In addition to the visible benefits of loyalty programmes, surprise rewards may be of value. They often may have a bigger impact on true customer loyalty than ongoing monetary rewards. Rewards received at irregular intervals maintain interest for a longer time than regular rewards. Surprise rewards and campaigns can be used to level off seasonality of business, and can also create new 'seasons' in otherwise slow times. Naturally, it has to be taken into account how relevant the rewards are to customers. Retail loyalty programme development will have an emphasis on 'concealed' benefits, which are not announced to customers in advance but involve an element of surprise.

The basic rules of loyalty programmes will most likely remain simple for the customer, but more complex campaigns and customer rewards are targeted at carefully selected customer segments. Lightweight marketing programmes will be replaced with increasingly high-quality programmes, which attract customers to the extent that some may even be ready to pay for joining them. When a customer pays for a magazine or some other additional service of the loyalty programme, a new level of customer loyalty has been reached. Quality naturally incurs costs, and these costs are very seldom covered with direct payments for the service, but a well-managed loyalty programme has a clear business case that justifies the investment.

Partners and joint programmes

The service portfolio required by customers, together with the costs of running a loyalty programme, have encouraged retailers to invite partners in their loyalty programmes and to set up joint companies to run the programmes. Joint companies may consolidate bonus collection or customer rewards, and often do both. Collaboration is also conducted in marketing, for example through joint customer magazines.

The reasons for creating joint loyalty programmes are clear. In a competitive situation, collaboration enables more attractive rewards for customers than individual players can provide. Hence, customers may be prompted to concentrate their purchases. With many players, various costs can be shared, leading to smaller relative costs per company. These cost savings can be achieved typically in IT, marketing and mailing (if joint communication is included), contact centre service, and many other daily activities needed to run the programme. Beside cost savings, joint loyalty programmes can also drive top-line growth, when companies carry out effective cross-selling campaigns to the customers of other companies in the programme. For some companies, the joint loyalty programme may be a crucial channel for new customer acquisition.

One of the best-known consolidated programmes is Nectar in the UK. Impressively, more than 50 per cent of British households are members. The four main sponsors of the programme (Sainsbury's, Barclaycard, BP and Debenhams) offer customers points on daily purchases. In addition, the programme has about 10 other collaboration partners. Joint financing by many players enables greater rewards for customers, which may serve to increase customer commitment.

Malls may also carry joint programmes for stores operating in them. One example is the VIP Shopper Club, which operates in close to 50 Chelsea Premium Outlets, providing access to hundreds of retail brands to consumers. The programme rewards customers with online coupons, vouchers, special discounts, and if the customer is willing, also targeted e-mails from participating retailers.

Retail loyalty schemes have been partnering actively for many years, and as far as big players are concerned, the markets have been largely divided up. In many markets, most of the major players in retail banking, hotels and gas stations belong to a retail loyalty programme or have one of their own. The effectiveness of joint loyalty programmes to the participating companies can be determined fairly accurately, and it has been seen that after the first year's enthusiasm, the activities typically slow down somewhat. Joint programmes nearly always have a food retailer chain as the 'locomotive'. Depending on the format and service portfolio of the company, other players may be included. Typical partner industries are shown in Table 7.2.

Joint programmes also have their share of challenges. With many separate companies managing the work involved, its linkage to each company's management system and everyday processes may be deficient. Similarly, the prioritization of development work as well as investment ability may vary significantly by company. This has often led to situations where joint programmes focus on the basic loyalty services, whereas more insightful shopper analytics and integration into key business processes such as category management and format development are implemented at company level.

Table 7.2 Joint programmes include several partners

Business area	Examples of retailer own label operations in a loyalty programme	Partner examples (+ retailer)
Credit card	ICA, M&S Money	Visa, Mastercard (plenty of retailers)
Retail banking	Migros Bank, M&S Money	OP-Pohjola (Kesko)
Insurance	Tesco, M&S Money, Carrefour	OP-Pohjola (Kesko)
Travel	Carrefour, El Corté Inglés	Fritidsresor (ICA)
Furniture retail	Micasa (Migros)	Argos (Nectar)
Car rental	Systéme U	Avis (Delhaize)
Mobile telecom	Migros, Delhaize, Carrefour	Telia-Sonera (Kesko)
Broadband	Tesco	Elisa (S-group)
Fuel stations	King Soopers (Kroger), Carrefour	Neste (Kesko)
Car service	Automaa (S-group), VV-auto (Kesko)	Nationwide Autocentres (Tesco)
Airlines	–	Air Miles (Albert Heijn), Condor (Metro)
Health	Target Clinics, Kroger Pharmacy	Nutricentre (Tesco)
Wellness	Fitness Park (Migros)	Cannons Health Clubs (Nectar)
Hotels	Sokos Hotels (S-group)	Marriott (Tesco)
Restaurants	Migros Restaurant	Beefeater (Nectar)
Legal services	Tesco Legal Store	Familjens jurist (Coop MedMera)
Utilities	–	EDF Energy (Nectar)

Opt-in customer clubs

Opt-in customer clubs are one way to implement targeted customer communication. With these clubs, customers opt in to the programme and notify the company that they wish to receive communication, benefits or other services concerning the subject of their interest. Experience shows that the commitment of customers is significantly better in opt-in clubs than in conventional targeted communication. Consequently, the marketing communication of opt-in clubs usually leads to remarkably higher pull percentages. On the other hand, as joining an opt-in club is completely in the hands of a customer, it may be challenging to reach a critical number of customers to ensure effective operations.

A simple opt-in marketing list is the easiest way for a retailer to start targeted customer communication. Many retailers, especially in speciality retailing, collect customer contact details for communication purposes. This has been the traditional way of receiving store catalogues, but today communication is increasingly conducted through digital channels, resulting in significantly lower costs to the retailer.

Opt-in clubs can be implemented based on the interests of customers and communication can then be targeted better and more effectively. Examples of programmes include Sainsbury's PetClub and Tesco's Wine Club. When a customer joins these programmes, he or she starts to receive relevant communication and offers from the company. A drawback of the clubs is that once a customer has been offered certain benefits, it is not easy to take them away. For this reason, clubs and other similar programmes require sufficient resources for continual development of customer services and communication. The content of the club must be relevant and up to date to ensure a good customer experience, especially for those who have been customers for a long time.

There are two key types of opt-in clubs: fixed-term clubs and continual clubs. Fixed-term clubs always relate to a certain customer situation. Classic examples include programmes for people moving to a new home or communication targeted at the parents of new babies. The customer has particular needs related to this situation, and can be provided with relevant communication. To take the example of the new parents, as the baby grows older they shift to the next communication package, which gives them new and interesting information. The retailer naturally continues the programme for parents of new babies, but communication is targeted at new customers who have entered this phase. The retailer can use a major part of the communication package for a long time almost unchanged, thus the relative cost of producing it is low over the long term.

Similar fixed-term clubs can be planned for almost all critical changes in the customer's life. The company can then support the change by providing new information on products and services to the customer. Opt-in clubs provide the option to offer the service only to those customers who are genuinely interested in it. It is vital in fixed-term opt-in offerings to agree with the customer about stopping communication when the service is no longer relevant to avoid wasting marketing resources and sending irrelevant communications to the customer. To ensure efficient operations in fixed-term customer communication packages, retailers need automated IT solutions supporting event-based marketing.

Continual communication programmes aim at strengthening the customer relationship over the long term. For instance, customers interested in a healthy diet or wine enthusiasts usually stay in a club for a long time, and when customers read the club magazine during their seventh membership year, they do not want to see the same communication package as previously, but require new content to maintain interest in the programme. This sets high requirements for a retailer's competence and calls for significant investment. It is, therefore, necessary for a retailer to consider carefully whether to set up a continual club, as it always entails a large long-term investment. In the first year, content production is fairly easy, but it is worthwhile also to think ahead to the future target state regarding customer communication. This sounds simple, but relatively few retailers have defined a clear long term vision for their opt-in clubs including the definition of the elements creating customer value and a business case. On the other hand, companies that are able to create good continual programmes may build permanent, loyal customer relationships. Most of the successful continual communication programmes focus on customers' high-priority interests. A good characteristic of a successful opt-in club is that customers look forward to the magazine and pick it up first from the pile of post when it arrives.

Product personalization may also be linked to retailer opt-in services. For example, Footjoy offers personalized golf or baseball shoes – Custom myjoys – as an online service, where customers can vary product colours, including base, saddle, accent and lace colours, according to their wishes. Logos, icons, flags or text can also be added, and different sizes for right and left foot may be ordered. Another similar example is Leftfoot Company that provides made-to-measure shoes delivered to the customer's home. Once the customer's feet have been scanned in a store, he or she can order the shoes via Leftfoot's web pages. Customers can choose shoe design, colour, leather type, outer and lining. Shoes are manufactured according to customers' choices and marked with the name of the customer and customer number onto the leather insole of the right shoe. Leftfoot Company has a multi-channel strategy where, for example, large department stores play a key role. Personalized details gained in these programmes create a good platform for continuous customer dialogue.

Opt-in clubs work best when a customer is involved in the process, for example by producing content, which might not always be directly related to the retailer's assortment. The best clubs host discussion forums, and become communities around the club theme. Notably, though, a retailer cannot fully control the content in these communities, and the risks can be great if the discussion is not properly facilitated. The operations require expensive resources in an area where retailers do not necessarily have them already in place. On the other hand, if retailers are not involved in this development, other players will implement the services, if the consumer demand exists for them. Many suppliers have set up clubs as part of their consumer communication that offer information in a similar way that retailers do. For example, Huggies (a nappy manufacturer) has a web-based baby club. Parents of babies can, for instance, share information with other customers, ask advice from experts and design a virtual nursery on the website.

Most customer communities, especially on the web, however, are outside the control of retailers and manufacturers. For instance, in car sales customers often look for facts, reviews and tests on the internet before making their decision. The content they view may well come from magazines, clubs or discussion forums, and these sources may play a significant role in the buying decision. As far as food is concerned, different magazines related to cooking and gourmet cuisine run active communities, which create many future consumer trends. Obesity is another important trend, as noted in Chapter 1, and there is now a host of related clubs and services, such as WeightWatchers, which may also have a great impact on consumers' purchase decisions. Information gathering about products is increasingly done at home over the web, and retailers in most cases are not in control of this process, which might change the power dynamics in the value chain rapidly in some product areas.

Customer communication through communities and opt-in clubs is a crucial development area for retailers, whether they build the services themselves or acquire them from collaboration partners. One enabler is Web 2.0, facilitating the participation of an individual consumer in the services. Public and non-profit services like Wikipedia also lead the way in developing similar activities. It is also important to note that it is not always necessary to set up a loyalty programme in order to carry out effective customer communication by the principles of the opt-in philosophy. There is no need to give additional monetary rewards to the customer if communication is sufficiently relevant and provides value. On the other hand, it is natural to link these clubs to a loyalty programme if the retailer already has one in place to 'close the loop' and enable measurement of marketing activities.

Web marketing will also affect this area significantly during the coming years. Currently most retailers do not have a very strong presence on the web, and often even product information is not available on retail websites. Search engines help consumers find information about products easily, and search engine optimization helps new, smaller players to gain customer share with services that are easy to use. Mobile web interfaces will take this new information to the shop floor, and retailers will face a new situation, where they are not the only ones managing the product information available in stores. This also provides manufacturers with new ways to gain consumer trust through good information services.

Use of shopper data

Retailers have traditionally used sales data in business development and tactical decision making. Adding a customer dimension to the analysis brings many benefits to retailers. Rob Turtle from dunnhumby stated in our interview that the sales data tells you what happened, but the shopper data may tell you why it happened. The 'why' is important for two reasons: it may provide an understanding of what to do differently next time, and it can also provide justification for actions.

The use of shopper insight for business development and customer communication is typically one of the key processes of a loyalty programme. Collecting and analysing shopper information as such yields nothing, but the benefits can be realized in some of the key retailing processes, where facts can be used to evaluate efficiency of activities or change ways of operating. Areas where customer insight can be used include:

- targeting of customer communication and marketing;
- measuring the efficiency of marketing and sales activities;
- format development in accordance with the retailer's target customer groups;
- range planning according to the customer base structure of catchment area;
- automating assortment planning in accordance with the retailer's target customer groups;
- planning of local assortments;
- store site analyses to support retail network planning;
- personalized customer services and communication.

Retailers' new insight into their customers' needs is one of the main reasons for the power shift from suppliers to retailers that has taken place within the value chain. Shopper information helps retailers plan assortments independently based on consumer demand. Retailers using shopper data themselves are less dependent on the consumer knowledge and assortment recommendations of suppliers. Furthermore, customer knowledge provides a good foundation for independent new product development and private label (own label) design, serving to further increase the power of retailers.

Segmentation

Behaviour-based segmentation creates a foundation for systematic tracking of shopper segment dynamics and enables the same customer focus throughout the retail core processes. This may be called customer portfolio or customer equity management. Some segments may be highly transitory or tied to a particular time period, such as families with small children and those spending time at their summer cottage. For a retailer, these segments may be permanent but customers in the segments keep changing. Apart from these, many narrow niche segments can be identified, such as people with allergies or wine enthusiasts. For these segments it may perhaps be worthwhile to track their behaviour separately and to plan communication for their needs. Some examples of retail customer segmentations are shown in Table 7.3 and described in more detail on the following pages.

RFM (recency, frequency and monetary value) segmentation is typically the first segmentation applied by most retailers. Most food retailers use

Table 7.3   Examples of customer segmentation in retailing

Segmentation approach	Description	Segmentation basis
RFM	RFM-segmentation classifies customer into segments based on purchase recency, shopping frequency and customer monetary value (often annual sales)	Customer loyalty data – eg annual sales volume and number of shopping visits. Sometimes also recency, last shopping visit (especially in home electronics and DIY)
Shopping mission segmentation	Classifies shopping missions (= receipts) into segments based on products and services in the shopping basket	POS receipt level data. Also customer loyalty information may be included, but is not mandatory
Shopper-relationship segmentation	Classifies customers into segments based on purchases of products and services over a certain time	POS data of all customer purchases on individual customer level, often over a 12-month time period
Customer-lifestage segmentation	Identifies typical customer lifestages for customer dialogue differentiation	May use several segmentation bases and event triggers, eg POS data and external data about customers
Geodemographic segmentation	Classifies customers into segments based on where they live and what are the area demographics. Often used for new customer acquisition purposes	Segmentation often bought from external data provider, and based on customer address and area demographics

only the last two dimensions, as shopping in food stores is a very frequent activity. However, the recency dimension in segmentation may still be of great importance in other retail areas such as home electronics and DIY. Customer buying frequency is often counted as visits during the past 12 months, which gives a good indication of customer loyalty and share of purchases, especially if it is linked to customer household size information.

Monetary value often refers to the annual sales to the customer. This is common information also for the customer and can be used as the basis for loyalty programme tiers. If customer margin or customer profitability is used, the segmentation information is most often used only in internal business development activities. However, even if the segmentation is done with sales figures, sales margin with customer communication and service costs should be considered as background information and can provide interesting insights into customer profitability.

In shopping-mission segmentation the retailer segments single shopping visits, which are actually individual receipts. The receipt information about products bought is the core information for segmentation. The shopping-mission segmentation does not require a loyalty programme, so this behavioural segmentation can be used by any retailer. However, a loyalty programme and linking shopper information from past behaviour and customer demographics can add value to segmentation. A shopping mission basically refers to customers' baskets. The company that collects, stores and analyses Tesco's shopper data, dunnhumby, has put it simply 'you are what you eat'. The segmentation is carried out mainly on the category or subcategory level, or using special product attribute classifications. Item-level segmentation would not be sustainable, since assortments change constantly.

When scored to whole data, shopping-mission segmentation illustrates key retailer basket types, volumes and products and services bought in the basket. This information is useful in category management and planning store-level promotion activities. Shopping-mission segmentation can also show the main customer routes through the store based on product placement, and provide useful insight for format development. When shopping-mission segmentation is applied with the retailer's full year data, we typically see a clear, natural shift in different baskets because of retail offerings in different seasons. For example, at summer time fresh produce sales go up; Christmas and Easter have their own distinctive shopping patterns. Shopping-mission segmentation can be used as background information for designing seasonal shopping areas and product displays.

Shopper-relationship segmentation is based on customer behaviour over a longer time frame. Typically 12 months of continuously updating customer data will serve the purpose well using this approach, and it evens out seasonal fluctuations in demand. Shopper-relationship segmentation always requires customer identification, so it can only be used by retailers with a loyalty programme. Just as with shopping-mission segmentation, this form of segmentation is most often carried out using sales in different product categories or subcategories, or special product attribute classifications. Customers are then segmented based on their shopping behaviour, ie what kind of products they buy. Product attributes may also be used, such as health-related products, inexpensive products and premium products. Shopper-relationship segmentation provides useful information for business development about retail core customer segments, for instance identifying the key products and services bought, how often customers visit the store, how well different campaigns and promotions work in the segment, and what the customer profitability is in each segment.

Another approach for shopper-relationship segmentation is to use shopping missions as the basis for segmentation – in other words how many times the customer has been shopping in different shopping-mission roles during the year. This approach needs a well-established shopping-mission segmentation to function well. At the same time we might lose some information about purchases of individual categories or product attributes, and a parallel shopping-mission segmentation is needed especially for category management decisions.

Customer-lifestage segmentation is one kind of customer-relationship segmentation, where customer segment dynamics are actively monitored. It can be done with shopper-relationship segmentation, where the retailer actively tracks customer segment changes from one segment to another. Most benefits of customer-lifestage segmentation can still be achieved with a much simpler approach using changes in customer demographics and purchases of 'marker' products. A customer moves from one lifestage to another by buying certain products; for example, buying nappies for the second time might tell the retailer that the customer has just had a second baby.

Another approach is to buy the same information from external data sources. The most useful offerings for certain lifestages can be turned into proactive offerings that customers can apply themselves. Examples of this are opt-in clubs covered earlier in this chapter. Customer-lifestage segmentation uses principles of event-based marketing. Events can be actively monitored using POS information, and can also benefit from customer master data changes (such as address changes) and externally available information (like household size, number and age of children).

Geodemographic segmentation is most often used to complete other segmentations and is applied in parallel with other approaches. The segmentation is often bought from an external data provider, and is based on customer demographics linked with geographical information. The main users of geodemographic segmentation in retail are store site planning and new customer acquisition, where the retailer can buy lists of interesting customers to contact. Brief examples of geodemographic segmentation were discussed in Chapter 6.

Several segmentation approaches were described above, but it is important to note that not all retailers conduct active customer segmentation, at least not at the individual customer level. For example, hard discounters do not even try to meet all customer needs, but want to reap success with certain volume products. In other words, they will exclude many shopping basket types and consumer groups because the service level required is not in line with their strict retail format. Customers understand this, as the retailer value proposition does not promise one-stop shopping, often only value for money. Heavy analytics and segmentation models would bring in little value for the customer in this environment.

Many different approaches have been presented for assessing the effectiveness of segmentation, both in academic literature and as a practical management tool. The following list includes key assessment criteria collected from a wide range of materials (for example, Wedel and Kamakura, 1999). They can be used in the assessment of segmentation for retailers and many other industries:

- *Identifiability*. All customers can be classified into one or more segments.
- *Substantiality*. Segments are sufficiently large commercially to enable segment-specific planning and actions (such as new product development or targeted customer communication).
- *Accessibility*. Customers can be reached in accordance with the retailer's needs, either at a store or through customer communication.
- *Responsiveness*. Customer segments react differently to activities and require their own service or communication models.
- *Stability*. Segments are sufficiently permanent to enable the planning of activities and, when needed, even organization based upon them.
- *Usability*. The service models for customer segments are sufficiently different to justify the segmentation.

Key retail processes often need different segmentation solutions, and advanced retailers use several parallel solutions at the same time. Where one segmentation model may work very well in personalized marketing, its usability in planning local assortments may be inadequate. In particular, retail strategic planning may benefit from several parallel segmentation models that enrich the retailer's customer insight. For store-level implementation segmentation has to be very clear and straightforward. Criteria of effective segmentation should always be assessed with a particular retail process using the segmentation.

Active customer portfolio management

Retailers, like any business, gain and lose customers all the time. Many customers are not loyal to one retailer, and regularly visit many retailers. In addition, customer needs change over time and customers change segments. Customer portfolio management is a systematic way actively to monitor and develop a retailer's customer portfolio. Retailers need to understand how to attract new customers and how to reduce attrition, but also how to help customers to shift to other, more profitable segments. Planning and operations are done on a customer-segment level, and objectives can be set on a segment level to optimize the structure of the customer base. Examples of segment-specific objectives include:

- number of customers;
- average purchase value;
- average number of items on receipt;
- category-specific sales;
- sales of new products or services;
- number of new customers;
- acquisition cost per new customer;
- level of customer attrition;
- number of customers shifting to more profitable segments (to be defined by segment);
- customer loyalty (eg share of wallet, shopping frequency);
- customer profitability;
- customer satisfaction (vs. key competitors).

Whatever the basis for segmentation, it creates a foundation for managing the retailer's customer portfolio. Customer portfolio management prioritizes the retailer's development resources in terms of the chosen customer groups and objectives set for them. Segment-specific reporting is also vital. This can be illustrated with the following example. A retailer collecting accurate shopper information gets good tools for understanding local customer behaviour. When, for example, a new premium store is opened next to the retailer's store, customer attrition can be analysed including what these customers have purchased earlier. The tracking of shopper behaviour also makes it possible to see which customers return and which permanently change their behaviour. When the lost customers can be identified, they can be targeted with activities such as direct marketing without having to lower prices to all customers. The impact of most sales and marketing activities can also be tracked with these metrics. Though some activities will be successful and others not, retailers can learn from all of them, and when the situation reoccurs, the lessons learned can be used.

Vital questions related to the retailer's customer portfolio management are as follows:

- How have customers moved from one segment to another, and why?
- How can the retailer help the customer to 'grow' into more valuable segments?
- In which segments has the retailer lost customers to the competition, and why?
- Into which segments has the retailer gained new customers, and which activities have been efficient in new customer acquisition?

Customer portfolio management is used to allocate resources in a way that maximizes retailer profitability and minimizes risks. It deals with different customer lifecycle phases: creating new relationships, maintaining and developing relationships and winning back churning customers. There is a link between acquisition and retention, the customer acquisition and retention strategies should be aligned. If a firm acquires customers not aligned with retail positioning, it will be difficult to maintain them or maintaining them might be unprofitable. For example, aggressive price reductions might bring lots of new customers, but they are probably not profitable and/or loyal. Acquiring the wrong kind of customers can also affect the existing customer base negatively, especially in services where customers may interact with each other.

Customer portfolio management deals with managing the retailer's core processes, such as category management, concept development, network planning and marketing, setting the customer segment objectives for each function. The major part of conventional reporting and objective setting in retailing has, however, been largely based on average customers. Customer portfolio management brings two important new characteristics into the measurement process: tracking customer segments and tracking change. In other words, it all boils down to a more accurate measurement of business dynamics. Analysing customer segment shifts reveal a lot about the development of business and help in forecasting trends further into the future than average figures could show. Understanding the dynamics of customer segments enlightens key business successes and failures, and learning from them creates a good foundation for retail business development.

Effective customer portfolio management requires clear objective setting. Advanced companies prepare their budgets based on objectives set for each core customer segment. As mentioned above, the objectives may concern the number of new customers acquired for different segments or the active guidance of customers from one segment to another. Moreover, cross-sales targets may be assigned, for example to make customers familiar with new product or service areas.

Customer attrition and slowdown should also be managed, though it is important to realize that some loss is natural and inevitable. Examples of natural churn include the moving of a customer to another town or to a nursing home or assisted-living facility, or change in transport connections. In these cases, the retailer cannot win the customer back no matter how much it invests in the customer relationship. However, retail customers usually defect only partially. But as a customer begins shopping in another shop, he or she might eventually defect totally. Hence, it is important to manage partial defection, too. Some grocery retailers have noticed with in-depth customer analysis that, once churned, customers are very hard to gain back. Shopper analysis also typically shows that certain demand fluctuations compared with customers' typical behaviour are a key impulse of attrition risk. The earlier retailers identify this risk, the easier it is to make corrective actions with positive surprises. Predictive modelling techniques from other industries can be of great help in this process. However, very few retailers have systematic and responsive processes in place for attrition risk identification and customer win-back campaign execution.

The goals of customer portfolio management should also involve customer satisfaction in different segments, indicating future trends in the customer base. In an ideal situation, the retailer benchmarks the satisfaction of its own customers compared with key competitors' customers or the whole population, but this requires the use of appropriate syndicated metrics or market research carried out by the retailer itself. An example of standard metrics is the ACSI (American Customer Satisfaction Index), developed and used in the United States to study customer satisfaction on a large scale among different industries and companies.

Customer portfolio management should also take into account the significance of local presence, at least to some extent. Competitive situations vary significantly between store locations, and an identical assortment or pricing does not always work optimally in every store. For instance, supermarkets in the same chain may be in quite a different situation depending on whether they are situated next to a hypermarket or a hard discounter or are the biggest store in the region. Other essential considerations in customer portfolio management are the targeting of marketing investment and the use of loyalty programmes in the development of chain operations. Retailers need to determine the amount of resources to be allocated in new customer acquisition and strengthening existing customer relations, in order to increase the value of the customer portfolio as a whole.

Category and activity management

Shopper data can be used in many ways in business development and operations, of which category and activity management operations often bring most benefits. The data is usually available almost real time and on a very detailed level: individual products, stores and days or even hours can be used in analysing the behaviour of customer segments.

Category management achieves totally new possibilities with shopper data, but also brings in complexity. The sales of each category, subcategory and product can be measured at shopper segment level, and hence assortment and range planning can be executed according to the demand of target segments. Shopper information provides from the outset the same measures and language for category management, marketing and format development, and all departments can work towards the same objectives. The basic measures are pretty much the same as in traditional category management, but now they include also the important customer segment dimension and basket information, revealing more about what is bought together and key customer basket types.

Shopper information can provide valuable new insights in category management, especially when choosing lines to be deleted in the assortment. If retailers are only looking at the sales figures, some products important for key customer segments or shopping baskets might be deleted as total sales are low. However, if customers do not find these products in the assortment, they might need to visit a competitor's store, and the retailer faces a real attrition risk. Shopper information enables retailers to check important products for each customer segment, and this process is relatively easy to automate. Taking it to daily use is a business and change management challenge, and needs clear measures that support the same customer metrics. They provide the reasoning why a category manager should keep an unprofitable product in the assortment, lowering individual category results, even though the decision is important for the whole concept.

New product launches also benefit from shopper information in several ways. Besides typical measures such as sales, penetration in stores, and category growth, retailers can gain insight related to several other questions, for example:

- Which shopper segments buy the product? Are there any regional differences?
- How often do customers buy the product?
- How do repeat purchases develop? Which segments bought the product again?
- What products are bought with the new product (basket information)?

With shopper information retailers can make a detailed buying profile for all new product introductions. They can get information about adopter segments, followers, and especially about repeat purchases of the product. In our experience, the repeat purchases of new products compared with marker products and category benchmarks can forecast the future performance of the product well. It is also useful to see the information about shopper segments that tried the product, but never bought it again. Also, the cannibalization effect of new product introductions (NPIs) can be analysed at a very detailed level, as we can see the past behaviour of customers and the products they used to purchase.

The most advanced retailers and consumer products companies update a rich variety of product attributes to classify products, and this information helps to identify trends and hidden purchasing patterns. Retailers often update only the most important product attributes, as the amount of products is huge, but manufacturers may have an interest in more in-depth updating, especially as many attributes are still category specific. The majority of consumer products manufacturers have rich product attributes already available for their own products, but the tricky part is to update the data also for competitors' products and private labels. Most consumer products companies have not yet defined clear master data management policies for competitors' products, so this is on the development path for many companies in the near future. Besides analysing the development of category trends, product attribute information is also very useful in customer analytics, as products change often, but different characteristics and product attributes relatively seldom.

Shopper data particularly benefits activity management in enabling the tracking of those customers who reacted to the activities and at what time, but also reveals the customers who did not react to the campaigns, and benchmarks these results actively to preset objectives. As the data is usually available almost in real time, tactics can be changed while the activity is still running. For example, the sales of a new product can be analysed during the first weeks and the following marketing activities can be adjusted according to the results. Activities and their results can be analysed in several ways, for example with the following questions:

- How did the campaign affect product- and brand-level sales during and after the campaign?
- How did the campaign affect category and segment sales during and after the campaign? What were the effects on category profitability?
- Regarding cannibalization – how did the campaign affect substitute products?
- Which shopper segments bought from the campaign? Which did not?
- How many times did the customers buy the campaigned product?
- How did the campaign affect the value of the shopping baskets?
- Did the campaign change shopping frequency in different segments?
- How did the post-campaign sales develop in different segments?
- When was the campaign efficient (compared with retailer customer flows and category benchmarks)? What were the particular hours or days?
- How did the campaign perform in different regions?

As seen from the above, there are several ways to analyse campaigns. However, the analyses are complex, and executing them manually is often not worthwhile or would require a considerable amount of resources, and thus is not done. In the past this has been a good excuse for not accomplishing the analysis, but new IT solutions have changed the field. Retailers need to automate the follow-up of campaigns to ensure efficiency, and can use campaign management solutions for this. Best practice retailers already have them in place, and others are likely to follow suit soon. With advanced tools retailers can pilot several campaigns in parallel, and leverage the best ones in the whole chain. Beside promotions, several other activities may be tracked similarly, such as price changes, new layout solutions, new planograms, and several others. Defining control groups for all campaigns is important, and enables retailers to evaluate the real effects of the activity.

Shopper data can also be used in planning local assortments for different regions. As the store-specific customer structure and purchase behaviour can be analysed, the assortment can be mass customized according to local needs. This of course adds much complexity to category management, and the achieved additional sales need to cover the costs involved. But when automated, retailers can continuously and systematically track successful local products or pilots, and leverage them in other areas where the customer structure is similar.

Range management is also an important part of the use of shopper data. Layout and space allocation for different categories can be done based on the demand of key customer segments. More space can be allocated to categories that are popular among the target customer segments, and also the store layout may have specific solutions for different segments. For instance, shopping routes can be designed to serve the needs of families with small children. Decisions about product placement can be done by analysing shopping basket structure. One example is Best Buy, that redesigned some of its stores based on loyalty information. Assortments, layout and other store solutions have been arranged according to the needs of key customer segments as solution areas. The experiment has been successful and the concept spread to other stores in the chain. Sometimes segmentation might also lead to different formats for different segments. Based on a large segmentation study, Delhaize differentiated its Food Lion format into three different store formats – Food Lion, Bottom Dollar and Bloom – and the format used in each location depends on the balance of local customer segments.

Shopper data provides benefits not only for retailers, but also for the consumer products companies. Later in this chapter, the section 'Data sharing in the retail value chain' introduces shopper data sharing possibilities in retailer–manufacturer collaboration.

Targeted communication

With loyalty programmes, targeted customer communication has become common in retailing. When a retailer knows its customers and their main characteristics, marketing can be planned and targeted more accurately. In addition to data received from loyalty programmes, effective targeted communication requires the selection and management of communication channels suited to the specific purpose and situation. Furthermore, targeted communication can be directed at attractive but relatively small groups with certain special needs. Such niche groups can include owners of a certain kind of pet, people on special diets, parents of babies or small children or people interested in a particular hobby. These groups can of course be identified based on the customer's purchase history, but another option is to give the customer a chance to indicate his or her interest in a subject field, as is done in opt-in clubs discussed earlier in this chapter.

In retail direct marketing, customer-specific bonus statements are a natural format for personalized messages. Tesco sends six personalized coupons with its Clubcard quarterly bonus statements. Of these, four relate to products that the customer has bought earlier. Two coupons are used for selling new products or services. These coupons can be used to entice the customer to visit new departments or to become familiar with a new product. For instance, a customer who buys a laundry detergent but never a softener, can be offered one, or a user of a basic detergent can be enticed to start using a more expensive premium brand.

Targeted marketing also enables multi-phased campaigns where customers can be contacted several times. For example, the first message can be directed to certain customer groups and the second only to those who did not respond to the first message. This kind of approach is already widely used in, for instance, catalogue and online retailing. The development of customer relationships is a continual activity, and it can be done in several channels. As the retailer knows all the communication the customer has received previously, new messages can build on the previous ones. As simple as it sounds, most retail marketing organizations do not have a clear plan for educating customers about new products and services, and continually building the customer relationship. To do it well requires tight collaboration of marketing and category management organizations.

Communication can also be targeted in accordance with customers' life situations (often called event-based marketing). Communication is then focused on the customer's current life situation and does not necessarily continue after the situation has changed. Classic examples of customers' critical changes in life situations include moving to a new home, the birth of a child, changes in the life of couples (cohabitation, marriage, divorce), starting a new hobby, having the children move out, moving to a new employer, retiring, and suffering serious injuries, for example leading to immobility. In event-based marketing, conventional campaigns related to a certain period and the accompanying campaign calendars lose their significance, and the focus shifts instead to following the customer from one life situation to another. A company always has up-to-date material for each customer life situation and it uses it at the moment suitable to the customer. This kind of communication is effective since it reaches the customers at the right time and offers relevant information to the customer. However, this kind of communication is not yet widely used since retailers do not typically have processes (for example, marketing planning) tuned up for event-based marketing. In addition, marketing budgets and traditional collaboration models with manufacturers might not support the continual actions needed in event-based marketing. In many cases, the data for event-based marketing already exists, but the business might still lack tools that are easy to use for campaign business-rules management.

Targeted communication is closely related to personalized services. Shopping history can be relied on to produce added value for a customer. For instance, the customers of the University Pharmacy in Finland have access to their medication history through loyalty cards, which may be very useful in patient treatment, and customers can take a printout about earlier medications with them to their doctor. In-store communication can also be targeted at an individual shopper if the store uses PDAs on trolleys or POS displays with the possibility of customer identification. At Boots in the UK some convenience stores have touch-screen kiosks (Advantage Point machines) where members can use their card and receive a printout of special offers that are personalized to their buying history. With new printing technologies, tailor-made customer magazines are another option to personalize messages to customers. An extreme case of targeted customer communication could be dynamic pricing for each individual customer at the point of purchase in the store.

Targeted marketing can also be a collaborative effort between retailers and manufacturers. Ziliani and Bellini (2004) have introduced some interesting examples of collaborative marketing efforts. An Italian retailer, Interdis, joined forces with Kraft to promote Milka and Interdis' own label juice. Coupons offering free juice with the purchase of three Milka chocolate bars were mailed to customers who had bought chocolate products during the last six months. Only customers who had bought several different chocolate brands were targeted, since it is easier and less aggressive to target customers who are not totally loyal to competing brands. Precise targeting based on shopper data can also be used as an aggressive marketing strategy. For instance, another Italian retailer Nordiconad, together with Procter & Gamble, wanted to increase the market share of Swiffer (Procter & Gamble's floor cleaning brand). Coupons were mailed to club members who had purchased Pronto, a rival brand of floor cleaners. The campaign was a success – Swiffer became the leading brand in the category. However, this is an aggressive and ethically questionable tactic, where retailers can discriminate suppliers heavily.

The aggressiveness of targeted marketing tactics may be reduced by focusing on retention campaigns rather than trying to acquire competitors' customers – in other words, retailers targeting only those customers who already buy their own brand. Targeting their own, profitable customers with cross-sell campaigns also has other benefits: the cost of marketing actions stays low and customers are more likely to react to the campaigns. However, direct customer communication is often about cross-sales and product upgrades for retailers, and new customer acquisition for manufacturers, so we are likely to see tough competition in this field.

Innovative retail companies make good use of targeted customer communication. Whereas conventional retail competitor activity tracking has been conducted by reading local newspapers, with targeted communication the company often does not know what the competitor does with its customers. A small share of campaigns can be recognized afterwards, but even then a competitor cannot be sure to whom the campaign was actually directed. This is good news for innovative companies, making it possible to develop their customer relations fairly undisturbed. By contrast, the situation is challenging for followers, who have become used to selling products advertised by a competitor at an even lower price. In the worst case, a company does not even notice that a competitor's customer communication has shifted its focus. How many retailers really track their main competitors today and know the communication they are using to develop their customer relationships?

Data sharing in the retail value chain

Transparency within the value chain is one of the key principles of efficient customer response (ECR), and data sharing across the value chain is a key dimension of it. However, surprisingly few companies have realized this vision even though the concept has been under discussion since the 1980s. The data shared by retailers can be used in many collaboration areas like category management, new product introduction tracking, marketing effectiveness measurement, optimization of field activities, and development of logistics and optimization of warehouse levels. The areas of application are wide, and the data requirements vary in different areas. The following figure shows a rough range of potential utilization areas.

Collaborative planning, forecasting and replenishment (CPFR) only requires sales data on the sales volumes of a supplier's products. The sales information of competitive products is useful particularly while analysing the impact of campaigns, but it is not necessary. The data can be given, for

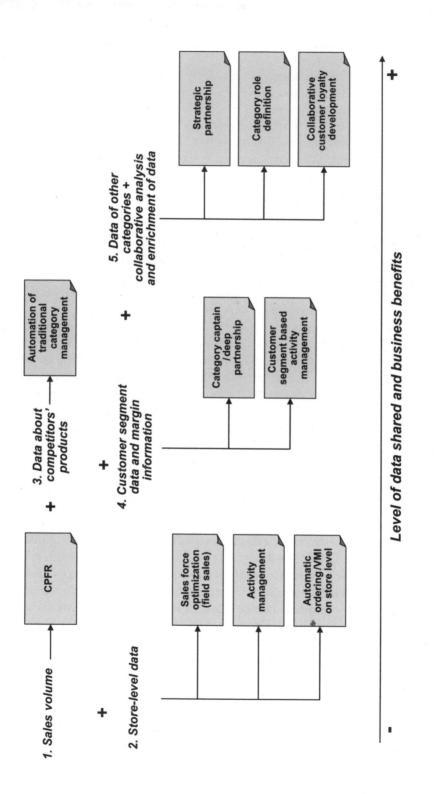

Figure 7.1 Potential application areas of retail sales data at different data levels

example, at chain level. What counts is the speed of data sharing, since production planning needs the data as soon as possible, for instance. Almost real-time availability is the objective but also daily updated data can lead to considerable benefits.

In the case of store-specific data, new options for using the data open up. A supplier may check store penetration of its products and manage its field organization in a more efficient way. With this information, the effectiveness of local campaigns and product demonstrations can also be analysed. Store-specific sales data combined with inventory balances would enable suppliers to use store-specific vendor-managed inventory (VMI) if the retailer wants to outsource the ordering and replenishment process and feels that the supplier can deal with it most efficiently.

When complemented by sales data of competitive products, the information can be used in conventional category management. There is actually nothing new about sharing information in this area since many retailers have distributed this kind of information on paper, shown it to suppliers or sent it in Microsoft Excel format. The biggest procedural change is that up-to-date information should always be easily accessible to suppliers, and at the same time the retailer could require suppliers to conduct certain analyses based on the data before making assortment recommendations. Also, using joint reports and measures helps in setting up mutual objectives as well as tracking them.

When information sharing is discussed, a concern is often raised about how to prevent the data from getting into the wrong hands. Wal-Mart is a good example of a company that shares data with suppliers systematically. Wal-Mart President Lee Scott has stated at an ECR Europe seminar that the share of suppliers who abuse the information is not more than 5 per cent, and that most of them will get caught sooner or later. At the same time, he posed a rhetorical question: Taking into account the undeniable benefits brought by the data sharing, should 95 per cent of suppliers be punished for the mistakes made by 5 per cent?

The sharing of sales data at shopper segment level will revolutionize retail–manufacturer collaboration. Information at shopper segment level enables suppliers to help retailers differentiate and increase customer loyalty in the target customer groups. Without this information, the recommendations given by manufacturers are based on average consumption, and their support for developing the shopper-driven retailing business model remains incomplete. Data at shopper segment level also gives suppliers information on shoppers who buy the products: their profiles, other products included in their shopping basket, the value of the average shopping basket and many other things. Significant benefits can be achieved in trade promotion activities when retailers and manufacturers together learn about how activities have impact on different shopper segments. Even if there is no desire to use segment-level shopper data actively in everyday collaboration, the data may have monetary value if the retailer sells information to its suppliers. As the retailers will collect data anyway and have tools for analysing it, it is nice to have some suppliers sharing the costs. Additional cost for opening up modern data warehouse systems are marginal compared to even direct benefits.

Product margin data approaches the sphere of trade secrets. Many collaboration contracts forbid dissemination of this data to competitors, which is very natural. In genuine category captain relationships, the supplier must try to help retailers succeed in the category. The real metric of success is, however, not the sales but category profit. Because of this, it should be possible to provide margin data, if needed, at a suitable level, for example at subcategory or segment level to strategic collaboration partners.

Data sharing goes furthest when a supplier begins to receive information on the sales of other categories, too, and starts to understand the shopper's overall behaviour in the store. This data can be used in, for example, category definitions along with category role and strategy development. Similarly, the information is most useful when category roles are considered in terms of the main shopper segments. It remains to be seen whether any supplier will reach this strategic level in retail collaboration. On the other hand, it should be estimated what resources should be allocated to ensure that the analyses are beneficial for all parties. It is often wise to over-resource the initial collaboration project, then when the results are seen it is easy to identify the focus areas for daily collaboration with fewer resources.

Independent of the level of data sharing, new solutions are needed in order to share data. As simple as it sounds, fully open data sharing would be the easiest, cheapest and quickest option with the supplier getting direct access to the retailer's reporting systems. Naturally, this is not possible because the majority of this data is considered trade secrets. Access rights management is a vital matter in the implementation of supplier reporting. As implied above, suppliers can be provided with very different information; it may also vary by a supplier or collaboration level, and these might also change on occasion. It should be possible flexibly to link access rights to detailed data (for example, product data, categories, suppliers) depending on the rules agreed upon with the supplier. Access to sales data can be built via many routes. Suppliers can be given access to the retailer's own systems with certain access rights, or data sharing can be organized through an external partner. For example, Sainsbury's transmits some data to its suppliers via Nectar, the loyalty programme run by Loyalty Management Group.

As far as value chain efficiency is concerned, it is vital to ensure that the systems chosen can be shared and are easy to integrate into other necessary applications. They must enable sufficient value chain transparency so that the most efficient player in the value chain can carry out the analyses and redundant work is avoided.

In the United States, targeted marketing and customer analytics have already become a significant business. Catalina Marketing collects the purchase history data of customers from more than 30 retailers and drugstores, altogether from more than 29,000 outlets. The number of new transactions is more than 250 million each week. Analyses based on these data are sold both to retailers and to manufacturers. The number of messages tailored to customers and sent through the company amounts to billions annually. Dunnhumby, which collects, stores and analyses Tesco's shopper data, is another company actively offering its services to suppliers. In addition, it has started growing in the United States by setting up a joint venture with Kroger, capitalizing on the lessons learned in collaboration with Tesco.

Using an external service provider may sometimes be profitable in terms of collaboration. It should be possible to tailor a given number of tables and attributes in the data warehouse to suit supplier needs. Examples include supplier-specific categories, product attributes, division of stores in accordance with supplier sales area classification and the supplier's own campaigns. Retailers are not necessarily interested in building all these features in their data warehouse even if suppliers pay for it. This is because the immediate benefit to the retailer is low, the task would involve a lot of work in coordination and data cleansing and would also explode the complexity in the data model.

From the manufacturer point of view, the rules of the market economy apply – in other words, the manufacturer often gets the desired reports by paying for them. On the other hand, it is not worthwhile for all suppliers to tailor reporting just for themselves, because the IT needs among suppliers are very much alike. Because of this, it is probable that there will be third parties or joint ventures in the business to deal with data processing for suppliers. This is also supported by the fact that in the future, suppliers can possibly receive information from many retail groups, and it would be practical to get the information from the same reporting system. None of the suppliers will have resources to build competences for several separate retail systems across different functions. Horizontal collaboration of different suppliers is likely to yield benefits, but it remains to be seen if they can make direct investments for it, or if the services will be operated by third parties.

Collaboration can also begin in an evolutionary way since the benefits of data sharing are significant. Forerunners will gain competitive advantage, and it does not seem likely that there would be drivers for joint venture solutions for a whole industry as in product data management. When one retail group conducts this kind of collaboration with its major partners and thereby reaps competitive advantage, the same model can then be spread to other suppliers as well. Suppliers can also use similar reporting solutions with other trading partners if possible and, as a result, systems develop along with this evolution. However, data sharing will be a retailer-led activity, and manufacturers will have a major challenge in keeping up with different retailer systems and harmonizing the data for internal use.

Common information systems quickly identify the suppliers that genuinely believe in the benefits of ECR activities. Compared with earlier ECR pilots, these decisions require resources and monetary investment and have far-reaching consequences in collaboration models. Decisions require the participation of not only marketing and sales but also at least the IT department. New solution investments, even if implemented as joint purchases, require board level approval at many companies. Top management needs firm commitment in the matter before taking it forward. This may slow the starting of collaboration, and dynamic companies will grab the pioneering advantage. On the other hand, boards with customer equity management competence may also ask top management about these plans, and the comments and preparation for the board may considerably promote the matter, as we have seen happening in some companies.

Shared information has a certain monetary value, and the members of the value chain have to agree upon benefit sharing. It is vital to realize that unless operational changes are made, more accurate information will not yield any benefits and costs will only rise because of new systems. On the other hand, information not shared also has no value. The benefits of collaboration can only be realized through operational activities. Agreeing upon the rules for data sharing is up to top management, and it is the retailer who sets the pace. Examples and experiences already exist, as does the technology for sharing data. Retail management defines collaboration willingness with its trading partners, and those aiming at true ECR operations will stand out from the rest during the next few years. Data sharing will add the required concreteness and a systematic touch to collaboration, enabling the parties finally to shift from pilots and development projects to daily joint operations.

Customer information sharing study

To identify key trends and future directions in customer data sharing, we carried out a study for 16 leading retailers from 11 countries (Spain, Sweden, Finland, Estonia, Germany, Switzerland, the United Kingdom, the United States, Belgium, Denmark and Italy). Most of the interviewed retailers had loyalty programmes, representing a total of 42 million club members. Interviews were conducted by the authors and a few other Capgemini consultants in February–April 2007. Most of the interviews were done face to face and some over the telephone.

Key questions of the study were:

- What type of shopper data is collected and shared in the value chain?
- How is shopper data analysed and leveraged in key retail business processes?
- What are the roles of retailers and manufacturers in shopper data analysis and use?
- What are the key challenges and success factors in shopper data sharing and analysis?

The following section introduces the main findings of the study.

What data is shared?

Overall, looking at the results, retailers seem to be open with manufacturers and share data with most of them. Only a couple of the retailers are in the piloting phase, and some of those who do not share data refuse to do it because of a conscious strategic choice. Hence, most of the retailers that are willing to share data are already doing it in one way or another with their key manufacturer partners.

Why is the data not shared? An interesting comment from a retailer that we consider advanced in customer analytics was that they want to differentiate from competitors and therefore do not share data at all. They do not want the manufacturers to leak the data to other retailers. Some retailers classified suppliers as pure private label suppliers and other manufactur-

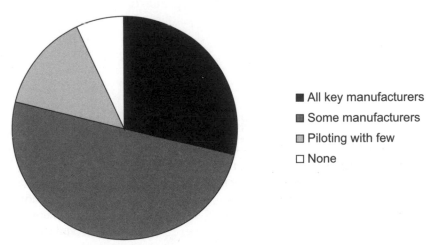

Figure 7.2 Shopper information sharing with manufacturers

ers, and interestingly pure private label suppliers were often considered as more strategic partners and open for data-sharing activities. Some retailers are very picky when choosing with whom to share information. They are often only willing to share it if the manufacturers are able to create value by using the data. At the same time, some retailers share or sell data to manufacturers very openly.

Most retailers share information only about manufacturers' own products. Some also share competitor information, and some at stock keeping unit (SKU) level and some only on a high level. Information about sales of manufacturers' own products will help with logistics development and demand forecasting, but will give little support to category management, as a large amount of data is missing. After many years of ECR collaboration, where information sharing is the core principle behind the movement, these results are very interesting. Only 27 per cent of retailers provide manufacturers with information that is needed for true category management collaboration. Getting information only about their own products will force the manufacturers to use other data sources, mainly syndicated data, in their category management suggestions. This means that retailer and manufacturer are using different data sets in joint category management discussions.

Many retailers (40 per cent) also share margin information with manufacturers alongside sales volume and price information. However, this information is shared only about manufacturers' own products, and manufacturers would also be able to access it using their own data. Only two of

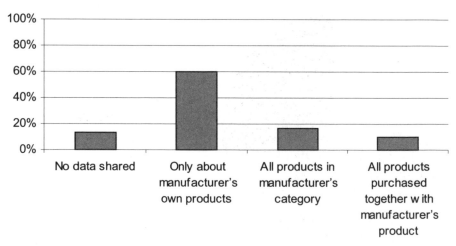

Figure 7.3   Product sales data sharing

the interviewed retailers shared margin information with their manufacturers about competitors' products, and this was done on a product segment or some other aggregate level and only on a project basis. However, it is important to consider sharing margin information as an option, because if the only data shared is sales price and volume, this is the data that will be used for defining the optimal solution for the category. Maximizing category margins should play a more important role in category management thinking than currently is done in most companies. After all, margins are the key measure that should be optimized in the long run.

None of the participating retailers shared shopper data on an individual customer level. Privacy policies in most programmes as well as legislation in many markets prohibit this action. About 20 per cent of the retailers shared segment-level shopper data continually with manufacturers. Many retailers have several segmentation models, which are shared with manufacturers. These can be based on, for example, lifestyles and demographics. Each retailer has its own way to segment customers, which makes it difficult for manufacturers to compare sales in diverse consumer segments in different chains. Some of the retailers do not have customer segmentation in place yet, and hence shopper information sharing is not possible; only POS information is shared. However, most of these retailers plan to start sharing shopper information as soon as possible.

For most retailers, data sharing is still manual work using Microsoft Excel and e-mail. After about 20 years of ECR collaboration this result is astonishing. Many retailers are also using electronic data interchange for data sharing, some are using data pools like WWRE, 1Sync or Sinfos, and some have opened up direct links to data warehouses with manufacturer-specific user rights. Most advanced retailers also offer manufacturers the ability to update and modify data. The most typical modifications are classification information such as brand classifications, product attributes, manufacturers' own category structures, manufacturers' salesperson-based sales areas and many others.

Many retailers are still in the piloting phase, and are sharing data only in joint projects or on an ad hoc basis. Some retailers share information on a regular basis, for example once a month. Most of these retailers also

Table 7.4 How is the data shared with manufacturers?

How is the data shared with manufacturers?	
Manufacturers have direct access to our database, and can modify data	23%
Manufacturers have direct access to our database to run reports	31%
Data is shared manually or via e-mail	38%
There is no data sharing at all	8%

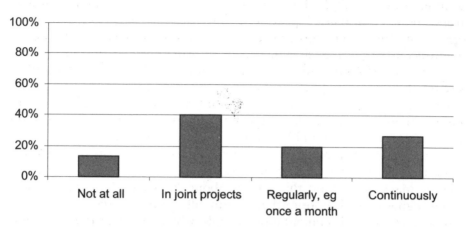

Figure 7.4 How often is the data shared?

share data on an ad hoc basis, if needed. One key question is: If information is not available daily for decision making, will it be used at all? To be honest, people tend to be lazy; if we do not have the information easily accessible, we might skip it in decision making. In addition, manual transfer of information consumes resources and the information is not often as up to date as it should be, especially for campaign management and follow-up of new product introductions.

The best retailers share information with manufacturers continually and real-time data sharing is seen as an example of best practice. Continual data sharing enables both parties to develop systematic use of shopper data which helps to build long-term understanding of customer behaviour through continual learning. Continual data sharing requires automated systems and clear rules for efficient cooperation, and most of the retailers sharing the data continually have given manufacturers access to their data warehouses or use some other mechanism (for example EDI, WWRE). Some of the retailers that share information continually have advanced models for collaboration. They can require the manufacturer to carry out a certain analysis set in order to get the information. However, some retailers did not see any benefits in continual data sharing and are not planning to start it in any phase.

The price and value of shopper information was defined in many ways by the retailers. Of the interviewed retailers:

- For 50 per cent of the retailers, manufacturers pay for shopper information.
- 29 per cent of retailers share data for free.
- 21 per cent of retailers do not share data.

Often shopper information sharing is linked to a wider collaboration contract between retailer and manufacturer, and shopper information is included in the contract fee. Some retailers also use the information tactically in pricing negotiations. In addition, mixed models exist – some information might be shared by typical contract, and other data on a project or needs basis. Some of the retailers that share the information for free at the moment are planning to start charging for it after the piloting phase. One interesting way of sharing data is a case where the retailer has agreed on specific business targets with manufacturers, and the service package including analytics was linked to that. If the retailer does not meet the jointly agreed targets, the manufacturer does not need to pay for the data. There were also comments that in true collaboration, data should be shared for free. However, retailers that mentioned this do not share data for free themselves.

How is the data used?

Shopper data can be used in many decision-making situations both internally and with partners. Both retailers themselves and manufacturers conduct analyses based on shopper data, which are then used in, for example, category and campaign management. Figure 7.5 shows the main areas of retailers' internal use of shopper data. The four most important areas are strongly linked to demand-side aspects: retail positioning, format development, customer communication and category management.

Shopper information is used least for personalized communication in stores. Most players in retail currently have no chance to personalize in-store customer communication, because of the lack of communication tools in stores. Similarly, measuring media marketing effectiveness and demand forecasting are not among the most popular uses of shopper data.

The interviewees also mentioned other uses for shopper data, including store site planning, space management, product recalls as well as customer retention and activities management. According to a few executives, the best practice is to manage shopper information as a whole, and to use this information in all key retail demand-management processes. This ensures a uniform business model for the retailer as well as the ability to differentiate and target the chosen customer segments. Common objectives for both parties as well as tracking them systematically are also an essential part of collaboration.

As we can see in Figure 7.6, retailers see room for development in manufacturer data analysis competences and results. Some retailers said they had to support manufacturers heavily to get acceptable results from the analysis. However, there seems to be substantial variation in the skills of the manufacturers' shopper data analysis. Many manufacturers are not given

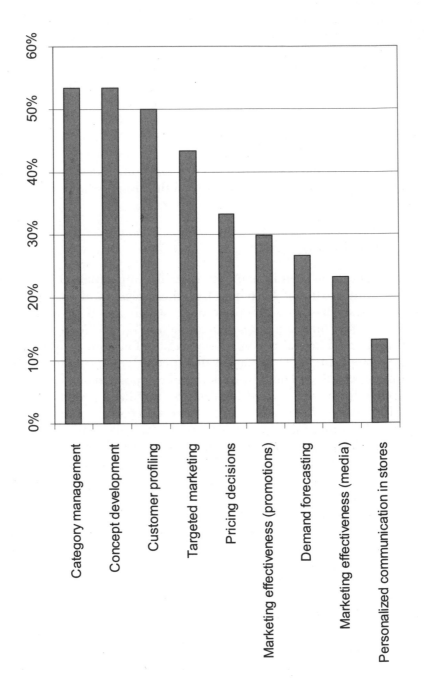

Figure 7.5 Areas where shopper information is in active daily use

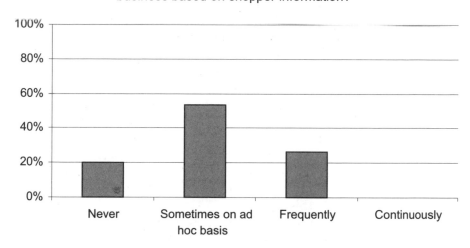

Figure 7.6 Retailers' evaluation of manufacturer competences in shopper data analysis

data continually and thus they do not have the possibility to use the data daily and learn from it. Most analyses are still done on a project basis on a specified subject. A few retailers mentioned that sometimes manufacturers lack the culture of focusing on the shopper and this makes the analysis challenging. This is due to the traditional category management process that focuses on products sold to the average consumer when collaboration partners work with syndicated data.

Some retailers indicated that large multinational manufacturers can provide examples of best practice in shopper data analysis. This was the case especially in less-developed and emerging markets. Interestingly, some other retailers noted that multinational companies in fact are behind local manufacturers in shopper data analysis competences. Even though they can provide some examples of best practice, their local implementation skills were not on the same level as those of local players. Thus, even large manufacturers have challenges in the consistency of their shopper analysis skills that may vary greatly among countries.

Defining distinct roles in shopper data analysing for the retailer and suppliers is also seen as important. Some retailers have a strong view that it is up to the retailer to lead the effort because of their direct link to final customers. Then again, one interviewee mentioned that retailers expect strong support from suppliers as the analysis capabilities of retailers are still relatively undeveloped. They expect a supplier's help in analysing shopper behaviour and detecting trends in the supplier's own category. It is anticipated that suppliers understand the retailer's objectives and offer an optimal solution to reach them. Retailers expect suppliers to think like a retailer and focus on the final customer.

An interesting finding in the study was that return on investment (ROI) measurement of campaigns and promotional activities is very seldom completed jointly by the retailer and manufacturer. We have also carried out several ECR scorecard sessions during our careers, and the results have been similar. Retailers and manufacturers are very good at planning campaigns and promotional activities, and some can also implement them out in the field successfully, but very few measure and learn systematically from old campaigns. Another interesting finding was that those best practice companies that measure ROI systematically in all campaign activities had all implemented clear processes and campaign management tools for supporting the process. Companies without proper campaign management tools were not able to do this.

Top management support was seen as essential in successful shopper information use and sharing, and many felt that top management in their company supports use of shopper data well. In several companies, top management also uses shopper information in key decision making, and customer measures are integrated in the company's strategic key performance indicators (KPIs). But only in a few companies do top executives use the systems themselves. Some interviewees mentioned that top management will never use the systems themselves, because they have a good

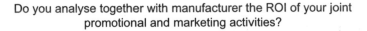

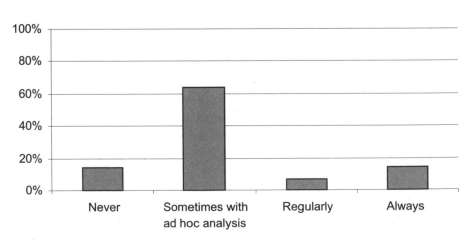

Figure 7.7 Collaborative evaluation of ROI in joint promotional and marketing activities

Table 7.5 Top management involvement with shopper information

Does top management use shopper information in key decision making?	
Daily, and they can use the systems by themselves	7%
Often	43%
Sometimes as ad hoc analysis	43%
Never	7%

analyst team that takes care of the analysis. Still, as we move forward with shopper data analysis and integration of new information into daily processes, top management sets an example for the company with its own behaviour. One interviewed company that we consider to be very advanced in shopper analytics mentioned that all key initiatives in the company need a business case based on shopper information before approval.

Customer portfolio development is reported to the board level in many companies. Almost 40 per cent of the interviewed companies report changes in customer portfolio to the board continually and over 50 per cent do it frequently or on an ad hoc basis. There were only a couple of companies in the study that do not report customer portfolio development to board level at all.

Key challenges in shopper data sharing

We also asked the interviewees about the key challenges in data sharing and analysis. The biggest challenge is integrating the data into daily processes. The key topic is how to move from nice-to-know reports and pilots to really implementing the results into daily operations. Key areas include, for instance, category management and trade promotion management. Getting shopper data to work well in different daily operations calls for clear processes and measures, and also requires new competences for many people. One of the biggest hurdles in this area is unlearning, leaving old traditional methods and data behind in order to start using shopper data.

Many of the key challenges relate closely to competence development, both for manufacturers' and retailers' internal organization. Shopper information offers a new way of working, and this also poses challenges in terms of competences in many daily processes. If things are done on an ad hoc or pilot basis, analyses require quite some time and analytical competence. This shows that many companies, especially those that are in the early phases of analysing shopper data, also face challenges in terms of having sufficient resources. However, the retailers that we consider as most advanced in customer analytics argued that the competences are pretty

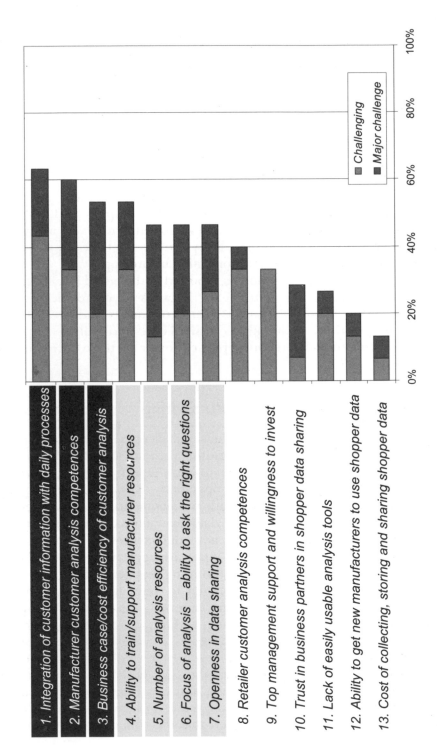

Figure 7.8　Key challenges in shopper data sharing

much in place since they have built up the required skills during the past few years. They have already used the data for years, and put the required competences in place, as the business required. For them, shopper information use in key processes is the way to do business. Automated solutions in, for example, campaign management support this business model.

Some retailers also find it challenging to focus on the right questions in analysis. It is not easy to identify the right KPIs and concentrate on relevant data as shopper data provides numerous possibilities for analysis perspectives. However, those who have used shopper data for a long time do not find it difficult to focus on the right analysis. Practice makes perfect in this area, too.

Some companies regarded openness and trust in data sharing as challenges. The opinions in this area, however, were divided in half, and some did not see trust as a problem. For some, collaboration is strongly based on trust, whereas other retailers had crafted supplier contracts with lawyers and made them so clear that there is little risk of mistakes. In particular, companies operating in smaller markets had a more reserved attitude toward the importance of trust in collaboration.

The future of shopper data sharing

Figure 7.9 sums up the views of the interviewees on the key areas of shopper data sharing in the future.

The results clearly show that the main focus so far has been to support the core processes of demand management. Trade promotion effectiveness and category management are the most vital collaboration areas. In other words, collaboration will focus on the daily core processes of retailing. However, personalized customer communication is also seen as a crucial area of collaboration. Some companies found the areas in Figure 7.9 important for shopper data use in the future but only in their internal operations. For example, pricing, concept development and the development of local assortments were seen in some companies as solely retailer operations and therefore not as candidates for collaborative actions.

It is interesting to see product development high on the list. In almost all of the interviews the development of private label products was given a high priority. Data sharing for the product development of suppliers' own products was in many cases found to be far less important. The development of private label products is a key factor in retail differentiation, and many companies invest heavily in it.

Based on the results, we have classified retailers into four groups according to the level of data shared and the degree of automation and advancement in data sharing. Figure 7.10 illustrates the classification.

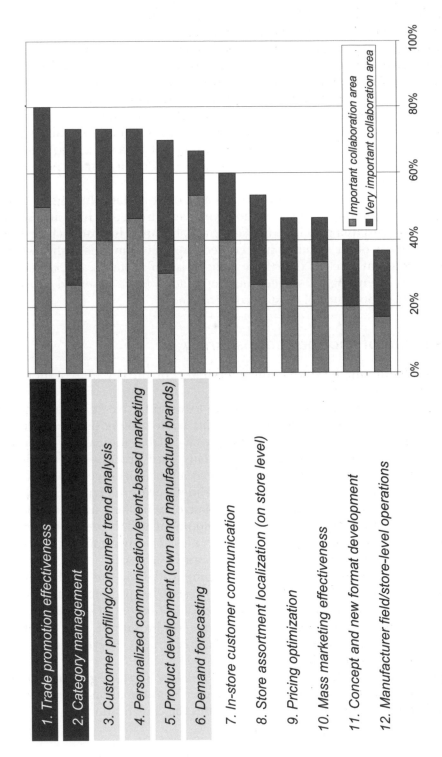

Figure 7.9 Business focus areas of shopper data sharing in the future

No data sharing companies do not share data at all with their suppliers. This group includes many different types of retailers. For some, data sharing is not yet technically possible or sufficiently feasible even if it were desired. However, some other companies have proceeded quite far internally in use of data but data sharing with suppliers has not been seen to bring enough value. Some of these internally advanced retailers also felt that data sharing threatens differentiation opportunities, and data sharing is avoided partly for ideological reasons. At these companies, a very high share (over 40 per cent) of sales typically comes from private label products.

Supply management partnership retailers actively share data with suppliers but only on the suppliers' own products. This information is most useful in demand forecasting related matters, ensuring good on-shelf availability at stores. Many cited Wal-Mart's Retail Link, providing information to several thousand suppliers, as an example of best practice. Data sharing is often automated and implemented using either EDI, data pools (such as WWRE or 1Sync) or the retailer's own or outsourced data warehouse solution. Presumably, similar data sharing will define the 'minimum level' for future data sharing in the value chain. This is because of the significant benefits realized in terms of on-shelf availability and integrating demand planning with production planning in the retail value chain.

However, these companies withhold from sharing data concerning their own shopper segments and demand data for the whole category, including sales data for competitors' products. Thus, it is extremely difficult for a manufacturer to support the retailer in, for example, category management and trade promotion management activities since it does not know the target groups set by the retailer nor the total category demand. These retailers do not carry out true demand management collaboration with suppliers. A manufacturer sells products relying on its own arguments and market information, while the retailer conducts category management independently, often with limited resources compared with the manufacturer. This solution still supports differentiation quite well, but a retailer needs to consider whether its own competence is so good that it can afford to leave all the analysing resources of manufacturers for competitors to use.

In non-food and speciality retailing, there are several success stories of vertically integrated retailers such as IKEA, H&M and Gap, so the model can work even at extremes. It is still also highly probable that companies in the group that do not share data will move into this class later on because of the obvious benefits in supply chain collaboration. Hiding the one-to-one collaboration data does not yield benefits to any parties.

The *ad hoc and piloting* group comprises most of the retailers in the study. The companies are in different phases of advancing data sharing but all believe in the model of collaboration with suppliers. Many retailers have

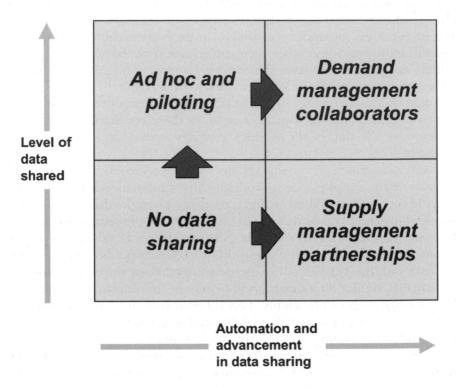

Figure 7.10   Retailer classifications in shopper data sharing

done a lot of work in this area but mainly on a project basis. The results gained from pilots and projects have been encouraging, and belief in the benefits of data use is strong. Depending on the company, pilots have typically taken place in the areas of category management and collaborative management of customer relationship or trade promotion. When asked about examples of best practice, these companies cited among others Tesco and ICA in Sweden as pioneers and role models for development.

Data sharing is, in many cases, still based on e-mail or Microsoft Excel, and is neither automated nor integrated into the daily processes. These companies usually cite competences and lack of resources as the biggest challenges for data sharing and analysis. Manual analysis and data sharing methods consume a lot of resources, most of which could be automated. Typically, these companies do not have solutions supporting trade promotion management, and hence all activity management measurement has to be done manually.

Demand-management collaborators are advanced companies that share data as part of their daily operations and have created a true demand-management collaboration model with suppliers. A few companies in our study clearly stood out from the rest in terms of data sharing sophistication. At these companies, management actively uses shopper data in its decision making. Indeed, according to an executive a clear business case is established for all key development projects run in the company, and the calculation often relies on shopper data to the appropriate extent. Shopper information is used in accordance with an integrated business model ranging from category management to concept development and even to store site planning. Ongoing tracking of promotions and other activities is part of everyday business operations, and it is also supported by the company's operational campaign management solution.

Interestingly, the advanced companies usually did not regard resource issues as big challenges. The data transfer to manufacturers is automated, and most have direct access to the retailer's data warehouse. Manufacturers are given information on all products in the categories they serve, and also often on adjacent products in other categories on the customer's receipt. Sales volumes and prices are continually shared, but every now and then the retailer might also supply profitability data, though this data is summed up to a certain aggregate level.

Manufacturers' skills in data analysis vary greatly. This creates opportunities for some suppliers, whose ability to carry out better analysis may bring them competitive advantage. Even though easy-to-use systems are being developed continually, the fact remains that data analysis is hard work and new to most suppliers and retailers. Logically, partnering in shopper data analysis probably mainly favours large suppliers, at least at the beginning.

Traditionally, suppliers have had a large amount of resources dedicated to category-related analysis compared with retailers, and it is likely that the same practice will continue – both parties will focus on their core competences. Shopper data provides new insight to category management analytics. The crucial question for a retailer is how to exploit the resources available from suppliers in the analysis of their categories. Our observations indicate that openly operating pioneering retailers have been able to use a considerable share of manufacturers' analysis resources. How would you allocate analysis resources if you could have 20–40 full-time analysts studying the categories of your chain?

Our experience indicates that retailers so far have not been very effective in managing the analysis work of suppliers. Therefore, suppliers have been given a fairly free hand in this respect, which has still yielded at least good or decent results for participating retailers. The situation may change in the near future as collaboration models and metrics become more precise. Retailers will learn from manufacturer best practices and will start to demand similar analysis and services from other manufacturers too.

To sum up, data sharing to suppliers seems to be a kind of 'acid test' for retailer–manufacturer collaboration. Is it only lip service, is it a pilot scheme or is it true everyday activity? Unfortunately at many companies, on the basis of this brief study, collaboration is seen in many companies only as supply management collaboration, and openness in the area of demand management is seen in only about half of the companies. Many companies are still in the piloting or testing mode. The next step forward is automation of analyses and integrating them into retailers' daily core processes. This will be facilitated with pilot projects that have yielded good results, and by global best practice examples from pioneering companies. Quick wins in collaboration can be achieved, for instance, in category management and campaign management.

Key future trends in customer loyalty

Loyalty programmes keep developing, and many trends affect the development. Some players totally dismiss loyalty programmes, and others develop better and more extensive ways to improve customer loyalty, and loyalty programmes can be a strong differentiator in future retailing. Running a loyalty programme is relatively expensive, so they need to bring measurable benefits. When the use of shopper data becomes a daily routine, the benefits will be considerably bigger and loyalty programmes will be able to yield significant competitive advantage. Retention may grow as customers begin to receive more personalized service and feel that their needs are responded to. The number of soft rewards will increase, and competing on rebates and bonus percentages alone will decrease. Some players will base customer loyalty more on emotional bonds and not on direct monetary rewards. Systematic actions to build emotional bonds for a retail brand takes time and money, but it may well be worth it, because of increased customer loyalty in the long run.

One of the biggest benefits of loyalty programmes and shopper data is the opportunity to conduct targeted customer dialogue and set clear, measurable targets for it. New products and services are introduced at an accelerated rate, and it may be difficult for customers to notice them among thousands of other new products and services unless targeted communication is used. The role of retailers will also be emphasized as an information source for consumers as healthiness, sustainability and local focus shape retailers' offerings. With good understanding of customer behaviour and personalized communication, these matters can be effectively communicated. Retailers offer customers not only campaigns and product information, but also surprises, and shift more and more clearly to the demand-generation business.

Besides conventional direct marketing, targeted customer communication will be seen in customer magazines, the internet and at stores. Sophisticated retailers will develop a multi-channel media format where suppliers can buy space for their products and services, according to the standards of the retail format. Smaller and smaller micro-segments can be reached effectively, and this is a high priority at retail companies running loyalty programmes since it provides an opportunity to stand out from the competition. Most consumers belong to one or more micro-segments, which may also be used to improve loyalty in terms of total purchases. Micro-segments are also interesting to suppliers because they offer opportunities for higher-margin value-added products. As retailing is basically about selling products and loyalty programmes support product communication, it is only natural that suppliers will have a stronger role in strengthening retailers' customer loyalty.

Event-based marketing will induce a significant change in retail marketing. Increasingly, campaigns will be prepared in a modular fashion in advance and sent to customers when the need arises. The best players may conduct up to hundreds of concurrent promotions related to changes in customers' life situations. As retailers use shopper data actively, customers should be able to gain benefits from the more relevant communications and better-targeted products and services. The amount of targeted communication is on the rise and this will continue. The customer can also be involved in the retail operations, as, for example, Amazon has already done. When a customer participates in the retail operations (thereby improving the retail offering) the degree of customer commitment increases. Loyalty programmes and shopper data will play a key role in retail expansion to consignment goods and services, and increasingly shift into e-business.

Using shopper data requires simple solutions that are easy to use, examples of which were given in Chapter 6. Targeted customer communication is largely a technology-enabled change, and new solutions play an important role. During the next few years, many retail players will implement campaign management and optimization tools, if they haven't already done so. These will be supported by sophisticated rules management, personalization, forecasting and data-mining systems. The principle is that all key retail activities are measured and learned from. Systems do not decrease the need for creativity and innovation but they can be used to measure what works and what doesn't. Retailing will become a systematic piloting business where successful products and services will be quickly leveraged across the chain. These changes will pose great challenges to analysis competences in the main functions of both retailers and manufacturers. As the analytics affect retailers' core operations, such as operational category management and customer communication, it cannot be entirely outsourced even if solution providers and consultants can be used to support the change.

Customer portfolio management will become more systematic, and the aim is to increase the profitable customer base. The preset objectives based on shopper segments will be measured more accurately than ever. Customer profitability, customer attrition rate, conversion rate (by category or activity) and customer lifetime value are examples of new key metrics. Retailers will increasingly understand what kind of new customers they have won and lost. Shopper segment development will be part of ongoing management and board reporting, when customer equity management will also enter the world of retailing. As a new metric, retailers emphasizing service in their positioning can start reporting customer satisfaction in comparison with their main competitors. Customer satisfaction in relation to the current profit generation capability of the company may provide a good indication of the company's future success.

8 The future

This chapter summarizes key topics from earlier chapters and introduces the authors' views about key development trends and future directions in the retail industry. The views presented are somewhat speculative, and some even a bit provocative, and do not necessarily represent our employer's official view. The future is always a fascinating topic, and we all as individuals might have quite different views about it. Instead of offering decisive and safe answers, our objective in this chapter is to raise new thoughts and questions for readers.

Retail trends and their relationships are complex, which can be illustrated with a mindmap we prepared when planning this chapter. In this exercise, some key retail development areas were linked to the threshold versus customer value framework designed by Treacy and Wiersema. The exercise could have been easily carried further, but the key message is that there are plenty of strategic initiatives for retailers to pursue, and the focus areas differ depending on the retailer's positioning and format strategy. This chapter covers some key retail development areas that we authors see as critical success factors in the near future.

Globalization and consolidation

Globalization and consolidation in the retail and consumer products industry will continue in fast pace as price competition remains tough and economies of scale provide the required cost advantages. Retail market shares on a global level are still tiny, and there are few truly global retailers that operate in over 50 countries, especially in grocery retailing. Hence, several regional retailers merge or acquire other players in the market to gain sufficient size. It will also be seen that many retailers face a saturation point on a regional or national level, and extending geographically is a natural next step. Adding new formats and product or service lines in the home market will not pay off forever, so expanding internationally with selected success formats will be a viable option for profitable growth among many retailers.

The focus of internationalization for many retailers continues to be in emerging markets such as China, India, Russia and South America since they provide huge sales potential with their enormous population and growing middle class. The focus formats when expanding to emerging markets are often hypermarkets or warehouse clubs. These are also successful in Western countries, but the possibility for fast growth is limited due to regulatory restrictions. Internationalization to Western countries will focus on hard discounters, convenience stores, and mall formats that provide more easily accessible locations. If a retailer has good space profitability and the ability to pay higher than average rent, there is always plenty of space available, especially for smaller formats.

The growth of emerging markets will have several consequences for many players in retailing. The population of emerging markets is vast, so the economies of scale will reach totally new levels. As retailers achieve double-digit market shares in China and India alone, the volumes compared to, for example, any European country are well beyond any current figures. The products and services produced, especially for emerging markets, may also be sold in Western markets and significantly lower price levels may be seen. However, the growth of consumption in emerging markets will also change the game. There will be a shortage of raw materials and resources in several areas and, hence, prices of the products affected by the shortage will go up.

The very low prices of products from the Third World will test the free-trade policies, especially in the European Union and the United States. It

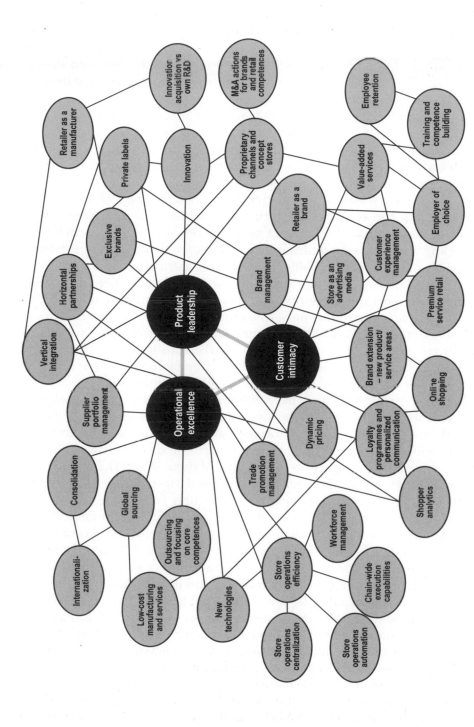

Figure 8.1 Key retail development areas linked with the threshold versus customer value framework

will be interesting to see the development of tolls and restrictions, as cheap products increasingly enter the Western markets, resulting in domestic factory closings and layoffs. Manufacturing of many standard consumables in Western countries will not pay off, and new production plants will be built only in low-cost countries. Consequently, globalization and ethical sourcing will involve significant political discussion during the next decade. Most of the politicians making noise about layoffs and unemployment are unfortunately not the ones driving growth initiatives in Western countries, and the discussion is more about outcomes of the development trend, rather than the ways to avoid these situations in the future. Consumer products companies need to teach lobbying governments to turn the trend, or gain sufficient offshoring competences to survive.

Sustainability is also a key matter, both in developed and emerging markets, and the ecological footprint of products will increasingly be a point of discussion and focus area both for retailers and manufacturers. Recycling and environment friendly products are becoming more valued, especially in consumer durables. The required infrastructure for recycling needs development and standards, and this might also need legislative changes and government support to happen. Sustainability might be an area that polarizes production – cost-efficient production and low prices for emerging markets, whereas the same factories deliver more sustainably produced product lines to Western markets with a premium price. Sustainability in production and product characteristics is driven by the consumer demand, in emerging as well as Western markets.

Retail ownership structures have differentiated retail globalization strategies, and are likely to do so in the future too. Entrepreneur or single-family owned retailers most often stay focused and expand to new markets only with greenfield operations using their standardized success format. This has been proved true already in cases like Mango, Aldi, IKEA and DM Drogeriemarkt, where the focus has remained clear despite their strong growth. Companies that have quarterly pressures from stock markets will more likely have 'several horses on the run', and build a multi-format strategy. In addition to organic growth, mergers and acquisitions will continue at a high level to keep activity level up and investors satisfied. Hard discounters are probably not rushing to be listed as the business of most of them would be too stable, even boring, for stock markets, and most of the current owners have little reason to take the companies public. Hard discounters will, however, still be yielding excellent results year over year, and will gain market shares in the coming years. Cooperatives and employee-owned retailers are likely to focus on regional operations, as the ownership structure might hinder quick growth and significant international pursuits.

Due to the capital-intensive nature of retail, store properties are likely to be owned by real estate investors to keep the costs away from retailers' balance sheets, especially in publicly rated companies. After a decade or so there will be a lot of store properties available for rent, as the current contracts with real estate investors will run out. Consequently, the chains with good rent paying ability (ie space profitability) will gain more market share.

The number of retail players will go down both regionally and globally. Barriers to entry are high, especially in grocery retail, and gaining satisfactory size to achieve economies of scale takes time and resources, and requires a capability to invest significantly up front. As the consolidation trend continues, most regional markets will have only a few grocery retailers left, and those retailers will have ever-increasing power in collaboration with suppliers. The competitive authorities will be interested in retailers' growing power, and the rules of the game will be clarified and tightened by regulators. The consolidation trend will also continue in the consumer products industry, which will balance the power in the retail value chain, at least for some players. However, some companies might gain competitive advantage by not exerting and revealing their power, but by smooth collaboration in the retail value chain.

Operational efficiency

Cost efficiency will continue to be a priority focus for retailers as it opens the path for price advantage and therefore also top-line growth. Price wars will ensure that all retailers analyse their own operations as well as those of the whole value chain to discover cost-reduction opportunities. Hard discounters and other value retailers with their highly effective and cost efficient operations are here to stay, providing a great benchmark for others. Automation of operations will continue in all levels of the retail value chain, including stores, chain units, warehouses and production. In particular, stores will be the next source for major efficiency improvements.

Retail task management is still in its infancy in most companies, but will be driven enthusiastically during the next five years. New solutions support modelling of store operations, and when linked with workforce management solutions, best practices in different store processes can be systematically identified, documented and leveraged in other units. Workforce management solutions enable continual optimization of store resources, which is the next big step in retail operational efficiency after demand forecasting and product flow optimization.

New value-added services to support store operations will be established in retail logistics terminals as 'factories' making the products ready for sale in a cost-efficient way. Besides retailers' own logistics, many new services will be provided by third party logistics operators or subcontractors. Manufacturers will also do much of the preparation work for stores; this development will be managed through retailer-led but jointly agreed collaboration models and annual contracts.

Demand forecasting will be done collaboratively by retailers and manufacturers and is based on sharing real-time POS information, since the same information can be used in the whole retail value chain from store ordering to production planning. Manual collaborative planning, forecasting and replenishment (CPFR) projects and joint demand forecasting meetings between retailer and manufacturer are replaced, as the trading partners discover the real costs involved in joint activity-based costing projects. In some categories the best competences for demand forecasting exist at the manufacturer's organization, and in real partnerships the manufacturers might also have the responsibility of sales forecasting and store ordering as a vendor-managed inventory (VMI) operation. In an extreme case collaboration might include demand forecasting for competitors' products as well.

Automatic store ordering is already used by many retailers, and in the future ordering will not be part of store operations in most chains. Campaigns and seasonal products will be included in automated operations and the demand will be forecasted centrally based on earlier consumption patterns of similar products. The forecasting models may be optimized in Eastern Europe or India, where employee costs are only a fraction of traditional store-level ordering costs. Many new external service providers for demand forecasting will emerge, and retailers start to use them due to measurable results compared with their own operations. Advanced statistics is not, after all, most retailers' core competence. However, buying analytics services and directing them to right purposes should be one, if retailers' in-house competences are not strong enough.

Self-service checkouts will become more popular, allowing alternatives to consumers and significantly affecting store personnel costs. Most automatic checkouts might not accept cash, which makes them simpler and low maintenance. Even though many retailers achieve some savings with current technologies, most benefits will be gained when RFID is a standard for product identification. Hard discounters and other retailers with centrally managed trimmed assortments (based on own labels to a large extent) are likely to drive this adoption trend, as they can control the value chain easily due to the small number of stock keeping units (SKUs). Large-scale adoption will pick up quickly as the price of RFID tags drops and reading technologies overcome some of their current challenges. In addition, large manufacturers are likely to contribute to RFID development, but for a very different reason. As the near field communication (NFC) function in mobile phones becomes standard, consumers will have more information available about products via a mobile web channel, which changes the dynamics of shopping on the shop floor in some categories.

The costs of retailer–manufacturer collaboration will be under the spotlight, which may lead to retailers trimming their supplier portfolio.

Collaboration models will be more streamlined and supported with score-cards and e-learning solutions, and regular, personal contacts with purchasing departments will be reserved only for selected suppliers. Many manufacturers have already closed or cut back their field sales organizations, and the actions (as well as the results) delivered by those that are left will be under thorough examination. Traditional roles in purchasing and sales will change to expert roles in jointly agreed collaborative processes between retailer and manufacturer. Also, price negotiations will often happen without any physical meetings, as they ultimately create little value for the final consumer. 'Free' lunches and business entertaining expenses will be reduced, as the examples of value retailers will force traditional retailers to set new standards and culture for cost efficiency. In addition, the overall changes in work ethics and tight public sector regulations relating to business giveaways will support this trend. Top management needs to serve as an example – cost efficiency is not simply a management issue, but more of a cultural and organization-wide leadership theme.

The whole retail value chain will be more transparent, as both retailers and manufacturers start to share information about the costs involved in joint ABC-projects. These projects need to start, because the price advantage of value retailers grows significantly, and others need to follow suit. Vertical integration is one option when the value chain agility or key resources need to be secured, but otherwise the focus will be on the development of the existing partner network. The value chain cost structures will be analysed more thoroughly than ever, and tasks delegated to the most efficient operators in the value chain. For example, logistics will be defined in most cases as a non-core process in retail, and is likely be outsourced. Efficient operations are supported by data sharing and integrated IT solutions. Value chain IT development and governance models over traditional company boundaries will be major challenges for most retail IT organizations in the near future. The integration will be supported by new ERP modules, data pools and several other service providers. As the field is still very fragmented and many solutions customized, systems integrators will also get their share of the development.

The capability to execute new operational models and concepts cost efficiently will be the key to achieving sustainable competitive advantage in the fast-changing environment. Because of this a major part of retailers' development resources will be focused on execution capabilities, as good planning without implementation will not deliver any results. New methods and approaches for store-level implementation will be introduced, as companies also take advantage of new technologies like video on demand, e-learning solutions, PDA solutions and others. The workload estimates of all changes in the stores will be known both at store and chain level, and the key responsibility of retail chain management will be to prioritize and schedule the projects to be implemented in the stores. Changes will be more thoroughly assessed than previously, when the true costs are known.

The quality, speed and cost efficiency of store-level implementations will be measured systematically using new metrics. Operations planning in several processes will be carried out in the real store environment instead of desk studies conducted at head office. The 'grassroots-level' experience will be valued and also expected in several retail head office roles. Howard Schultz (CEO of Starbucks) will not likely be the last CEO (re)hired with a passion for store-level operations. The store will remain the core unit of all retail operations and planning, and hence, all supporting head office functions should be directed to enable efficient and profitable store operations to serve the selected customer segments.

Fact-based management

Fact-based management will be a part of all key operational processes in retailing. Customer loyalty programmes play an important role in data collection and enable segment-based analysis of customers. Retail offerings, assortments and communication can be more customized for selected segments and based on actual demand. Some retailers will take the lead role in the use of shopper information, and teach customers to use personalized services. The best customer loyalty programmes will also raise the level of customer expectations, and consequently some companies decide not to follow suit and will close down their programmes. These retailers need to start aggressive high-low pricing with visible campaigns to ensure customer loyalty after ending their programme. This will impact price competition in certain categories, and might also have a significant effect on a retailer's total profitability level. However, running a loyalty programme is expensive too, and having one should yield considerable add-on sales. Cooperative companies are likely to continue with loyalty programmes regardless of retail format strategy, as they provide a modern way for distributing cooperative capital.

Almost all real-time information of actual demand enables process efficiency in many new ways. The same shopper segment-based measures will be used in different parts of the organization – format development, category management, marketing, pricing, store site planning, demand planning and several other functions. New operating culture emphasizing continual piloting is likely to emerge. The basic principles are: all actions can be measured, and the organization can learn from all actions, including actions carried out by competitors. This will raise an organization's intellectual capital, the value of which is hard to measure, but which can still be a key competitive differentiator, especially in the long run. Continual measurement of activities also requires systems that are efficient and easy to use, so those retailers that do not yet have campaign management solutions in place are likely to have them implemented during the next couple of years.

Fact-based management also affects pricing. Consumers remember only a limited number of prices, so not everything needs to be discounted. Optimized pricing is a key enabler of retailer profitability, especially when a retailer carries a wide assortment. Analytical solutions will facilitate the efficient markdown management for seasonal products and dynamic pricing already used in several service industries such as hotels and airlines. This means prices can be changed daily or hourly as needed, and might even be differentiated among customer segments. Retired customers and other people free during office hours will be attracted to stores with lower prices when the capacity is in partial use and the shopping experience is more pleasant than during rush hours. Retailers will create new seasons and themes to attract customers to store, and the focus of marketing will move from seasonal campaign planning to filling the store with customers when there isn't a traditional season on. Why waste money on marketing during high seasons, when customers come in anyway? Customer loyalty programmes already execute differentiated pricing with coupons and free product introductions, and measures like these are expected to increase massively in the near future, including yield management targets for retail capacity optimization.

Data sharing and joint measures also enable new business collaboration models. Advertising agencies may be briefed with clear target segment-specific objectives and rewarded with success fee-based contracts. In addition, category captains may be compensated with risk- and revenue-sharing models focused on total category sales and profitability, including competitors' products. This approach supports objectivity in assortment and campaign planning.

Syndicated data sources will lose their significance in decision making as retailers will learn to use their own data sources. POS and shopper information are accurate, almost real time and include the customer dimension. This information will be shared – or sold – to key manufacturer partners. As most retailers and manufacturers do not have sufficient resources for data analysis, this opens business opportunities for external research agencies and analytical service providers. Outsourcing some analytical activities helps balance the costs and benefits, as the projects are more transparent than in internal organizations. In addition, project management and objective setting for analysis projects is often more prompt when outsourced.

Some retailers are likely to limit participation in syndicated data pools to reduce the information available about their successful products and services. Currently, the followers may identify emerging successful products with syndicated data, and include them in the assortments as they have reached a required demand level, without having the costs and risks of product development and piloting. The separation of information flows in retail will boost differentiation, and assortments will become genuinely different as all companies use their own information sources. In concentrated markets open data sharing via syndicated data pools might also raise questions among competitive authorities. Manufacturers will have a hard time figuring out the total picture of the markets in the new situation, and they will need new information sources for analysing market trends. Consumer panels are expected to increase in importance and new players are likely to emerge in the market research field. As the retail and consumer products business becomes more international, market research is also likely to become more international.

Fact-based management will come to all key retail processes. In, say, 10 years time it will be hard for any retail professional to understand how the business could be managed without this accurate and timely information. How would you feel now working without mobile phones and e-mail?

Innovation and exclusivity

Innovation and brand management will continue to be strong keys for success, both for retailers and consumer products companies. The share of private labels (own labels) is likely to increase, in the most strategic categories as well as others. Retailers and competing manufacturers will 'borrow' new ideas in the market and apply them quickly to own labels, as only a few products will have strong enough patent and immaterial rights covered and not many manufacturers really want to sue their clients publicly.

The success of the copycat companies will force other businesses to cut down R&D budgets or refocus on new areas. Significant R&D projects might take years to yield results, and only in a few companies does top management have time to wait for the results with the pressure of the quarterly economy. Technically challenging products cannot be copied as easily, and many R&D budgets will be focused in these areas, where the differentiation can be guaranteed. Most product innovations will be focused on items that can be leveraged globally and are suitable to brand extensions.

Typically manufacturers counter private labels with strong brand management. As retailers are operating private labels often with only a few brands, manufacturers also need to consolidate their brand families to gain cost efficiency. Brands are built on several levels – global megabrands, national brands and local brands – and all levels will have a significant role in the future. Most new brands are still launched to either end – global or local, and few players focus on national markets. 'Co-branding' will also gain share, as it is often a politically easier solution for most manufacturers than producing private labels. However, many of the co-branding activities will be small-scale tactical actions, and do not yield real growth and sustainable long-term results. Brand ownership is an interesting question, even though the consumer does not often care about it. Retailers buy and innovate new brands to gain exclusivity and achieve cost leadership, and manufacturers build brands to gain space in consumers' minds and also on retailers' shelves.

Retailers are also willing to use manufacturers' strong brands to support the retail brand in customer communication, in-store activities and displays. Particularly in department stores, manufacturers are able to provide high-quality shop-in-shop concepts that add value to consumers above retailers' own solutions. Department store businesses will focus on selecting successful brand portfolios, and hiring store space to selected suppliers in line with the store's positioning. Some department stores begin to operate more like malls than traditional department stores. Typical store operations like cashiers, security and customer service will still be provided by the retailer as shared services to gain cost efficiency.

Shop-in-shops will become more popular also in other areas, as manufacturers can ensure the customer service experience and help retailers gain a premium price. As manufacturers gain knowledge and competences in retail operations, a number of them will start their own concept stores – that is, become retailers. The path showed by many current concept stores will be followed by other manufacturers. A manufacturer's own retail chain is a visible marketing channel and provides direct access to the consumer interface. Many manufacturers will run concept stores along with traditional retail channels, but some will make them proprietary channels as the sales grow. Manufacturers can appropriately ask: Why should the retailers gain profits for innovations and exclusivity, particularly if the manufacturer's own sales channel has a reasonable geographical coverage with a better customer experience?

Consumer product companies and retailers will become active innovation identifiers and buyers. Large multinational consumer product companies, in particular, will systematically hunt for innovations for their marketing and sales machine. This will provide attractive opportunities for small entrepreneurs that have interesting innovations but do not have resources for sales and large-scale production. New innovation reseller markets are likely to be established, and some manufacturers will invest in deep product development collaboration with universities and other third parties nesting innovations.

Retailers will innovate exclusive private labels, buy some manufacturer brands off the market and build horizontal partnerships. As retailing is still regional, horizontal partnerships with other retailers in different markets will provide cost-efficient collaboration models for 'innovation'. Leveraging other retailers' private labels as exclusive products in home markets will help differentiation, whereas the other party gains economies of scale in private label production and also gets a small sales royalty. Many markets are small, so horizontal partnerships are needed to provide sufficient demand and justification for own label development.

Retailers will also extend their brands to new service concepts and solutions for customers. There are many ways to support the consumer with value-added services closer to the point of consumption, but most retailers still operate a long way from the consumption, running pick-up warehouses. If traditional retailers will not innovate and offer solutions closer to the consumer, it is likely that other players will take the space. A few examples of these are provided later in this chapter.

Customer dialogue management and service extensions

The nature of retail marketing will change and an increasing share of marketing funds will be spent close to the point of purchase, as stores become a major media for consumers. Personalization of marketing messages will become common, and marketing efficiency will be measured for all key activities. Store-level marketing will be conceptualized and retailers will be able to offer distinct marketing packages for selected manufacturers and other partners. Stores will become a major competitor for traditional media like newspapers and television. The price of retail marketing space will be significant, even though its value is hard to measure, as it is allocated in most cases to manufacturers as part of partnership agreements that will not be reported externally.

Customer identification currently done at the checkout will be completed earlier, so the shopper can receive personalized messages during the shopping trip, for example on a PDA device attached to the shopping trolley. All actions are of course optional for consumers, but are often taken because of interesting benefits provided. Personalized messages can also be targeted to small niche segments that broaden retail assortments and open up new, profitable niche product opportunities for manufacturers that are able to create small product volumes efficiently. The in-store activities will be funded by manufacturers that are keen to influence shopping decisions at the point of purchase. Personalized actions become sellable resources like traditional end cap promotions. Joint key performance indicators (KPIs) based on shopper information, and success fee contracts with media and advertising agencies will also work as a catalyst in the development.

Information availability in stores will increase as interactive touch screens become common, and they can be used to enrich the customer shopping experience with new content and value-added services. At a minimum, customers will receive the same information they would get at home on the internet. Some advertising agencies will focus purely on retail store-level devices like PDAs, touch screens and video on demand. The effectiveness of these tools is easy to measure, which speeds up the adaptation.

Personalized marketing will be performed increasingly using digital media. This is a high priority on retailers' marketing agendas, as the cost of advertising is minimal compared with traditional mailings. Sustainability issues will drive the development in the same direction, as it will be relatively easy for consumer activists to calculate the waste involved in sending traditional marketing flyers with low pulls, and public opinion will change consumers' habits towards eco-friendly digital marketing. Retail forerunners in digital marketing might also put indirect pressure on other retail players regarding the sustainability of marketing activities, and this will particularly affect retailers relying on mass marketing without loyalty programmes and direct contact to customers.

One of the critical questions for the future is: Who owns the channel for customer information? When a customer is shopping and needs information about a product or service, will the customer use the devices and services provided by the retailer to get the information, or just use his or her own cell phone and the internet? If the internet is used, will the customer use the retailer's information pages, manufacturers' web pages or a third-party service such as WeightWatchers or an external price-comparison service? Search engine marketing might also become important in several categories.

The winners in this competition will be the companies that can provide the easiest and most reliable way for consumers to get the information they need. Ownership of the information channel is always close to the sale – as the consumer is online, the purchase might be only a click away. Both retailers and consumer products companies will face a new environment, as customers with their own mobile phones and web access might have more information on the shop floor than a retailer's own salespeople. The balance of power in the retail value chain will be shaken as consumers and information providers gain significantly more power.

Web sales will increase in several categories, and quite a few new category killers will emerge around consumer interest groups and hobbies. Traditional retailers will use web sales and personalized marketing, especially to extend to new areas and services close to the customer's annual routine services. Key areas might be travel, financial services, insurance, ticket sales, mobile phone subscriptions, music and videos, and several non-food product categories. Purchase frequency in food retail is the key competitive advantage compared with other industries, and retailers learn to use purchase visits as active cross-sales opportunities, as they serve as pick-up points for online stores with extended assortments.

In the next couple of years we might need to redefine retailing, as convergence will increasingly blur traditional channels. Besides the online services mentioned above, new service areas like clinics and restaurants will be added to the retail offering. Retailers have been losing share of consumers' wallets for decades, but this is the time to change this loss to growth. In the new environment, retailers need new competences in several areas such as contact centres and customer service, service marketing, revenue management and yield management (to optimize consumption and delivery of services) and also heavy analytics capabilities. Retailers' key competitive advantages in selling the new services are the richness and frequency of shopper data that provides a good platform for add-on and cross-sales. Digital marketing and the ability to deliver personalized messages at the point of purchase will also give retailers a distinct advantage that is enhanced with the high frequency of shopping visits, especially in grocery retailing.

Adapting to the local environment

Locality in retailing will become increasingly important in the future as the use of local suppliers and assortment offer an option for differentiation. There are big regional differences in demand structure, so those who are able to mass customize assortments locally will gain a competitive advantage. Local sourcing capability will also be a key differentiator for some retailers as the business models of most value retailers and tightly controlled chains cannot adapt to local products and suppliers. This development is already clearly seen in some markets, but its importance will continue to grow.

There are different ways to use locality: most retailers will use somewhat localized assortments, where part of the assortment is localized through mass customization. This is a cost-efficient way for centrally managed chains to add some local flavour to the assortment. Some of the retailers will handle local products through sourcing offices, where finding local products and handling relationships with local suppliers becomes easier. However, this approach is not as cost efficient as central operations. Some retailers will also have at least some of the local sourcing at store level.

The importance of local initiatives varies by consumer segment, but local products may be a value as such and increase the trust level among customers. Local products often carry a story, and narrative marketing may justify the higher prices. Pictures of local producers are already visible in some chains and information about local products is often emphasized.

Some retailers will arrange the whole shopping experience around their locally sourced products, creating an old marketplace feeling, and adding a sense of romance in shopping. Local suppliers may also have the opportunity to sell their products directly to customers in different kinds of events. Locally grown products are often seen as a more sustainable and safer choice. They do not require long transportation, and will become more popular as discussions about CO_2 emissions continue.

The position of local suppliers as retailing partners is still challenging, but might become easier than in the near past. Small manufacturers are usually not able to supply products to all of the retailer's stores, but serve only a pre-selected area or store type. Large retailers typically have quite a few requirements for suppliers, and small players are usually not able to deliver according to them all. Hence, the retailers that are willing to focus on local products need to find ways to train and support the local suppliers in a cost-efficient way. These programmes will become more popular in the future as more retailers need to differentiate. Retailers will support local suppliers, and sell products under a 'sustainable sourcing' banner, and this development might even increase the number of small suppliers in the next few years. Actually, some retailers will be competing for the local suppliers with exclusive products, as the supply will be scarce for unique local products that could enhance the shopping experience.

Getting products into major retailers' assortments can offer tremendous growth opportunities for some small suppliers. The success of the products can be easily monitored with real-time demand information, and the best products can be leveraged in the chain assortment nationally or even globally. We will see some sky-rocketing growth figures for small manufacturers that are able to grow with the demand. However, not all of the suppliers are able or willing to grow. Many of the firms are small family farms that are not willing to change their business considerably, or do not have resources to make the growth. Some retailers might also buy local suppliers or make exclusive contracts to guarantee differentiation. Also, large manufacturers might buy them, keep the brand, and invest in further production capabilities to fulfil the demand.

Local sourcing also affects the surrounding communities. Usually when a new large-scale store opens, many conventional stores lose customers and often have to shut down. This can lead to unwanted consequences such as unemployment and migration, decreased purchasing power in the area due to lower salaries and empty city centres, as one store after another closes and services move elsewhere. Hence, supporting local communities will be increasingly important to companies that wish to act in a sustainable way. Local sourcing is a way to support local communities, but many other programmes for supporting and ensuring their future vitality may also be introduced. New store openings may become more public, and retailers need to show a good track record in supporting local communities to be welcome in new areas. It is not only about money anymore, and a retailer's impact on the community will be assessed by new criteria in public decision making.

Success formats

Several retail formats will be successful in the future as they fulfil the needs of the different customer segments and shopping occasions. One size will not fit all, and as consumers get new options, some segments will turn to them. Format polarization will occur as value and premium retailing develop in different, opposing directions, and some traditional players are stuck in the middle.

Value retailing will continue growth in some markets, but development will slow as narrow assortments attract only a limited portion of customers and their shopping baskets. At the other end of the market spectrum, premium retailers will achieve success as consumers enjoy the shopping experience, variety, freshness and friendly service. Malls maintain their role as shopping paradises with continually changing store portfolios, and convenience stores serve as quick shopping destinations close to the customer. Category killers in speciality retailing will keep growing and making life difficult for many department stores and hypermarkets. What's more, their online presence with huge assortments will make it hard for any brick and mortar store to compete.

In the future, many new store formats will most likely emerge and some will succeed. Each will attract and serve different customer segments and needs. To illustrate the development, we have briefly described some examples of possible future retail concepts. The examples might be somewhat extreme but they provide a view of the development trends and the reasons behind them.

Hard discounters increase their cost efficiency to extremes with highly optimized operations, and will be price leaders in the market. The key savings are achieved by reducing employees and automating operations. The few employees needed in stores concentrate mostly on filling the shelves and guarding the store. Checkouts are totally automated and customers scan products themselves. Cash is not accepted anymore due to cost and security reasons, and payment is made with the retailer's own credit card to avoid unnecessary handling costs. The most advanced chains use RFID technology at the checkouts, so customers do not have to scan the products themselves. Ordering is fully automated and order quantities are decided centrally, and only whole pallets or other full supply packages are delivered. The store looks more like a simple warehouse than a supermarket and customers collect products straight from the pallets. These kinds of stores do not draw in all customers but the most price-sensitive segments find them very attractive. To keep costs down loyalty programmes or other expensive marketing activities are not used. Instead, good word of mouth from satisfied 'bargain hunters' is the retailer's main marketing tool.

A *neighbourhood store* with friendly service is the meeting point for local customers. The store manager knows all of the 1,000 to 1,500 regular customers, and the success of the store is mostly based on the characteristics and personality of the store manager. The assortment provides all basic products easily and quickly. The assortment is simple but offers carefully selected fresh and high-quality products. The store is also an important pick-up point for a number of online category killers, and can also offer an extended food assortment with online order or discussion with store employees. After shopping, customers may stay for a cup of cappuccino at the store's café and meet the other regulars. This is the best place to hear the latest gossip and local news as the store manager knows everyone. No loyalty programme or heavy data analysis are needed, as the store manager knows customer needs, and can reward and surprise customers without any formal programmes. Franchising is common with this concept, as the store manager's feasible personality is essential, and the best people running the store can make good money. Franchising also helps to ensure employee retention, which is vital for customer loyalty.

Concept stores enable suppliers to get close to customers and gain extra sales. The number of concept stores has risen as several manufacturers, squeezed by retailers for years, saw the light in establishing their own retail channel. Enthusiastic brand lovers love to shop in the stores filled with their favourite products, which continually change, providing variety for different seasons. The shops offer experiences for all the senses where customers can see, feel, hear, smell and even taste the large selection of the branded products. The store staff is very knowledgeable about the products – training days are well above industry average – and service, including after-sales service, is of high quality. The total brand experience is secured as the suppliers coordinate the whole value chain, and in most cases control is maintained with vertical integration and ownership structures. Media marketing expenditures are getting smaller, and the traditional marketing investments are now directed to retail channel development. Window dressers and in-store design agencies are in high demand. Most manufacturers have found new pricing options, as the brand image and customer service experience have been enhanced to new levels.

Malls continue their success and look alike in different regions, as they have mostly the same stores. However, some have taken on a role as important community centres. The retail offering within a mall is refreshed all the time, as new stores enter and others close. Facility management in malls provide very high service levels, and most stores even use the same POS systems that have become a commodity because of standardization. As retailers pay a success fee based on the number of visiting customers, malls are very active with customer acquisition events. Most retailers in malls spend very little on traditional marketing, but stores are designed and implemented very well, especially store-front campaigns. It is the retailer's job to get the customer in the store after the customer is in the mall. The toughest competition comes from other malls – even big-box retailers have a hard time competing for customers' leisure time, as they are 'jack of all trades but master of none'. New malls can be built only rarely, as earlier development led to too many deserted malls due to fierce competition. Old malls are renovated to ensure sustainable continuation of business, as required now by the regulators. Besides local malls there are a number of large destination malls with different kinds of attractions. For example, instead of a traditional city vacation, a top promotion might be a weekend relaxation and shopping package in a mall spa.

The *grocery shopping* paradises full of experiences are combinations of old marketplaces, supermarkets and gourmet shops. Assortments are extremely wide and new product introductions often enter here before other stores. Customers interested in slow food and culinary experiences can find all kinds of exotic, high-quality foods and add variety to their shopping routines. In one example, the store is packed with service encounters, and top chefs, among other experts, give fascinating cooking tips. Customers often attend the high-end cooking courses, which are constantly evaluated by other retailers that consider the retailer involved as a forerunner and trendsetter. Continually running themes and events make shopping exciting and fresh every time. The retailer's food magazine is an international bestseller, and compared to other retailers, it is not a giveaway, but an own business area and tightly integrated into the retailer's product and format development. Manufacturers are keen to use the magazine for new product introductions, as they can reach important opinion leaders through it. The retailer's revenues are small compared to some large retail chains, but the retailer still has a significant effect on customer behaviour. There are only a few shopping paradises regionally, but people travel to them from miles away. However, several additional regions can now enjoy the market feeling as some premium supermarket chains have started to offer continually changing theme departments, where the same new products and events are introduced on a smaller scale under the same banner.

Online category killers boosted growth in several areas, as consumer masses got used to the benefits of online buying. Most of these companies work on a global scale, with assortments no brick and mortar retailer can compete with. Personalization has made shopping easy and fun; for example, shopping for clothes is now much easier and faster with 3-D pictures of people on which to try new clothes. Since cost-efficient mass customization and production capabilities gained ground, sales of personalized products have risen in many areas. Customers like to be involved in the process, by designing their own clothes, for example. Many customers also make good money with their own designs, as retailers pay a success fee for all similar items that are ordered. Category killers use customers' shopping history wisely for cross-sales and personalization, and activate customers regularly. The best players achieve over 90 per cent opened e-mail rates, as the content is very relevant and creates value for the customer. The growth of online category killers has forced brick and mortar stores to focus only on mass items, and their share of total volume is continually declining. There are plenty of delivery options, from using postal services to delivery at neighbourhood stores or workplaces.

A *fridge refill service* together with household cleaning services offer an effortless way to shop and get rid of 'bulk shopping' routines. The service makes life easier for customers as key household purchases are delivered weekly and the house is cleaned. This is not a privilege of the rich anymore, as the same services can now be mass produced cost efficiently and afforded by the middle class. The service had quick success especially in the new-generation segments that are accustomed to buying services. Home delivery is popular for beverages, dairy and other heavy items, but all key grocery products are available. Other items can be added to the delivery using the online store and additional services are also provided, like dry cleaning and laundry. The delivery person makes a suggestion for the next order during each visit, and in 80 per cent of the cases it is accepted as such, without any changes, as the order is easy and 'good enough'. The margin level is completely different from that in conventional retailing, but customers are paying for the convenience of getting the products delivered straight to their fridge. Since these services came to market, the average shopping frequency in traditional supermarkets has gone down significantly in several segments.

In addition to home delivery, deliveries to the workplace make life easier for busy customers. Employee restaurants have *shop-in-shops* where customers can buy basic necessities, such as milk and bread, as well as takeaway meals. It is an easy way to get something to eat, readily prepared if needed. Consumers save time since there is no need to drive to the store, find a parking space and queue to get to the cashier. These shop-in-shops also serve as delivery spots for groceries and other products that are ordered online. Delivered foods are kept in the restaurant's cold storage, so the customer does not need to wait for the delivery at home at a certain time. This is convenient and easy, and the retailer also benefits, as deliveries can be taken care of during quiet store hours. As foodservice operators in most markets had limited competences for this type of operation, several joint ventures and partnerships with retailers were established to provide the services.

As shown, the future may bring many new store concepts for customers to choose from. In addition to the somewhat extreme and niche examples mentioned above, the current, more mainstream, formats will also continue to develop. Some of them will be more successful, and some will vanish from the market as time goes by. However, the differences among markets will be huge, some focusing more on value retailing, while premium formats gain more market share in others. Big markets will have the whole spectrum of retail formats, while smaller markets are likely to be more focused on selected formats. Price competition will continue to become fiercer, and some retailers will not survive when big players bring prices down with the help of huge economies of scale as the consolidation trend continues. As the prices continue to fall and margins diminish, operational excellence becomes more important, and retailers need to be innovative to find new ways to create revenue.

In the end, customers decide with their behaviour in which direction the retail industry will develop. The power of consumers is remarkable, much more than most of them realize. The power is just not used in a systematic and centralized way, but all purchases are monitored actively by retailers. The paradox is that as retail automation continues and competences in data analytics develop, retailers' operative systems and processes might focus too much on the past and existing assortments, and not on the real needs of the customers. The use of internal data is too convenient and provides hard facts for decision making, so the weak signals from the market are easy to ignore in decision making.

However, innovative retailers and suppliers will develop new forms of dialogue with customers, and discover ways to identify and fulfil the needs of the target segments. Even small niche segments can be served as retailers learn more about customer behaviour and can personalize communication and service. Value retailers are successful with cost-conscious customer segments, whereas premium retailers with large assortments succeed with great customer dialogue skills, both in store and with personalized customer communication. Customer dialogue and personalization capabilities will drive the growth of the retail industry, stretching the boundaries of the traditional retail value chain, most likely with online and multi-channel retailers leading the way.

References

Brandes (2004) *Bare Essentials – The Aldi Way to Retail Success*, Campus Verlag GmbH, Frankfurt/Main, Germany

Finne & Kokkonen (2005) *Asiakaslähtöinen kaupan arvoketju – kilpailukykyä ECR-yhteistyöllä*, Ekonomia-series, WSOYPro, Finland

Roush (1999) *Inside Home Depot*, McGraw Hill, Columbus, OH

Treacy & Wiersema (1995) *The Discipline of Market Leaders*, Perseus Books, New York

Wedel & Kamakura (1999) *Market Segmentation: Conceptual and Methodological Foundations*, ISQM, Kluwer Academic Publishers, The Netherlands

Ziliani, Cristina and Bellini, Silvia (2004) Retail micro-marketing strategies and competition, *Int. Rev. of Retail, Distribution and Consumer Research*, **14**(1), pp7–18

Index

NB: page numbers in *italic* indicate figures or tables

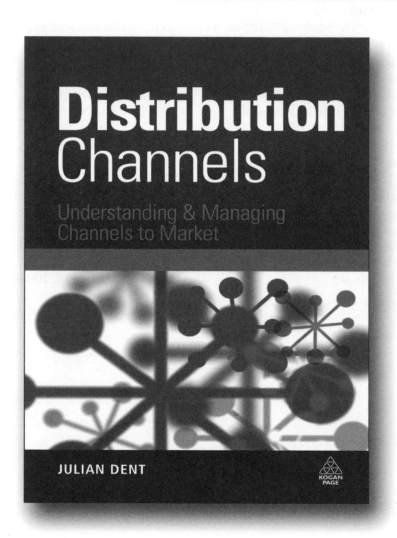

ALSO AVAILABLE FROM KOGAN PAGE

ISBN: 978 0 7494 5016 8   Hardback   2007